The Witches' Goddess

Janet & Stewart Farrar

By the same authors:

WHAT WITCHES DO
EIGHT SABBATS FOR WITCHES
THE WITCHES' WAY
THE WITCHES' GOD
SPELLS, AND HOW THEY WORK

With Gavin Bone:

THE PAGAN PATH

THE WITCHES' GODDESS

The Feminine Principle of Divinity

by
Janet and Stewart Farrar

With line illustrations by Stewart Farrar

PHOENIX PUBLISHING INC.

This edition printed 1995

PHOENIX PUBLISHING, INC.
Portal Way
P.O. Box 10
Custer, Washington USA 98240

Distributed in the U.K. by
ROBERT HALE LTD.
Clerkenwell House
45-47 Clerkenwell Green
London EC1R 0HT

Distributed in Canada by
PHOENIX PUBLISHING INC.
#276; 20465 Douglas Crescent
Langley, BC V3A 4B6

ISBN 0-919345-91-3

Cover art and design by Bob Birtch

Printed in the U.S.A.

This book has been manufactured on recycled paper using vegetable based inks.

List of Photographs

PHOTOGRAPHIC CREDITS

British Museum: 1, 10, 13, 22, 25, 30; Newcastle-on-Tyne Museum of Antiquities: 2; National Archaeological Museum, Athens: 3; Heraklion Museum: 4; Claire and Bill Leimbach: 5; Tate Gallery: 7, 8, 26, 31; Doreen Valiente: 16; Bel Bucca: 18; George Morrison: 23; Museo Nazionale di Napoli: 29; Stewart Farrar: 6, 9, 11, 12, 14, 15, 19, 20, 21, 27, 28.

Contents

Her names are innumerable ... In naming all these, we are practising an age-old rite. Such lists as we find in Apuleius, who identifies Isis with innumerable kindred goddesses, are a form of ritual worship. The abundance of manifestations is a characteristic of the archetype, and the plethora of names by which the powers are invoked among all peoples is an expression of their numinous ineffability.

Erich Neumann

Introduction

After centuries of banishment, the Goddess has returned. Few are aware of her re-emergence yet, but it may well prove to be one of the most significant spiritual, psychic and psychological developments of our lifetime.

'Returned' is, of course, not quite the right word. She has always been here, as the soul of our living planet, the hidden wisdom of our inner selves, the urge to relatedness without which we are empty shells. We have simply refused – at least in Europe and in white America and Australia – to acknowledge her. Millions of our fellow-humans (in India, for example, and among the aboriginal peoples of America and Australia) have been wiser. With them, in her many faces and her many names, she has remained honoured and enthroned.

Europe (to use a single label for the 'developed', essentially patriarchal societies of the past two millennia) has been spiritually the poorer for her banishment. Even the God has suffered, for without his complement he is emasculated, his image distorted and impoverished. As we have said elsewhere, God is not dead, as many claim: he is a grass widower, awaiting the readmission of his banished consort.

1

It has never been possible for the banishment to be complete; grass-roots human instinct could not tolerate it. In Christianity the Goddess, though never acknowledged as such, very early had to be readmitted through the back door in the carefully circumscribed, desexualized and subordinated form of the Virgin Mary – at the Council of Ephesus in AD 431, to be exact, when she was promoted to Theotokos, Mother of God. Judaic symbolism, particularly of the Sabbath, is full of 'bridal' connotations. Even in Islam, the three goddesses condemned by name in the Koran – Al-Lat, Al-Uzza and Manah – are popularly known as the Three Daughters of Allah; and the magical power of the name of Fatima, the Prophet's own daughter, is obvious to anyone who has ever visited a Moslem country.

But the real breakthrough – the acknowledgement and honouring of the Goddess as such, in those cultures which had for so long rejected her – has come with the major pagan revival of this century, and particularly of the past decade or two.

It may be said to have started with the occult revival which began to gather momentum around the end of the nineteenth century and which still continues. Occultism overlaps paganism, as it does the more thoughtful elements of Christianity, Judaism and Islam; but only in paganism is the occult principle of the complete and necessary equality of the male and female creative polarities – of the God and the Goddess – openly and joyfully proclaimed.

What is the essential philosophy of paganism? We write as practising witches, and Wicca (as modern witches call their Craft) is perhaps the most typical and widely followed of today's pagan paths; so we shall be forgiven if we express ourselves in Wiccan terms. We regard all those paths as equally valid, and we hope their adherents will recognize the following outline as basically characteristic of the whole.

Paganism, like the occultism from which it is inseparable, holds that reality exists and functions on many levels – spiritual, mental, astral, etheric and physical, to give a generally accepted set of definitions. The levels are interdependent, interactive and all essential to cosmic activity and evolution; they do not, as so often in patriarchal thinking, range in that order from 'good' to 'bad'. As the Cabalists express it, 'All the Sephiroth are equally holy'. Surprisingly, as some may find it, the frontiersmen of science are being forced more and more by the nature of their studies to a similar conclusion; typical of this development is the Gaia Hypothesis, which we consider on pages 15–16.

Paganism regards the whole cosmos as alive, both as a whole and in all of its parts. The frequency on which that life operates varies widely: we can recognize the life-principle in a mouse or a rose, because its frequency is close to our own, but to recognize it in a diamond, a planet or a solar system requires a conscious effort to put ourselves in tune with it. Paganism makes that conscious effort.

Two things follow from this. First, paganism (and perhaps the Craft in particular) is strongly Nature-based. Both in their worship and in their daily lives, pagans love, respect and endeavour to attune themselves to their natural environment, in all its aspects and on all its levels. They recognize themselves as being an integral part of that environment, and of its currents and rhythms.

Secondly, on a wider scale, pagans do not regard the ultimate creative force (in its complementary aspects of the God and the Goddess) as something 'up there', separate from its creation. They regard the cosmos as a total organism, of which they are individual cells. The health and evolution of that organism – ultimately, one may say, of the God and Goddess themselves – depend, however minutely, on the health, and healthy activity, of each of those constituent cells. 'As above, so below': we are not separate from the God and the Goddess but part of them, sharing their nature – and sharing too, at our own microcosmic level, their macrocosmic responsibility for the total organism. (This attitude, incidentally, encourages a much greater emphasis on 'Blessed is he who ...' than on 'Thou shalt not'.)

Such an organic view of the cosmos cannot be fully expressed, and lived, without the concept of God and Goddess. There is no manifestation without polarization; so at the highest creative level, that of Divinity, the polarization must be the clearest and most powerful of all, reflecting and spreading itself through all the microcosmic levels as well.

We are at a period in history when that truth is forcing itself on our attention, because the patriarchal epoch which denied it is dying on its feet. For humanity to find its way again – even, perhaps, to survive – it must rediscover the Goddess.

This book is intended as a contribution to that rediscovery.

It is in three parts. Part I explores the history of mankind's thinking about the Goddess, and the various aspects which go to make up her complex nature. Part II takes a selection of individual Goddess-forms which mankind has envisaged, examines their mythology and symbolism and suggests a ritual for each by which we may attune ourselves to her particular aspect. Part III is a directory of Goddesses of the world, both past and present, with a brief description of the aspect which each expresses.

It may be asked why it is necessary to delve so much into the past, sometimes into the thinking of long-vanished cultures, in order to rebuild a picture (or set of pictures) of the Goddess which will be valid for us today.

It is necessary because in the enterprise of readmitting her, so many of us are starting from scratch. We may know in theory, and feel in our gut, that her readmission is vital. But we need the wisdom of those to whom she was (or still is) a living part of their daily experience. We even need the occasional inadequacies of their vision to avoid or correct inadequacies of our own.

Communion with the Goddess is not a one-way process. We reach out to and worship her, and the more effectively we do so, the more she reaches out to and enlightens us. So the experience of the Goddess-acknowledging cultures, whether past or present, and the mythologies by which they express what they learned from such feedback, can help us immeasurably in establishing our own communion. An overall view of the many Goddess-forms evolved by mankind is the best possible start to evolving our own.

But it should always be remembered that such communion is not a purely rational activity. Attunement with the Goddess is a mystery, activating far more than the ego-consciousness. Its truths are expressed in mythology and ritual, not because the people who evolved those myths and rituals were ignorant but because mystery-truths can be fully expressed only in that way, just as a poem can express truths which a technical treatise cannot – and, of course, vice versa.

Part of the process is to absorb all we can of men and women's experience of the Goddess, and their expression of that experience. The rest is the psychic fermentation which cannot be hurried but which gradually transmutes knowledge into personal awareness.

Janet Farrar
Stewart Farrar

Herne's Cottage
Ethelstown
Kells
Co. Meath
Ireland

Part I

Discovering the Goddess

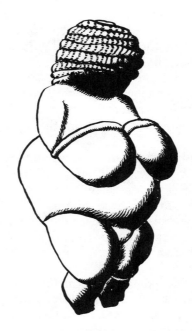

I The Goddess in History

The Great Goddess ... is the incarnation of the Feminine Self that unfolds in the history of mankind as in the history of every individual woman; its reality determines individual as well as collective life.

Erich Neumann

In the beginning was the Mother.

We have no direct evidence, naturally, of just when and how *Homo sapiens* became a religious animal – that is, when he first began to symbolize abstractions in his mind and to worship, plead with and propitiate them. Or in psychological terms, when he first became aware (to begin with unconsciously) of numinous archetypes which transcended his individuality.

But we do know when he began to express that awareness in art: in the Palaeolithic or Old Stone Age, when he had become a tool-making animal. It was then that he first produced what may be called cult-objects.

To quote Erich Neumann (*The Great Mother*, p.95): 'Of the Stone

Age sculptures known to us, there are fifty-five female figures and only five male figures. The male figures, of youths, are atypical and poorly executed, hence it is certain that they had no significance for the cult. This fits in with the secondary character of the male godhead, who appeared only later in the history of religions and derived his divine rank from his mother, the Goddess.'

In primitive societies known to history, the male role in procreation was not realized. Intercourse and pregnancy both began with puberty, and there was no evident reason to regard one as the cause of the other. Women were believed to conceive from the light of the Moon or from ancestral spirits.

It was not surprising, therefore, that woman became the symbol of the Earth Mother. Both mysteriously produced life and nourished it. The Palaeolithic female sculptures (of which the so-called Venus of Willendorf, depicted at the head of this chapter, was typical) were powerful fertility symbols, with huge belly and breasts. They were not, as Palaeolithic human skeletons prove, faithful representations of living women but deliberate exaggerations of their life-creating and life-nourishing aspects.

Nor did Palaeolithic woman have the massive buttocks and tiny legs of the goddess statues. These evidently represented the goddess as immobile, seated on the Earth and identified with it.

The first deity that mankind conceived, then, was the Earth Mother. We shall consider her further in the next chapter; it is enough here to emphasize that a male deity was a later development. Early human society was inevitably matrilinear, since the male role in biological parentage was not realized. There is still argument about whether it was almost universally matriarchal, though some societies certainly were.

Some still bear traces of it; compare, for example, the status of women in the Berber tribes of Morocco with that of their Arab fellow-countrywomen. The matriarchal Berbers were there before the patriarchal Arab invasion, and their women are still free, unveiled, and of powerful standing in their tribes. They have contempt and pity for the Arab 'femmes voilées', who are the mute property of their husbands or fathers. The difference is obvious even to a foreign tourist.

With the emergence of recorded mythologies, around the fourth millennium BC, we have evidence not only of the religious thinking of the time of their writing but also of the earlier ideas out of which that thinking had developed. Man had already reached the stage of not only reacting to the reality which surrounded him but also speculating about its origins.

Dig far enough back into any mythology, however refashioned by patriarchy, and the Primordial Mother is there. In Egypt, as a priest told Cambyses, King of Persia: 'It was Neith, the mighty mother, who gave birth to Ra; she was the first to give birth to anything; she did so when nothing else had been born, and she herself had never been born'. In Greece, Gaia was the first being to emerge from Chaos; from her was spawned the universe, including the earliest gods and mankind. In Assyria, Tiamat was the primeval ocean from whose fertile depth sprang every living thing. (Tohu, the 'waters' of Genesis 1:2, is the Hebrew form of Tiamat.) In India, Aditi was the self-formed Cosmic Matrix, mother of the Sun and the Moon, and ultimately of everything else. In Hebrew tradition, the Primordial Mother survived as Lilith, transformed by patriarchy into a demoness (see Chapter XVIII.) To the Gnostics, Sophia gave birth to the cosmos by a self-induced orgasm, desiring 'to generate out of herself without spouse'. To the witches of Tuscany, Diana was 'first created before all creation', and initiated that creation by separating out a part of herself as Lucifer, the principle of Light. And on the other side of the world, Australian Aborigine myth says that the Sun goddess Yhi, the Great Spirit, the Mother, created her counterpart, Baiame the All-Father, and together they created animals and mankind.

Even in the Cabala, with its subtle and profound balance of polarities, it is Binah, the Supernal Mother, who first initiates creation by giving form to the raw directionless energy of Chokmah, the Supernal Father. Not until Binah has given birth to Chesed (as Diana to Lucifer) does the masculine aspect emerge as an organized entity, as distinct from pure energy.

This is the pattern of all primordial Creation legends: the self-created Mother who gives birth to her Son/Lover, from which initial polarity all manifestation springs.

Such a pattern was an inevitable inference from the first of all deity-forms, the life-giving Earth Mother. Woman's, and the Goddess's, mysterious gift of creating life out of herself had an even more mysterious dimension: she could produce life which was different from her own, and in a sense alien to it – the male. But he was her creation, secondary to her, dependent on her in infancy and mating with her when he became adult. He was first the Son/Lover; only later did he become important as the Father. In human terms, of course, the Son mated with the Daughter, not the Mother, but the Goddess was the *Ewigweibliche*, the Eternal Feminine, Mother and Daughter in one, so in relation to her, Son and Lover were also one.

Whether or not prehistoric societies were matriarchal or characterized by matrilinearity plus a simple division of functions between the sexes, the time came, in the last two or three millennia BC, when the male began to take charge. Several factors entered into this development.

First, the increasing complexity and productive efficiency of human society, with its resulting appropriable surplus of those products. Man, as the more aggressive and mobile sex, because of his hunting background and his independence of childbearing and rearing, had the advantage over woman when it came to taking charge of that surplus, organizing it, defending it against predatory neighbours (or seizing it from weaker neighbours), and thus claiming to own it.

Second, the change-over from hunting and nomadism to settled agriculture as the main basis of society meant that woman was no longer the sole organizer of the home base.

Third, the comparatively new realization of the male role in procreation encouraged man, from his growing position of dominance, to regard women and children as part of the property of which he claimed ownership.

Fourth (and stimulated and accelerated by the first three factors) the conscious ego, the linear-logical, left-brain function of the human psyche, was undergoing an evolutionary leap. It had been emerging for hundreds of thousands of years, unique to humans among the land animals of this planet, and for most of that time it had contributed tremendously to the technical achievements of the race, from fire- and tool-making through pottery, weaving, home-building, the domestication of animals, agriculture and so on – but in creative partnership with the intuitive, instinctive, right-brain function.

Now, however, it began to flex its muscles and take charge, struggling to change the partnership into a master-and-servant relationship.

The left-brain function is masculine in emphasis, a gift of the God; its operational headquarters is the individual conscious ego, its strategy that of rationalized thinking, linear and analysing. The right-brain function is feminine in emphasis, a gift of the Goddess; its operational headquarters is the Collective Unconscious, its strategy that of intuitive awareness, cyclical and synthesizing.

We say again – 'in emphasis'. No man is, or could be, purely left-brain; no woman is, or could be, purely right-brain; the degree of emphasis (and of integration of the two functions) varies widely from individual to individual. But the emphasis remains, because it is rooted in the biological vehicle with which the individual is equipped in any one incarnation; and that polarized emphasis is the basis of human creativity.

But to return to those few crucial millennia BC. The creative balance was being upset, and in the more dangerous of the two possible directions. In religious terms, to honour the Goddess alone is a step backwards in human development, but at least she is rooted in reality, in life-creating instinct and in the fruitful Earth; by her nature she cannot help rebirthing the Son/Lover who is her complement, and thus forcing us once again onto the forward path. To honour the God alone is to cut one's roots off from the source of life, and to value categories and abstractions above the realities which they represent.

During those millennia, the God, the King, the Priest, the Father steadily supplanted the Goddess, the Queen, the Priestess, the Mother. The process was uneven, but overall in the one direction, and it culminated (in Judaism, Christianity and Islam) in the attempt to banish the Goddess altogether.

We have dealt in some detail with this patriarchalization process in the Introduction to *Eight Sabbats for Witches* and in Chapter 25 of *The Witches' Way*; perhaps the best recent work on its historical development is Merlin Stone's *The Paradise Papers* (see Bibliography).

Throughout this book we shall see the effect of this patriarchalization on religious thinking and practice, and on the mythologies which symbolized it. And in Chapter XI we shall try to see where we go from here, in the struggle (which has already started) to restore the creative balance, and the forward march of evolution, by reuniting the God and the Goddess and all that they stand for.

A final thought before we start on our voyage of exploration. We have talked of the Goddess and the God as evolving human concepts, symbolizing attitudes to life and our environment. But are they real in themselves? Or are they mere projections, however useful, of elements in the human psyche, and of our attitude to the planet on which we live?

To answer this, we must look back at our fundamental pagan concept of the cosmos as a living organism of which we are constituent cells.

Any organism has a vital centre, a creative force which gives it life and determines its form. So does the cosmos – and that force is real (or we should not be here), conscious, immeasurably greater than ourselves although we reflect its nature, and concerned about our healthy functioning for the sake of the whole. We can call it 'God', provided we recognize the polarity which it contains within itself.

But we can become aware of it, and communicate with it, only when it manifests. And manifestation can begin only when there is polarization. So 'it', as the first step in cosmic creation, polarized into the two fundamental aspects which we have defined ('as above, so below') as the feminine and masculine essences – formative and fertilizing, cyclical and linear, synthesizing and analytical, monolithic and mobile, and all the other complementary sub-polarities that contribute to manifestation.

These two aspects we call the Goddess and the God. Mankind has built up many thought-forms as channels to them or to one or more of their sub-aspects, and these thought-forms bear the hallmarks of human imagination; but the more apposite that imagination, the more the God or the Goddess ensouls them and gives them genuine life. So Isis, and Pan, and Demeter, and Thoth, and Aphrodite, and Herne, and Arianrhod and the rest are all alive, real and responsive, each showing us as much of the face of the Goddess or the God as we can apprehend at any one time.

This book is about the Goddess, the exile who needs to be re-acknowledged for our own health, sanity and survival. So, as we explore her myriad names, remember that each of them is a genuine face of Her, even if some are more clearly envisaged than others.

The Goddess is indeed real, and waiting for us to speak with her.

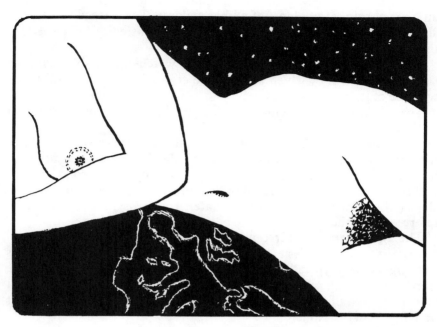

II   The Earth Mother

Earth's crammed with heaven.
Elizabeth Barrett Browning

The Earth Mother is the most vivid and immediate face which the Goddess presents to us. She is fertility itself, for mankind and for all creatures and plants. She gives birth to us and to them; she nourishes us and them throughout life, and in death receives the empty physical shell back into herself and transforms it into new fertility; for she is both the womb and the tomb, which is again the womb. She maintains the eternal, rhythmic balance by which plant feeds animal and animal feeds plant, and each moreover breathes out the air which the other needs to breathe in.

She can be merciless in defence of that balance. When it is threatened by one part of her family of children, she will take action, as drastic as may be necessary, before the situation gets out of hand.

She herself presents many faces, from the Arctic icefields which support a surprising variety of life-forms to the almost frightening exuberance of the tropical jungles; from the gentle richness of the

13

corn-plains to the deserts where plants sleep for years just below the surface, ready to spring up in an ephemeral green bridal veil after an hour of rain. Man alone, of all her children, has learned to adapt to all those faces and bears a corresponding responsibility for respecting them.

She has watched us grow up, and is still watching, for she is also the shifting ocean out of which all land life crawled and which still teems with life of its own.

She is Isis Veiled, the Goddess robed in the multi-coloured garment of Nature.

It is not surprising that Palaeolithic man first envisaged the Goddess with massive buttocks, firmly enthroned on the Earth and identified with it. Nor that mountains, visible symbols of that solid Earth-enthronement, have been sacred to her from time immemorial and, like ships (which are also, though much later, goddess-symbols), tend to be referred to as 'she'.

The *hieros gamos* – sacred marriage – by which the King had ritual intercourse with a priestess representing the Goddess to confirm his sovereignty, was typically celebrated on a mountain-top. For it was the Earth herself with whom the King was mated; the right to rule a part of her, on behalf of the community which inhabited it, was seen as deriving from her alone.

This concept of the Goddess as the source and confirmer of sovereignty is ancient, widespread, and still survives, enshrined in language and ritual. Even today, after a sovereign has succeeded to the title through the death of its former holder, he still, in any kingdom, has to go through a coronation rite whereby he 'ascends the throne'. The earlier forms from which that ritual derives made it quite clear that the throne was the lap of the Goddess. The royal symbolism of many ancient cultures represented the King as being suckled by the Goddess, and the name of perhaps the greatest and longest-lasting of all the pagan goddesses, Isis, was in Egyptian Aset, which means just that – 'seat' or 'throne'.

Even in those countries which are now republics, the President (unlike ordinary members of the legislature) does not assume office merely by election; he must then go through a solemn inauguration ceremony before he is felt to be 'really' President, human symbol of the nation's identity. The instinct survives in the ritual remnant, however deeply buried. And the formal 'seat' of the President, the plot of Earth identified with his authority, is the magical symbol of that authority, continuous through all its occupants; one speaks, for example, of 'the White House', 'the Elysée Palace' or 'Áras an Uachtaráin' as embodying the essence of the American, French or Irish Presidency. Each is, in a sense, still a temple of the Goddess of Sovereignty, the

Earth Mother wearing her regional face.

All goddesses are one Goddess, but the cosmic organism is made up of many entities at many levels, some 'bigger' than others. If we are individual cells in that great organism, we must recognize that it also has 'limbs' and 'organs' – multi-cellular entities on a much larger scale than ourselves but still only a part of the whole.

In this sense, we may regard the Earth Mother in two ways, each of them valid in its own context. On the one hand, she is the face of the One Goddess most immediately available to us for communion and attunement. But as a planet she is a separate entity, existing and active on all the levels – one planetary entity among countless others, one 'organ' of the total cosmic organism, and we in turn are cells of that organ.

The concept of the Earth Mother as the body-plus-soul of the fertile planet beneath our feet is of course common to many religions and to occult thinking, but a few years ago it received unexpected support from the carefully worked-out theory of two distinguished British scientists.

In the *New Scientist* of 6 February 1975, Dr James Lovelock FRS and Dr Sidney Epton published the outlines of their Gaia Hypothesis, and in 1979 Lovelock gave a fuller account of it in his book *Gaia: A New Look at Life on Earth*. They based the Gaia Hypothesis on two propositions:

'1. Life exists only because material conditions on Earth happen to be just right for its existence;

'2. Life defines the material conditions needed for its survival and makes sure that they stay there.'

Proposition 1, they pointed out, 'is conventional wisdom. It implies that life has stood poised like a needle on its point for over 3,500 million years. If the temperature or humidity or salinity or acidity or any one of a number of other variables had strayed outside a narrow range of values for any length of time, life would have been annihilated.'

Proposition 2 is the unconventional one, and it sums up the Gaia Hypothesis: 'It implies that living matter is not passive in the face of threats to its existence. It has found means, as it were, of driving the point of the needle into the table, of forcing conditions to stay within the permissible range.'

For example, the Earth receives between 1.4 and 3.3 times as much solar energy as it did when life first started. Yet the atmospheric blanket, with its heat-retaining properties, has altered its composition at just the right rate to keep the Earth's surface within the extremely narrow average temperature range (between about 15°C and 30°C) needed to sustain life – whereas even a few decades above or below those limits could have destroyed that life entirely. And not only its heat-retaining function: 'Almost everything about its composition seems to violate the laws of chemistry' – yet its composition, too, has remained consistently life-supporting.

That (and the fact that we have always taken it for granted) is astonishing enough, but the Gaia Hypothesis examines a host of other factors – the degree of salinity of the ocean, for example – and shows how these, too, have stayed within narrow life-supporting limits against all calculable probability.

Lovelock and Epton's conclusion from this staggering array of scientific improbabilities (which were nevertheless scientifically demonstrable facts) was that the whole system – the Earth and its biosphere – 'seemed to exhibit the behaviour of a single organism, even a living creature'.

They called this creature Gaia, 'the name given by the ancient Greeks to their Earth goddess'.

The whole theory deserves careful study by every witch, pagan or occultist – preferably from Lovelock's easily available book, for it typifies a steadily growing development: the discovery, by the frontiersmen of science, of the coherence of that multi-level reality which occultism has always recognized.

(The Gaia Hypothesis, incidentally, cannot be dismissed as wishful thinking or selective argument by inadequate scientists. 'Fellow of the Royal Society' is one of the few honours which can genuinely be said to be granted only to first-class minds. If the pagan movement had an Honours List, it should give Lovelock a knighthood at least.)

The Earth, then, by human experience, occult theory and scientific fact, is a living entity.

One other conclusion of Lovelock and Epton's should be quoted. 'In man, Gaia has the equivalent of a central nervous system and an awareness of herself and the rest of the Universe. Through man, she has a rudimentary capacity, capable of development, to anticipate and guard against threats to her existence.'

The Earth, like the whole cosmos and every one of its parts, is evolving. And with the emergence of mankind, she has made the evolutionary leap of developing that 'central nervous system'. The responsibility which that puts on our shoulders is awe-inspiring.

So back to the Goddess, the Earth Mother and our two ways of looking at her. On the one hand, she is one of the constituent entities of the cosmos, needing mankind's conscious self-awareness as a new stage in her ability to maintain the conditions necessary for life – her own and that of all her creatures. That ability has proved itself, over 3,500 million years, to be resilient and unconquerable; she always finds a way. So if mankind lets her down, she will write us off and find something else.

On the other hand, she is a Face of the One Goddess, the Mother aspect of our ultimate divine creative source, and our most immediate way of contacting that source.

If we can hold these two concepts in our minds and our actions and realize that both are true – then we are really coming to understand, and work with, the Earth Mother.

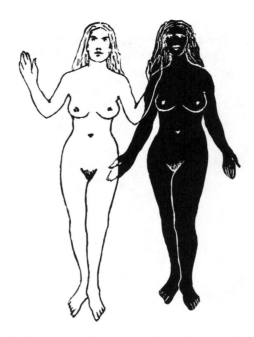

III   The Bright and Dark Mother

Why fear ye the Dark Queen, O men? She is the Renewer.

Dion Fortune

One of the major weaknesses of patriarchal thinking is that it debases the concept of the creative polarity of complementary opposites (male/female, light/dark, fertilizing/formative, intellect/intuition and so on) into a mere conflict of good and evil, of God and the Devil.

We have seen, and shall continue to see, how it strives to ignore the polarity of the God and Goddess principles. It does this on the one hand by trying to abolish the Goddess altogether (i.e., by denying the polarity principle at divine level), while at the human level it tends not only to subordinate woman but also to regard all the Goddess-aspects for which she is a channel (intuition, psychism, earthiness, her cyclical nature, even her sexuality) as suspect, dangerous, subversive to the tidiness of patriarchy – in short, as belonging to that same Devil. It is almost surprising that Satan has not been characterized as female.

Typical of this attitude are the statements of St Paul. That man 'is the image and glory of God; but the woman is the glory of the man' (1

Corinthians xi:7). 'Let the woman learn in silence with all subjection. But I suffer not a woman to teach, nor to usurp authority over the man, but to be in silence' (1 Timothy ii:11-12). 'It is good for a man not to touch a woman ... I say therefore to the unmarried and widows, It is good for them if they abide even as I. But if they cannot contain, let them marry: for it is better to marry than to burn' (1 Corinthians vii:1,6-9). And so on – all of it presumably still officially Holy Writ (though one wonders what Jesus, who treated women as human beings, would have said about it).

This denial of a balanced polarity between the male and female principles has now become a matter of public debate and active confrontation on many fronts, from women's liberationists to Jungian psychologists – and about time too. The public argument is a symptom of the growing realization that the patriarchal epoch has had its day.

But there is another and subtler denial, of which even many progressives – even some who accept the Goddess principle – are guilty. That is a denial of, or a failure to realize, the internal polarity within that principle: the polarity of the Bright Goddess and the Dark Goddess, who are one and inseparable.

At the heart of the Bright Mother is the Dark Mother, and at the heart of the Dark Mother is the Bright Mother. If it were not so, there would be no life.

In fact, this internal polarity of the Goddess, which is intrinsic to her cyclical nature, is the key to all life and all renewal. Life is a process, not a state. The Goddess is both the womb and the tomb; she gives birth, she creates form, she nourishes, and she reabsorbs the outworn preparatory to its reshaping and rebirth. If she were not the destroyer, she could not be the renewer.

This is most obvious in the process of organic life and death but it is also true on all the levels and in all phenomena. It is true in the development of the individual, physically, mentally and spiritually – where each stage of growth is at first a step forward, having its phase of useful functioning, but finally tends to become fossilized; when that point is reached, if it is not discarded or reshaped, it becomes a brake on progress; if that discarding is resisted, it may turn poisonous.

The Goddess's demand that an outworn stage be discarded may be seen, by the individual, as a threat to his integrity, his image of himself, but the Goddess knows better and keeps up the 'threat' with increasing pressure. The individual (or on a larger scale, for instance, the patriarchal order) therefore sees her as 'dark' in the evil sense.

That is the fundamental mistake. The devouring Dark Mother is not evil; she is our friend, if we are not to stagnate and thus truly die. She urges us forward to new life, and to her other self, the Bright Mother.

Another manifestation of the Goddess's internal polarity is (as we

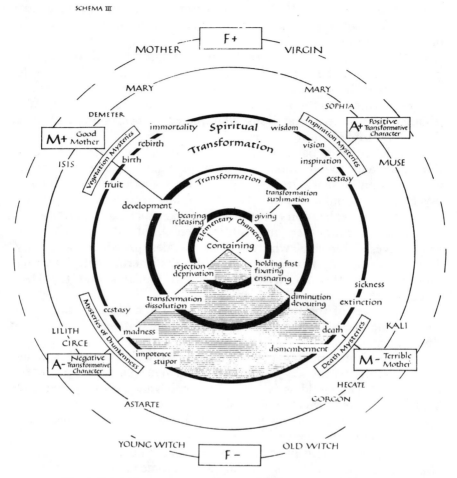

Fig. 1. Erich Neumann's analysis of the Bright and Dark Mother.

shall see in the next chapter) the menstrual cycle of woman. At the ovulation peak, she is the Bright Mother, concerned with impregnation and birth. At the menstruation peak, she becomes the Dark Mother of inward-looking renewal, prophetic and visionary. There is more than poetic significance in the correspondence between a woman's cycle and that of our supreme Goddess-symbol, the Moon – not only in its number of days but in its light and dark phases.

A profound and thought-provoking analysis of the complexities of the Bright and Dark Mother will be found in the Jungian psychologist Erich Neumann's book *The Great Mother*. We reproduce here, by kind permission of the publishers Routledge & Kegan Paul, one of Neuman's diagrams (see Figure 1). It will be seen that one axis has the poles of birth and death, and the other the poles of positive and negative transformation; every Goddess form that mankind has conceived can be placed somewhere (or even in more than one place) on the schema. But, as Neumann emphasizes, each pole can transmute into its opposite – death into birth, and apparently negative transformation into positive. (We would point out, in passing, that Neumann's use here of the terms 'Young Witch' and 'Old Witch' refers to the old frightening image created by the propaganda of persecution, which has become a negative thought-form in itself. One knows what he means – but that image, too, can transmute!)

Approaching it from another angle, the Bright Goddess represents the light of consciousness – not the intellectual analysis of that light (which is a God function) so much as the direct awareness of our environment, of the manifestations of fertility, of pleasure and comfort, of fulfilment, of overt sexual attraction, of relatedness in action. The Dark Goddess, on the other hand, represents the mysteries of the Unconscious, both personal and collective, the indirect awareness of intuition, of instinctive attunement to the environment and the processes of fertility, of the useful warning stimulus of pain or discomfort, of the instinctive urge to achieve and create, of the merging of identities in sexual union, of relatedness as a 'wavelength'.

In this sense, the Dark Goddess can appear frightening or disturbing, particularly to the defensive ego-consciousness, obsessed with its own independence. But that independence is a dangerous illusion; ego-consciousness has its living roots in the Unconscious. It is a useful, and peculiarly human, function and extension of the total psyche. Unless it acknowledges and accepts the Dark Goddess as a positive factor in the whole, it cuts away its own roots and will rapidly wither and collapse. The attempts of ego-consciousness to achieve independence (in other words, to regard the Dark Goddess as the Devil) is the prime mistake of the patriarchal era, and its correction is an urgent task of our time if we and Gaia are to survive.

One way to achieve understanding of, and harmony with, the Dark Goddess is to realize that she is the Goddess of the unconscious senses, and the key to the expanding of consciousness, to 'opening up the levels' (a primary aim of all genuine witchcraft and occultism).

By 'unconscious senses' we mean, obviously, those which can loosely be called psychic, but we also mean the subtle bodily senses which are generally (or through neglect have become) operative below the threshold of conscious awareness, or operative only on a very muted level. These are the senses which other animal species live by in varying degrees – the dog's sense of smell, the bat's sense of echo-location, the pigeon's orientation by the Earth's magnetic field, the ape's sense of body-language, the moth's attunement to the most attenuated pheromones, certain fishes' radar abilities and so on.

Now mankind has all these senses (except perhaps the radar one) to a subliminal degree, but all capable of development. Blind people prove it by the way they expand, sometimes spectacularly, their sense of smell and of echo-location. (Stewart was once given an afternoon's training, blindfolded, in echo-location by a Royal National Institute for the Blind instructor and was astonished to find how quickly he was beginning to make it work.) And it may be news to most people that we are all potential homing pigeons. Robin Baker of Manchester, in a series of experiments with students whom he blindfolded and sent on bus journeys, found significant success in their ability to point in the direction of their homes (the women substantially more so than the men). When he fitted them with helmets containing bar magnets, to screen them from the Earth's magnetic field, the ability disappeared.

Kirlian photography, and the use of Kilner screens, has proved that the human aura and the etheric body are not the fantasies of imaginative occultists but objective phenomena. Many people (including Kilner himself) have found that they are able to see the aura not only of humans but of other animals and of plants, and many more are developing the latent ability by deliberate experiment and practice.

Dowsing, too, is an 'unconscious sense' of long-established validity, which far more people than realize it are capable of exercising and improving.

Bringing all these senses to the level of conscious use is one excellent way of opening up the levels and of attuning ourselves to the Dark Goddess and everything that she has to offer.

Peter Redgrove put it thus in his 1984 J.R.R. Tolkien Lecture to the Lincoln Clinic and Institute for Psychotherapy:

Why then is this Goddess black? Let us say again because she is the symbol of all the things we could know in the blackness beyond visible sight. Because she represents all the forces that surround us which are not perceived in the eyes, but which extend from the visible spectrum into unexplored modes of being. Because she is the Goddess of the vision of the night, the dream, and all those things we see by inner light when our eyes are closed. Because she is the Goddess of Second Sight, and of First Sight too, the touch in the womb, and the lover's light of touch in bed. She is the Goddess of intimacy, of being 'in touch'. And perhaps because she lives in the blackness which men have created by their blindness she is therefore sometimes represented as blind, the Goddess of Justice, the blind Sheckinah weeping for the exiled people, Jung's blind animal figure, Salome.

The Dark Mother, then, is two things. She is everything in the Goddess principle which men and women fear because they fail to understand her. And she is the key to greatly expanded awareness, including awareness of herself.

She is no threat; she is the key to renewal and rebirth. And sooner or later we must come to terms with her, if she is to cease to weep for her exiles.

IV   The Menstruating Goddess

That which is below is like unto that which is above, and that which is above is like unto that which is below, to achieve the wonders of the One Thing.

Hermes Trismegistos

When the Christian puts on his Sabbath best, or the Jew wishes his neighbour 'Gut Shabbus', or the witch casts her Circle for a Sabbat festival, etymologically at least they are all doing the same thing. They are paying due homage to the menstrual cycle of the Moon Goddess.

Prehistoric and early historic mankind knew very well that women's menstruation was a central fact of existence, and that at the period of menstrual flow woman was at her most magically powerful, shamanistic and mysterious. Since the parallel between the Moon's phases and women's was obvious, the dark of the Moon was equally obviously the Goddess's menstrual peak. Then she, too, was at her most powerful and mysterious, and humans were very careful about what they did, or refrained from doing, at that awesome time. The New Moon became hedged around with a host of prudent taboos and propitiatory rituals.

In due course, these observances were extended to the four quarters of her cycle. The Assyrians marked not only the day of the New Moon but also the seventh, fourteenth and twenty-first days of the cycle with special ceremonies. Each of these days was called *sabbatu*.

It is from the Assyrian *sabbatu* that today's Sabbath, observed every seventh day, and with taboos on various kinds of activity, directly descends.

One interesting *sabbatu* has disappeared: the Assyrians also marked the nineteenth day. Now days 14-19 of a woman's menstrual cycle are nearly enough her ovulation peak, when the possibility of conception is at its maximum. So this ancient civilization, millennia ahead of Dr Billings, were aware of the fact and honoured the Goddess's period of maximum fertility as it deserved.

All very humanly and symbolically understandable, at that epoch, the cynic might say; nevertheless an obvious fantasy, from our better-informed standpoint.

But is it? Or were the Assyrians propounding a psychic and spiritual truth – that the Goddess menstruates?

The ultimate polarity of the cosmic creative force – the God and the Goddess – is reflected on all the levels and in all manifestations; as Hermes Trismegistos put it, '*ad perpetranda miracula Rei Unius*' ('to achieve the wonders of the One Thing'). In other words, Creation is inevitably of the nature of the Creator; the universe is One.

And the more evolved an element in that creation, the more complex and complete its reflection of the creative source.

(Hermes Trismegistos was a legendary sage said to have lived in Egypt about 1900 BC. He was in fact a form of Thoth, Egyptian God of Wisdom, and his famous 'Emerald Tablet' – from which this quotation comes – was a Latin text probably deriving from Thoth rituals and much cited by medieval philosophers.)

To say that mankind is the most highly evolved factor on this planet is not to be arrogant; it is to admit an almost frightening responsibility. A mother turtle reflects one or two comparatively simple aspects of the cosmic feminine principle, the Goddess; a mother cat or dog considerably more. A male salmon reflects a few simple God-aspects; a stag many more.

But when we come to our own species, a woman is the most complex reflection of the Goddess, and a man of the God, in Gaia's multiform repertoire. How clearly that reflection shines, varies widely from one individual to another; in some it seems distorted beyond recognition, while in others it approaches completeness. But the closer we approach to that completeness, the more genuinely human we are.

The same may be said of the Goddess-forms and God-forms which mankind has envisaged. Some of them have taken animal forms or, while being anthropomorphic themselves, have been associated with totem animals. But this has been an instinctive emphasis only on the particular Goddess-aspect or God-aspect represented by the deity concerned. And the more complete a deity-concept becomes, the more it is envisaged in human form. Ishtar, Isis or Arianrhod is Woman-shaped; Apollo, Christ or Lugh is Man-shaped.

This is not due to the inadequacy or egocentricity of the human imagination. It is an admission of responsibility, an acknowledgement that, potentially at least, we are capable of reflecting the whole spectrum of aspects of the Goddess and the God. Envisaging Isis as Woman, or Apollo as Man, is not an attempt to drag them down to our own level; it is a striving to raise ourselves to theirs.

'In the image of God created he him; male and female created he them.' The truth cannot be hidden even by the patriarchal bias of Genesis; the image of Divinity is male and female.

Let us look at it, then, from the other end: by examining the male and female essences at human level, we can apprehend the essences of the God and Goddess which they reflect. (We discussed this in some detail in the chapter on Witchcraft and Sex in *The Witches' Way*.) In brief: the male essence is linear, analytical, with concentrated and logical awareness; it takes things to pieces to see what they are made of; it is fertilizing energy, force rather than form. The female essence is cyclical, synthesizing, with diffuse and intuitive awareness; it puts things together to see how they relate; it receives the male energy and gives it form.

(This is not to say, of course, that a man is purely the one, and a woman purely the other. Each healthy human contains both; the 'essence' is a matter of creative emphasis. See the passage on Animus and Anima on pages 59–61.)

Either without the other is incomplete, distorted and vulnerable. Working together, they generate immense creative power, whether at human or divine level. Their polarity is the dynamo of the universe.

As we shall discuss more fully in Chapter VI, the outstanding symbols of the God and Goddess, the Sun and the Moon, express these qualities vividly.

The Sun gives a bright, fertilizing light; he is constant in contrast with the Moon (though he has his own, long-term cycle); he illuminates dark corners and banishes ambiguity; sometimes his heat can be merciless, driving us into shelter to moderate it.

The Moon, on the other hand, is the bright jewel of the dark Unconscious. She takes the Sun's light and tempers its fire, making something different of it. Her cyclical nature is inescapable. At one phase, she manifests entirely as the Dark Mother; at another, she is wholly the Bright Mother; in between, she is both at once, in one perfectly integrated whole. She also has a mysterious face forever invisible from Earth (but beginning to yield its secrets to us, now that mankind's probing intelligence has learned to orbit around her; so, if we are wise, can our Sun-aspect be used to understand our Moon-aspect instead of ignoring or smothering it).

Woman, reflecting the Goddess, has all these qualities and, being (like Man) a multi-level entity, her bodily nature mirrors that of her non-material levels.

Her one inescapable physical difference from Man is menstruation. Her capacity to mate and bear children is a potential which the individual may or may not fulfil, but lover or virgin, mother or nun, from puberty to menopause (the Mother phase of her triple nature) she menstruates. And the point to realize is that she menstruates on all her levels – physical, etheric, astral, mental and spiritual. It is the ultimate expression of her (Goddess-like) cyclical nature.

Under patriarchy, with its distorted (because unbalanced) thinking, menstruation has become 'the curse', and by and large it has been so accepted by women as well. Even biological and psychological science has ignored its true implications, markedly more so than in other fields of research – until Penelope Shuttle and Peter Redgrove's revolutionary 1978 work *The Wise Wound: Menstruation and Everywoman*, which should be compulsory reading for every witch and pagan.

Shuttle and Redgrove point out that patriarchal science, interested only in the procreative aspect, has concentrated on the ovulation peak of the cycle, treating the menstrual peak as purely negative, a mere preparation for the next ovulation. But the cycle is an integrated whole, with deep psychic significance as a cycle, and not merely as a string of repetitions.

At ovulation, woman is the Bright Mother, the fecund womb of the race, the extrovert carrier and passer-on of everything that is encoded in its DNA molecules. Sexually, she tends to be receptive, desiring penetration and fertilization. At menstruation, she is the Dark Mother, the seeress, the introvert midwife of mysteries – carrier, if you like, of the DNA molecules of the Collective Unconscious. Sexually, she tends to take the erotic initiative, desiring experience for its own sake, divorced from the procreative urge.

There is a difference, too, in her image, whether conscious or unconscious, of the male. At ovulation, he is the potential father (whether wanted or feared). At menstruation, he is the brother or the non-impregnating lover – or maybe the psychic intruder.

Strangely enough, it is menstruation which makes *Homo sapiens* essentially human. 'It is received opinion in zoological science that the development of the menstrual cycle was responsible for the evolution of primate and eventually human societies. (*The Wise Wound*, p.142). The oestrus cycle of other mammals is purely procreative, sex being 'switched off' when the female is not on heat – i.e., at her ovulation peak. But the development of the menstrual cycle produced continuous sexuality – what Shuttle and Redgrove call 'sexual brightness'. This in effect is an urge to relatedness transcending that of other social animals, an evolutionary leap which (like all such leaps) had survival and development value for the species.

It was, we suggest, an important step in the process we mentioned earlier – mankind's increasing capacity to reflect the whole spectrum of the God and the Goddess. For although the God is essentially linear, and the Goddess essentially cyclical, the creative polarity between them operates all the time, through all her phases and on all their levels. So it is with Man and Woman, and with the buried masculine elements in Woman (the Animus) and the buried feminine elements in Man (The Anima), for as Shuttle and Redgrove emphasize in a thought-provoking remark, 'What should never have been forgotten is that *the anima menstruates*' (*ibid.*, p.130).

As above, so below. We strive to understand the God and Goddess by understanding ourselves, and vice versa, because we are of their nature.

So in answer to our question: both as a truth in itself and as a helpful concept in learning to understand her – yes, the Assyrians were right. The Goddess menstruates.

V   The Triple Goddess

Diana in the leavës green,
Luna that so bright doth sheen,
Persephone in Hell.
                    John Skelton

The theme of the Triple Goddess is found in the mythology of all lands
– a Trinity many millennia older than the Christian one. She is Maid,
Mother and Crone; Enchantment, Ripeness and Wisdom; the waxing,
full and waning Moon.

Behold the Three-Formed Goddess;
She who is ever Three – Maid, Mother, and Crone.
Yet is she ever One;
She in all women, and they all in her.
Look on these Three, who are One, with a fearless love,
That you, too, may be whole.

She is found in all cultures because she is archetypal. The female
aspect of divinity (as of humanity) is, as we saw in the last chapter,

cyclical – seductive, nourishing and counselling, by turns and simultaneously. Every fulfilled, self-aware woman knows this of herself, if only instinctively, and every thinking man who has ever loved a woman knows it too.

Just how old the concept is can be seen from the earliest known representation of a European religious ritual: an Old Stone Age cave-painting at Cogul in north-eastern Spain, described in detail by Robert Graves on p.399 of *The White Goddess* (third edition, Faber, 1952). Nine women are dancing in a crescent, facing an exhausted-looking young man with huge genitals – the human representative of the Dying God. Deosil (clockwise) round the crescent, the women's clothing and figures make it clear that they grow progressively older, starting with three young girls and ending with the most ancient and emaciated woman of all, who has the face of a waning Moon (she is the only one who is dancing widdershins – anti-clockwise). The only other figure, riding a fawn away from the group but facing backwards, is a young boy 'as clearly as anything the escaping soul of the doomed Dionysus', Graves comments. 'For the wild women are closing in on him and will presently tear him in bloody morsels and devour him. Though there is nothing in the painting to indicate the season, we can be sure that it was the winter solstice.' The Triple Goddess, re-tripled for emphasis, is also a frequent theme (see our remarks on the Muses, and on the Crone, below).

This was the dark, sacrificial-mating aspect of the Triple Goddess, but she crops up again and again in all her aspects.

Thousands of years later, patriarchal monotheism (with a crucial contribution from St Paul) completed the process which late patriarchal paganism had started: denial and suppression of the realities of sexual polarity, whether dark or light. The earlier pagan world-view had taken these realities as self-evident and had envisaged its Goddess-forms to express them.

'In a Gallo-Roman "*allée couverte*" burial at Tresse near St-Malo in Brittany two pairs of girls' breasts are sculptured on one megalithic upright, two maternal pairs of breasts on another; the top of a third upright has been broken off, but V.C.C. Collum who excavated the burial suggests that it pictured a third pair – probably the shrunken breasts of the Hag' (Graves, *The White Goddess*, p.387).

So again and again we meet the Triple Goddess – always with the emphasis on her essential oneness (a concept taken over, whether consciously or unconsciously, by the Christian Trinity). As often as not a Triple Goddess would have only one name, yet her legend would emphasize that there were three of her. Even sometimes her places of worship; for example, at Stymphalus in Greece, Hera had three temples – to the child-goddess, the wife-goddess and the widow-goddess. Hera was one of the worst sufferers from the patriarchal take-over: originally a powerful mother-goddess in her own right, she was demoted by the newcomer Zeus to a mere consort. So it is not surprising that even at Stymphalus her titles of 'wife' and 'widow' related to her consort status, instead of to herself as 'mother' and 'wise old woman'. But her Triple Goddess nature was still unobscured. (It would be illuminating to know just what form the rituals took in those three temples.)

Hecate of the Three Faces, guardian of crossroads (where the traveller faces three choices), was typical. So were the Three Fates, in pantheons from the Greek Moerae to the Teutonic Norns. Moerae and Norns, incidentally, are both clearly divided into the three functions: she who spins the thread, she who shapes destiny and she who cuts the thread when the time comes.

Greek triads of the darker kind were the Erinyes, goddesses of divine vengeance and justice (called the Furiae by the Romans), and the terrifying Gorgons, whose gaze turned men to stone – symbolizing the hidden depths of the unconscious which few are well integrated enough to face directly.

At the other extreme stood the Charites or Graces, goddesses of splendour, joy and good cheer, and naturally a favourite subject for artists.

Apollo, shining epitome of the male aspect of divinity, had nine Muses – the old Triple Goddess multiplied by herself and reduced to a team of assistants. Earlier Muses on Mount Helicon and at Sicyon had all been three in number, as they were at Delphi, the greatest centre of feminine clairvoyance and prophecy, before Apollo seized it.

Carmenta, a Roman goddess of childbirth, and thus a Mother, had as Maid her sister Antevorta ('Looking Forward') and as Crone her other sister Postvorta ('Looking Back').

In the Hindu pantheon, Bhavani is one clear example among many. She is known as the Triple Universe and is depicted in three forms: as a young woman crowned, containing within her body all the potential of creation – Earth, Sea, Sun and Moon, or as a mother with the Sun and Moon at her breasts, or as dark and awe-inspiring, with a necklace of skulls.

The Chinese have a Buddhist triad called the Triple Pussa, who have affinities with beneficent Kwan-Yin.

In the Slavonic pantheon we find the three Zoryas, goddesses of dawn, evening and midnight – a somewhat crucial triad, this, because they have charge of a dog chained to the constellation Ursa Minor – and when the chain breaks, it is said, the world will end.

Even popular Christianity smuggled in the Triple Goddess, by way of the South of France. Here, at Les Saintes Maries de la Mer, the Virgin Mary, Mary Magdalene and Mary Cleopas are believed to have landed after Jesus's Ascension; the worship of the Three Maries is very deep-rooted in Provence (see Chapter VIII).

Another emigrant triad – from Dahomey in Africa to Haiti – is the Voodoo Erzulie. The Mother figure is Erzulie Freda Dahomey, goddess of love, known as Maîtresse and often identified with the Virgin Mary; the Maid is La Sirène, with her sea-like voice; and the Crone is the aged and protective Gran Erzulie.

The Triple Goddess survives very ambivalently in Islam, as Al-Lat, Al-Uzza and Manah. Al-Lat, an ancient Moon goddess, is etymologically the feminine form of Allah. Al-Uzza was originally the goddess of the Ka'aba, the sacred stone of Mecca. Manah means 'time' or 'fate'. All three are condemned in the Koran, Surah liii:19-23: 'What think ye of Al-Lat, and Al-Uzza, and Manah, that other third goddess? Have ye male children, and Allah female? ... They are no other than empty names, which ye and your fathers have named goddesses.' And yet they are known in Moslem tradition as 'the Three Daughters of Allah'.

The richest surviving goldmine of Triple Goddess evidence is Celtic.

Celtic culture, unlike that of most of Europe, did not turn the gods of the old religion into the devils of the new. It turned them into racial heroes and heroines, whose body of legend was even written down by medieval Celtic monks with remarkable sympathy and faithfulness (as in the *Lebor Gabála Érenn, The Book of Invasions* – see Bibliography under MacAlister). Nor did it suppress the old folktales; it simply transferred them virtually unchanged from (for example) Lugh Lám-hfada to St Patrick, as Máire MacNeill has shown in *The Festival of Lughnasa*.

On the female side, this transferring was even less disguised. The supreme example is Brighid (which is variously interpreted as deriving from *Breo-saighead*, 'fiery arrow', or *Brigh*, 'power'). Brighid was a Celtic goddess of inspiration, fertility and fire; her festival of Imbolg ('in the belly') was on 1 February, and one of her principal cult centres was Kildare.

As we shall see in Chapter XIV, the historical St Brighid or Bridget, who died about AD 525, took over her characteristics, legends and holy places – even her feast day, Lá Fhéile Bríd, 1 February – lock, stock and barrel.

Brighid was a major Goddess throughout the Celtic lands. Brigantia, which covered much of the North of England, was named after her, and many surviving British place-names derive from her. In Gaul she was known as Brigindo, and in other parts of the Continent as Brigan or Brig. Small wonder that, even in her Christian guise, she ended up as 'the Mary of the Gael', the Foster-Mother of Christ; folk devotion is indifferent to anachronism.

And here is our Triple Goddess clue: time and again, even in Christian legend, she is referred to as 'the three Bridgets'. No plausible historical evidence is cited for this, and indeed the historical St Bridget is shadowy enough behind all the splendid legends of her magical powers. But the triple nature of a much-loved Goddess survives in folk memory as the mysterious tripling of a saint. (She even has three feast days: 1 February already mentioned, 10 June for her translation and 24 March for the supposed discovery of her body, along with those of Patrick and Columba, by Malachy at Downpatrick in 1185.)

(St Augustine, attacking the worship of the triple Moon Goddess, wrote: 'How can a goddess be three persons and one at the same time?' Apparently only a male deity is allowed that.)

To turn to unchristianized pagan figures, the most striking example is perhaps that of the three queens of the Tuatha Dé Danann – Eire (Eriu, Erin), Banbha and Fodhla. When the Milesians (Gaels), last conquerors of Ireland in the mythological cycle, defeated the Tuatha Dé Danann ('the People of the Goddess Dana'), these three ladies asked Amergin, bard and spokesman of the Milesians, that Ireland be named after them, and their request was granted. (Banbha and Fodhla may be forgotten today as names of Ireland, but they crop up as such in passages of the *Lebor Gabála Érenn*.)

These three were daughters of the Dagda ('the good God') and, interestingly, they had elemental consorts. Banbha's husband was Mac Cuill, Son of the Hazel, described elsewhere as 'he whose God was the hazel', or 'his God the sea'. Éire's was Mac Greine, Son of the Sun (or 'the Sun his God'). Fodhla's was Mac Cecht, Son of the Plough (or 'whose God was the plough' or 'whose God was the earth').

Here we not only have the Triple Goddess, with an awareness of her complex polarity with the male divine aspect, but can actually allot a role in the trinity to at least one of them: to Banbha as the Crone. Banbha told Amergin 'I am older than Noah; on a peak of a mountain was I in the Flood'. She claimed to have come to Ireland with Cessair (Cesara), granddaughter of Noah and legendary first occupier of this island. Another passage in the *Lebor* goes even farther and says Banbha was the first woman who found Ireland before the Flood.

From their consorts, we might even guess at the roles of all three; antediluvian Banbha as the Crone, mated to the primordial Deep; Fodhla as the Mother, mated to the Earth; and Éire as the Maid, bride of the Sun.

The Morrigan, Irish battle goddess, is also sometimes envisaged as combining Anu, Banbha and Macha in a Three Fates triad.

The Triple Goddess is hinted at in less prominent Irish legendary women too: for example, the three sisters the Cailleach Bheara (the Hag of Beare), the Witch of Bolus and the Witch of Dingle.

Significantly, one of these again was reputedly very ancient; the Witch of Dingle lived to be 300.

Coventina, patron goddess of the sacred well at Carrawburgh, Northumberland, is represented in a relief there as a trio of nymphs.

Thanks to Wagner, everyone knows one version of the story of Tristan (Tristram) and Isolde (Iseult, Essylt Vyngwen 'of the fine hair'), but in fact Celtic legend links three Iseults to Tristram. First, a Queen of Ireland who had great healing powers, by which she cured Tristram when her brother Morold wounded him. Second, the promised bride of King Mark of Cornwall who became Tristram's lover when they drank a love potion by mistake; when they had to part, she gave him a ring as token of her love, to be used as a signal if he ever needed her. And third, the daughter of a King of Brittany who became Tristram's wife.

Here again the Triple Goddess theme is expressed, in polarity with the young hero-god. Iseult the Maid becomes his lover; this spring-time phase does not last, but she will always be there if he really needs her. Iseult the Mother becomes his wife and bearer of his children. And Iseult the Crone, with her magical arts, heals his wounds. Yet their shared name indicates that they are three aspects of the same goddess, to each of whom the god must relate to fulfil his destiny.

Less clear, but still unmistakable, is Arthur's Queen Guinevere (Gwynhwyfar). According to *The Triads of Britain* (see Bibliography under Morganwg), medieval manuscripts whose material stems from oral tradition of the sixth or seventh century and perhaps earlier, Arthur had three wives called Gwynhwyfar, daughters respectively of Gwythyr son of Greidiawl, of Gawrwyd Ceint and of Ogyvran Gawr.

Medieval romance has greatly distorted the archetypal themes which earlier crystallized about the real historical figure of Artorius, the *Dux Bellorum* who united the British Celts against the Saxons after the collapse of Roman Britain. These archetypes, one can distinguish, represented the honoured Old King, his brilliant Young Heroes and the Goddess-Queen who kept the balance between them – her roles of consort, lover, mother, counsellor and inspirer overlapping with a splendid pagan lack of inhibition. This must have been the true Gwynhwyfar of Celtic legend, whatever the facts about Artorius's actual wife; and only a Triple Goddess (or her human expression, which every real woman is) could have measured up to that position as the vital focus of the Court of Heroes.

There are possible hints of this in the three Gwynhwyfars' 'Fathers', paralleling those given by the elemental mates of Banbha, Fodhla and Éire. Gwythyr was a type of the hero who must battle annually with his rival other-self for the Goddess-heroine's favour (like the Oak King and Holly King); Ogyrvan Gawr was a giant (Earth?), and so on.

Lancelot was a late addition to the original Celtic body of Arthurian legend; his disastrous affair with Gwynhwyfar may hark back to a seasonal dying-god prototype.

It is sad that, at the hands of the medieval romancers Gwynhwyfar degenerated into a rather colourless puppet, beguiled into adultery by Lancelot and thus disgraced – the very opposite of the sacrificial-mating theme.

But the archetypes can still be discerned behind the distortions. The Triple Goddess is not easy to hide. And as far as Arthur himself is concerned, she was with him to the end – as the three mysterious ladies who took his body by boat to Avalon.

What is the nature of the three aspects that make up the Triple Goddess?

First, the Maid. She is Enchantment, the bright magic of the female principle, the fresh light of dawn that sweeps away weariness with the promise of new beginnings. She is the adventurous young flame that banishes indifference and leapfrogs obstacles, the lively curiosity that blows the dust off stale knowledge and gives it new perspectives. She is springtime, the first daffodil, the hatching egg. She is excitement, she is the carefree erotic aura that sets men and gods preening themselves. She is unselfconsciousness in a mini-skirt – the cosmic pin-up, innocently skyclad (the Wiccan word for 'ritually naked') or unapologetically dressed up to the nines as her mysterious fancy takes her. She is the huntress, running free through the woods in pursuit of her quarry (which might be you) with her hounds beside her. She is danger if abused; she is joy itself if respected. Her traditional colour is white.

Among the goddesses typical of the Maid are rosy-fingered Eos, the Greek dawn goddess who daily teased the Sun out of his bed and who turned the heads of mortals and Olympians alike, embracing either when she felt like it; her Hindu counterpart Ushas, whose lover was Fire; Renpet, Egyptian goddess of springtime and youth, significantly known as 'Mistress of Eternity'; and the Assyrian Siduri, who ran a seaside pub and tried to persuade the young hero Gilgamesh to enjoy life as it came and not be so damned earnest.

Even when the names are different, the other aspects of the Three are seldom far to seek. Eos, for example, grows naturally into Hemera, the Day Goddess, as Mother; and Hemera's own mother was Nyx (Night), the Crone aspect.

Second, the Mother. She is Ripeness; she moulds life within the womb, gives birth to it, nourishes it, teaches it and slaps its bottom when necessary. She is mentally, spiritually, emotionally and physically full-blooded and powerful. She may give open advice or exert shrewd influence which is unnoticed at the time but which achieves its ends.

The male principle is both her husband and her child. As mate, she does not tantalize, which the Maid may sometimes do; she will restrain him if the time is not ripe – or if it is, she will give all, transmuting him to gold in the furnace of her love, just as she transmutes his seed into new life. Against anything which threatens what she loves, she is merciless and terrible. And when she destroys the outworn, or whatever impedes the development of that which she loves, she may seem merciless. But that is only in the eyes of those who do not understand her (which sometimes includes those whom she loves). She is fertility itself – yet her fecundity, which appears unbounded, is not blind or aimless; it has an overall balance, a symphonic richness, which tunnel vision cannot perceive. It is that overall balance which determines her actions; ephemeral standards of morality or equity, believed eternal by those who hold them, mean nothing to her. Her traditional colour is red.

Mother goddesses are numberless, because the Great Mother was the first image of divinity that evolving mankind grasped. But outstanding among them in recorded history are perhaps Gaia, the Greek Earth Mother who was the great womb of the gods and of humanity; the Roman Juno, too powerful even for imperial patriarchy entirely to subordinate her; and above all Isis, the supreme flowering of the Mother aspect before male monotheism tried to banish the Goddess altogether.

And lastly, the Crone. She is Wisdom, the Jewelled Hag. She has seen it all; she has compassion for it all, but a compassion undistorted by illusion or sentimentality. Her wisdom is much wider than intellectual knowledge, though it includes intellect and does not despise it. Maid and Mother live within her as stored experience, and she within them as potential. (In this sense, the Three are Nine; for each contains all three, though with her own characteristic emphasis.) When called for, the Crone is baby-sitter for the Mother, and chaperone for the Maid, keeping a shrewd eye on both and maintaining the overall balance. To the male aspect she is a steadying influence, and an enriching one if he listens to her; she adds another dimension to his linear-logical thinking and prevents it getting the bit between its teeth. Like the other two, she is Love, but hers is a calm understanding love, complementing the heady love of the Maid and the incandescent love of the Mother. She too can seem terrible, because she is the gateway to Death. But she is also the Psychopompos who guides us through it, pointing the way to the new life where she will again be all the Three. Her traditional colour is black.

And now comes the mental leap, the key to understanding. Contemplate each of these aspects in all its complexity, and then try to hold all three in your awareness at once. Realize that the whole spectrum, with its shifting colours, is the one glowing rainbow. To pursue the analogy further – red/orange for the Mother, yellow/green for the Maid, and blue/indigo/violet for the Crone. (Think of that next time you see a rainbow.) Which wavelength predominates for you at any one moment depends on your own tuning. But make the effort to grasp the whole rainbow, and you are face to face with the manifold Goddess herself.

You are also face to face with Woman, the manifested feminine principle – and with the reason why the High Priestess is the integrating focus of the Wiccan coven.

But that is a matter for Chapter XI.

VI The Moon Goddess

She is the ruler of the tides of flux and reflux. The waters of the
Great Sea answer unto her, likewise the tides of all earthly seas,
and she ruleth the nature of woman.

Dion Fortune

It is not surprising, in view of what we have said about the Triple
Goddess, that the outstanding Goddess symbol is the Moon. Cyclical
and eternal at the same time, waxing and waning, dark and light,
ruling alike the tides of the primordial ocean, and of women.
Fundamentally unchanging, always showing the same face, but
illuminating it differently from day to day – and, if you watch her
closely enough, from hour to hour.

Yet we find an apparent puzzle, for there are Moon gods too.

The gender of the Moon and Sun varies from pantheon to pantheon
– and sometimes within the same culture. What may be called the
'standard' pattern is feminine Moon, masculine Sun. The classical
Greek and Roman pantheons adhered consistently to this: Sun gods
Apollo, Helios, Sabazius, Sol; Moon goddesses Artemis, Hecate,

Bendis, Brizo, Callisto, Selene, Prosymna, Diana, Luna. (Though there is evidence that both Artemis and Diana may have absorbed a pre-Indo-European Sun goddess.)

Tuscany, as we shall see in Chapter XXII, had (and still has) Diana, Aradia and Losna as Moon and Lucifer as Sun. The Americas, too, had Moon goddesses, Auchimalgen and Mama Quilla (Chile), Chasca (Inca), Ka-Ata-Killa (pre-Inca), Chia (Colombia), Hun-Ahpu-Myte (Guatemala), Metzli (Aztec), Komorkis (Blackfoot Indian) and various corresponding Sun gods. (Though again, the Cherokees had a Sun goddess, Igaehindvo.)

The Hebrew Jarah, after whom Jericho was named, was goddess of the New Moon and bride of the Sun; Levanah, the Moon of the Song of Solomon, was also Chaldaean; and another Chaldaean Moon goddess, Sirdu, wife of the Sun god Shamash-Bubbar, may also have been the bride of the Hebrew Iao (Yahweh). The Essenes, however, linked their Earthly Mother with the Sun, their Heavenly Father representing only abstract concepts. An ambivalent Moon deity was Sams, a southern Semitic goddess who was the male Samas to the northern Semites.

On the other side of the world, the Polynesian Sina was Moon-sister to the Sun god Maui.

The Hindus, with their complex pantheon, tend to the 'standard' pattern, though their Sun god Surya is sometimes feminine, but their Moon goddess is personified in phases – Gungu, Kuhu and Sinvali (New, Sinvali being a wife of Vishnu), Raka (Full), Anumati (Waning) and Jyotsna (Autumnal). But there are also the brothers Mitra (Sun) and Varuna (Moon), sons of the primordial Mother Aditi.

(A similar family in Africa is the Dahomey Mother Goddess Lissa with her sons Maou, the Sun, and Gou, the Moon.)

Egypt had its Sun god, Ra, and its Moon God, Thoth, but with both there is a hint of the other aspect. In surviving legend, Rait is Ra's wife, and mother of the goddesses Ma'at and Selkhet, but her name is merely the feminine form of Ra ('Sun'), and she may well have been the earlier Sun deity. And although Thoth is the Moon god, he is not identified with the Moon, as we shall see below. A Moon goddess Sefkhet-Seshat appears as his wife as well as Ma'at; and when he visits the Moon, he is looked after by a goddess of its dark side, known as Woman-Light of the Shadows.

When we come to the overlapping pantheons of Sumer, Assyria, Babylon, Caanan and Phoenicia, there is also ambivalence. Ishtar, greatest of the Middle Eastern goddesses, was daughter of the Moon god Sin and sister of the Sun god Shamash. (Mount Sinai was named after Sin, and the Levites were originally Moon priests, wearing the lunar crescent as a headdress.) Over the centuries Ishtar acquired many

of her father's lunar characteristics and even came to be referred to as
the Mother of the Moon (see Chapter XV). There was also an
Assyro-Babylonian Moon goddess Mylitta, whose worship overlapped
Ishtar's, and a Phoenician Moon goddess Re; to confuse things still
further, the Sumerian and Canaanite Sun goddess Shapash, and the
Syrian Sun goddess Nahar.

Slavonic Sun and Moon are usually both male, but Myestas appears
sometimes as a Moon god and sometimes in an Earth role as the Sun's
beautiful young bride whom he marries each Spring and abandons each
Winter. The Romanians had a male Sun with an incestuous passion for
his sister the Moon, who kept herself to the night to escape him.

To the Eskimos, on the other hand, the Sun is female, and the Moon
is her lover who visits her by night.

The Japanese pantheon also reverses the 'standard' pattern
completely. Their supreme deity, ancestress of the Japanese Emperors,
is the Sun goddess Amaterasu. The Moon god Taukiyomi is her
brother. The Chinese Li represents the female solar aspect, though in
general the Sun is associated with the male Yang aspect and the Moon
with the female Yin. And to the Australian Aborigines, the Great Spirit
and prime creatrix is the Sun goddess Yhi; her lover is Bahloo, the
Moon god.

The Celts seem to be the only major culture to whom both Moon and
Sun were feminine. Surviving legend, which has converted the original
deities into folk-heroes and heroines, does not name any solar or lunar
deity as such. But *Grian*, 'Sun', is a feminine noun in both Irish and
Scottish Gaelic, as is the Welsh *Huan*; it was also, for example, the
name of a Co. Tipperary fairy queen; and Markale (*Women of the
Celts*, p.112) says that the Provençal legendary heroine Brunissen was
probably originally a Celtic Sun goddess. As for the Moon, *Gealach*
and *Ré* ('Moon') are also feminine in both Irish and Scottish, as are
Lleuad and *Lloer* in Welsh; Áine of Knockaine was a Munster Moon
goddess (Graves, *The White Goddess*, p.370); the Welsh Cerridwen had
lunar associations; and the markedly triple nature of so many Celtic
goddesses points unmistakably to a lunar origin.

An apparently confusing picture; but it is worth looking at it closely
to see how it makes sense – particularly in relation to the Moon, which
is the subject of this chapter.

Why does the Moon, whose dramatically feminine symbolism is
obvious even to a modern town-dweller, appear as a male God in so
many ancient cultures?

The essential key is that the Moon was mankind's first precise
time-measurer. Its phases are absolutely regular, and one does not need
even the crudest of instruments to pinpoint them. It may be said that
the Moon was the first object of precise observation by the emerging

consciousness of *Homo sapiens*; everything else in his environment was either variable (like the weather, the scarcity or plentifulness of food, the height of the tides) or so long-term and slow-changing as to have no easily definable 'milestones' (like the solar year).

As economic, social and ritual life became more complex, man began to need a calendar of some kind, and he turned naturally to his one clear and dependable clock, the Moon. All early calendars were lunar – and this fact survives in our months ('Moonths'), even though we have had to falsify their length to fit the solar year, in our seven-day Moon-quarter week, in the lunar dating of Easter and more obviously in the Jewish, Moslem and Chinese ritual calendars, which still co-exist with the practical solar ones.

It is clear from a study of pagan pantheons that mankind knew instinctively from the start, long before any conscious analysis of them, which were God functions and which Goddess. Precise measurement, including predictive measurement, was a gift of the God; so the Moon, at least in its time-defining function, was a god.

The Egyptian religion – the longest-lasting and most complex and subtle in pagan history – illustrates the development typically, if only because it never abolished old concepts and symbols when a new stage was reached but preserved and adapted them, sometimes paradoxically, within the overall framework.

Thoth, as a Moon god, recalled his primordial time-measuring function – and developed naturally into a god of wisdom and knowledge. Then, when the divergence between the lunar calendar and the solar year became obvious (and inconvenient because of the vital annual importance of the Nile flooding), to whom did the Egyptians equally naturally appeal for a solution? To the god of wisdom and logical reasoning. It was Thoth who went back to his own source, the Moon, and beat it at draughts to win the intercalary days (see p.171), the first major step in solving the problem.

In a sense this action separated Thoth from his lunar nature. Intellect had won independence from its starting-point, and the Moon's equally obvious feminine symbolism (which had doubtless co-existed from the start – Isis and Hathor were both linked with the Moon) also emerged as independent, in the form of Sefkhet-Seshat and the Woman-Light of the Shadows.

But the Egyptians always got the balance right. Independence did not mean competition, but collaboration. The most powerful magic in Egyptian mythology was always worked by Isis, the intuitive essence, and Thoth, the logical essence, operating as a harmonious team.

The stage where conscious intellect conquered the problem of defining the solar year is also marked by the remarkable neolithic structures such as Stonehenge in England and Newgrange in Ireland, whose astronomical accuracy and sophistication have only recently been appreciated.

If the measurement of time is a God function, time itself is a Goddess one. 'Since she governs growth, the Great Mother is goddess of time. That is why she is a moon goddess, for moon and night sky are visible manifestations of the temporal process in the cosmos, and the moon, not the sun, is the true chronometer of the primordial era. From menstruation, with its supposed relation to the moon, pregnancy, and beyond, the woman is regulated by and dependent on time; so it is she who determines time – to a far greater extent than the male ... And this temporal quality of the Feminine is bound up with the moon' (Neumann, *The Great Mother*, pp.226-7).

So just as consciousness is the son of the unconscious, the Moon god comes to be seen as the son (and lover) of the Moon goddess, being sacrificed and reborn with her phases (a relationship parallel to that between the Earth Mother and her annually sacrificed and reborn vegetation son/lover). The young crescent Moon was the son fighting off the dragon of darkness that had consumed his father, whose renewed self he was.

Even the Babylonian Moon god Sin was often depicted seated in the Moon-tree which was a Goddess symbol. He was the fruit of that tree, not the tree itself. The ambivalence of the Moon as both Goddess and God is reflected in the prayer to him: 'Mother Womb, begetter of all things, O Merciful Father who hath taken into his care the whole world.'

The role of the human male in parenthood was not a sudden discovery; it overlapped and interwove with the primordial belief (among the Maoris, for example) that the Moon was the true impregnator of women. Some tribes believed that man's function was merely to rupture the hymen or dilate the vagina to open a path for the fertilizing Moon. Others believed that, while most pregnancies were now the result of human intercourse, it had not always been so, and that certain special babies were still Moon-children. Genghis Khan was said to be the descendant of such a Moon-child, and many kings claimed Moon parentage. They wore crescent crowns to declare this – hence the symbolism of horns as meaning divinely bestowed power, as they do throughout the Old Testament.

(This belief in the Moon-parentage of kings or chiefs may have been the origin of the '*droit du seigneur*', the alleged right of a feudal lord to take the virginity of a bride on her wedding night. Proof of this actually having been a custom is hard to find; lords may well have cited a half-remembered ancient tradition as an excuse for levying a tax in lieu. The ancient tradition certainly existed – the human representative of the Moon ensuring the fertility of the marriage.)

Another widespread belief was that menstruation was the monthly abortion of an imperfect Moon-child. The gradual emergence of the Sun god, taking over much of the earlier Moon god's fertilizing and time-measuring functions, hastened the stage (typified by Greece and Rome) where the Moon became entirely a goddess. We believe this can be called a step forward in symbolic thinking; and the Sun-god, Moon-goddess pattern has certainly become fittingly expressive of psychic truths, at least in the West.

(At least one Christian thinker – the outstandingly Nature-conscious St Francis – had a similar outlook, expressed in his famous Canticle to Brother Sun and Sister Moon; and he included Mother Earth for good measure.)

The Sun symbolizes the light of consciousness, illuminating the dark corners of doubt and uncertainty. It symbolizes the annual impregnation of Mother Earth. It symbolizes purposeful, deliberate activity and clarity. All of these are God functions.

The Moon symbolizes repose, the gentle illumination of the riches of the unconscious, intuition, magic and mystery. And these are Goddess functions.

To which may be added that the Sun's cyclical frequency is long and only gradually apparent, while the Moon's is monthly and unmistakable – phenomena which match human male and female experience of themselves and of each other.

Neither is fruitful without the other, any more than permanent day or permanent night could support terrestrial life.

Just as man's psyche includes his anima (buried feminine aspect) and woman's her animus (buried masculine aspect) – a subject which will be more fully dealt with in Chapter VIII – so these Goddess and God functions interpenetrate. Jung has suggested that the Moon represents not only the female consciousness but also the male unconscious, and that while the daytime Sun represents male consciousness, when it descends into the darkness at night, it represents female consciousness penetrating and comprehending that darkness. That would appear to leave woman without an unconscious – but the answer is that she is the key to the unconscious for both of them, being by nature in closer and more understanding touch with it, while his nature is more 'at home' with consciousness.

Symbol is the language by which the unconscious speaks to consciousness; and ritual, which is dramatized symbolism, is the language by which consciousness communicates with the unconscious.

The choice of symbols with which one works is therefore a two-way process. On the one hand, one listens to the unconscious and tries to grasp the meaning of the symbols it puts forward. On the other, one tries out symbols which seem appropriate, and numinously charged, for ritual call-signs to the unconscious.

The symbols which prove successful will come from two sources (which of course overlap). First, from the Collective Unconscious, symbols which have attached themselves to archetypal concepts, thought-forms which have been built up and strengthened by the beliefs and practices of countless generations of our ancestors. Second, from one's personal unconscious, engendered by one's individual experience, one's cultural environment and the concepts with which one feels personally in tune.

On both these grounds, most Western pagans will work most naturally with the Moon-goddess, Sun-god symbolism which has evolved in the family of cultures in which our roots are deepy planted. And even the Celts, one of the most magically powerful of the Western cultural streams, with their minority-view feminine Sun, are wholeheartedly with the majority in seeing the Moon as feminine.

For us, then, the Moon is the archetypal symbol of the Goddess. The Earth Mother beneath our feet is Isis Veiled, the Goddess robed in the infinite variety of Nature; and her other self, the Moon, is Isis Unveiled, goddess of the night sky, quietly pouring the secrets of her mystery through the windows of our soul.

All we have to do is to open the curtains and let her in.

VII   Blessed Among Women

I sing of a maiden
That is makeless.
Anonymous carol

Patriarchy's first assault on the Goddess took the form of subordinating her. Her acceptable aspects were put under the charge of male masters, mothers becoming wives (as Hera) or sisters (as Artemis) or daughters (as Britomartis), or being masculinized altogether (as Danae). Her uncomfortable or (to the patriarchal mind) frightening or dangerous aspects became demonesses (as Lilith), dragons that had to be tamed (as Tiamat) or glamorous sorceresses who had to be outmanoeuvred (as Circe).

The final assault, inevitably, was a determined attempt to abolish her entirely. This may be said to have begun with the heretic Pharaoh Akhenaton, though even he honoured Ma'at, goddess of justice and the divine order, by name. But the really sustained attempt began with the Hebrew priestly establishment.

They were less successful in this than is generally realized. For $2\frac{1}{2}$

centuries Ashera was worshipped in the Temple at Jerusalem along with Jehovah, as his wife and sister, and her image publicly displayed. Her cult was deeply ingrained in the old farming population of Israel. The tribe of Asher was named after her. Jeremiah (vii:18; xliv:17-25) thundered against the 'great multitude' who made offerings to the Queen of Heaven. And the Essenes, strict followers of the Law whose teachings greatly influenced Jesus, worshipped the Earthly Mother and her angels in polarity with the Heavenly Father and his angels.

Patriarchy in the shape of the Byzantine Church finally, if tacitly, had to admit the impossibility of the total abolition of the Goddess. At the Council of Ephesus in 431, it elevated the Virgin Mary to the position of Theotokos, Mother of God.

Mary is the Goddess of Christendom, let in through the back door, nervously denied actual divinity by the hierarchy but effectively acknowledged as such by the ordinary worshipper.

Apart from the Nativity story (given fully by Luke, briefly by Matthew and not at all by Mark or John), the Flight to Egypt (Matthew only) and twelve-year-old Jesus's visit with his parents to the Temple (Luke only), Mary is barely mentioned in the Gospels. John alone tells of the marriage at Cana and of Mary's presence at the Crucifixion. Matthew, Mark and Luke relate the incident where Jesus was told 'Thy mother and thy brethren are without' and gave the hardly complimentary answer that his disciples were his mother and his brethren. (His retort to her at the Cana wedding, and his reply to the woman who praised her in Luke xii:27-28, seem equally unfilial.) A single verse in Acts mentions her in prayer with the disciples in Jerusalem. And that is all.

The Nativity story, with its virgin birth, is agreed by scholars to be a later addition. (So, incidentally, are the last twelve verses of Mark — that Gospel's only account of the risen Christ.) The birth and childhood of Jesus are not even mentioned by Mark, whose Gospel was the earliest; and John, who seems the only one to have made use of eye-witness memories of the adult Jesus's mother, merely refers to the birth obliquely in i:13-14, the wording of which many scholars believe to have been tampered with.

To understand all this, one has to realize that although Jesus was one of the greatest spiritual and ethical teachers in history, the actual form of his ministry, and his approach to it, were very much the product of his time and culture. The Jews, suffering under the Romans and their quisling Herodian kings, were in the grip of a Messianic fervour. They understandably believed that this was the scripturally predicted End of Days, when their suffering would be worse than anything which had gone before, and that the promised Messiah would come to end it and establish the Kingdom of God on Earth. It is hard to grasp, two thousand years later, just how powerful and universal this belief was – and nowhere was it stronger than in Jesus's native Galilee.

It is evident from all Jesus's words and actions that he, too, believed in it utterly, was genuinely convinced that he was that Messiah, the Suffering Just One, and consciously did everything to fulfil the scripturally predicted pattern. Arguments have persisted as to whether he regarded this Messianic Kingship as purely spiritual or as political as well, but contemporary thought did not distinguish between the two.

This is no place to go into the subject in depth (except to observe in passing that to have claimed to be God Incarnate would have been totally incompatible with the belief, and a blasphemous concept both to Jesus and to his hearers which would have killed his mission stone dead). A clear explanation of the background is Hugo J. Schonfield's book *The Passover Plot*. One does not have to accept all his conclusions, some of which he himself describes as tentative, to accept his deep knowledge of that background, as a Jewish scholar with a profound admiration for the teacher Jesus.

Another book, which draws different but overlapping conclusions, is Donovan Joyce's *The Jesus Scroll*; journalistic rather than scholarly, it nevertheless contains many interesting facts.

Our point here is to underline that the first Christians believed the same, scriptural predictions and all; the very word Christ is merely a Greek translation of the Hebrew word Messiah, both meaning 'the anointed one' – which anointing was reserved exclusively for the King of Israel. But as the originally Jewish movement became a Gentile one, especially after the Roman destruction of Jerusalem in AD 70, other mythic elements were bound to enter in – in particular, the traditional hero-birth by divine impregnation of the mother, in the pattern of Alexander the Great and many others. (Actually this was a popular Jewish belief too; similar legends existed about the birth of Noah, Abraham and Moses.)

More than this: the Canaanite Anat was worshipped alongside Yahweh by many Jewish apostates, including the Jewish soldiers at Elephantine. Anat was (like the Egyptian Neith) Virgin Mother of all things, including the male God, conceiving all of her own volition and without outside impregnation. She became (in a mystery typical of many primordial goddesses) at the same time mother, consort, sister and daughter of the male God. Like Neith, 'She was the first to give birth to anything, and she had done so when nothing else had been born, and she herself had never been born.' Something of this concept (however unofficially) undoubtedly influenced thinking about Mary. As Geoffrey Ashe puts it (*The Virgin*, p.61): 'If any hint from the constellation of senior deities crept into Christian minds, it was probably subconscious and its nature is quite uncertain. But they are relevant to Mary as the divinely fertilized women are not, even though their own motherhood is outside history and humanity.'

The early Christians, both Jewish and Gentile, believed that, as a result of Jesus's coming, the Kingdom of God on Earth was imminent. (Its continued non-arrival dictated the gradual shift of emphasis from Earth to Heaven.) And in spreading the message, they naturally, and doubtless sincerely, emphasized the scriptural and mythic appositeness of the whole Jesus story. This required a miraculous birth, and the growing body of tradition supplied it – not necessarily a deliberate forgery for propaganda purposes; more probably a genuine belief that it must have been so, and a corresponding interpretation of scraps of second-hand memory. Luke, it should be pointed out, was writing perhaps half a century after the death of Jesus and was himself a Gentile.

Pauline Christianity, with its hatred of sex, added an element to the miraculous-birth legend: the perpetual virginity of Mary. This certainly was not required of earlier divinely impregnated mothers, and in fact any unbiased reading of the Gospels would seem to deny it of Mary.

Three centuries of totally male-chauvinist Christianity followed, during which what Geoffrey Ashe has called the 'Goddess-shaped yearning' of the ordinary worshipper built up a pressure which seriously threatened the whole structure. An answer was ready to hand: the mother of Jesus. He had become God Incarnate, and she the divinely impregnated mother of that God (to which image were later added her own immaculate conception and perpetual virginity; and even, with a prurient obsession over the physical details of virginity, the dogma that her hymen was unbroken before, during and after Jesus's birth).

Meanwhile a quite independent cult took root, non-Christian yet stemming from the Gospel story. Most of our knowledge of it comes from the fourth-century writer Epiphanius, who condemned it as a heresy. It consisted mostly of women, who were known by the nickname of the Collyridians, and its groups ranged from north of the Black Sea to Arabia. They worshipped Mary as Queen of Heaven, who had never suffered physical death but, like Elijah, for whom a place is set at every Jewish Passover, had been 'translated' (thus anticipating the Christian Assumption dogma). They, too, kept an empty chair for Mary at their rituals. They accepted Jesus as her divine son, but as secondary to her. They were noticeably feminist, resenting the male-dominated Church and claiming that Mary had cancelled the inferiority of women.

The whole Collyridian story is told in Chapter 7 of Ashe's *The Virgin*.

Being women, in those days they wrote little themselves and received little notice from male writers, until Epiphanius saw fit to damn them. But they must have posed a threat to the official Church – and another reason for neutralizing them by absorbing their ideas and making them safe and respectable.

So for all these reasons, Mary was elevated – though not officially to Goddess status, of course. She was allowed *hyperdulia* (super-veneration) but not *latria* (the adoration due to divinity). The ordinary worshipper, with his or her Goddess-shaped yearning, could not have cared less about the theological niceties. The Mother was back home, and there she has remained.

To quote Ashe again (*op. cit.* p.4): 'Far from treating Mary-worship in Protestant style as a disease of Christianity, we should confess that in at least one crisis it actually saved Christianity, which would have dwindled to nullity for the lack of what it supplied.'

The Jewish teenager who bore Jesus, and then may have gone on to bear his brothers and sisters, would have been astonished at what had been made of her. But the power of the Madonna symbol, the Goddess-form the centuries have created, is real enough; the pretence that it is history does not matter. Many historical men and women have provided crystallization-points for archetypal concepts and have been transformed into effective call-signs for the power behind those concepts.

So it has been with Mary.

Both officially and popularly, her role is intercession with God on behalf of her supplicants. But there is a difference. Officially, since she is not herself divine, she can do no more than plead mercy for the sinner with the masculine God, and even that she can do only if the sinner is truly repentant (which one would think would be enough without her intervention).

In the popular mind, however, she is the one who can bend the rules, who can cajole and pressurize her Son and even cheat her way round the cold, harsh logic of the male Trinity to whom ultimate power is officially reserved.

Janet once saw in a Dublin ladies' toilet the succinct graffito: 'Holy Mary, conceived without sin – help me to sin without conceiving!' On the face of it, no more than a blasphemous witticism, but it typifies a genuine and deep-rooted popular attitude. Jesus too, after all, is believed to have been 'conceived without sin' – but it would have been unthinkable to make the plea to him, even as a lavatory joke. Mary is seen as the one who understands the human heart and who cares more for it than for the letter of the patriarchal law. In other words, the one who answers the 'Goddess-shaped yearning' in the Bright Mother aspect.

But the instinctive 'yearning' is for the whole Goddess – which, as that instinct well knows, includes the Dark Mother too. How can the sinless, sexless Madonna, officially without experience of the very things for which she is being asked to seek forgiveness, fill the whole of the Goddess-vacuum?

Symptomatic of this aspect of the 'yearning' are the many Black Madonnas to be found throughout Christendom, and the powerful popular veneration (and official unease) which attaches to them. Explanations are many: the favourite evasion being that these images have been blackened naturally by centuries of incense-smoke – which ignores the fact that eyes and teeth are not also black. Another suggestion is that many of them were originally Isis-and-Horus images, of Egyptian complexion, adapted to Christian use. This explanation forgets what Egyptian murals reveal – that the Egyptian convention was usually to depict female complexions as creamy and male ones as ruddy. All the same, there is a germ of truth in the idea. Veneration for the many-aspected Isis certainly carried over into Mary-worship, injecting concepts into it which strained the official Madonna concept at the seams. One of the reasons for Mary's elevation to Mother of God was to counter Isis-worship, which had spread throughout the known world (see Chapter XXIII). Mary took over many of Isis's attributes and titles (including 'Star of the Sea' and 'Redemptress'), and the first churches dedicated to Mary in Rome were requisitioned Isis temples, with repainted statues. (Mary also took over the doves of Aphrodite; and interestingly, there are, too, a few known statues of Black Aphrodite – Aphrodite Melainis – of periods and places where she may have overlapped with Isis.)

As David Wood puts it (*Genisis*, p.49): 'The almost inescapable conclusion is that the Virgin Mary is a remodelled image superimposed on the cult of the Black Madonna because it was too strong to destroy. Furthermore the image of the Black Madonna has more in common with Magdalene than with the Virgin Mary.'

This brings us to another element in the paradox of Christianity's readmission of the Goddess 'through the back door'. To quote Marina Warner (*Alone of All her Sex*, p.225)

> The Catholic religion does not admit sins or even faults in its God, not even in his mother. The image of human error is relegated to the lesser ranks of the fellowship of saints ... The Virgin Mary could not meet this condition, for in her absolute purity and her exemption from the common lot she could not sin. Another figure consequently developed to fill this important lacuna, that of St Mary Magdalene, who, together with the Virgin Mary, typifies Christian society's attitudes to women and to sex. Both female figures are perceived in sexual terms: Mary as a virgin and Mary Magdalene as a whore – until her repentance. The Magdalene, like

Eve, was brought into existence by the powerful undertow of misogyny in Christianity, which associates women with the dangers and degradation of the flesh. For this reason she became a prominent and beloved saint.

The official image of the Magdalene is quite unsupported by the Gospel evidence, contradictory though that evidence is. Mark and Luke both describe her as one of the women who 'ministered unto' Jesus during his travels – 'out of their substance', Luke adds. In other words, well-to-do women who, out of conviction, travelled with him and looked after him, at their own expense. Another of them was Joanna, wife of Herod's steward, high in the social register and most unlikely to work alongside a notorious prostitute. 'Magdalene' means 'of Magdala' (Migdal, Mejdel), a flourishing Jewish town on the west coast of the Sea of Galilee, which was the main breeding centre of sacrificial doves for the Temple – another hint that Mary was a woman of means. In John, she is at the Crucifixion with Jesus's mother, and she alone meets and talks with him at the Tomb. Mark and Luke have her at the Tomb with others; Mark has Jesus speaking to them; Luke has her returning alone and meeting Jesus.

The only other information on her is that Jesus had 'cast seven devils' out of her – mentioned by Mark and Luke but not by John. In biblical language, that could imply actual exorcism but could also (and more probably) mean that he cured her of serious psychiatric problems. Luke says he cured others of these women fellow-travellers of various 'evil spirits and infirmities'.

The confusion starts with the quite unjustified identification of Mary with the repentant woman who washed and anointed Jesus's feet, weeping, when he was dining at the house of a Pharisee called Simon, in Nain. Simon was shocked, because of 'what manner of woman this is', but Jesus rebuked him and forgave her her sins.

The chapter-heading summary in the Authorized Version names this woman as Mary Magdalene, but even that standard work *Peake's Commentary on the Bible* says categorically: 'Mary of Magdala must not be identified with the woman that was a sinner mentioned in Luke vii:37.'

The anointing story is further confused with that of Mary of Bethany, sister of Lazarus and Martha, performing a similar action, but with no implication of sinfulness or repentance; in fact, Jesus makes it quite clear that it is a ritual act: 'She did it for my burial.' The incident is related by Matthew and Mark as happening at the house of 'Simon the leper' (Lazarus means leper), but neither names the woman; John does name her, as Lazarus's sister Mary.

Out of these three quite separate elements, early Christian orthodoxy invented a penitent whore (the sin it would automatically attribute to a woman, though the Gospels do not define the weeping woman's sins) and called her Mary Magdalene.

This synthetic Magdalene admirably fitted the Christian stereotype of the woman who has known the delights of the flesh and abandoned them as sinful. As an officially authorized saint, she also appealed to the grass-roots worshipper: she was someone who knew what sin and forgiveness were all about, from the inside – a direct knowledge forbidden to the impossibly pure Virgin.

It must be remembered that saints are for the Christian what god-forms and goddess-forms are for the pagan; a means of contacting particular aspects of the ultimate Divinity. An artilleryman invoking St Barbara, or a Celtic warrior invoking the Morrigan; a car-driver touching his St Christopher medallion, or an ancient Greek traveller making an offering to Hermes: all four are doing exactly the same thing, though many Christians would be shocked to admit it. Tuning in to aspects of Divinity is the only human way of approaching it; the pagan does so directly through a pantheon of aspect-forms, but the monotheist Christian has to move the aspect-function downwards to human saints. These saints are often fictional, idealized or simply old pagan deities given a Christian image, like Brighid/St Bridget.

The two Maries – Virgin and Magdalene – may thus be said to have provided between them a more rounded answer to the Goddess-vacuum created by the early Church Fathers. Both for the official theologians, reflecting their stereotyped image of woman (a mixture of their wishful thinking and their fears) and for the rank-and-file, reflecting their instinctive yearning for the Light and Dark Mother in all her fulness.

Significantly, the archetypal Triple Goddess in due course entered the Mary concept. French tradition has it that the three Maries – the mother of Jesus, Mary Cleopas (or Mary Salome) who may have been her half-sister, and Mary Magdalene, bringing with them the Holy Grail, landed in the South of France at Les Saintes Maries de la Mer. The cult of the Three Maries is very deep-rooted in Provence, which was the area of the Cathars – who were exterminated with Hitlerian thoroughness in the Albigensian Crusade for their heresies, one of the most shocking of which was the complete equality of men and women. The Three Maries cult persists there, as does the particular veneration of the Magdalene; some of the Provençal Black Madonnas can be shown to have been originally Magdalenes.

Meanwhile, apocryphal and Gnostic tradition assigned a far more important role to the Magdalene than did the official Gospels. The Gospel of Mary, for example, portrays her as a high initiate into Jesus's mysteries, and a teacher of the other apostles. The Gnostic Gospel of Philip emphasizes that the union of man and woman is a symbol of healing and peace and stresses the relationship between Jesus and the

Magdalene, who was 'often kissed by him' and is referred to as his 'companion' or 'spouse', her sexuality rescued from its 'sinful' image.

Modern works (such as William Phipps' *Was Jesus Married?*, Joyce's *The Jesus Scroll* and Baigent, Leigh and Lincoln's *The Holy Blood and the Holy Grail*) examine the possibility that Jesus and the Magdalene were man and wife; and Wood's *Genisis* maintains that, in addition, she was High Priestess of a Temple of Ishtar at Magdala.

Whatever one thinks of such suggestions, ancient or modern, they certainly bear witness to the impact that the Magdalene, as a symbol of female sexuality (whether condemned or approved), has had on human imagination and thinking.

The Dark Mother role of the Magdalene remained very necessary during the High Middle Ages, as the Virgin Mary became exalted to ever more ethereal and remote heights of purity and non-humanity. Today the medieval excesses have softened, at least in the popular mind, and the Virgin Mary has regained her position as the unchallenged, if officially unacknowledged, Goddess of Christendom.

(Sadly, perhaps, she has even been cast in the ancient role of Goddess of Battle. Christian militia in the Lebanese civil war carried her picture on their rifle butts.)

In 1964 she was proclaimed *Mater Ecclesiae*, Mother of the Church – and thus *causa efficiens* of Redemption. Theoretically, Catholics since 1964 may speak to God only through the Redemptress; without her intercession, God's grace cannot come through to mankind.

What has all this to do with witches? Are we really concerned with the legal niceties of Latin phrases or with Gospel textual criticism, except as matters of academic interest?

'All goddesses are one goddess'. Since most of us live in a Christian environment (some of us in a Catholic one), the significance of the Madonna is anything but academic. We would be most unwise, as witches, to let anti-Christian prejudice blind us to the fact that, whatever the theologians say, for our Catholic fellow-citizens the face of the banished Goddess shines in their Lady Chapels, in the loved maternal figure of the wayside shrines, in the mother-and-child statuette on the mantelpiece. We have talked with priests and nuns who will privately admit this and seem unperturbed by its technical heresy.

To descend from theology to practicality, known witches, whether they seek it or not, have people coming to them for advice and help; and in Ireland, for example, most of these will be good Catholic women – often with problems they are reluctant to take to a celibate male priest. In many cases, the witch will know that an appeal to the Goddess principle is called for; and why should she not be prepared to say so, in terms which have a real meaning to the person she is helping?

The world urgently needs a reawakening of the Goddess – or, more precisely (since she has always been there), a reawakening of mankind's awareness of her, in all her aspects and with all the faces she wears. And sectarianism should not prevent us from acknowledging that, for millions of our fellow humans, her face is that of the Madonna, *Stella Maris, Redemptrix*. We should let her in through whichever door she knocks at.

At the heart of Wiccan ritual is Drawing Down the Moon – the invocation of the Goddess (who is partner with the God) at human level, and the attunement of the human to her influence.

Is there so much difference, in principle and practice, between that and the time-honoured call: '*Ave Maria, gratia plena, Dominus tecum, benedicta tu in mulieribus*'?

VIII   Psyche and Goddess

This archetypal psychical world which is encompassed in the multiple forms of the Great Goddess is the underlying power that even today ... determines the psychic history of modern man and modern woman.

Erich Neumann

Every good witch, and particularly every good High Priestess, has to be something of a psychologist. The human psyche is, after all, her main field of operation; even when she is dealing with animal, plant or so-called inanimate Nature, her own psyche is a major factor.

Being 'something of a psychologist', in ordinary speech, usually means having a shrewd intuitive grasp of the workings of the human mind – which every good healer and teacher has, and most active witches are both of these. It does not necessarily mean an academic knowledge of the subject.

Fair enough. We do not suggest that every dedicated witch should take a university course in psychology; apart from anything else, she or he would be cluttered up with a lot of chaff along with the wheat.

But a little attention to one particular school of psychological thought – that of Jung and his followers – would, we suggest, prove very fruitful to any witch or occultist. Even a single reading of such a 'potted' exposition as Jolande Jacobi's *The Psychology of C.G. Jung* is likely to whet your appetite for more.

Carl Gustav Jung, quite apart from being a profound and creative thinker, was himself a natural psychic (to the considerable annoyance and bewilderment, on at least one occasion, of the teacher from whom he had to break away, Sigmund Freud).

Four of Jung's concepts in particular will immediately ring a bell with most witches: that of the Collective Unconscious; that of the Archetypes; that of the Animus and Anima; and that of Synchronicity.

The first three are all highly relevant to the subject of this book, the Goddess, but the theory of Synchronicity expounds what witches and magicians have always known, but what no modern scientist or academic before Jung has dared to put forward, so it is worth mentioning in passing, before we get on to the other three.

It is the theory of meaningful coincidence, of an acausal connecting principle in events, which Jung claimed operates alongside the known laws of cause-and-effect; and he made out a formidable case for it. It prompted him, for example, to write the Foreword to Richard Wilhelm's classic book on the I Ching, and since that is on the book-shelves of, or at least available to, most practising witches, we refer our reader to it and leave the subject at that.

The theory of the Collective Unconscious accords perfectly with the basic occult view of the cosmos as an integrated living organism, which we put forward on pages 2–3. It maintains that each of us, at the unconscious level, is in touch with, and indeed a part of, the total psychic identity of the human species, with all its built-in concepts and attitudes, and its half-million years of experience; and that the Individual Unconscious is, so to speak, a single outcrop of this, formed by the individual's own experience and unique identity, but nevertheless rooted in the Collective Unconscious and overlapping it.

In occult terms, the Collective Unconscious defines mankind as an 'organ' of the cosmic whole, on the non-material levels, and the Individual Unconscious defines each of us as a cell in that organ.

We need hardly point out that this is a fruitful way of looking at such phenomena as telepathy, clairvoyance, divination, psychic healing and many other aspects of Craft practice.

The Archetypes – a central Jungian concept – are, so to speak, the building blocks of the Collective Unconscious. Jung himself defined the term Archetype as being 'not meant to denote an inherited idea, but rather an inherited mode of psychic functioning ... a "pattern of behaviour" '. This is on the biological level; but looked at from within

Bronze head of Aphrodite from Satala, Armenia

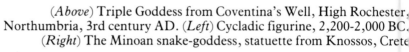

(*Above*) Triple Goddess from Coventina's Well, High Rochester,
Northumbria, 3rd century AD. (*Left*) Cycladic figurine, 2,200-2,000 BC.
(*Right*) The Minoan snake-goddess, statuette from Knossos, Crete

Worship of the Sea Goddess by the Macumba of Brazil

Bábóg mhara (sea doll). An Irish
fisherman's token sacrifice to the Sea
Goddess. Seen at Belmullet, Co Mayo

Beatrice addressing Dante from the Car by William Blake. Beatrice is a classic personification of the Muse Goddess

Queen Guinevere by William Morris. The Guinevere of medieval and Victorian romance must be a pale shadow of the Celtic archetype

Lilith offers the apple

Egyptian sky goddess Nut carved inside the lid of the sarcophagus of Ankh-nes-nefer-ib-re, daughter of Psammetichus II. Nut was often portrayed on the inside of coffin lids

Bright Isis and (*below*) *Black Isis* by Janet Farrar

Isis protecting Osiris. 26th Dynasty,
Temple of Karnak

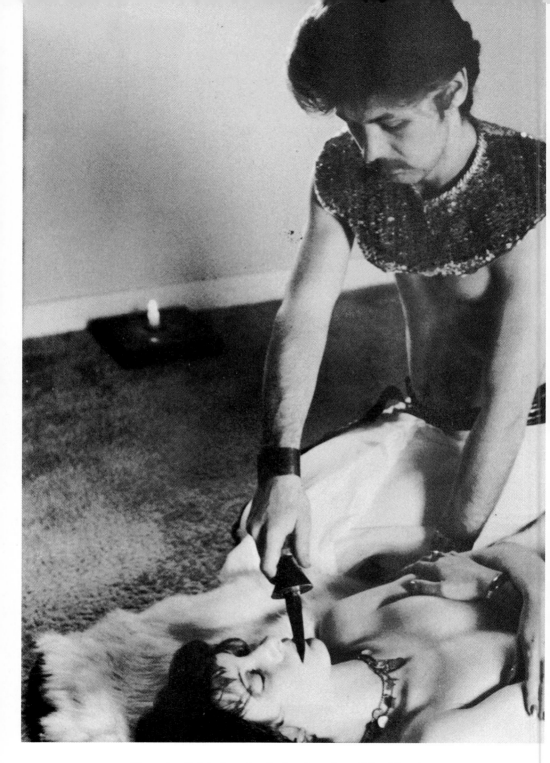

Egyptian Initiation ritual: the Opening of the Mouth

the subjective psyche, an Archetype 'presents itself as numinous, that is, it appears as an experience of fundamental importance. Whenever it clothes itself with adequate symbols, which is not always the case, it takes hold of the individual in a startling way, creating a condition of "being deeply moved" the consequences of which may be immeasurable.' (Jung's Introduction to Esther Harding's *Woman's Mysteries*, pp.ix-x.)

Jung and his followers gave names to many of the universal Archetypes – and one of the most important of these is the Great Mother.

From the human point of view, God-forms and Goddess-forms are Archetypes. We dealt with this question more fully in the chapter 'Myth, Ritual and Symbolism' in *The Witches' Way*; within the theme of the present book, it is enough to emphasize that every one of the hundreds of Goddesses named herein is an aspect of the numinous Great Mother Archetype which is an ineradicable element of our racial Collective Unconscious, and also (whether acknowledged or not) of everybody's Individual Unconscious.

Let us be clear about this. An Archetype is unknowable directly; it makes itself known to consciousness only through symbols – which, as Jung said, may or may not be adequate ones. A Goddess-form is a complex of symbols to enable us to interact fruitfully with the (ultimately unknowable) Goddess herself. So the building up of such a Goddess-form is a two-way process. On the one hand, it is man-conceived: Ishtar or Brighid or Aphrodite or Parvati or Amaterasu is a product of the human imagination. But the Archetype itself is real; the Goddess exists. So the more adequate the man-conceived symbols, the more strongly the Goddess is contacted, and the more she feeds back improvements to the symbols. Ishtar and the others come more and more to genuine life; they too exist.

We cannot say it too often: the Goddess exists. Strict psychological theory, cautious about stepping outside its own terms of reference, may leave open the question of whether an Archetype is merely (so to speak) a building-block of the human racial psyche or represents a reality above and beyond *Homo sapiens*.

To the pagan world view, with its organic cosmos, only the second conclusion is tenable. Archetypes are functions of the cosmic organism; and the Great Mother Archetype, the Goddess, represents the feminine polarity of the ultimate creative force – one of the two most 'real' components of the universe.

So, too, are the various Goddess-forms we have 'created' to put ourselves in tune with her. The Goddess herself is both infinitely simple and infinitely complex, unknowable in her totality, at least at our present stage of evolution. But if (say) we invoke her as Aradia, with all the symbols and concepts we have come to associate with that name, then the Goddess comes through to us wearing her Aradia-face, as the magical teacher-Maiden, special patroness of those who follow the path of the Craft. We are not being fanciful (not even 'constructively fanciful', using a legitimate psychological trick, as some would maintain) if we regard Aradia as a 'person' – because she is.

Mankind is always constructing such thought-forms, at various levels of importance, as symbol-complexes for communication with archetypal elements of the Collective Unconscious. This is the essentially human way of mutual feedback between the conscious Ego and the Unconscious, without which the psyche would disintegrate.

For an apparently trivial, but in fact classic, example of how such thought-forms can be instinctively created when they meet a need, let us look at the Teddy Bear.

Toy bears must be as old as toys themselves, but Teddy in his present form, as he is known throughout the English-speaking world at least, seems to be a twentieth-century phenomenon. He was named (with visual appropriateness) after Theodore Roosevelt, who became US President in 1901, and the name stuck. So did the concept; Teddy is with us to stay.

Commerce has cashed in on him, of course, but his popularity and permanence seems quite independent of this. Other toys, from Sindy Dolls to Action Men, are loved in childhood; Teddy remains an honoured pensioner of countless adults – including men – and is often handed on, carefully patched and restored, from generation to generation. A census of our own coven revealed that the majority of them still had their Teddies, or at least that their sisters or children held them, and we do not think that we are untypical.

(Nor is it untypical that Stewart's sister's bear, over sixty years old now, is known as Pooh, like many others of his vintage; for A.A. Milne not only to rode to popularity on Teddy's established reputation, he also added brilliantly to his body of legend.)

Seriously – why has it happened? Why does Teddy hold such a unique position in the history of toys?

It can only be because he more than adequately personifies an Archetype, and its corresponding need. He is, for our epoch, as much the living god of childhood as (for example) Pan was for the Greeks the living god of nature. Teddy represents reassurance, cuddleability, warmth, innocence, dependability, unruffled wisdom and a complete absence of sharp corners or of ambiguity. He personifies most of a child's emotional needs – which remain with the adult, however deeply they are buried.

The occult maxim applies to him as it does to every deity-form: 'All Teddies are one Teddy' – yet each aspect-Teddy has his own personal

Fig. 2. The Yang-Yin Symbol.

characteristics, on the wavelength of his individual devotee.

And however well the toy manufacturers (the money-changers in the Temple?) have done out of his cult, the cult itself is a cultural and psychic phenomenon, not a commercial one.

Floreat Teddy!

But to return to the fourth of Jung's concepts which we mentioned – that of the Animus and Anima. This, too, tallies remarkably with occult thinking.

The Anima, briefly, is a man's buried feminine aspects, and the Animus is a woman's buried masculine aspects. Either, if unacknowledged, can turn apparently malignant; healthy integration of the Animus or Anima with the rest of the psyche is a major aim of Jungian therapy, as it should be of occult self-development.

The Chinese Yang-Yin symbol (see Figure 2), perhaps the most vivid expression we have of male-female polarity, embraces this concept. At the heart of the light, masculine Yang is a dark Anima-spot; and at the heart of the dark, feminine Yin is a light Animus-spot. This is true of all creative polarities; each contains the seed of the other, enriching their interaction.

But for the occult outlook, with its belief in reincarnation, the Animus/Anima concept is really inescapable. If each immortal Individuality is bisexual, containing within itself both polarities – and if, in each incarnation, the temporary Personality which it assumes is either male or female – then a man's total self, Individuality-plus-Personality, must include the feminine aspect of his Individuality, temporarily unemphasized in a male incarnation, because the main 'work' of that incarnation centres rightly on the male aspect. Similarly, the masculine aspect of an Individuality is temporarily unemphasized in a female incarnation.

This is as it should be, of course. Male and female incarnations are constructive steps in the evolution of the Individuality and contribute constructively to the overall cosmic evolutionary process. But the degree of advancement of a human Individuality, in any one incarnation, is measured by the amount of fruitful communication between the Personality (from which the Individuality learns by broadening its experience) and the Personality (for which the Individuality is a unique source of nourishment, inspiration and accumulated wisdom).

So the Anima or Animus, in fact, is this temporarily unemphasized aspect of any one human's total self. And a healthy recognition and integration of it are essential to the development of that total self. It must be neither suppressed (in which case it will fester and cause trouble) nor allowed to overwhelm the natural emphasis of a particular incarnation (in which case the Personality will become distorted – in psychological terms, neurotic or psychotic). And certainly no pagan, with his or her organic view of the cosmos, should allow either imbalance to develop.

Another implication for the practising witch. The Craft bases much of its working on male-female polarity. In practice, and naturally, this means at its simplest a man and a woman (or men and women) working together, each contribution one 'pole of the battery' to produce the necessary current. And again, at its simplest, there is a tendency to think of the God speaking entirely through the male witch and the Goddess entirely through the woman. But we should always remember that it is not as simple as that. Also contributing to a man-woman working partnership is the man's Anima and the woman's Animus. The Goddess may speak out loud through her natural channel, the woman, and the God out loud through the man. But the Goddess is also whispering meaningfully to the man's Anima, which speaks her language, as the God is to the woman's Animus. And both man and woman, if they are wise, will learn to listen to the whisper as well as to the clarion-call.

To pursue the metaphor – a man-woman working partnership is not just a battery; it is a tetrapolar magnet, the field-windings of a powerful generator which should be understood and kept in working order.

A final tip on the psychological theme. The two best books on the Great Mother Archetype are Erich Neumann's *The Great Mother* and Esther Harding's *Woman's Mysteries*. Both are well worth study.

In the old pagan world, the psychological truths we have been discussing were still mysteries clearly understood only by the wisest of the trained priesthood. But today we are in an epoch where much that was once only intuitively grasped is now surfacing and becoming articulate and available to anyone who is prepared to look at it. Call it, if you like, a turning-point in the evolution of the relationship between the conscious mind and the goldmine of the Unconscious.

We would suggest that the thinking of Jung and his followers is one of the spearheads of that breakthrough – one field in which advancing science no longer explains away or belittles the religious and psychic outlook (as it did in the nineteenth century) but strengthens and clarifies it.

IX   *Woman as Goddess*

For in old times, Woman was the altar.
Great Rite declamation

We have been studying some of the many faces of the Goddess – and when in Part II we consider some of her individual manifestations, we shall be studying more, for her faces are infinite, and the study is never-ending.

We have seen that she is the Earth Mother, the womb which bears us, the breasts which feed us, the hands which guide us, and the womb-tomb which reabsorbs our physical shell. That she is Isis Veiled, clad in the robes of Nature. That she is Isis Unveiled, revealing her mysteries as we are ready to understand them. That she is the Bright Mother and the Dark Mother, beautiful and terrifying at the same time, each eternally containing and leading us to the other. That she is the Moon Maid, the Moon Mother and the Moon Crone, ever Triple and ever One. That she takes the bright energy of her son/lover the God and creates living form with it. That she in turn is the Muse, inspiring him to his own forms of mental creation. That she is the inexhaustible treasure-house of the Collective Unconscious, and he the penetrating light of Consciousness. That without her he is spilled seed, and without him she is sterile. That for 2,000 years and more we have dangerously undervalued her.

And we have seen that Woman, her most complete channel is Gaia's family, is also all of these things.

The recognition of Woman as the reflection of the Goddess goes back to very ancient times. Discussing the late obscenity of the Black Mass (a purely Christian heresy, and nothing to do with witchcraft), Doreen Valiente says that within its theatrical trappings there is nevertheless 'one genuinely ancient figure – the naked woman upon the altar. It would be more correct to say, the naked woman who is the altar; because this is her original role ... This use of a living woman's naked body as the altar where the forces of Life are worshipped and invoked, goes back to before the beginnings of Christianity with its dogmas about Satan; back to the days of the ancient worship of the Great Goddess of Nature, in whom all things were one, under the image of Woman' (*An ABC of Witchcraft*, p.44).

Strangely enough, this concept has persisted in a veiled form in the places of worship of Judaism, Christianity and Islam. In his manual *The Symbolism of Temple Architecture*, Lawrence Durdin-Robertson argues, with convincing scholarly detail, that every church, synagogue and mosque is in fact the body of the Goddess, symbolically and conceptually. Or not so strange, perhaps; Christian dogma (revealing more than it realizes) has always insisted that the Church is the Bride of Christ; and the stone building, after all, symbolizes that Church. (In the old Law of Sanctuary, there is maybe buried the knowledge that the Goddess protects all her creatures, whether they are seen to deserve it or not.)

The Craft holds to the original concept, not concealing it in stone or bricks and mortar. The witches' place of worship, the Magic Circle, is neither male nor female; it is a power-house for the polarity of the two, and the whole ritual of Circle-casting emphasizes a deliberate balance of aspects, including that of the elements. It is the body, mind and spirit of the High Priestess which are seen as the channel for the Goddess, and the opening-up of that channel is a central feature of Wiccan ritual.

This ritual opening-up is called, very appropriately, Drawing Down the Moon. (The actual ritual is given in the Appendix, on pp.292–3.) Its various stages illustrate all that we have said about the relationship between the male and female principles on the one hand, and about the relationship between Woman and the Goddess on the other.

First the High Priest approaches his High Priestess as a human woman. It may be said that, for this particular ritual, there is no need to start by invoking the God into the man; he already represents, by his nature, the 'raw directionless energy' of the male principle, so, provided he plays his part reverently, that in itself is enough to trigger off the form-creating female principle; and giving form to something is what the ritual is all about. For other rituals, where more God-aspects are involved, an invocation such as Drawing Down the Sun (see our *The Witches' Way*, pp.67-70) is called for.

He greets the human woman by means of the Fivefold Kiss, a salute which acknowledges her as his sister witch, fellow-worshipper and complementary polarity at the human level.

Next he addresses the Goddess independently of the woman, invoking her to 'descend upon the body of this thy servant and priestess'.

Next he addresses the Goddess in and through the woman, confident that his invocation had been answered. He praises her and appeals to her to help him, 'who without thee am forlorn.'

And finally the woman, speaking as the voice of 'the Mother darksome and divine', answers his appeal by giving her blessing to him.

In the full Opening Ritual, this is normally followed by the High Priestess delivering the Charge, the traditional (in Gardnerian and Alexandrian witchcraft at least) address of the Goddess to her followers. This was originally written by Gerald Gardner, using the Tuscan witches' invocation from Leland's *Aradia* as a starting point, and later revised by Doreen Valiente with Gardner's approval. It is the most moving, and best-loved, passage in the modern Craft liturgy, and when Doreen perfected it, the Goddess must truly have been speaking through her. (See Appendix pp. 293-4 for its full text.)

Anybody who has witnessed Drawing Down the Moon regularly must agree that it works. Time and again, an 'ordinary' human woman seems transformed by it, so that the coven has no difficulty in reacting to her as the voice and presence of the Goddess. This often begins with her speaking of the Charge; her style of delivery may vary widely from Circle to Circle, prompting the perfectly natural question 'Who was it tonight?' In other words, 'Which aspect of herself did the Goddess find it appropriate to reveal to us on this occasion?' It might be a Mother aspect such as Dana if encouragement and reassurance is called for; or the fiercer Hecate if the coven is getting lazy; or Aradia if more teaching is needed; or Ma'at if a clearer sense of justice is required; or Gaia if the relationship with Nature is out of key; or the Morrigan if evil is to be fought; or Brighid if creative inspiration is sought; or Aphrodite if men and women are becoming insensitive to each other; or even someone unnamable but with a clear and relevant message taking everyone by surprise.

Nor is it always just a matter of the tone of delivery. Many times we have known the familiar words of the Charge to be unexpectedly replaced by something quite different, communicating advice or reprimand, illumination or warning.

In either case, the delivery is not usually determined by the High Priestess's conscious decision. Every experienced High Priestess is familiar with the strange feeling of observing from a corner of her own mind, of listening to the Goddess using her vocal cords, and wondering what will come next.

Incidentally, this is a good reason why every High Priestess (indeed every woman witch, for each one should be ready to take a Circle, however inadequate she thinks she is) should learn the words of the Charge by heart. Reading it from a book tends to inhibit this channelling process.

Drawing Down the Moon, and the treatment of the High Priestess as representative of the Goddess for the rest of the Circle, is of course not a matter for the High Priestess and High Priest alone. Every woman in the Circle should identify with and psychically support the High Priestess, and every man the High Priest, during the Drawing Down; this helps the leaders to attune themselves to the cosmic female and male principles – to the Goddess and the God – and it also turns the power-raising polarity within the Circle into a group effort, which is what coven working is all about.

We say 'for the rest of the Circle' but we find it a sound rule that, even during the often cheerful relaxation which follows the Banishing, the High Priestess (or whoever has acted as such for the Circle) should continue to be treated as someone special and not subjected, for example, to the kind of boisterous teasing or romping which is perfectly natural in a healthy (and particularly a young and healthy) group of friends after serious work. 'All acts of love and pleasure are my rituals', including the exuberant ones; but to treat with special respect the one who has been the channel of the Goddess during the serious work is to acknowledge that the Goddess, once invoked, does not pack her bags and leave the moment the Circle is banished. It is also, if you like, an acknowledgement which invites her to join the party afterwards and to preside over the exuberance, but from a fitting distance. Her woman-channel can be given till next morning to become 'merely' human again – if any woman is ever 'merely' that.

In fact, of course, she never is. Drawing Down the Moon is a ritual intensification of a quality that always exists. 'As above, so below': every woman, with greater or less success, is a human expression of the cosmic feminine principle; and every man should, in the words of Penelope Shuttle and Peter Redgrove (*The Wise Wound*, p.33) 'be the guardian and student of these abilities in the woman', instead of being, as all too often in this age, 'the proud and envious aggressor'.

Another important Wiccan ritual which involves the concept of Woman as the altar is of course the Great Rite. We have described it in two forms — a simpler form in *Eight Sabbats for Witches*, pp.48-54, and the longer form from Gardner's Book of Shadows in *The Witches' Way*, pp.31-9. In both, the woman is not only the expression of the Goddess principle; her body literally is the altar of the Goddess.

> Assist me to erect the ancient altar, at which in days past all worshipped,
> The Great Altar of all things;
> For in old times, Woman was the altar.
> Thus was the altar made and placed,
> And the sacred point was the point within the centre of the circle.
> As we have of old been taught that the point within the centre is the origin of all things,
> Therefore should we adore it.
> Therefore whom we adore we also invoke ….

The Great Rite is the Craft's version of the immemorially ancient *hieros gamos* — the ritual mating, by human representatives, of the Goddess-principle and the God-principle. It is fitting that one of its uses is for the initiation to the Third Degree, the Craft's highest, and also that the ritual should be the same whether the man or the woman is the initiator, because at that level both principles are and must be equal and complementary.

The Great Rite can be either symbolic, with the man's athame and the woman's chalice representing the moment of union, or actual, with that union consummated in intercourse — the latter in private, the rest of the coven withdrawing. But both must be enacted with reverence and seriousness, because the couple are, so to speak, Drawing Down both the Moon and the Sun upon themselves and acting as channels for the two great cosmic forces. The Goddess and the God are invoked on all the levels, so, for the actual Great Rite at least, only a partnership which is already integrated on all those levels should invite the power which it can raise.

Male-female polarity, expressed in man-woman working partnerships (whether married, lovers or simply harmonious friends), and within the coven as a whole, is a basic principle of the Craft. So every man witch, by being 'guardian and student' of the Goddess-principle within his partner, is in effect continuously Drawing Down the Moon on her and helping her to live that principle and realize her whole self. He is also, of course, coming to fruitful terms with the Goddess-Anima principle within himself and giving free rein to the God-principle which is his own true nature.

The conscious awareness of this polarity, and its creative use in magical and personal practice, is one of the most important contributions the Craft can make to the race as a whole at its present stage of evolution, because it is a principle which has been denied and distorted for centuries, and its reinstatement is an urgent task if Gaia is to survive.

Not every woman is a witch. But every woman is a face of the Goddess.

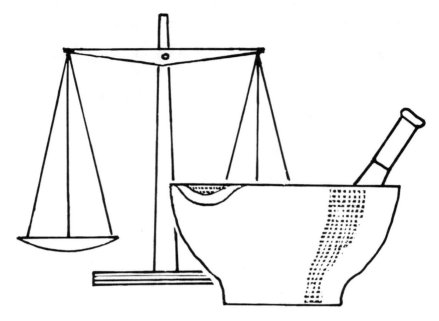

X   Some Goddess Recipes

Round about the cauldron go
Macbeth

Perfume – whether worn or as incense – is a great help for creating the appropriate atmosphere in the Circle. It appeals directly and powerfully to the psyche on all the levels, from spiritual attunement to bodily awareness.

It is also accepted occult experience that perfumes have a real (and therefore magical) effect on the etheric plane, some perfumes a very powerful one. And it is the etheric plane which links (in both directions) actions and phenomena on the physical plane with those on all the other levels.

Dion Fortune has some illuminating things to say about ritual perfumes and incenses on pp.278-9 of *The Mystical Qabalah*. She divides them into (a) those which exalt consciousness and (b) those which stir the subconscious to activity. Type (a) includes particularly (and for ecclesiastical incense exclusively) the aromatic gums and also certain essential oils, especially the aromatic and astringent ones. Type (b) she divides into Dionysiac (aromatic, spicy, such as smouldering cedar or sandalwood or pine-cones) and Venusian (sweet, cloying, such as vanilla); these tend to shade into each other – 'Many perfumes which by themselves are crude and acrid, or cloying and sickly, become admirable when blended'.

There is no reason why both women and men should not use perfume ritually (the key word again being 'appropriate', as the designers of after-shave lotions know). But for women there is an extra consideration, apart from the fact that they are the traditional perfume-users. In the Circle, the High Priestess represents the Goddess and is her principal channel, and all the other women should reflect aspects of her, even though on this occasion they are not the central focus of that channelling. So a suitable perfume not only helps each woman to feel in tune with the Goddess-aspect invoked, it also helps the others, including the men, to 'see' her thus.

In celebrating the worship of the Goddess, ritual food has always played a significant part, and since the Goddess has many aspects, it is only reasonable to suit that food to the aspect being invoked.

In the choice and preparation of ritual food and ritual perfume, there is plenty of scope for creative imagination. But in this chapter we give a few suggestions to get that imagination working. Some of the recipes are traditional, some we or our coven members have designed ourselves.

Perfumes, Oils, Incenses

These three overlap; an anointing oil may be modified as a perfume or a cologne, for example, and drops of oil may be put on the glowing charcoal like incense to produce a preliminary atmosphere. (Using oil this way during the ritual usually requires too constant attention, and perfumes or colognes are usually too rapidly volatile.)

Moon Priestess perfume
    1 drop Queen of the Night oil
    3 drops rose oil
    1 drop lemon verbena oil
    4 fl. oz (120 cc) white spirit
Blend the three oils in a bottle. Add the white spirit, and shake vigorously.

A cologne form can be made by adding another 1 fl. oz (30 cc of white spirit and 3 fl. oz (90 cc) of distilled water.

Moon Priest cologne
    1 fl. oz (30 cc) lemon verbena or lime oil
    2 fl. oz (60 cc) coriander oil

$\frac{1}{2}$ fl. oz (15 cc) camphor or myrrh oil
$\frac{1}{4}$ fl. oz (7 cc) white spirit
$3\frac{3}{4}$ fl. oz (105 cc) distilled water
Blend the oils in a bottle, add the spirit and water and shake vigorously.

Increasing the myrrh oils gives a darker perfume; increasing the camphor, a lighter and more spicy one. All perfumes 'behave' differently on different skins, so it is worth experimenting to find your own balance.

Earth Mother perfume
    Musk oil
    Patchouli oil
    Rose oil
Blend equal parts, bottle and shake well.

Isis perfume
    Rose oil
    Blue Lotus oil
Blend equal parts, bottle and shake well.

Sun Goddess perfume
    Cinnamon oil
    Lemon verbena oil
    Ylang-ylang oil
Blend equal parts, bottle and shake well.

Oil for the Dark of the Moon
    2 fl. oz (60 cc) tincture of myrrh
    1 fl. oz (30 cc) oil of cinnamon
    $\frac{1}{4}$ fl. oz (7 cc) Queen of the Night oil
    1 fl. oz (30 cc) oil of rose
Blend, bottle and shake well.

Oil for the Rites of Isis
    7 drops oil of rose
    2 drops oil of camphor
    2 drops tincture of myrrh
    3 drops oil of blue hyacinth
Blend the oils of rose, camphor and blue hyacinth during the waxing Moon. Bottle and keep till the Moon wanes. Add the myrrh as near as possible to the New Moon, but not after it.

Kali incense

This is an individual and personalized priestess incense, for attunement to your own Dark of the Moon.

1 oz (30 gm) sandalwood chips
1 oz (30 gm) dried jasmine flowers or 6 drops jasmine oil
½ oz (15 gm) dried rose petals
2 drops of your own menstrual blood

Blend and use for private meditation during the onset of menstruation.

Morrigan incense

1 oz (30 gm) musk amberette
½ oz (15 gm) dragon's blood (resin used in violin staining)
4 drops patchouli oil
4 drops civet oil
4 drops of blood from your own finger

Blend at the dark of the Moon, put in a jar and bury in the earth for six weeks (a flower-pot of peat in a cool cupboard will do).

Athene oil and incense

The olive is sacred to Athene, so use pure olive oil as an anointing oil; in particular, rub between the palms of your hands and anoint your feet, forehead and lips. For the incense:

1 oz (30 gm) cedarwood chips
½ oz (15 gm) camphor
7 drops musk oil
Female sweat (as much as possible)
6 olives, unstuffed and preferably black

Blend the first four ingredients well, at the full Moon, and add the olives. Put in a jar and leave for one month to mature. Then remove the olives (which will have imparted their essence to the rest) and throw them away.

Stuffed olives, both black and green, are an obvious food for a ritual of Athene; also stuffed vine leaves, a very Athenian dish. If possible, of course, the wine should be Greek – especially retsina, though that is an acquired taste.

Pre-ritual bath sachets

To cleanse and relax the body before a ritual, and to energize the psychic centres. This recipe was given to us by Paul Demartin of Anubis Books (see Kyphi Incense, p.72). Fill small sachets of muslin cloth with equal amounts of the following herbs:

Basil (for psychic energy)
Borage (to strengthen the inner self)
Lavender (to banish mental and emotional stress)

Centuary (a traditional witch herb)
Rue (a traditional bathing herb)

Put a sachet into your bath five minutes before you get in, to give the aromatics time to work.

Diana of the Moon incense

This simple yet effective recipe is another of Paul Demartin's. He recommends that it be made in the hour and the day of the Moon – i.e. the first or eighth hour after sunrise, or the third or tenth hour after sunset, on a Monday.

(The full list of planetary days and hours is given in many books, including Appendix III to Stewart's *What Witches Do*. Here we will just note that the purely Goddess hours are (Monday) first, third, sixth and eighth after sunrise, and first, third, eighth and tenth after sunset; and (Friday) first, third, eighth and tenth after sunrise, and third, fifth, tenth and twelfth after sunset. Other day/hour combinations, involving Goddess/God (or purely God) aspects, are obviously also useful but too complex to be given here.)

Thoroughly mix equal amounts of the following:
Gum mastic
Jasmine
Mandrake
Orris root

Add a few drops of wintergreen oil and moisten with a little clear mineral oil.

Kyphi incense

This was an important Ancient Egyptian ritual incense, and its sixteen ingredients are listed in the Ebers Papyrus, *c.*1500 BC. Since the proportions are not given, and some of the ingredients are not easy to obtain, its complex preparation is a job for specialists. Most good occult suppliers, such as John Lovett's Occultique (73 Kettering Road, Northampton NN1 4AW) and Paul Demartin's Anubis Books (218 Bamford Road, Heywood, Lancs), offer their own versions of it, and we recommend that you try these.

Áine of Knockaine incense

The Irish Moon goddess Áine of Knockaine is said to have given the meadowsweet its splendid scent. We have been unable to find an explanation for this tradition, but Francis, our coven Fetch and a born Donegal storyteller, has come up with one of his own. When St Patrick was chasing the goddesses out of Ireland, he sent his hounds after Áine, who found they were overtaking her. So she broadcast her perfume over all the meadowsweet, which was in bloom at the time, and the hounds were confused and lost her. Áine was thus one goddess who escaped Patrick's purge. We like it – and we like the incense which Francis devised to illustrate it. (Incidentally, 'Áine' is pronounced 'Oyn-yeh'.)

> ½ oz (15 gm) meadowsweet flowers and leaf (gathered when the plant is in full bloom, and dried)
> ½ oz (15 gm) finely chopped pine needles
> ½ fl. oz (15 cc) lemon verbena oil

By the way, meadowsweet blossom also makes a delicious wine.

Planetary perfumes and incenses

We have suggested one or two perfumes and incenses above for working with particular feminine planetary aspects. For further experimenting, Pat Crowther's lists of suggested ingredients given in her *Lid Off the Cauldron* may be found helpful. Her lists for the feminine planets (including the sometimes-feminine Sun and Saturn) are:

Sun: Heliotrope, orange blossom, cloves, frankincense, ambergris, musk, mastic, paliginia, sunflower oil

Moon: White poppy, white rose, wallflower, myrtle, mugwort, camphor, cedar

Venus: Stephanotis, apple blossom, musk, saffron, verbena, damiana

Saturn: Hyacinth, pansy, pepperwort, asafoetida, black poppy seeds, henbane (note that henbane is poisonous if eaten!), lodestone, myrrh. (Why do we include Saturn as 'sometimes feminine'? Because for witches who use Cabalistic symbolism, Saturn is the planet of Binah.)

Crowley's attributions

Aleister Crowley, in his *777*, gives perfume correspondences for the following goddesses: Aphrodite, Artemis, Athene, Bhavani, Ceres, Cybele, Demeter, Diana, Frigg/Freya, Hathor, Hecate, Hera, Isis, Juno, Kundalini, Lakshmi, Lalita, Ma'at, Minerva, Mut, Nephthys, Nike, Nut, Persephone, Psyche, Rhea, the Valkyries, Venus and Vesta. These perfumes are named in the goddesses' alphabetical entries in Part III.

Food

Diana honey-cakes

According to the Tuscan witches' tradition (Leland's *Aradia*, p.13), 'You shall make cakes of meal, wine, salt, and honey in the shape of a (crescent or horned) moon, and then put them to bake.' The Aradia chapter includes the invocations to Diana that accompanied the baking. No quantities are given, but the ingredients are similar to those

of oat fingers or flapjacks; so we suggest you experiment with the
following:

    4 oz (120 gm) coarse porridge oats
    2 oz (60 gm) butter
    Enough honey to bind
    A little wine
    Salt

Melt the butter with a teaspoonful of the honey in a saucepan, then add
the oats and a dash of wine and a pinch of salt. Add more honey till the
consistency feels right, and stir together over a gentle heat for a few
moments. Turn into a buttered baking-tin, and bake till brown (fifteen
to twenty minutes) in a moderate oven. Cool in the tin, turn it out and
then cut into crescents.

Demeter cakes

According to Tom Chetwynd (*A Dictionary of Symbols*, p.117), during
the rituals of the corn-mother Demeter, the corn was 'threshed,
ground, made into man-shaped cakes (like gingerbread men) and eaten.
The whole is broken down into bits, but the bits are formed into a new
whole: there is continuity through the change.'

It is yourself you eat; breaking down the ossified, outworn
personality you have been hiding behind, and reabsorbing and
recombining its elements (whose raw materials are the gift of Mother
Earth) 'into a new whole' and a healthier one.

The symbolism is valid and vivid, well worth using ritually, provided
its meaning is held clearly in mind while you are doing it. No recipe is
needed; the figures are made from pastry (which is Demeter-based) and
baked flat 'like gingerbread men'.

But obviously the men should eat men-cakes, and the women
women-cakes; and if they can be made to represent the individuals –
slim, plump, currant-bearded, long-haired, or whatever – so much the
better. Everyone must be aware that it is his or her old self being
reabsorbed and revitalized.

Aphrodite cakes

    Fresh peaches or nectarines
    Short crust pastry

Cut the peaches in half, removing the stones. Lay the halves face
downwards on slightly larger discs of pastry on a baking-tray and cover
each of them with a dome of pastry. Press the edge of each dome onto
its disc to seal it. Punch a hole with a matchstick in the top of each
dome. Bake till golden brown. Juice rising from the fruit will create a
little dark patch around the hole.

The symbolism of these delicious cakes (which were devised by our coven member Martin) is as clear and unapologetic as Aphrodite herself. And why not?

Sally Lunns

2 lb (900 gm.) flour	1 oz (30 gm) yeast
4 oz (120 gm) butter	2 oz (60 gm) lump sugar
Cream	A little castor sugar
1¼ pints (700 cc) milk	

Make a thick batter with most of the flour, yeast, a little castor sugar and a pint (570 cc) of warm milk. Cover and leave to rise in a warm place for two hours. Dissolve the lump sugar in the rest of the warm milk and add it to the batter. Rub the butter into the rest of the flour, mix it with the batter and knead lightly. Leave to stand for thirty minutes. Make into round cakes on a baking tray, and leave till they rise. Bake in a hot oven for thirty minutes. Split and spread with cream.

It may seem strange to find this traditional Devonshire recipe in our list, but Sally Lunns are believed to have their origin in the offerings made to Sul or Sulla, the Celtic Sun goddess and patroness of hot springs – whose most famous temple was, and indeed still is, at Bath (Aquae Sulis). West of England witches in particular may enjoy using them for their original purpose.

Brighid cakes

For a ritual of Brighid, the traditional Irish soda cake is a very appropriate choice.

1 lb (450 gm) plain flour	1 heaped teasp cream of tartar
4 oz (120 gm) margarine	1 heaped teasp bicarbonate of soda.
4 oz (120 gm) sugar	4 oz (120 gm) sultanas or stoned
2 oz (60 gm) mixed chopped peel	raisins
½ pint and 6 tablesp (375 cc) sour milk	
1 level teasp salt	

Have ready a fairly hot oven. Grease a seven-inch cake tin with melted margarine. Sieve the flour, bicarbonate of soda, cream of tartar and salt together in a mixing bowl. Rub in the margarine piece by piece till the mixture is crumbly. Stir in the sugar, sultanas and peel. Add the milk and mix with a knife to a fairly soft dough. Knead lightly on a well-floured board. Put the dough in the tin and press to the sides. Mark a suitable design on the top. Bake for one hour on the middle shelf of the oven, then for another thirty minutes with the oven turned down to moderate.

If you have no sour milk, half a pint and five tablespoons (360 cc) of fresh, plus one tablespoon (15 cc) vinegar, will do; mix together (and if necessary heat gently) till the milk curdles. And for variety, try two heaped tablespoons (50 gm) caraway seed instead of the sultanas.

Moon food

Dion Fortune's moon-food menu, as described in *The Sea Priestess* (hardback p.204, paperback p.111), gives interesting suggestions for lunar rituals. 'Almond-curd such as the Chinese make; and scallops in their shells; and little crescent honey-cakes like marzipan for dessert – all white things. And this curious pallid dinner-table was relieved by a great pile of pomegranates.'

Wine

It helps, both psychologically and magically, if you can choose a wine appropriate to the ritual. For example, an Aradia ritual would be well suited by the north Italian Valpolicella, easily obtainable and not expensive; or, if you can get it, the delightful liqueur Strega (which means 'Witch')..When Stewart was in Morocco, he became familiar with a French wine called La Reine Pédauque; he's never seen it since but wishes now he could lay his hands on it for a Lilith ritual (see p.133).

Celtic countries, except for Brittany, are no longer noted for their wine industries; but home-made wines are another matter. This is not the place to go into the subject in depth, but the fact that home wines are based on flowers and fruit offers limitless scope. For example, elder is one of the most important Goddess trees – and uniquely (so far as we know) among plants, the same tree provides both a splendid red (including a port) and a fine white (either still or sparkling), from the berries and the flowers respectively. What could be more appropriate? – one for the Dark Goddess and one for the Bright Goddess.

Hawthorn is another outstanding Goddess tree, offering a delicate white wine from its May blossoms; those blossoms steeped for six weeks in vodka (or, even better, the illicit Irish poteen!) make an excellent liqueur.

On the subject of Goddess liqueurs – blackthorn is a tree of the Dark Goddess, and its fruit supplies sloe gin by similar steeping; though again, for our own taste we find vodka (or its unmentionable counterpart) preferable to gin.

Other home-brew suggestions – for Demeter or any harvest Goddess, barley wine; for any Celtic or Nordic Goddess, mead; for any ritual with Avalon or Glastonbury associations, cider; for any Oriental Goddess, rice wine; and so on. All are to be found in any standard home wine-making book.

XI The Goddess Today

You can't push the toothpaste back into the tube.
                              American nun to Pope John Paul II

The re-emergence of the Goddess is a major revolution of our time, though not all its revolutionaries are fully aware of its implications.

The revolution has many fronts. At the one extreme there are Catholic nuns (particularly in the United States) demanding ordination for women, the readmission of the priestess function on a basis of full equality – a demand pithily summed up in the quotation at the head of this chapter.

At the other extreme are the sub-atomic scientists who have been compelled, by their own researches, to discover that the fundamental structure of the universe consists not of 'things' but of inter-relationships – a concept which is already beginning to have a far-reaching, and sometimes traumatic, effect on science as a whole. (On this, read Fritjof Capra's fascinating book *The Tao of Physics*.)

In between these two is a wide spectrum of units in the revolutionary army.

There is the feminist movement – a wide spectrum in itself, from constructive to unreasonable. But as Shaw pointed out, the reasonable man tries to adapt himself to the world, while the unreasonable man tries to adapt the world to himself – which is why all progress is due to unreasonable men; and today, more than ever we may add, to unreasonable women.

There are the environmentalists, from the simplest back-to-Nature activists (some of them very successfully organized) to the gallant battlers of Greenpeace, willingly gambling their lives (and in at least one recent case, losing).

There are the Jungian psychologists, exploring and mapping the Collective Unconscious and, with their theory of synchronicity, closely paralleling the sub-atomic physicists' reassessment of the nature of reality.

There are the genuine fringe-medicine practitioners (ignoring the inevitable quacks) who work on principles that transcend mechanistic logic, yet achieve undeniable results.

There are many far-sighted educationalists, and even some politicians, who know that the technological revolution not only makes possible but demands a fundamental shift of emphasis from the work ethic to the human-fulfilment ethic, with all that that implies.

There is another wide spectrum of campaigners, from the Greenham Common women to Bob Geldof, who in their various ways are rubbing our noses in the fact that the human race is one whole family and that it is vitally urgent that we start behaving accordingly.

One could continue the list indefinitely, with ever more subtle subdivisions, but one cannot escape the fact that it seems to include all the most forward-looking, genuinely hopeful and creative elements in contemporary thought and action.

What do they have in common?

All, whether they realize it or not (and an increasing number of them do), are battling for an end to the patriarchal phase in human evolution. Against the materialist view of the cosmos as a mere machine, however complex. Against the dominance of linear-logical thinking to the exclusion of the intuitive. For a living integration of ourselves with our environment, instead of a headlong and disastrous exploitation of it. For a recognition that we are Gaia's children – indeed, her evolving 'central nervous system' – not her overlords. For a recognition that relationships matter more than things.

This does not mean that they would throw out the baby with the bathwater, and reject the positive achievements of the patriarchal phase – the vastly expanded understanding and use of the laws of the physical level of reality in particular. On the contrary, they would accept and build on those achievements by getting them into correct proportion and achieving a balance with their banished complementary aspect. To take one example: the sub-atomic physicist who has realized that the laws of Newtonian physics cease to apply on the frontiers which he is exploring does not reject those laws altogether. He merely points out that they are valid, and extremely useful, within a certain limited field but that to continue to regard them as universal destroys our grip on cosmic reality.

All revolutionary periods in human history are reflected by corresponding developments in religious thinking and practice. This is inevitable, because all genuine religions express, in symbol and ritual, archetypal truths which cannot be expressed otherwise. And if changing circumstances bring a change in the impact of those archetypes on our awareness and our behaviour, their religious expression will change accordingly.

So the common ground between the various forward movements we have described expresses itself in religious terms thus: a vigorous revival of the Goddess-principle in restored balance with the God-principle. Such a development is essentially pagan, in the sense in which we defined the pagan outlook in the Introduction.

Not all who are contributing to the general forward movement would agree with that conclusion, of course. The nun who demands the right to act as an ordained priestess, for example, knows perfectly well that the priestess-function is different in kind from, and should be complementary to, the priest-function. She may well feel, consciously or instinctively, that the creation of such a complementary balance is the only way forward if Christianity is again to become a living faith in harmony with its founder's teaching, instead of a rapidly fossilizing dogmatic structure. But she is unlikely to take the logical step of extending that concept from the human to the divine level. Yet that is where it leads. The priestess is the human expression and channel of the Goddess; readmit her, and you readmit Her.

We have spoken privately with one nun who is fully aware of this and is undeterred; perhaps she is not so untypical. The shrewd and apprehensive hierarchy are surely aware of it; hence their vigorous resistance to the growing demand.

Survey all the overlapping elements in the revolution we have spoken of, and the emergence throughout the spectrum of pagan ways of thought, symbolism and action, whether conscious or involuntary, becomes obvious and striking.

Overlapping all of them, either by unanimous support for their ideas (such as for the environmentalists or the enlightened educationalists) or by individual involvement (such as with the anti-nuclear protesters, scientific research, or the Third World activists), stands the Craft.

Of all the popular pagan movements, the Craft in its various forms is

probably the clearest expression of the readmission of the Goddess. It is
also the fastest-growing. The very nature of its work – the development
and use of the psychic levels – inevitably means an emphasis on the
feminine, Goddess-aspect (and for male witches, on the Anima,
Goddess-aspect); and in its ritual and organization, it means an
emphasis on the Goddess and the primacy of the High Priestess. The
balance between God and Goddess is accepted, the High Priestess is
only first among equals, and the basic feature of the Wiccan coven is
the male-female working partnership, but the emphasis is intrinsic to
the working purpose.

In any revolutionary period, the significant spearheads are those
which emphasize the aspect which is pressing for introduction or
reintroduction. So the Craft, with its emphasis on the Goddess, is one
of the key factors in her readmission from the limbo to which
patriarchy has tried, for 2,000 years and more, to banish her.

The Collective Unconscious – and Gaia herself – know that the time
is ripe and the need pressing for her readmission. It is this need, not the
coincidental arcane studies of a Gardner, or the poetic scholarship of a
Graves, or the brilliant insight of a Jung or a Fortune, that has
triggered the avalanche of the witchcraft revival movement. The time
and its need produce the articulate voices.

The more the need continues to become conscious, the more will
people turn to such paths as the Craft to express it.

XII   The Grail

If that which thou seekest, thou findest not within thee, then thou
wilt never find it without thee; for behold, I have been with thee
from the beginning, and I am that which is attained at the end of
desire.

The Wiccan Charge

We have studied the Goddess in many aspects, but before we go on to
look at some individual goddesses, one thought is worth emphasizing.

We have used, and shall be using, the Gifts of the God to study the
Goddess. In other words, we have called on recorded history; we have
tried to marshal facts in an orderly manner; we have analysed those
facts and drawn conclusions from them.

That is as it should be. The communication of human knowledge
from past to present, and between elements of the present, is one of the
most precious Gifts of the God. We cannot tap the experience of past
cultures and past generations, or of present cultures outside our own
experience, without that knowledge as a basis, or without analysing it
to the best of our ability and consciously relating it to our own
knowledge and experience.

But by itself it is not enough. The Gifts of the God – ego-consciousness, intellectual analysis, articulate communication – are only a part of the cosmic whole and of the human psyche. They rest on, and should be integrated with, the Gifts of the Goddess – the individual and racial unconscious, intuition, the instinct for relatedness.

In seeking the Goddess, both are necessary. The Father can help us to understand the Mother, but only she herself can bring about communion with her.

Communion with the Goddess is one of the great Mysteries, in the sense that, when all is said and done, it can only be experienced, not communicated.

When we think we have found the Grail, its legend emphasizes that, before we can win it and heal the Fisher King and his barren land, we must ask the right questions. Awareness of what we must ask and its articulation are a Gift of the God. But the communion itself, the taking of the Grail in our hands and drinking from it – that is the greatest Gift of the Goddess, which we can achieve only by entrusting ourselves to her.

We hope we are helping you ask the right questions. The rest is up to you.

Part II

Invoking the Goddess

XIII Demeter and Persephone

Virgin and mother stand to one another as flower and fruit, and essentially belong together in their transformation from one to the other.

Erich Neumann

Woman invented agriculture. Confined by child-rearing to the home base, while her man roamed hunting meat, she (helped by the children) supplemented the family diet by gathering berries, nuts, roots and other edible vegetation. Naturally, therefore, it would be she who first discovered by accident that one could not only gather but also plant, grow and harvest, and she who first experimented with, and took charge of, the process.

'In agricultural communities woman was often clothed in an extraordinary prestige ... In a mystical sense the earth belonged to the women; they had a hold, at once religious and legal, upon the land and its fruits ... All nature seemed to him [man] like a mother: the land is woman and in woman abide the same dark powers as in the earth' (Simone de Beauvoir, *The Second Sex*, pp. 98-9).

Correspondingly, the Earth has always been a Goddess, the Great Mother who gives birth to us all, and to the food which nourishes us.

An exception may appear to be the Egyptian Earth god Geb; but the Egyptians, because of their unique environment, distinguished between the Earth as a whole (which was mostly desert) and the only fertility they knew, the Nile Valley; so it was that valley which was the obvious home of the Great Mother.

The crops to which the Great Mother gave birth could be envisaged in two forms: as her annually dying and reviving son/lover or as her annually disappearing and reappearing Other Self, her daughter.

The first form (which is perhaps the commonest) is exemplified by Ishtar and Tammuz; we discuss them, and their predecessors and successors, in Chapters XV and XVI.

The classical (in both senses) example of the mother-and-daughter visualization is that of Greece's Demeter and Persephone.

Demeter, goddess of the Earth's fruitfulness in general but of barley in particular, was one of the great Olympians (though herself of pre-Olympian origin) and held in peculiar honour by the others. She was severely beautiful, with hair like ripened grain. She was the daughter of Cronus and his sister Rhea, and thus herself sister of Zeus, Poseidon, Hades, Hestia and Hera.

Poseidon and Zeus both desired her, but she resisted their advances. To escape Poseidon, she took the shape of a mare among the herds of King Oncus. But Poseidon shape-changed to a stallion and took her. She bore him Arion, a horse with the gift of speech, and a daughter whose name remained secret but who was referred to as Despoena, 'the mistress' (much worshipped in Thessaly).

Furious at Poseidon's trickery, Demeter left Olympus and had to be persuaded to return by Zeus, which she did after purifying herself in the River Ladon. She also cursed the River Styx on his account and guarded it with snakes. (The symbolism of both acts may suggest the distinction between fresh water which gives life to vegetation, and the deadly brine of Poseidon.)

Zeus, in his turn, used a similar trick on her, taking the form of a bull, and by him Demeter became the mother of Persephone – more usually known by her title of Kore, 'the maiden'. This daughter was Demeter's great love.

Now Demeter's third brother, Hades, ruler of the Underworld, entered the seduction scene, but desiring the daughter rather than the mother. One day when Persephone was picking flowers in the fields of Nysa, she stopped to admire a particularly beautiful narcissus. At this moment the ground opened, and Hades emerged and carried her down to his kingdom. (Significant of the universality of the myth is that other sites in Greece, Sicily and Crete also claimed to be the place of the abduction.)

Demeter was desolate. Throwing a dark veil over her grain-gold hair, she 'flew like a bird over land and sea, seeking here, seeking there' but finding no trace of the missing Kore. After nine days, on Hecate's advice, she consulted Helios, the Sun god who sees all. Helios blamed Zeus, saying that he had granted Persephone to his Underworld brother.

Once again Demeter left Olympus in anger and, disguising herself as an old woman, roamed the cities of men. She was treated kindly at the Court of King Celeus of Eleusis, in Attica, and became nursemaid to Demophoön, baby son of Celeus' wife Metaneira. As a result of her secretly divine care, the boy grew like a god, but she was prevented from making him immortal by bathing him in fire, when Metaneira interrupted her and screamed. Demeter then revealed herself as the goddess and ordered that a temple of her mysteries should be built at Eleusis. (This whole sequence in her story is remarkably similar to that of Isis at Byblos, see p.171, which was also part of the Goddess's search for the lost vegetation-deity.)

Demeter continued her wanderings, visiting various Courts, including that of Phytalus to whom she gave the olive tree.

But Persephone was still missing; and finally, in despair, Demeter returned to Eleusis and her new temple, where, as the Homeric account says, 'She prepared for mankind a cruel and terrible year: the earth refused to give forth any crop. Then would the entire human race have perished of cruel, biting hunger if Zeus had not been concerned.'

The gods pleaded with Demeter, but she was adamant; the Earth would remain barren until she was reunited with her daughter. So Zeus sent Hermes to command Hades to return Persephone to her mother. Hades obeyed – but before she left, he persuaded her to eat a few pomegranate seeds, symbol of indissoluble marriage.

So Demeter and Persephone were joyfully reunited, but when Demeter learned about the pomegranate seeds, she feared that she had been defeated after all.

To save the situation, Zeus proposed a compromise. Persephone should spend a third of each year with her husband in the Underworld, and the other two-thirds with her mother on Earth.

Rhea persuaded her daughter Demeter to accept the arrangement, and Demeter lifted the curse of barrenness from the Earth. So flowers, fruit and crops appeared again with the Spring return of Kore, 'a wondrous sight for gods and men'.

At Eleusis, Demeter gave to Triptolemus, Celeus' eldest son, the first grain of corn and taught him the art of ploughing and harvesting. Triptolemus roamed Greece spreading this knowledge – Demeter frustrating at least three attempts by kings to murder him, the last by

Celeus himself, who was compelled to yield his throne to Triptolemus. (In later versions, Triptolemus was identified with Demophoön.) The name may be cognate with *tripolos*, the 'thrice-ploughed furrow' in which the grain was sown and where Demeter, in another story, obviously related to a crop-fertility rite, lay with her lover Iasion (perhaps her original consort).

Demeter thus represents both the fertile Earth and the ripened grain of harvest; while Persephone/Kore represents both the young vegetation of Spring and the Underworld in which the seed is buried during the barren Winter months.

Demeter was probably of Cretan origin (some mythographers identified her with Rhea, her mother in the Homeric version). Her worship spread to the Romans via Greek colonists in Sicily; she and her daughter were known in Latin as Ceres (whence our word 'cereal') and Proserpina, but their myth was the same.

Persephone, during her annual sojourns with Hades, was no prisoner but acknowledged Queen of the Underworld. By Olympian standards, Hades was a remarkably faithful husband; she had cause to complain of his infidelity only twice – once with the nymph Minthe, whom Persephone trod mercilessly underfoot and who became the plant mint, sacred to Hades; and once with Leuce, daughter of Oceanus, who died a natural death and became the white poplar, tree of the Elysian Fields. It is said, however, that Persephone herself was one of the many lovers of Hermes, the *psychopompos* who conducted souls to her realm.

Demeter means literally 'Earth-Mother', and primordially she seems to have been Goddess of both the Earth's aspects – its fertile surface and its dark Underworld. Later the two became distinct, at least in name: as Demeter of field and orchard, and Persephone of the hidden depths. Yet as mother and daughter they were still essentially one, as are flower and fruit. In her Underworld aspect, she was generally known as Persephone, and in her role as the new young vegetation which springs from those depths (like her narcissus from its buried bulb) she was more usually Kore,* the Maiden.

Sacred to Demeter were the horse, the bee, the poppy, the snake and the torch; pigs were sacrificed to her, and her sickle was made by Hephaestos himself. The willow was sacred to Persephone.

In many parts of Greece the rites of Demeter and Kore remained orgiastic. But at Eleusis they evolved to a deeper and more spiritual mystery, the most important festivals of the Greek world. As psychic power-centres, Eleusis and Delphi, in their separate ways, towered above all the others.

The details of the Eleusinian mysteries remained secret to initiates,

* Pronounced 'Koray'.

but there are enough hints for us to be able to reconstruct something of the picture.

Eleusis means 'Advent', and the town was said to be named after the legendary King Eleusis. His mother was Daeira, 'Wise One of the Sea', daughter of Oceanus, and his father was sometimes said to be Ogygus of Thebes, in whose reign a great flood inundated the Boeotian corn-lands. Eleusis himself appeared in the Greater Eleusinian Mysteries in Autumn, as the Divine Child in an osier harvest-basket, for the adoration of those taking part. Graves (*The White Goddess*, pp. 157-88) notes the similarity to the myths of Moses, Taliesin, Llew Llaw Gyffes, and Romulus.

The calendar of the Mysteries was quite complicated. The October Thesmophoria marked the departure of Kore for the Underworld; they lasted for three days and were confined to married women.

The Greater Eleusinia took place every five years, in September, and seem to have involved the son/lover theme which is absent from the Demeter/Kore myth. Athenian youths (*ephebi*) brought Demeter's sacred objects (*hiera*) in solemn procession from Eleusis to the Eleusinion in Athens. Selected devotees would purify themselves in the sea and also wash pigs which were sacrificed to Demeter. The *hiera* would then be returned to Eleusis, equally solemnly, behind the statue of Iacchus, a title of Dionysus, who was linked with Demeter from the earliest times.

At Eleusis the secret mysteries were then celebrated, by initiates only. There were two degrees of initiation, the second (*epoptai*) requiring an extra year's probation.

The initiates (*mystai*) seem to have shared the sacred barley drink (*kykeon*) and the sacred cakes, and then ritually to have enacted the abduction of Kore by Hades. This seems to have been followed by a second ritual drama, attended by the *epoptai* only, in which a *hieros gamos* between the priestess and priest symbolized the union of Demeter and Zeus.

The seventh-century BC Homeric Hymn to Demeter, the classic exposition of the Demeter/Kore myth, includes veiled indications of the nature of the rituals. 'Amongst the rites as to which the poet thus drops significant hints are the preliminary fast of the candidates for initiation, the torchlight procession, the all-night vigil, the sitting of the candidates, veiled and in silence, on stools covered with sheepskins, the use of scurrilous language, the breaking of ribald jests, and the solemn communion with the divinity by participation in a draught of barley-water from a holy chalice' (Frazer, *The Golden Bough*, p.519).

Another element in the mysteries seems to have been the revealing, and contemplation, of a single ear of grain.

The Lesser Eleusinia, at the beginning of February, celebrated the return of Kore from the Underworld and the rebirth of vegetation.

Initiation into the mysteries of Eleusis was open to men and women alike. The mysteries 'stood in this respect between the older, matriarchal mysteries intended only for women (preserved in Rome, for example, in the cult of the Bona Dea) and the male mysteries (such as those of Mithras) with their purely patriarchal foundation' (Neumann, *The Great Mother*, p.324). 'The male was enabled, through his experience of the creatively transforming and rebearing power of the Great Mother, to experience himself as her son – i.e., to identify himself both with the newborn, divine spirit son, as child of the great Goddess, and with Triptolemus, the son invested by her with the golden ear of grain.'

Above all, it is emphasized again and again that initiation to the Mysteries of Eleusis offered immortality. The Greek concept of the Underworld of the Dead was a place of pale shades, mere wraiths of their former selves; only to heroes was genuine immortality sometimes granted, in the form of admission to Olympus as junior members, so to speak. But the Eleusinian initiate was confident of true survival. As the Homeric Hymn declared: 'Happy is he among men on earth who has seen these mysteries; but he who is uninitiated and who has no part in them, never has his lot of like good things once he is dead, down in the darkness and gloom.'

Or as Robert Graves expressed it, some $2\frac{1}{2}$ millennia later:

My feet have borne me here
Out of the weary wheel, the circling years,
To that still, spokeless wheel: Persephone

The Demeter and Persephone Ritual

At least two rituals spring to mind with this theme: a dramatization of Persephone's abduction, Demeter's mourning and the final compromise which symbolizes the annual cycle of nature; and an attempt to recall the spirit of the Eleusinian mysteries themselves. We have chosen the former, if only because so many interpretations and degrees of emphasis are possible with the latter that it is perhaps better to leave it to covens, if they feel drawn to it, to experiment and devise their own.

All the rituals suggested in this book (with the exception of the Isis ritual in Chapter XXIII) are designed for the normal Wiccan Circle and intended to begin and end with the normal opening and closing rituals of Casting, Drawing Down the Moon and Banishing. For completeness, and so that the interested non-witch reader can see the rituals in context, we have included these as the Appendix on pp.290-5. They are in the Gardnerian/Alexandrian form, but we hope that witches of other traditions will find that our various Goddess rituals can be easily fitted in with their own opening and closing methods.

The Preparation
Witches are chosen to enact Demeter, Persephone, Hades and Hermes. Purely dramatically, Demeter should be a mature woman, Persephone a young one, but as every woman witch ought to be able to acknowledge each of the Triple Goddess aspects within herself and give expression to it as the situation demands, there is no need to insist on this.

In the centre of the Circle is a dish or tray of fruit and blossoms. Beside it is a dark cloth ready for covering it, and a dark veil ready for Demeter to put over her head.

Beside the West candle is a single long-stemmed flower in a vase. Ideally it should be a narcissus.

Outside the Circle to the North-West is a single fruit, the coven's white-handled knife, two goblets of wine and a crown for Hades to put on Persephone. Again, for strict adherence to the legend, the fruit should be a pomegranate, but these are not always easy to come by, and any fruit which can be cut in two, such as an apple, pear or peach, will do just as well.

Personal accessories of the four actors give scope for imagination. Hades, for example, could wear a dark crown or a crown securing a dark head-cloth to his scalp and shoulders. Persephone could wear a necklace of flowers, and Demeter one of ears of grain, poppies or both combined. Hermes should carry a wand, preferably transformed (either simply or elaborately) into a caducaeus.

The Ritual
The Opening Ritual is entirely as normal. After the Witches' Rune, all but the four actors seat themselves around the perimeter, but leaving the North-West segment clear. As far as possible they sit in couples, man and woman close together.

Hades stands beside the altar at its East end.

Demeter and Persephone start a happy deosil (clockwise) dance around the Circle.

Hades takes his athame from the altar and opens a gateway in the North-West. He steps through it, closes the gateway behind him, lays down his athame outside the Circle and sits down. (Note that once cast, the Circle must never be entered or left without ritually opening a gateway with a widdershins gesture, and reclosing it afterwards with a deosil one – widdershins and deosil as seen from within the Circle, that is.)

Hades remains outside the Circle for the whole of the ritual, except when he comes in to abduct Persephone.

After a while Demeter stops dancing and sits (with her back to the West) close to the tray of fruit and blossoms in the centre, enjoying the look of it and touching it lovingly.

Persephone continues her happy dance for a while, then notices the flower by the West candle. She goes and kneels by it, still swaying to the rhythm of her dance. She touches the flower as though wondering whether to pick it.

Demeter, with her back to Persephone, is oblivious to what she is doing. But Hades, watching her with interest, is stealthily rising to his feet.

Persephone makes up her mind and plucks the flower. While she is smelling and admiring it, Hades quietly picks up his athame, opens the gateway, lays down his athame and creeps round behind her. Neither Demeter nor Persephone is aware of him.

Suddenly Hades seizes Persephone from behind, pulls her to her feet and hustles her through the gateway out of the Circle. While Persephone looks around, wondering where she is, Hades picks up his athame and closes the gateway. Then he turns to Persephone.

Persephone (realizing): *'You are Hades!'*

Hades: *'Yes, Persephone. I am Hades.'*

Persephone: *'And this is your Kingdom, the Underworld!'* (Looking around, alarmed.) *'There is no light here – no warmth ...'*

Hades picks up her crown and puts it on her head.

Hades: *'For me, you are its light, and its warmth. And now you are its Queen, and my bride.'*

Persephone: *'But I belong in the sunlight – on the living Earth.'*

Hades: *'I am your mother's brother. She rules the fruits of the light, and I the mysteries of the dark. Both are living. But my mysteries need your youth and beauty to give them meaning.'*

Hades picks up the two goblets of wine. Persephone comes and looks in his face, at first nervously, then with a growing fascination.

Persephone: *'Your mysteries call to me. I do not know why.'*

Hades: *'Because you have become their Queen.'*

He holds out one goblet and, after hesitation, she takes it. Facing her, he puts his elbow inside hers so that their drinking-arms are linked. He drinks and Persephone, as though hypnotized, drinks too. After the first sip she is won over, and they both drain their goblets.

Hades: *'So. It is done.'*

Demeter, still with her back to them, breaks off from her pleasant meditation and suddenly looks alarmed. She jumps to her feet.

Demeter: *'Kore?'* (Then crying out.) *'Kore!'**

* Pronounced 'Koray'.

As though not hearing her, Hades and Persephone sit down outside the Circle and murmur together – she questioning and he answering. She is absorbed in his answers.

Demeter runs hither and thither in the Circle, increasingly frantic, and calling '*Kore! Kore!*' Hermes watches her. Hades and Persephone are in another world and hear nothing.

Hermes goes to the West candle and looks across at Hades and Persephone. Then he turns his back on them and goes to Demeter. Demeter sees him.

Demeter: '*Hermes! I have lost my daughter – my beloved Kore, my Persephone!*'

Hermes: '*Your brother Hades has taken her to the Underworld, to be his Queen.*'

Demeter puts her face in her hands and sobs. Then she goes and sits as before. She picks up the veil and shrouds her head in it, then picks up the dark cloth and covers the fruit and blossoms with it.

Demeter (sombrely): '*Until she returns, the Earth shall remain barren. No plant shall blossom or bear fruit. No harvest shall spring from the thrice-ploughed furrow.*'

Hermes puts a hand on her shoulder, but she shrugs it away angrily.

Demeter: '*Until Kore returns to me, man shall not lie with woman. Love and desire shall lose their power, and the seed and the womb shall be as ghosts.*'

Round the perimeter, men and women turn away from each other and slump wearily. Solo men and women hang their heads. Demeter, too, hangs her head.

Hermes: '*Demeter – you cannot do this!*'

Demeter (not looking up): '*Until my daughter returns, it is already done.*'

Hermes walks about the Circle, frowning. He looks at all the slumped men and women, across the West candle at Hades and Persephone (who are still murmuring animatedly) and back at Demeter. Then he goes and kneels before the altar, looking up beyond it. After a while he rises and returns to the West candle.

Hermes (calling clearly): '*Hades!*'

Hades (rising to face him.): '*Hermes! What brings you to the gates of my Kingdom?*'

Hermes: '*Thus Olympus ordains: Persephone shall return to her mother, that the Earth may be fruitful again.*'

Hades: '*Is that the will of the Gods and Goddesses in council?*'

Hermes: '*It is their will. You dare not resist it.*'

Hades pauses. Then he smiles, as though hiding a secret. '*So be it.*' Hades returns to sit by Persephone. '*Persephone – the gods and goddesses have decreed that you must go back to Earth.*'

Persephone: '*But I am content, ruling here with you.*'

Hades: '*I too am content. But we cannot disobey.*' He picks up the single fruit and the white-handled knife and cuts the fruit in two. He hands one half to her. '*The Underworld, too, has its fruits.*'

He waits until she bites her half, and then bites his, smiling. Then he goes and picks up his athame and opens the gateway for her. She goes through it, looking at him a little sadly. He bows as she passes, and then closes the gateway, puts down his athame and sits down by himself.

Hermes smiles and bows to Persephone, who smiles at him in return. Hermes then goes and kneels before the altar as before, looking up and beyond it.

Persephone goes to the centre and takes the dark cloth off the tray of fruit and blossom. The action arouses Demeter, who lifts her head and sees her.

Demeter (joyfully): '*Kore!*'

Demeter throws off her veil and embraces Persephone. The men and women round the perimeter shed their despondency, smiling and hugging each other.

Persephone: '*I am back, mother.*'

Demeter: '*My daughter is back, and the Earth shall be fruitful again.*' She lifts up a flower in one hand and a fruit in the other, and holds them high. '*And you did not eat of the fruit of the Underworld?*'

Persephone: '*I shared fruit with your brother, yes.*'

Demeter drops her hands to her lap, and her smile vanishes. The men and women on the perimeter are still, watching.

Demeter: '*Then are you his bride forever. You are lost to me, and to the Earth.*' She starts to sob, and Persephone puts an arm round her, trying to comfort her. Demeter: '*Without you, the Earth will die again!*'

Hermes (calling clearly): '*Not so!*' He rises and turns, and everyone looks at him expectantly. '*Hear again the decree of Olympus. Persephone shall spend one-third of each year in the Underworld, for she is its Queen; and two-thirds on Earth, for she is its blessing.*'

Demeter (still unsatisfied): '*One-third of each year as Hades' prisoner?*'

Persephone: '*Mother, no! Not as his prisoner but as his bride. I belong here, and I belong there. If I stay forever in the Underworld, the Earth dies. But if I stay forever on Earth, the Underworld is without light, and the Earth itself grows weary, having no rest.*'

Hades rises and stands outside the edge of the Circle, watching.

Persephone takes the single fruit and flower from Demeter's hands and holds them up joyously. The men and women around the perimeter rise and start circling round Demeter and Persephone. As Persephone speaks, she is handing flowers and fruit one by one to the circling men and women.

Persephone: *'I am the young seed and flower of the Earth, as my mother is its fruit and harvest. I rest in the Underworld while the Earth sleeps in winter, and in Spring I come again to bring new life and joy to the world.'*

She rises, pulling Demeter to her feet with her, and they join the circling coven.

Hermes: *'Yet is Persephone more than seed and flower. She is Queen of the Underworld, bringing light and warmth to its mysteries, and the gift of those mysteries to the people of Earth.'*

Hermes himself now joins the circling coven. Then Hades picks up his athame, opens the gateway, walks into the Circle, puts his athame on the altar and he, too, joins the others. The circling becomes a joyous dance, until Persephone cries *'Down!'* and they all sit on the floor.

Persephone and Hades consecrate the wine, and Demeter and Hermes the cakes, and they are passed round.

XIV   Brighid

May Brigit give blessing
To the house that is here;
... Brigit, the fair and tender,
Her hue like the cotton-grass,
Rich-tressed maiden
Of ringlets of gold.
          Scottish Gaelic invocation

Speaking of any of the major Celtic goddesses, one is really speaking of the primordial Celtic Great Mother herself. That is ultimately true of all the world's Goddesses, of course, but with the Celtic family of cultures in particular, the hints are always there. Dana, Anu, Brighid,* Arianrhod, Cerridwen, Modron, Epona and others – all were originally the one Great Mother. We shall probably never know her name, because Celtic beliefs were not committed to the written, or even the carved, word until long after she became (in name at least) diversified.

Two things brought about this diversification. First, the evolution of

* Pronounced 'Breed'.

the Celtic culture into two main streams – the Goedelic (Irish, Scottish, Manx) and the Brythonic (Welsh, Breton, Cornish). The common source is revealed, for example, in the parallels between the family trees of the Irish Dana and the Welsh Dôn (see p.153).

The second phenomenon, which is common to all religious development, was the expansion of aspect-concepts, and therefore of aspect names. The primordial Great Mother would be an Earth, fertility, love and war goddess, among other things, and the Primordial Son/Father the same, though with different emphasis – usually sky rather than Earth, for example. (Sun and Moon, as we saw in Chapter VII, would be variously allotted, though mainly as God and Goddess respectively.) So if Inanna of the dim Sumerian past, who was a fertility, love and war goddess, expressed herself much later in Greece as ripe Demeter, erotic Aphrodite and helmeted Athene, any deep study of these three 'individual' goddesses soon reveals that they are but aspects of the One.

Even Christianity did not escape this process. What would the teacher Jesus and his fishermen apostles have made of the Trinity, Virgin Mother and specialized saints of later centuries?

This aspect-diversity (except when patriarchy warped it) was not a retrogade step, of course. It made possible a finer attunement to the complexities of the deity, and a more vivid visualization and powerful invocation of the aspect relevant to any particular situation. But it is as well always to bear in mind the unity which underlies the diversity.

Brighid – or Bríd to use the Irish name – reveals the unity as well as the aspect-specialization. On the one hand, she was spread throughout the Celtic world. In Britain, as Brigantia, she was the supreme and all-embracing deity of the northern English Kingdom of that name, and there perhaps more than anywhere kept her original Great Mother form. On the Continent she was known as Brigindo or Berecyntia.

The abundance of her place-names reveals her Celtic universality. To name but a few – Bride Cross, Bride Stones, Bride Stones Moor, Bidstone hill, Bridekirk, all in northern England; Bridestow, Bridford and Bridport in the south-west; hundreds of wells, from Bridewell in London to the many *Toibreacha Bhríd* in Ireland; and among rivers, the English Brent, the Welsh Braint and the Irish Brighid.

In the Gaelic areas she developed a special, and much loved, character as a goddess of fire, inspiration, healing, craftsmanship and (in the Hebrides particularly) childbirth. She was patroness of poets, of smiths and other craftsmen, of doctors, of the hearth and of priests (whether Druidic or – thanks to Pope Gregory I, of whom more later – Christian).

She was also a goddess of sovereignty, obviously in Brigantia and in Ireland particularly of Leinster. As Proinsias MacCana puts it (*Celtic*

Mythology, p.95): 'The criterion of a rightful King is that the land should be prosperous and inviolate under his rule – and this can be achieved only if he is accepted as her legitimate spouse by the goddess who personifies his kingdom.'

The Irish, unlike most cultures, did not turn the gods and goddesses of the old religion into the devils of the new. They turned them into the heroes and heroines of the legendary past – in particular, of the last-but-one conquerors of Ireland in the mythological cycle, the Tuatha Dé Danann, Peoples of the goddess Dana. The Tuatha defeated their Fomorian predecessors and were in turn defeated by the Gaels, Sons of Mil, retiring to the hollow hills as the aristocracy of the fairy folk, the Daoine Sidhe. As such, they still hold magical sway over Irish folklore.

According to the *Lebor Gabála Érenn*, Brighid was daughter of the Dagda, 'the Good God' of the Tuatha. For dynastic reasons, she was married to Bres of the Fomors and bore him a son Ruadan. But peace between the Tuatha and the Fomors remained unstable, and in the First Battle of Mag Tuireadh (Moytura), King Nuada of the Tuatha lost his hand. Celtic kings had to be physically perfect, so Bres was elected (presumably in another peace-making attempt) as High King in his place.

But Bres failed to meet the standards of generosity required of the Ard Ri and also imposed excessive taxes on his subjects. Retribution was typically Celtic: the bard Cairbre satirized him and, as a result, boils appeared on his face and he too had to abdicate. This led to the Second Battle of Mag Tuireadh and the final defeat of the Fomors.

In this battle Ruadan was killed, and Brighid's lament for him 'was the first time crying and shrieking were heard in Ireland'.

The fact that Dana, though goddess/ancestress of the Tuatha, is sometimes referred to (like Brighid) as the Dagda's daughter; other overlappings between the myths of Dana and Brighid; the hints (see Graves, *The White Goddess*, p.101) that the Dagda was originally the son of this primordial goddess, then her husband, then her father; the dynastic marriage between Brighid and Bres – all these reflect a long process of integration of the pantheons of neighbouring tribes, or of conquerors and conquered, and also of patriarchalization.

Brighid survived them all, and still survives – which brings us back to Pope Gregory I, known as 'the Great'. This shrewd sixth-century pontiff instructed St Augustine, then evangelizing England, not to destroy pagan sites or customs but to take them over and Christianize them, so that the local people would take more easily to places and patterns to which they were accustomed. This ruling undoubtedly helped Augustine's mission, but it had an effect that Gregory cannot have foreseen: it preserved many things, even though in a disguised form, which might otherwise have been lost or distorted beyond recognition – including Brighid, who became a saint, retaining most of her characteristics in the process.

The human St Bridget, who is said to have died about 525, draws this comment from *The Oxford Dictionary of Saints*: 'Historical facts about her are extremely rare; some scholars have even doubted her existence altogether; her Lives are mainly anecdotes and miracle stories, some of which are deeply rooted in Irish pagan folklore.' And Frazer (*The Golden Bough*, p.177) puts it even more bluntly: 'It is obvious that St Bride, or St Bridget, is an old heathen goddess of fertility, disguised in a threadbare Christian cloak.' (Brighid, Bríd, Bridget, Brigit and Bride are all Gaelic or anglicized forms of the same name. We have chosen Brighid for the goddess and Bridget for the saint merely for clarity.)

St Bridget is believed to have been born near Kildare of humble parents. Baptized by St Patrick, she became a nun and founded the monastery at Kildare. It is historically true that Kildare later became an important double monastery, with shrines of Bridget and her friend the monk St Conleth.

Like Brighid, Bridget was the patroness of poets, blacksmiths and healers. Her legends make her, like the goddess, a personification of compassion and nourishment, both material and spiritual. Her goddess-roots shine through in the ecclesiastically impossible tradition that she was consecrated as a bishop by Bishop Ibor. (Druids, it is worth remembering, did ordain women.) She was also popularly identified with that other goddess figure Mary, as 'Mary of the Gael' (sometimes as her reincarnation), 'the Foster-Mother of Christ' and even Mary's midwife.

St Bridget's Day, *Lá Fheile Bríd* in Ireland, *Laa'l Breeshey* in the Isle of Man, and Wives' Feast Day in northern England (the former Brigantia), is 1 February, eve of the old pagan Spring festival of Imbolg, which also belonged to the Goddess Brighid. We describe the transparently pagan folk-rituals which still mark St Bridget's Day in all those places, and in Scotland, in *Eight Sabbats for Witches* pp.62-4.

Another feature which the saint inherited from the goddess was her triple nature. Brighid, typically, was a Triple Goddess, often subdividing her functions; in Cormac's Glossary (*c*.900) the poets' goddess was said to have two sisters, both of the same name as herself, and patronesses of healing and smithcraft respectively. In various versions, the Dagda was said to have married the Triple Goddess or to have had three daughters all called Brighid.

The saint, likewise, keeps appearing in popular tradition as three holy sisters, all of the same name. A Cornish invocation to her (a spell against a scald) runs:

Three ladies came from the East,
One with fire and two with frost.
Out with thee, fire, and in with thee, frost.

The great Kildare monastery was doubtless built on a sacred pagan site, and at least one of its rituals seems to have been continuous. Giraldus Cambrensis, who died about 1220, wrote that a perpetual fire had been kept burning there 'through all the years from the time of the virgin saint until now', tended by twenty nuns, in a circle of bushes which no man might enter – a typical pagan Celtic women's goddess-mystery.

Equally continuous, and still continuing, is the folk veneration accorded to the goddess-saint, and the nature of the inspiration and protection she affords. In Ireland she is second only to St Patrick in popularity, as the ubiquity of her magic wells bears witness. The quotation at the head of this chapter is from a Scottish Blessing of the House, collected and translated by Alexander Carmichael in his *Carmina Gadelica*. Brighid appears again and again in this collection, the goddess shining unmistakably through the 'threadbare Christian cloak'.

The fire goddess re-emerges in one of the saint's typical miracle stories. When a man in Ardagh accused her of not being holy at all, but wicked, she proved her holiness by putting a burning coal in her bosom and walking with it from Ardagh to the Pound of Killen without being burned. In one version of the story, a well sprang up where she dropped the coal; it has remained miraculous, and the means of countless cures, from that day to this. It is typical of the nature of Brighid/Bridget that she should have total command of the elements of fire and water. And it is not surprising that a favourite form of the Bridget's Cross, still the central symbol of the Imbolg folk-rituals, suggests a swastika or fire-wheel (see the design at the head of this chapter).

Typical, too, of her fertility aspect is the fact that a favourite date for patroness-rituals at her magical wells is 1 August, the old pagan harvest festival of Lughnasadh.

Another haunting poem from the *Carmina Gadelica* gives her an unnamed son, which the Kildare saint could surely not have had. They talk together.

Brid: Black the town yonder,
    Black those that are in it;
    I am the White Swan,
      Queen of them all.
Son: I will voyage in God's name
    In likeness of deer, in likeness of horse,
    In likeness of serpent, in likeness of king.
      More powerful will it be with me than with all others.

Graves (*The White Goddess*, p.412) comments: 'The son is evidently a god of the waning year, as the sequence of deer, horse and serpent shows.'

She, too, had her symbolic animals, according to the *Lebor Gabála Érenn*: 'Brigit the poetess, daughter of The Dagda, she had Fe and Menn, the two royal oxen ... She had Triath, King of the boars ... She had Cirb, King of the wethers' (rams).

A strange sentence follows the naming of Fe, Menn and Triath: 'With them were heard the three demon cries in Ireland after ravaging – whistling and wailing and outcry.' The *Lebor* says that the Tuatha Dé Danann invented battle shouting, outcry and barking: 'Shouting for fear of capture, barking against mischief and plunder, outcry for a fitting lamentation of their affliction.'

So did the creatures of Brighid, goddess of fertility and the arts of peace, raise their voices against violence and pillage? And did the divine Poetess herself, as befitted a bard, give expression to the emotions of her people, whether in tragedy or in rejoicing?

Brighid is a glowing example of the goddess who cannot be banished from the dreams of men and women; they turn to her in need, or for inspiration, whatever the religious forms of the time. As an aspect of the Great Mother, she has survived the onslaughts of patriarchy, both pagan and Christian.

And if today's witches – particularly those with Celtic blood in their veins – are looking for a form and a name to give to their newly acknowledged goddess, who better than the Triple Goddess of inspiration, healing and creativity, Brighid?

The Brighid Ritual

The emphasis we have chosen here is on Brighid's triple role as patroness of inspiration, healing and craftsmanship – and it has a practical magical purpose.

Every coven is likely to have among its members individual witches whose activities or ambitions lie in one or other of those three fields – of mental creativity, healing and manual skill. So we will invoke Brighid to help and encourage them.

The Preparation
Three people are chosen – we will call them the Poet, the Healer and the Craftsman or Craftswoman – who it is felt will most benefit from the power being invoked. (These labels are merely for convenience; the Poet, for example, may be a writer, artist or musician, and a sculptor may prefer to be categorized as a Craftsman if it is his technical

dexterity rather than his ideas which need strengthening.)

Each of these people can be either a man or a woman, depending on who is most in need of this particular kind of help and inspiration. They are referred to below as 'he' merely for brevity.

There is no reason, of course, why the coven should not invite a sympathetic non-witch friend or friends, who would benefit in this way, to take part, if coven and guest are happy about the arrangement.

It helps the dramatic symbolism if each of the three carries something symbolic of his or her activity – whether it be a pen, bunch of herbs, stethoscope, spanner, weaver's shuttle or what have you.

If there are two women witches to spare, they can emphasize the Triple Goddess theme by accompanying Brighid throughout the ritual, as her silent 'other selves'.

The Ritual

The Opening Ritual is as usual, except that Drawing Down the Moon is performed on the woman who is enacting Brighid, whether or not she is the High Priestess. (In fact, it is better if she acts as such for the occasion in any case.) If she has the two companions, they will stand silently on each side of her while it is done.

The Goddess and God names used for the Casting should preferably be Celtic ones.

The 'Hail Aradia' invocation is replaced by the following:

Hail, golden Brighid, inspirer of us all,
Mother of healing, mistress of the arts,
Lady of every skill – on thee we call
To pour thy magic into human hearts.
Bestow thy blessing on the poet's pen,
The craftsman's chisel, and the healer's hand;
And guide the work of women and of men
To bring thy beauty into this our land!'

After the Witches' Rune, Poet kneels in front of the East candle, Craftsman in front of the South, and Healer in front of the West, all facing inwards towards the centre.

The rest of the coven sit down around the perimeter.

Brighid goes to the altar and picks up the wand. (Her two companions, if any, accompany her from now on, just behind her to her left and right.) She then goes and faces Poet, who bows to her without rising.

Brighid: *'Who sits by the Watchtower of Air?'*

Poet: *'My name is ——, Lady.'* He then describes, in his own words, what he aims for in his art and what aspects he feels need strengthening, ending with: *'Give me your blessing, Lady.'*

Brighid. '*Air is the element of inspiration, of creative thought and of the power to express it. Let it be always so with you. May your words* [pictures, music] *inspire others as I inspire you. But remember always – look to the other Watchtowers also; for whatever your work, all must be in balance. So mote it be.*'*

Poet: '*So mote it be.*' He holds up his symbolic object, and Brighid lays her hand on it in blessing, while he bows to her.

Brighid goes and faces Craftsman, who bows to her without rising.

Brighid: '*Who sits by the Watchtower of Fire?*'

Craftsman: '*My name is* ——, *Lady.*' He too describes his aims and needs in his own words, ending with: '*Give me your blessing, Lady.*'

Brighid: '*Fire is the element of the smith's forge, of the potter's Kiln and of the magic of electricity. Let it be always so with you. May the things of skill and beauty which you fashion help others as I help you. But remember always – look to the other Watchtowers also; for whatever your work, all must be in balance. So mote it be.*'

Craftsman: '*So mote it be.*' He holds up his symbolic object, and Brighid lays her hand on it in blessing, while he bows to her.

Brighid goes and faces Healer, who bows to her without rising.

Brighid: '*Who sits by the Watchtower of Water?*'

Healer: '*My name is* ——, *Lady.*' He too describes his aims and needs in his own words, ending with: '*Give me your blessing, Lady.*'

Brighid: '*Water is the element of compassion, of cleansing, of the healing influence between one human and another. Let it be always so with you. May you bring the blessing of wholeness to others, as I bring it to you. But remember always – look to the other Watchtowers also; for whatever your work, all must be in balance. So mote it be.*'

Healer: '*So mote it be.*' He holds up his symbolic object, and Brighid lays her hand on it in blessing, while he bows to her.

Brighid goes to the altar, lays down the wand and takes up the chalice. She then stands with her back to the altar, holding the chalice before her.

Brighid: '*Know and remember, that I am always with you. You invoke me, but I am already there. The magic you seek is within your hearts and minds, waiting to be unlocked. Call on me as you work, and I shall bring you the golden key. So mote it be.*'

She holds the chalice high, and all rise, saying: '*So mote it be!*'

The High Priest joins her at the altar, and they bless the wine together for passing round.

* This is a traditional Wiccan – and Masonic – phrase meaning 'So let it be' or 'Amen'.

XV Ishtar

Creatress of mankind we call thee;
Mistress of all the gods be thy name!
Babylonian hymn

Ishtar was the greatest of the Middle Eastern goddesses. She was first
known as Inanna by the Sumerians; early in the second millennium BC
she became Ishtar of the Assyrians and Babylonians; and later she
became known to the Phoenicians as Astarte or Asherah, and to the
Philistines and Syrians as Atergatis. (This development is laid out in
family-tree form on p.113.) As Asherah she gave her name to the
Hebrew tribe of Asher, and she was widely worshipped by the farming
population of Israel as Queen of Heaven, to the horror of the priestly
establishment.

In all her forms, Ishtar was a very complete goddess, embracing both
the bright and the dark aspects, and this is reflected in the variety of
fathers, brothers and consorts attributed to her. As a goddess of love
and benevolence, she was said to be the daughter of the sky god Anu
and the fertility goddess Anat (not to be confused with the Canaanite

Anat, though they may have the same origin), and was associated with the fertility god Min. As a battle goddess, she was daughter of the Moon god Sin and associated with the slayer god Reshef.

Over the centuries, she took over many of Sin's lunar attributes, becoming in fact a Moon goddess (see, for example, the paragraph on *sabbatu* below).

Her consorts were the supreme god Assur, who was also a war god; or Marduk, god of the Spring Sun, originally a vegetation god, or Nebo, god of writing and speech. And, of course, Tammuz, the dying and resurrecting vegetation god, of whom more later. She had many lovers, and the Gilgamesh epic tells how the hero paid dearly for spurning the advances of so powerful a goddess.

She was also sister to the Sun god Shamash and, in her Hittite form, sister to the storm god Hadad.

In addition to her Moon aspect, she was the planet Venus, as both Morning and Evening Star; the Zodiacal belt was known as the Girdle of Ishtar. Her symbol was the eight-pointed star and also a loop-headed symbol rather like a comet. She was typically represented full face, naked but richly ornamented, elaborately coiffed and often crowned by a crescent with a jewel in the middle, and with her hands clasping her breasts from underneath. She was known as 'the Lady with the Beautiful Voice'.

Her cult animal was the lion and, in her dark, Underworld aspect, sometimes the scorpion.

As a fertility goddess, she was often depicted with flowers, branches or grain or dispensing water from a never-failing jar.

Water, whether nourishing or overwhelming, was very much associated with Ishtar; the Biblical Flood story is a revision of the Ishtar one. She inherited it from an earlier Babylonian Moon goddess, Nuah, whose name, masculinized, is the obvious root of Noah.

In the Ishtar account, as related in the Gilgamesh epic, no reason is given for the Flood (except in one Akkadian version, which says the gods were troubled by men's rapid increase and the noise they made); disaster is merely prophesied by Ishtar (who is powerful in prophecy and magic), and when it happens, she and the gods weep together.

> I the mother have begotten my people,
>   and like the young of the fishes they fill the sea.
> The gods concerning the spirits were weeping with me,
> The gods in seats seated in lamentation
>   covered their lips for the coming evil.
> Six days and nights passed,
> The wind, the deluge, storm overwhelmed.

Utnapishtim, the equivalent of Noah, had been advised by the god Ea to build an ark – whose construction is described in some detail. After seven days of the Flood, he sends forth a dove, which returns; then a swallow, which also returns; and finally a raven, which does not.

> On the seventh day in its course,
>   was calmed the storm, and all the deluge
> Which had destroyed like an earthquake
> Quieted.

According to one version (and in the Noah original), it is the Goddess herself who makes and sails the ark, and

> On the seventh day in the course of it
> I sent forth a dove ...

and after the Flood had subsided, 'Then at last Ishtar also came, she lifted her necklace with the jewels of heaven that once Anu had made to please her: "O ye gods here present, by the lapis lazuli round my neck I shall remember these days as I remember the jewels of my throat; these last days I shall not forget" ' – a detail echoed by the rainbow of Genesis ix.

The Hebrews, and their Christian and Moslem heirs, owe many unacknowledged debts to Ishtar – including their Sabbaths, as mentioned on page 25. The Babylonian word was *sabbatu*, derived from *sa-bat* – 'heart-rest', and was the day of the full Moon, when the goddess was held to be menstruating, and it was believed unlucky to do any work, eat cooked food or travel. All of these have been taboo to menstruating women in many cultures, but when Ishtar was menstruating the ban covered men as well as women. Later the *sabbatu* was extended to the four lunar quarters – i.e., every seven days, which is how the Hebrews inherited it.

The Hebrews also owe the biblical Book of Esther, and the Purim festival, to Ishtar. During the Babylonian captivity in the fifth century BC, the ordinary Jewish captives turned naturally to the worship of Ishtar. A vital part of that worship was the *hieros gamos* or sacred marriage – see p.108 below – between the king and the human representative of the goddess (chosen from the fairest of the virgin priestesses), a union which brought blessings on the people; and the story of Esther and King Ahasuerus reflects this exactly. Even her name does so; before the marriage she was Hadassah ('myrtle'), but from then on she was called Esther, a form of Ishtar. Significantly, the Purim festival is on the 14th and 15th days (i.e., the full Moon, sacred to Ishtar) of the month Adar; and the word Purim is non-Hebrew, from the Assyrian 'Puhru', the annual assembly of the Gods.

The present Book of Esther was written a generation or two BC, doubtless to make respectable a festival of ineradicable popularity. Scholars agree that it is full of interpolations; but its original meaning cannot be hidden. Not once does it mention the Jewish God – the only book in the Bible, apart from the splendidly erotic Song of Solomon, which does not.

The story of Ishtar and Tammuz is one of the classic versions of the theme of the fertility goddess and her lover the dying and resurrecting vegetation god, and its commemoration was one of the most important of the seasonal Middle Eastern rituals. (How it evolved both before and after Ishtar, or rather through her various forms, is also shown in the 'family tree' on p.113.)

Ishtar's lover Tammuz (who is also her son and brother) is killed by a wild boar and taken to the Underworld. Ishtar is desolate:

Alas, hero! My son, my faithful lord ...
Alas, hero! Thou who art my heavenly light ...

and all the women weep with her. She determines to go to the Underworld, ruled by her sister Ereshkigal (or Allatu), to get Tammuz back.

To the Land of No Return, the realm of Ereshkigal,
Ishtar the daughter of Sin set her mind ...
Where they see no light, residing in darkness,
Where they are clothed like birds, with wings for garments,
And where over door and bolt is spread dust.

At the first of the seven gates of the Underworld she threatens to break in by force. She is admitted only on condition that she sheds one of her ornaments or garments at each gate – her crown at the first, her earrings at the second and so on, until she finally stands naked and helpless before Ereshkigal.

Her sister refuses to surrender Tammuz and imprisons Ishtar. As a result, the Earth becomes infertile:

Since the Lady Ishtar descended to the Land of No Return
The bull does not spring upon the cow,
    the ass does not bow over the jenny,
The man no more bows over the woman in the street,
The man sleeps in his chamber,
The woman sleeps alone.

The gods are alarmed, and Ea, the god of water, wisdom and magic, intervenes to bring pressure on Ereshkigal. As a result, she gives orders to 'sprinkle Ishtar with the water of life and take her from my presence'. At each of the seven gates on the way out, Ishtar resumes her impounded finery.

As for Tammuz, the lover of her youth,
Wash him with pure water, anoint him with sweet oil;
Clothe him with a red garment,
    let him play on a flute of lapis lazuli.
Let courtesans turn his mood.

Thus the goddess returns with her lover, and life springs anew on Earth.

The annual mourning over Tammuz and rejoicing over his resurrection are described in the next chapter, on p.117.

In the Tammuz myth, Ereshkigal is Ishtar's sister, but in essence she is another aspect of Ishtar herself, because Ishtar was the triple Queen of Heaven, Earth and the Underworld. And the seven-stage shedding of jewels suggests the nightly 'bites' taken out of the Moon in its last quarter, which ends in complete Underworld darkness.

Ishtar, like so many other goddesses from the Egyptian Isis to the Irish Queen Medhbh, was also a goddess of sovereignty. Throughout Assyrian and Babylonian history, the King was regarded as married to the goddess, the true source of his authority. This sacred marriage was ritually consummated between the King and a priestess known as the *enitum*, who was forbidden intercourse with laymen. The King Sargon (2242-2186 BC) put it on record that he was the son of an *enitum*, and this too may have been typical.

Not only the King's authority depended on this *hieros gamos* (sacred marriage) but also the fertility of the land. This fertility magic was also the basis of Ishtar's sacred temple prostitutes – a subject discussed more fully in the next chapter. (She herself was known as 'Courtesan of the Gods'.)

Such courtesan priestesses were called *ishtaritu*; several Babylonian princesses were dedicated as such and were known as 'Lady of the House' or 'first priestess'. These would probably be among the few who had intercourse only with the representative of the god, 'but more often the sacred marriage could take place with any male worshipper or initiate who sought for union with the goddess. A sacred marriage of this kind probably formed part of the initiation of men to the mysteries of the goddess' (Harding, *Woman's Mysteries*, pp.134-5). In due course, it became the custom for all women, of whatever rank, to serve once in their lives as a courtesan priestess of the goddess – 'dedicating, as it were, the first fruits of their womanhood to her' (*ibid.*, p.135).

Ishtar was thus a goddess of love and fertility, and at the same time of battle and death, of the bright Heaven, the fertile but precarious Earth and the gloomy Underworld. She was both the Bright Mother and the Dark Mother, whose completeness was probably unique among the goddesses of the ancient Western world, until Isis surpassed them all.

A long hymn to her (of which the following are but a few lines, in L.W. King's 1902 translation) conveys both the love and the awe she inspired:

Thou art mighty, thou hast sovereign power, exalted is thy name!
Thou art the light of heaven and earth,
  O valiant daughter of the Moon god.
Ruler of weapons, arbitress of the battle!
Framer of all decrees, wearer of the crown of dominion ...
Thou judgest the cause of men with justice and righteousness;
Thou lookest with mercy on the violent man,
  and thou settest right the unruly every morning ...
O goddess of men, O goddess of women,
  thou whose counsel none may learn,
Where thou lookest in pity, the dead man lives again,
  the sick is healed,
The afflicted is saved from his affliction,
  when he beholdeth thy face! ...
O exalted Ishtar, that givest light
  unto the four quarters of the world!'

The Ishtar Ritual

The legend of Ishtar's descent into the Underworld will be recognized at once by witches as the inspiration for the Wiccan Legend of the Descent of the Goddess – although in that, the ruler of the Underworld is male, there is no equivalent of Tammuz, and the whole message of the ritual is different. It does not concern the seasonal fertility cycle but (so to speak) spiritual fertility through the integration of complementary aspects.

But the Wiccan Legend is such an integral part of Craft tradition, at least in the Gardnerian and Alexandrian streams, that it would seem a pity to confuse it by suggesting another version with a different message, and the Demeter and Persephone ritual we have already given parallels the Tammuz story, so we will leave that aspect, and take instead the Flood theme.

The Preparation
No special preparations are needed, except for any water symbolism which the imagination may devise. But the High Priestess (or whoever enacts Ishtar) must be wearing a necklace. Lapis lazuli would be ideal, of course, but in any case it should be a bright and colourful one.

The Ritual
The Opening Ritual is as normal, but using the Goddess named Ishtar

and the God name Ea (pronounced 'Eh-ya'), who was the Babylonian water deity. In the ritual itself, these two may be enacted by the High Priestess and High Priest, or by whatever couple they nominate. The third actor is Utnapishtim (which may require a little practice beforehand to articulate!). The rest of the coven are a *corps de ballet* representing the waters of the Flood.

If a woman witch other than the High Priestess is enacting Ishtar, she should be the subject of Drawing Down the Moon. And we suggest that the 'Hail Aradia' declamation be replaced by the Babylonian hymn we gave above, from 'Thou art mighty ...' down to 'the four quarters of the world'.

After the Witches' Rune, Ishtar and Ea stand with their backs to the altar; Utnapishtim sits in the centre facing them; and the rest of the coven seat themselves, man and woman alternately, evenly spaced around the perimeter, facing inwards. (If there are enough women, one will sit beside Utnapishtim as his wife, reacting as he does to the following action.)

Ea: '*Men and women have forgotten us who created them.*'

Ishtar: '*They are still our children.*'

Ea: '*They lay waste the Earth we gave them. They lay waste the creatures who live on it. They lay waste each other.*'

Ishtar: '*They are still our children. They will learn wisdom. Let us not punish them while they are learning.*'

Ea: '*It is not we who punish them – it is they themselves. See – they have unloosed the floodgates of destruction, and the waters are rising.*'

Ishtar: '*You are Lord of Water, Ea. Call a halt to the Flood!*'

Ea: '*It is too late. Look!*'

The coven are slowly rising to their feet, undulating like seaweed as they do so. They continue to rise to their full height, still in a swaying dance but without moving their feet. Utnapishtim, still seated, holds his head in his hands.

Ishtar (despairing):

I the Mother have begotten my people,
And like the young of the fishes, they fill the sea.
The Gods are weeping with me,
The Gods look on, lamenting.
Six days have passed, and six nights,
And still the wind rages, the waters rise ...
The storm is unending!

Ea: '*Look, Ishtar! One man alone has not forgotten us. I bade him build an ark to ride out the storm, and he heard my voice!*'

Ishtar (calling): '*Utnapishtim! Send forth a dove!*'

Utnapishtim rises to his feet, looking astonished, and mimes the releasing of a bird. He watches it circling and returning to his hand.

Utnapishtim: '*She has returned, Lady. There is no place for her to rest.*'

Ishtar: '*Utnapishtim! Try once more. Send forth a swallow!*'

Utnapishtim repeats his action and again mimes the bird's return to his hand.

Utnapishtim (shaking his head): '*He, too, has returned. It is hopeless, Lady.*'

Ea: '*Look, Ishtar! The Flood is abating.*'

Ishtar (to Utnapishtim): '*Have faith, mortal. Send forth a raven!*'

Utnapishtim again mimes the releasing of a bird. The coven's undulating becomes gentler, and while Utnapishtim watches the circling of the bird, they gradually sink to the ground and are still. Utnapishtim is now looking in one direction, into the distance.

Utnapishtim: '*Lady! The raven has found dry land. The Earth is saved!*'

Utnapishtim (and his wife if there is one) falls to his knees and bows towards Ishtar, afterwards sitting proudly upright.

Ishtar takes the necklace from her neck and holds it high above her head, stretched between her hands like a rainbow.

Ishtar: '*O ye gods here present, by this necklace do I swear, that I shall remember these days as I remember the jewels of my throat. O ye mortals here present, do ye remember them also.*' She puts the necklace back round her neck, and continues: '*The Earth is saved; by the wisdom we have implanted in you, watch that you keep it so ... Gather round, my children, and share with us the fruits of the reborn Earth.*'

The whole coven moves forward and sits at the feet of Ishtar and Ea, who bless the wine and cakes in the usual way and pass them round.

XVI Aphrodite

Hypocrisy and Aphrodite were not bedfellows.
Geoffrey Grigson

Foam-born Aphrodite was the last and the most splendid of the love goddesses of Western paganism. Also the purest – not in the puritan sense (may She forbid) but because she personified love and nothing but love. Earlier love goddesses had often been battle goddesses as well, or wisdom goddesses, or what have you. Aphrodite carried no such superfluous luggage. She was erotic, beautiful, uninhibited, desirous, desirable, unpredictable, overwhelming and single-minded. She was Love itself, with full orchestra – everything from the high strings of enraptured spirit to the percussion-section of engorged genitalia. She was all these things without qualm or apology.

We say 'the last' – but of course she has never died, and never will. There have merely been (and still are) a series of attempts, with varying but never complete success, to sweep her under the carpet.

The classical story of her birth takes us back to the beginning, to the pre-Olympian gods. When Cronus, on his mother Gaia's orders, castrated his father Uranus, he threw the severed genitals away so that some of the blood fell on the earth, and from this sprang the Furies, the Meliae (ash-tree nymphs) and various giants. But the genitals themselves fell on the sea, and from them sprang Aphrodite; she drifted first to Cythera, and finally came ashore on Cyprus – traditionally at Achnion on its south coast.

Not all her legends agree. Homer makes her the daughter of Zeus and the Nature goddess Dione. Hyginus, writing many centuries later, says she was born from an egg which dropped from the sky into the Euphrates and was brought ashore by fish. Doves kept it warm, and it hatched out Aphrodite (writing in Latin, he called her Venus), which is why fish and doves were sacred to the Syrians, who would not eat them.

In one sense, Hyginus was nearest to the truth; because Aphrodite in fact was the final development of a series of Middle Eastern goddesses. That development was as follows:

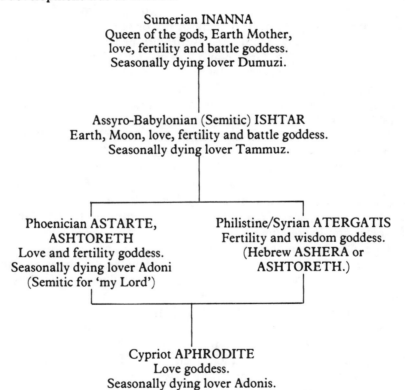

Sumerian INANNA
Queen of the gods, Earth Mother,
love, fertility and battle goddess.
Seasonally dying lover Dumuzi.

Assyro-Babylonian (Semitic) ISHTAR
Earth, Moon, love, fertility and battle goddess.
Seasonally dying lover Tammuz.

Phoenician ASTARTE,
ASHTORETH
Love and fertility goddess.
Seasonally dying lover Adoni
(Semitic for 'my Lord')

Philistine/Syrian ATERGATIS
Fertility and wisdom goddess.
(Hebrew ASHERA or
ASHTORETH.)

Cypriot APHRODITE
Love goddess.
Seasonally dying lover Adonis.

This evolution, from Inanna swearing by her lapis lazuli necklace not to forget the Flood, down to the lovely Aphrodite of Greek sculpture, took well over a thousand years. Inanna was becoming Ishtar early in the second millennium BC. About the same time, the Phoenicians and other western Semites were establishing themselves along the western Mediterranean coast, and in due course the same goddess became their Astarte.

Their southern neighbours, the Philistines of Askalon, called her Atergatis, and both these seafaring races – the 'Sea Peoples' watched warily by the Egyptians – had their trading posts and their places of worship in Cyprus. The name Ashtoreth would have been familiar there, too.

The Mycenaean Greeks, who began entering Cyprus about the thirteenth century BC, could not have pronounced 'Ashtoreth', so it may well have become something like 'Aphthorethe' and finally 'Aphrodite'.

Now *aphros* in Greek means foam and, having adopted a sea-people's love goddess and given her a pronounceable name, the Greek immigrants might naturally have envisaged her as born of that *aphros*, and evolved an appropriate legend for her origin.

Be that as it may, foam-born Aphrodite became one of the Twelve Olympians of classical Greece and was given by Zeus to the lame smith god Hephaestus as his wife. (Hephaestus, like her, was an immigrant to Greece; he was originally a fire god from the volcanic areas round Lycia, in the south of what is now Turkey.) She was thoroughly established in her Greek form by at least the eighth century BC.

She brought many things with her from her Middle Eastern homeland, including her doomed lover Dumuzi/Tammuz/Adonis, but the original theme of the sacrificed and reborn vegetation god changed its emphasis to that of a tragic love-story. (Also, of course, the death and rebirth of vegetation, and the goddess who successively mourns and rejoices over it, was already adequately personified for the Greeks by Demeter and Persephone.)

One other characteristic, apparently unconnected with love, she retained to the end: her connection with the sea. This was doubtless because the Sea Peoples who introduced her to Cyprus, and thus to the Greeks, were used to invoking her to protect their voyages, and her image was irrevocably perfumed with the sea and the *aphros* of her arrival. Also, at a deeper level, because the mysterious, fathomless, ever-shifting sea is an archetypal symbol of the essential female. Her own symbol became the scallop shell – *kteis* in Greek and *concha* in Latin, both of which also meant a woman's genitals. Many of her naked statues wear it like a fig-leaf. (It is ironic that it was much later worn in the caps of pilgrims to the Holy Land, Aphrodite's home ground, and became the symbol of such pilgrimages. Or were the locals having a quiet joke?)

She may also have brought the ritual use of incense to Greece with her; before then, the stench of animal sacrifice was tempered by burning it on fragrant wood.

And what of the battle goddess aspect common to her earlier forms? Aphrodite was no warrior, in the general tradition (though she was so honoured in warlike Sparta); the only time she was wounded in battle – an arrow-scratch on her hand when she was defending her son Aeneas – she left Apollo to look after him and fled back to Olympus, where Dione treated the scratch. Hera and Athene were predictably sarcastic. Zeus smiled and told her she was not meant to concern herself with war; she should 'attend to the sweet tasks of love'.

But perhaps there is a trace of her forebears in her adulterous affair with the war god Ares, which ended with her humiliation before the assembled gods by her outraged husband.

Maybe the Greeks felt instinctively that beauty, love, and passion are fittingly mated to craftsmanship; but that if they dally with violence, disaster results. A civilized concept, one must allow.

Beautiful she certainly was, and in a literally aphrodisiac sense. As F. Guirand puts it (*Larousse Encyclopaedia of Mythology*, p.144): 'Aphrodite was the essence of feminine beauty ... To be sure Hera and Athene were also very lovely, but the haughty beauty of Hera imposed respect and the severe beauty of Athene arrested desire. Aphrodite exuded an aura of seduction. To the perfection of her figure and the purity of her features she added the grace which attracted and conquered.'

The famous Judgement of Paris was really a foregone conclusion. Zeus asked the Trojan Paris to award the golden love-apple (in Greece actually a quince) inscribed 'For the Fairest' to one of those three goddesses. Hera offered him kingship, Athene victory in war, and Aphrodite merely unfastened her tunic and her girdle (quite enough in itself) and then offered Paris the most beautiful woman in the world, Helen, wife of Menelaus. She won the quince, and the destruction of Troy, and of Paris himself, was Hera and Athene's terrible revenge.

But in her own sphere, Aphrodite's victory was thereafter complete. Even Hera, when she wanted to win back Zeus's love, was not too proud to borrow her magic *kestos* (girdle), against which gods and men were powerless. (The *kestos* was a beautifully embroidered band worn not as a belt but round the neck and coiled between the breasts.)

A handful of her many titles reflects the completeness with which she personified love and sex in all their aspects – and with a whiff of the sea thrown in:

Urania – of pure and ideal love
Genetrix – protectress of marriage
Pandemos, Porne – of lust, patroness of prostitutes
Anosia – impious, irreverent

Peitho – persuasive
Epistrophia – heart-turning
Psythiros – she who whispers
Parakyptousa – the side-glancer
Baoiotis – of the little ears
Kallipygos – of the beautiful backside
Machinitis – she who contrives
Of the Mandrake – of aphrodisiacs
Pelagaia – of the ocean
Euploia – of good sailing
Galenaia – of the calm
Akraia – of the headland
Nympha – bridal
Harma – she who joins
Philommedes – lover of genitals
Philommeides – lover of laughter
Thalamon – of the bridal chamber
Praxis – of success, orgasm
Charidotes – giver of joy
Tymborochos – grave-robber (cheater of death)
Hetaira – courtesan
Androphonos – slayer of men
Pseliumene – of the bracelets or necklaces
Stephanousa – diademed
Paregoros – the soother
Antheia – of the flowers
Ambologera – postponer of old age

– which does not leave much of the spectrum unaccounted for.

The symbols sacred to her were many, too. Her animals were the dolphin and the goat; her birds the dove, sparrow, goose, partridge and wryneck, and occasionally the swan (borrowed from Apollo); and her plants the rose, myrtle, quince, rose campion and water-mint.

Quite apart from her adventure with Ares (to whom, somewhat surprisingly, she bore a daughter Harmonia), it was scarcely to be expected that she would be faithful to Hephaestus. To Hermes she bore the strange Hermaphrodite, who united with the nymph Salmacis to become one body, 'neither man nor woman, seeming to have no sex and yet to be of both sexes'. To Poseidon she bore Rhodos, bride of Helios the Sun, after whom the island of Rhodes was named.

The father of her son Eros was variously named as Ares, Hermes or Zeus himself. Eros was a charming but irresponsible child whose love-arrows could cause chaos and whose targets were often cruelly chosen. Even his mother had to punish him sometimes, but usually he was her obedient companion, and together with her attendants the Charites (Graces – themselves as much Love Goddesses as inspirers of art) he helped with her toilet.

In fact Eros, like Aphrodite herself, had been a much more ancient pre-Olympian deity – a primordial sexual force, brother of Gaia, the original Earth Mother; the unequivocal male counterpart of Aphrodite. A far cry from the naughty if endearing cherub he became on Olympus; and his original parent had been Chaos, not the shapely Cyprian.

This meaning of the name Eros should not be confused with the philosophical and psychological term Eros, meaning the principle of psychic relatedness, in contrast to Logos, the principle of logical reasoning. Jung correlated these two as characteristically feminine and masculine, respectively.

Another immigrant who became her son (by Dionysus this time) was the serio-comic Priapus. Originally a fertility god of the coasts of Asia Minor, he became popular in Greece and Rome, and installed (carved out of fig-wood, tiny and misshapen but with his huge erect member) in every orchard, garden and fishing-harbour. Prudent maidens, taking offerings to him, approached him from behind. A cruder and simpler personification of the same force as Eros and his elegant adoptive mother, he was regarded with humorous affection but taken very seriously; after all, fecundity depended on him.

Aphrodite had human lovers, too, the most famous being the Trojan shepherd Anchises to whom she bore Aeneas.

Her most significant divine (or semi-divine, as he became in Greece) lover was of course Adonis. The name was purely Greek, from the Semitic title 'Adoni' ('my Lord', 'my master') by which the Phoenician women addressed their Tammuz vegetation god during their seasonal lamentations for him. His Phoenician festival, just after the harvest, was dramatically beautiful, with little potted 'gardens' of quick-fading plants such as lettuce to accompany the mourning of his death, which were later thrown into the sea, streams or springs; afterwards came the joyous ritual of his resurrection. (It is these deliberately short-lived 'Gardens of Adonis' which are scornfully referred to in Isaiah xvii:10-11.)

Astarte/Aphrodite was said to have fallen in love with the beautiful youth and begged him to give up his passion for hunting, in case he should meet his death. He ignored her advice and was killed by a wild boar. (Symbolically, the boar was Aphrodite herself.) This became a favourite subject for Greek poets and artists, but the vegetation-god theme was never as central as it was in Phoenicia. Although the Greek Aphrodite inspired the mating urge in all creatures, not only in men and women, that urge in itself was her basic concern, its resultant fecundity much less so. The patronage of childbirth or of harvest she left to other goddesses, though the Middle Eastern goddesses from whom she evolved had embraced both the urge and its results.

This distinction is also to be seen in the history of the goddess's patronage of prostitutes, both sacred and ordinary.

In Sumer, Babylon and Phoenicia, Inanna/Ishtar/Astarte's temples had both holy professionals and holy amateurs, as Grigson calls them (*The Goddess of Love*, p.117). The professionals, attended by eunuch priests, sat in upper windows, attractively arrayed; Jezebel of the Bible was a Phoenician professional of this kind, and of no mean standing, for Jehu described her as a king's daughter (2 Kings ix:34) and, having brought about her death, would have had her buried as befitted her rank.

As for the amateurs, Herodotus describes the practice at Ishtar/-Mylitta's temple in Babylon in the fifth century BC. Once in her life, every Babylonian woman, rich or poor, had to go there and sit, wearing a plaited bandeau round her head, and wait until some man chose her. He would throw a silver coin into her lap and claim her in the name of the goddess. She would give herself to him and then go home, her duty to the goddess done.

This was the *hieros gamos*, the sacred marriage: an offering to the goddess of love and fertility (herself known as 'courtesan of the gods') to bring prosperity to the land; an act of ritual sympathetic magic, from which not even the highest was exempt – in Sumer, an important annual ritual was the sacred intercourse between the King and a priestess known as the Enitum.

The goddess took the practice of sacred prostitution with her to Cyprus, and eventually to the mainland of Greece. But by then, as we have pointed out, her emphasis was on love, and only incidentally on fertility. She was naturally adopted as patroness by Greek prostitutes, from the humble streetwalkers to the sophisticated and often well-educated – and rich – *hetairai* (usually translated 'courtesans'). In Cyprus and in Greek colonies on Sicily, her holy girls still served in her temples. But on the mainland, with the communal aim of fertility pushed into the background, and *aphrodizein* (to copulate) becoming a private rite, the only temples of Aphrodite staffed by sacred prostitutes were those at Corinth (the most important of which, on the height of Corinth's Acropolis, was one of the richest in Greece).

Professionals, sacred or otherwise, notwithstanding – there is evidence that loving couples also made appropriate use of her temple *tenemoi* or enclosures, which tended to be more garden-like than those of other deities. Grigson (*The Goddess of Love*, p.143) says: 'There were myrtles especially, because the myrtle was sacred to Aphrodite … there were planes, cypresses, bay trees, and plenty of the ivy and the grape-clustered vines of Dionysos (his wine being coadjutor to the business of Aphrodite).' After the ritual purification at the entrance to the *tenemos* and the offering within the temple itself, couples would withdraw to one of the secluded benches in the garden to please the goddess by pleasing each other.

Her temples (not to mention her countless humbler shrines) were in every city of Greece and its colonies. Few of them remain, for she was the particular target of Christian iconoclasts, who hated the 'lusts of the flesh' even more than they did 'idolatry'. But as a touching footnote, beside the ruins of the oldest and most famous of them, at Paphos in her own Cyprus stands the little white church of Katholiki – which used to be known as the Church of the Blessed Aphroditissa.

She extended her rule to Rome too, of course, where she completely took over the comparatively minor goddess Venus. Thanks to the fact that most of European civilization was built on Roman imperial foundations, with Latin as its *lingua franca*, Venus has been the name by which she has mostly been called. Even her best-known (if far from her best) statue, Aphrodite of Melos, is stuck with the title 'Venus de Milo'; perhaps her loveliest painting, thoroughly Greek in symbolism and spirit, is Botticelli's 'Birth of Venus'; and Shakespeare lyricized over 'Venus and Adonis'. But it was really Aphrodite they and countless others carved, painted or wrote about, and it is time she got her real name back.

We have heard Aphrodite described, even by informed pagans, as something of a 'dumb blonde' who could have done with a little of the wisdom of Athene, or the responsibility of Hera, to make her wholly acceptable. But this is to overlook the Greek genius for specialization, and what may be called 'aspect-purity', in their deities. Ares, for example, was not softened into a noble warrior; he was a destructive menace, unwhitewashed. No one god symbolized the perfect man, and no one goddess the perfect woman. Whereas the Egyptian Isis included within herself the qualities of Hera, Athene and Aphrodite, in balance with each other, and thus could be said to represent the ideal of womanhood, the Greek approach was to contemplate each aspect in isolation, undiluted by other aspects, the better to understand its true nature – the implication being that the human task was to strive for one's own balance of these fully understood aspects, without disowning any, and thus to achieve one's own perfection.

It was a noble ambition, and doubtless unconscious in the ordinary worshipper, but appropriate to the analytical nature of the finest Greek thinking, just as subtle synthesis flowered naturally on Egyptian soil.

There is much to be said for both approaches, and much to be said for the flexibility of today's Craft, which allows us to use the best of both. Thus a woman witch (or a man witch working to understand her) can acknowledge the Aphrodite in herself without shame, the Athene without priggishness, and the Hera without haughtiness – and so enter the shrine of Isis.

The Aphrodite Ritual

There is no need (indeed we feel it would be mistaken) to devise a special Craft ritual of Aphrodite, because one already exists: the Great Rite of male-female polarity.

It has two forms, symbolic (without intercourse) and actual (with intercourse), and at least two 'scripts' – the simpler one we gave in *Eight Sabbats for Witches*, the more complex one from Gardner's Book of Shadows in *The Witches' Way*. Here we suggest yet another, for this particular purpose.

We would emphasize again what we said in those two books: that while the symbolic Great Rite can be enacted by any couple the High Priestess finds suitable, the actual Great Rite should be performed only by married couples, or by established lovers of a marriage-like unity, and that the intercourse itself should always be private to the couple involved.

For a Ritual of Aphrodite, the actual Great Rite is the obvious choice; and there is an added reason (if one were needed) for observing these rules. On this occasion, the Great Rite would not be raising power on behalf of the coven or for directing to any non-personal end. It would be the ritual celebration, and enrichment, of the love between a particular man and woman, on all the levels.

The spirit of the ritual should be dedicated but joyous, serious and yet laughing, in the sense of the Charge: '*For behold, all acts of love and pleasure are my rituals. And therefore let there be beauty and strength, power and compassion, honour and humility, mirth and reverence within you.*' Aphrodite is anything but a solemn Goddess.

It should also be flexible. The 'script' is not the Law. We tend to agree with those witches who feel that, while the traditional 'scripts', with their lengthy declamations, are fine and moving for the symbolic rite, they can be cumbersome and inhibiting for the actual one, and this might be particularly true when Aphrodite herself is presiding.

The couple themselves – whom we will call the Man and the Woman – should conduct the ritual. Some couples may prefer to hold so intensely personal a rite entirely alone; if so, the following ritual can be simplified accordingly.

We shall discuss the Woman's adornment later, but it should include a girdle – either a *kestos* as described above, or a belt or sash round her waist – and it should be as beautiful as possible.

The Opening Ritual should include Drawing Down the Moon but omit the Charge and the 'Bagahi' and 'Great God Cernunnos' invocations.

The Goddess-name used should of course be Aphrodite, and the God-name could be Eros or Pan.

A foundling rook plays his part in a
Morrigan ritual

An unidentified painted wood panel in
the possession of Doreen Valiente. The
birds suggest the subject may be
Rhiannon or a raven goddess such as
the Morrigan

Sheila-na-gig from the Church of St Mary and St David, Kilpeck, Hereford & Worcester

Goddess woodcarving by Bel Bucca

Arianrhod ritual: The Dark Goddess and (*on the right*) the Bright Goddess

Arianrhod by Su Dixon

Bronze Kore (Persephone), *c.*480 BC

Arcadian Atalanta by Pierre Lepautre

The many-breasted Artemis (Diana) of Ephesus, c.150 AD

Mosaic of Atalanta hunting on horseback, from a villa at Halicarnassus

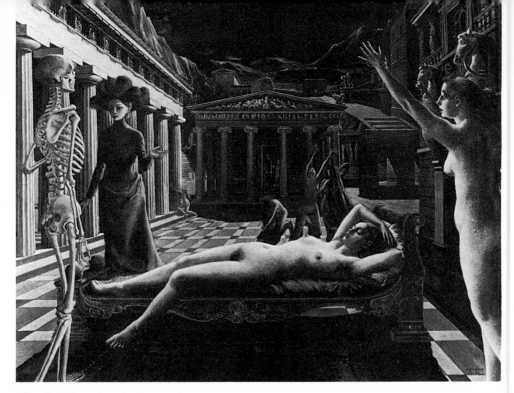

Sleeping Venus by the Surrealist painter Paul Delvaux

Birth of Venus by Uli Nimptsch. Part of the Battersea Park sculpture exhibition, 1963

Ishtar swears by her lapis lazuli necklace

The Three Graces, a mosaic from
    Pompeii

Egyptian relief of Canaanite goddess
    Astarte (known to the Egyptians as
    Qodshu) standing on a lion and offering
    a lotus to Egyptian god Min and
    serpents to Canaanite god Reshef

The Dweller in the Innermost by George Frederic Watts. Portrait of the Anima?

In *Drawing Down the Moon*, the Man's invocation is amended to: '*I invoke thee and call upon thee, Golden Aphrodite, Lover of Lovers; by seed and root, by stem and bud, by leaf and flower and fruit, by life and love do I invoke thee to descend upon the body of thy servant and priestess.*'

Instead of going immediately to the equivalent of the 'Hail Aradia' greeting, this seems a good occasion for the Woman to Draw Down the Sun on the Man (see *The Witches' Way*, pages 68-9).

The Woman now stands with her back to the altar, the Man facing her from in front of the South candle. The coven, men and women alternately, stand around the perimeter of the Circle. The Man says:

'*Assist me to erect the ancient altar,*
  at which in days past all worshipped;
The great altar of all things.
For in old time, Woman was the altar.
Thus was the altar made and placed,
And the sacred place was the point within the centre
  of the Circle.
As we have of old been taught that the point within
  the centre is the origin of all things,
Therefore should we adore it.'

All step forward (including the Man and Woman) to form a ring, with their hands on each other's shoulders as for a Greek dance, and start to move deosil, while the Man, looking straight across at the Woman, says:

'*Hail, Aphrodite! All I have to give*
Upon thine altar laid, is thine to take;
My spirit and my body here I bring
To thee in love, for my beloved's sake.
For me, her face is thine, her limbs, her hands,
The locks that crown her, and the eyes that shine;
Give us thy blessing, Cyprian, and know
That I am hers in love, and she is mine.'

The circling continues until the Woman again has her back to the altar, when she halts. Everyone halts with her, and arms are dropped from shoulders. The Woman says:

'*Of Aphrodite, golden and divine,*
Mine the embrace, and mine the kiss;
The five-point star of love and bliss –
Here I greet you, in this sign.'

She then ceremonially removes her girdle – the traditional Greek gesture of a woman signalling her invitation to her man – and drops it to one side.

The Man starts towards her, but another man steps between them, challenging him. They mime a brief contest, and the challenger steps back, bowing his head in surrender – but another man immediately takes his place. While he too is contesting with the Man, the first challenger puts his arm round one of the other women (if possible, his normal working partner) and they both leave the room. This challenge-and-surrender continues with each of the men, till the last is ready to leave. (If there are more men than women, or vice versa, two men will take out one women together, or one man two women; nobody leaves alone.)

The Woman watches all this from her place in front of the altar. As the last of the coven leave and close the door, the Man and the Woman start a spontaneous mating dance.

From this point, they continue as Aphrodite inspires them.

So much for the form. How about the incidentals?

Aphrodite's native incense is frankincense, but today we have many more ingredients at our command, so there is much more scope for exercising the imagination.

Personal perfumes or oils are just that – personal; the same formula on different skins may produce quite different aromas. Try experimenting with some of those given in Chapter X. But any woman will know what suits her, and what turns her man on, which after all is the guiding principle in this ritual.

The wine and cakes should be whatever both partners enjoy. A Greek wine should be particularly appropriate, of course, especially the aromatic retsina – but don't try that for so important an occasion unless you've already acquired the taste for it. And as for the food – what better than the Aphrodite cakes described on page 74?

Candles could suitably be red or orange, the colours of love in the passionate, urgent sense. But in the atmospheric sense, for most people love calls for a softer colour, such as blue; so the ideal setting might be an overall softness, with passionate accents such as the small bright candles.

Music – entirely personal. (But try Ravel's *Bolero* or African drum music!)

Some of Aphrodite's flowers should be on the altar – above all, roses, even if they're out of season, the occasion is surely worth the expense of at least one hothouse bloom from the florist.

Apart from that, the couple may like to have on the altar, or around the Circle, some of the little possessions which to them symbolize their love – the personal Lares we discussed on p.87 of *Eight Sabbats for Witches*.

The keyword throughout, you will notice, is 'personal'. And that applies, too, to the Woman's adornment.

Traditionally Aphrodite is lavishly bejewelled, and most women would feel it right on this occasion to make up carefully and somewhat dramatically. Then again, there are men who prefer their women 'as is'. The Woman will know what is called for and prepare accordingly.

There could hardly be a more suitable ritual for being skyclad, but if for their own reasons the couple prefer to start off robed (perhaps the Woman owns some emotionally charged garment), when the moment for shedding it comes, they have a wide and (may we say it again?) utterly personal choice ranging from a dignified disrobing to a deliberate and languorous strip-tease during the mating dance.

'The lover's unveiling of a woman's body is a sacred gesture as old as man himself. In our rationalized world, which no longer believes in ritual but which constantly and unwittingly re-creates it, this act has become the strip-tease, an aberrant form of religious worship debased to the level of commercial spectacle' (Markale, *Women of the Celts*, p.144). We mean it here in its original sacred sense.

Enough advice. May Aphrodite be with them.

XVII   Hecate

Witchcraft celebrates
Pale Hecate's offerings.
Lady Macbeth

Hecate is at the same time a goddess of the Moon, of the Underworld and of magic. She was pre-Olympian, Thracian in origin, but like other primordial deities was absorbed into the classical Greek pantheon (and also into the Roman one); thus she took part in the Olympians' war against the Giants, and from being a daughter of the Titans Perses and Asteria (both symbols of shining light), her parentage was later ascribed to Zeus and Hera. She was also said to be one of Hermes' many lovers.

Olympus, however, was never her home. She dwelt in the Underworld, alongside Hades and Persephone and the minor deities Thanatos (Death), Hypnos (Sleep) and Morpheus (Dreams). But like Persephone, she had power elsewhere as well; while Persephone, daughter and other self of the Corn Mother, fructified the Earth every Spring, Hecate held sway in the night sky, and on Earth was a protectress of flocks and of sailors – and, of course, of witches.

While Persephone was, so to speak, the bright link between the Underworld and Earth, Hecate was the dark link. One of the reputed entrances to the land of shades was Lake Averna in Campania; the hills around it used to be covered with trees sacred to Hecate and pitted with caves through which one summoned the souls of the dead. The night-calling owl was her messenger, and the dark yew and the willow or osier were her trees; witches' besoms were traditionally bound with osier – without that, they were said to be helpless.

Of all the Greek goddesses, she was the most markedly triple. She was at the same time the three-phased Moon and, in particular, its dark phase; to the Romans, 'Diana Triformis' consisted of Diana, Proserpina and Hecate. (In Greek terms, Artemis, Persephone and Hecate.)

She was depicted as three female figures or as one with three animal heads – of horse, dog and boar, or sometimes of three dogs. Lethbridge (*Witches*, p.26) suggests that these represented the amalgamation of totem-animals from her primordial past. Dogs were certainly associated with her (perhaps from their habit of howling to the Moon and from their pathfinding ability). Sometimes she was portrayed as a whelping bitch, and she shared with Herne of the North the reputation of leading the Wild Hunt of ghostly hounds through the night.

She was, to both Greeks and Romans, especially the goddess of crossroads, where the traveller faces three choices. Statues of her stood there, and food offerings – 'Hecate's Supper' – were taken there at dead of night, on the eve of the full Moon. One left the food and walked away without looking back, for none dared confront the eerie goddess face to face.

Her annual festival on 13 August in Greece (and that of Diana on the same date in Rome) was a propitiatory one, to avert the harvest-destroying storms which the Moon was apt to send at around that time.

She also haunted graveyards and the scenes of crimes – as a goddess of expiation and purification.

Hecate is the Dark Mother, in both the positive and the apparently negative sense. She can send demons to torment men's dreams; she can drive them mad, if they are not well integrated enough to cope with her; but to those who dare to welcome her, she brings creative inspiration. She is Hecate Antea, the Sender of Nocturnal Visions, and, typically of a Moon goddess, she has a son – Museos, the Muse-man.

For divination, the Greeks used an instrument called 'Hecate's Circle', a golden sphere with a sapphire hidden inside it – her mysterious Moon concealing the bright seed of understanding.

Her symbol is the torch, for the Dark Mother also holds the light which illumines the Unconscious and reveals its treasures.

Shakespeare, as usual, knew what he was talking about. His witches' deity was not Satan, as contemporary authority claimed, but the Dark Goddess, whose paradoxical function is to pierce that darkness, bring visions, call back the past, illuminate the present and give warning or promise of the future – the goddess of the moonlit crossroads, Hecate of the Three Faces.

The Hecate Ritual

We have chosen here to emphasize Hecate as the Triple Goddess of the crossroads, the place of choice. The women enacting her three aspects should ideally be young (the Maid), mature (the Mother) and old and wise (the Crone). But whatever their actual ages, they should think themselves into the attitudes of bright joyfulness, poised self-possession, and dark mystery, respectively.

Three other actors are required, and they may be either male or female: the Seeker, the Thinker and the Doer.

The Preparation
One of the three women enacting Hecate, if the High Priestess is not among them, should act as High Priestess for the occasion, so as to be the subject of Drawing Down the Moon. For perfect balance, this should really be the Mother.

Classically, when the three Hecates were depicted in woman-form, they were always identical and robed. Even if the coven is skyclad, our three should be identically robed, but the three aspects may be indicated – say, by a white belt or waist-cord for the Maid, red for the Mother, and black for the Crone – the traditional colours.

The cauldron is placed in the centre of the Circle, with incense burning in it, and a supply of incense beside it.

Part of the emphasis is on witchcraft as such; so if, for example, the coven possesses a broomstick, it should be prominently displayed – say, laid at the foot of the altar.

The Ritual
The Opening Ritual proceeds as normal. The Goddess-name used will of course be Hecate (stressed on the second syllable, by the way). Since she is so universal, the God-name may be from any pantheon – but perhaps again with a Craft emphasis, such as the horned Cernunnos or the night-riding Herne.

The 'Hail Aradia' invocation is replaced by the following:

'Hail, great Hecate! Goddess of the Moon,
Goddess of witches in the dancing ring,
To thee all roads must lead us, late or soon –
The end, and start, of all our wandering.
Thou offerest the never-ending choice –
Left, right or onward, every path is thine.
O great Hecate, let us hear thy voice!
Lighter of darkness, give to us a sign!'

After the Witches' Rune, the wine is consecrated and the chalice placed beside the cauldron.

The three Hecates arrange themselves standing South of the cauldron, facing North. The Mother is in the centre, the Maid on her left, and the Crone on her right.

The Thinker sits a pace or two behind the Maid, and the Doer a pace or two behind the Crone.

The Seeker stands with his or her back to the altar, and the rest of the coven seat themselves around the perimeter. When all are in place:

Mother: *'I see one who seeks us.'*
Maid: *'Why does he hesitate?'*
Crone: *'Let him come forward.'*

Seeker comes forward and faces the Three across the cauldron, then bows to each in turn.

Seeker: *'I am faced by three paths, and I know not which to take.'*
Mother: *'We three are one, and all paths are ours.'*
Maid: *'Mine is the bright path.'*
Crone: *'And mine the dark.'*

Seeker (after a pause): *'The bright path beckons most clearly.'*

The Maid smiles and takes a pinch of incense and drops it on the burning charcoal. When it is smoking well, she holds out her hand to Seeker.

Maid: *'Come, then.'*

The Maid leads the Seeker to face the Thinker, who looks up.

Thinker: *'Who comes now? Another Seeker? I am the Thinker, and you are no help to me. This way is all gentleness and clarity. There is no danger for me to challenge, no awareness of lurking evil for me to fight, no mystery for me to unravel. I grow weary of the day that has no night.'*

The Thinker drops his or her head, and the Seeker looks at the Maid questioningly.

Seeker: *'Did I choose wrongly?'*
Maid (smiling): *'That is for you to say.'*

The Maid leads the Seeker back to the cauldron, and both take their places as before.

Seeker: '*The dark path may hold the answers.*'

The Crone, unsmiling, takes a pinch of incense and drops it on the burning charcoal. When it is smoking well, she holds out her hand to Seeker.

Crone: '*Come, then.*'

Crone leads Seeker to face Doer, who looks up.

Doer: '*Who comes now? Another Seeker? I am the Doer, and you are no help to me. This path is all uphill, all dark thought. There is no dance in my step, no song in my heart, no laughing companions to take my hand. I grow weary of the night that has no day.*'

The Doer drops his or her head, and the Seeker looks at the Crone questioningly.

Seeker: '*Did I again chose wrongly?*'

Crone: '*That is for you to say.*'

The Crone leads the Seeker back to the cauldron, and both take their places as before. The Thinker and Doer quietly move to sit side by side a pace or two behind the Mother.

Seeker: '*All that remains is the middle path.*'

The Mother smiles, but more mysteriously than Maid. She takes a pinch of incense and drops it on the burning charcoal. When it is smoking well, she holds out her hand to the Seeker.

Mother: '*Come, then.*'

The Mother leads the Seeker to face the Thinker and Doer, who look up.

Doer: '*Who comes now?*'

Thinker: '*Another Seeker. He [she] is no help to me. I fear that he [she] is too much of the light – all deeds without thought.*'

Doer: '*He [she] is also no help to me. I fear that he [she] is too much of the dark – all thought without deeds.*'

The Thinker and Doer both drop their heads.

Seeker: '*You are both wrong! The light must not be without thought, nor the dark without deeds! The day must not be without night, nor the night without day.*'

Mother: '*You have glimpsed the truth. Come.*'

The Mother leads the Seeker back to the cauldron, and they take their places as before. The Mother picks up the chalice and holds it in front of her.

Mother: '*What have you learned, Seeker?*'

Seeker (after a pause): '*That you are not Three, but One. That all paths are yours, and that I must tread them all, to be whole.*'

Mother: '*And do you dare?*'

Seeker: '*I tremble, but I dare.*'

Mother (gesturing towards the Thinker and Doer): '*Then will you not end as they are, sorrowing.'*

The Maid and Crone reach out so that all three are holding the chalice. They hold it out to the Seeker.

Maid		
Mother	(together):	*'So mote it be.*
Crone		*Drink of us all,*
		and be whole.'

The Seeker puts his hands round theirs and drinks.

XVIII   Lilith and Eve

The disturbing Lilith ... being the most dangerous and subversive threat to the established male order, was buried in the furthest depths of the Hebrew unconscious.

Jean Markale

Nowhere is the vigorous determination of patriarchy to suppress memories of the Primordial Mother more evident than in the Biblical Garden of Eden.

The Genesis story is a patriarchal revision of earlier Middle Eastern Creation myths, and also of Hebrew tradition itself.

According to that tradition, as recorded in the Talmud, Adam's first wife was Lilith. Yahweh (or was it Elohim, that curious God-name which is feminine with a masculine plural ending?) created them both at the same time. But Lilith refused to subordinate herself to Adam, or to the male God – even physically: when Adam insisted that she must always lie beneath him during intercourse, she quarrelled with him, flew up into the air and vanished. Adam appealed to Yahweh to bring her back, and Yahweh sent the three angels Senoi, Sansenoi and

Samangloph to find her.

The angels caught her on the shores of the Red Sea (at the place where the Egyptians pursuing the Children of Israel were later engulfed), coupling with lascivious demons and giving birth to demonic children called *lilim* or *liliot* at the rate of over a hundred a day. She refused to return to Adam and was told that, if she did not, she would lose a hundred of her own children every day. She still refused, and the angels tried unsuccessfully to drown her. She was finally allowed to live on condition that she would never harm a newborn child on which she could see the angels' names written. Yahweh gave her to Samael (Satan) as the first of his four wives, and she became a persecutor of the newborn (presumably the unmarked ones).

Significantly, she was seen as most dangerous to male babies, who were vulnerable to her till they were eight years old, while baby girls were out of danger after twenty days.

According to the Zohar, Lilith later took part in the Fall, seducing Adam while Satan, as the Tempter, seduced Eve.

Lilith was not her original name, which appears to have been lost. She acquired it by identification with the Sumerian 'night hag' Lilitu. As such, she is the 'screech-owl' (Authorized Version) or 'night monster' (Revised Version) of Isaiah xxiv:14. Incidentally, the word 'lullaby' is said to be a corruption of '*Lilla, abi!*' – a Jewish banishing spell meaning 'Lilith, avaunt!'

So much for the blackening process. Lilith (whatever her own name was) is clearly a concept much older than Eve. Whether she was the First Woman, co-equal with the First Man – or farther back than that, the uncreated Primordial Mother who gave birth to the First Man (or first Male God) and then mated with him – she was totally unacceptable to emerging Hebrew patriarchalism. So Eve was invented – created by a male God out of Adam's male body, as complete a reversal of the natural order as Zeus's giving birth to Athene by swallowing her pregnant mother Metis.

The kind of First Woman that patriarchy required is grimly summed up in another passage from the Talmud:

> The Lord considered from what part of the man he should form woman; not from the head, lest she should be proud; not from the eyes, lest she should wish to see everything; not from the mouth, lest she might be talkative; not from the ear, lest she should wish to hear everything; nor from the heart, lest she should be jealous; nor from the hand, lest she should wish to find out everything; nor from the feet, in order that she might not be a wanderer; only from the most hidden place, that is covered even when a man is naked – namely, the rib.

As Markale puts it (*Women of the Celts*, p.145): 'Eve, the mother of mankind, is merely the castrated version of Adam.'

Even her name reflects her status: 'She shall be called Woman' (Hebrew, *Isha*), 'because she was taken out of Man' (Ish)', Genesis ii:23.

Graves (*The White Goddess*, p.257) has an interesting theory about the rib story – that it 'seems an anecdote based on a picture of the naked goddess Anatha of Ugarit watching while Aleyn, alias Baal, drives a curved knife under the fifth rib of his twin Mot: this murder has been iconotropically misread as Jehovah's removal of a sixth rib, which turns into Eve. The twins, who fought for her favours, were gods of the Waxing and the Waning Year.' ('Iconotropically misread' here means that the intended meaning of the symbols has been misinterpreted.) He maintains that, 'Jehovah did not figure in the original myth. It is the Mother of All Living, conversing in triad, who casts Adam out of her fertile riverine dominions because he has usurped some prerogative of hers.'

Eve, like Blodeuwedd in Welsh legend (see Chapter XXI), is a man-created image of woman as patriarchy would like her to be: subordinate, obedient, excluded from all positions of real power, and her sexuality confined to procreation.

But even this image, this shadow-woman, cannot be completely tamed. Eve and Blodeuwedd rebel against dictatorship; Blodeuwedd refuses to be told whom she may love, and Eve refuses to be told what fruits of knowledge she may not eat.

Both are damned for it, of course, by the male masters, to whom they had been allotted, and by patriarchal dogma (whether pagan, Hebrew or Christian). In Eve's case, the rebel is in fact Lilith herself, the real female principle, man's true but banished partner, bursting through the artificial stereotype. So she is branded the cause of all humanity's troubles – i.e., as the saboteur of the patriarchal structure.

It is significant that both Blodeuwedd and Lilith are condemned to become night-owls – a perfect symbol for the dark-side magic of the feminine principle, of which patriarchy is terrified.

Lilith's demotion to demoness betrays that terror, for even as demoness, haunting men's dreams – the succubus who mounts them astride – she retains her dangerous appeal. The Talmud describes her as a charming woman with long, wavy hair. Doreen Valiente (*An ABC of Witchcraft*, pp.225-6) sums up the accepted picture of her as 'the archetypal seductress, the personification of the dangerous feminine glamour of the moon. Like Hecate, she is a patroness of witches; but where Hecate is visualized as an old crone, Lilith is instead the enticing sorceress, the beautiful vampire, the *femme fatale*. Her loveliness is more than human; but her beauty has one strange blemish. Her feet are great claws, like those of a giant bird of prey.' (In this image, she has a medieval French equivalent in La Reine Pédauque.)

Truths banished to the unconscious do acquire talons – representing both our fear of them and their ability to tear a way through the veils of hypocrisy and distortion with which we have tried to surround them. Only when we come to terms with them and integrate them with consciousness is their loveliness restored, so that their talons become feet again. Only when the night-owl is admitted to the sunlight can we appreciate the beauty of her plumage.

Lilith, the true Mother of All Living, must be reacknowledged – so that she and Eve can become one again. For without that one, Adam is only half a man.

The Lilith and Eve Play

Not, you will notice, a ritual as such, but – for a change – a little drama. (In fact, all drama is in essence ritual.) It is light-hearted but, we hope, meaningful, and that is appropriate, because one of Lilith's most dangerous characteristics, from the patriarchal viewpoint, is her wicked sense of humour. She takes the mickey out of rigid attitudes and is quick to put out a foot (or claw) to trip up pomposity.

You can read it and think about it or try performing it, with any degree of realism or artistry you like; so we will not give any detailed stage instructions. (It would be fun to perform it in a private wood.)

We have found that dramatizations – including spontaneous ones – can be both enjoyable and instructive, as a Craft exercise. One spontaneous one we have used several times is to choose a legend – say that of Isis, Set, Nephthys and Thoth after the murder of Osiris, or Medhbh, Aillil and Cuchulainn, or Odysseus, Circe and Hermes. We then give everyone a few days to study it, and 'on the night' we either allocate roles or pick them out of a hat (or rather two hats, one for the men and one for the women). We then assume those roles, think ourselves into them and put forward our cases in turn. The occasion can develop into a lively argument, and it is surprising how much one can learn about the meaning of the legend – and about oneself – in the process. Anyway, back to the Garden of Eden.

In the Beginning
Sheila, a witch, born a Christian
Bernie, a witch, Sheila's husband, born Jewish
Eve
Adam
Lilith

Scene: Sheila and Bernie's living-room Circle. They have finished their ritual and are sitting on the floor, skyclad, relaxing over the last of the wine.

Sheila: *That was a good Circle, Bernie. If Harry doesn't pass his exam after that lot, it's not our fault.*

Bernie: *Well, I think we gave a boost to what he lacks. He's powerful in Hod – good brain, and all that – but he needs a dollop of Netzach for creative imagination.*

Sheila: *Not to mention Geburah for determination ...* (smiling) *You and your Cabala!*

Bernie: *I should abandon my cultural heritage, already? I don't bash your leprechauns.*

Sheila: *Leprechauns again! I've told you before – they're a very minor part of Irish mythology. The Tuatha Dé Danann and the Daoine Sidhe are the ones that matter.* [Pronounced 'Tooha day dahn'n' and 'Dweenuh shee'.]

Bernie: *Blinding me with science.*

Sheila: *Hark who's talking!* (Holding up hands in surrender.) *All right, all right. Call it a draw. Everyone's got his cultural heritage; you can't be born without one.*

Bernie: *Way back to Adam and Eve, who presumably hadn't.* (He sips the wine.) *Le Chaim.* [Pronounced 'lehayim'.]

Sheila: *Now there's a bit of Hebrew cultural heritage I'd like to know the truth about.* (Takes the chalice and sips.) *Sláinte mhaith.* [Pronounced 'Slawncheh voy'.]

Bernie: *That's easy. A priestly establishment rewrite of earlier Middle Eastern creation myths. They wanted to suppress Ashera-worship, which was rampant among the farming population of Israel. In the Sumerian version ...*

Sheila: *Hold it, hold it. I didn't mean that. I meant, what really happened.*

Bernie: *I hope you meant psychic truth, not alleged history.*

Sheila: *You know perfectly well what I meant.*

Bernie: *Let's go and see, then.* (He picks up the pentacle from the altar and holds it to shine light in Sheila's eyes, saying mock-dramatically:) *You are going back to the Garden of Eden ... You are going back to the Garden of Eden ...*

Sheila (laughing): *No, Bernie – not your hypnosis thing – you're too good at it, and I'm too tired ...*

Bernie: *It is too late ... You are already there ...*

(It is suddenly pitch dark.)

Sheila: *No, Bernie, no ...*

Bernie: *Oy, gevalt!*

(It is bright sunlight, Sheila and Bernie are sitting in the same positions, in a beautiful forest glade. She jumps to her feet.)

Sheila: *Bernie, you've done it again! You know how susceptible I am to it ...*

Bernie (getting up more slowly): *It certainly looks like the Garden of Eden.*

Sheila: *But how come you're here with me, this time? I mean, I've always been able to hear you, but ...*

Bernie (bewildered): *I don't know!*

Sheila (pointing): *Bernie – look!*

(Eve walks into the glade. She is exactly as we imagine her, naked, with long blonde hair. She sees Sheila and Bernie and halts, puzzled.)

Sheila: *Eve!*

Bernie (taking a couple of cautious steps towards Eve and speaking tentatively): *Shalom, Chava?*

Eve: *Shalom ... You're like him, I think – but what is that?* (pointing at Sheila).

Bernie (pulling himself together): *I'm Bernie, and this is my wife Sheila.*

Eve (examining Sheila and starting back): *You're another one!*

Sheila: *Another what, Eve?*

Eve: *Your voice is like mine and the Green One's. But his is like Adam's.*

Sheila: *That's right. You and I are women, and Adam and this one are men ... Who's the Green One?*

Eve: *Adam belongs to me. I don't want any more ... women. Go away.*

Sheila: *I will, I promise. I don't want your Adam, honestly.*

Eve: *The Green One does. She says she was here first.*

Sheila: *Who is the Green One?*

Lilith (from out of sight): *Actually, my name is Lilith ... Shalom.*

(Lilith, in green body make-up or leotard, slithers into view round a tree. All her movements are serpentine. Her hair is as black as Eve's is blonde.)

Sheila: *Er ... shalom.*

Lilith: *Some company at last.* (She slithers round the tree again, and reappears immediately with a red apple in her hand, which she offers to Eve.) *Well, Eve?*

Eve: *I don't trust you.*

(Eve starts to walk away. Lilith walks casually beside her, tossing the apple in her hand. Sheila and Bernie follow them.)

Lilith: *You learn fast, my dear. Dealing with concepts like 'trust' already, are we?* (Pointing ahead.) *It'll take him longer.*

(Adam comes out of the trees. He, too, is unself-consciously naked.)

Adam: *I've been looking for you, Eve. What are these creatures?*

Eve: *That one's a Bernie and that one's a Sheila. I don't know what they do. The Sheila says it's a 'woman', the same as me and the Green One, and I don't like that.*

Lilith: *Oh, poor Eve. She doesn't trust anyone.*

Adam: *What's 'trust'?*

Lilith (to Eve): *See what I mean?*

Sheila: *I'm not here for long, Eve. And I'm here as your friend.*

Lilith: *Good – Eve has a friend. Perhaps she'll advise her about the apple.* (Holds the apple in front of Eve's nose.) *Eve is trying to make up her mind. I'm sure you're aware of the background. What do you say?*

Sheila: *I only know one version of the background. I'd rather start from scratch. What is the apple?*

(They have reached a many-branched tree, bearing several of the same red apples. Lilith slithers onto a sloping branch and lies along it, with her head just above the head-height of the others.)

Lilith: *One of these. Adam thinks they're dangerous.*

Sheila: *Why, Adam?*

Adam: *God told me.*

Sheila: *Men always call their own taboos the Voice of God.*

Lilith: *I like this girl ... How long can you stay here?*

Sheila: *I don't know. Not long.*

Lilith: *Pity.*

Adam: *What's a 'taboo'?*

Lilith (throwing Adam the apple): *Here, eat that, and you'll stop asking such stupid questions.* (She picks another apple.)

Adam (catching the apple and looking at it): *I'm afraid.*

Lilith: *Of opening your eyes?*

Adam: *I can see well enough!*

Lilith: *The facts in front of your nose, yes. Not the truths behind them.*

Adam: *Oh.* (Studies apple thoughtfully.) *All right, then.* (He bites into it.)

Eve (anguished): *No, Adam! No!*

Lilith: *Too late, my dear.*

(Adam swallows his mouthful of apple, frowns and then comes to look up into Lilith's face from a foot or two away. Enlightenment dawns. Lilith toys with the other apple.)

Adam: *I remember now! You were here first – before me, even – you gave birth to me ...*

Lilith: *Go on. You're doing nicely.*

Adam: *You're Lilith – you're my first wife ...*

Lilith (to Sheila): *All genuine creation myths are both parthenogenetic and incestuous.*

(Eve has burst into tears and dropped to her knees on the grass. Adam goes to her and kneels beside her, putting an arm round her.)

Adam: *But Eve – don't cry – you're my wife, too ...*

Lilith (to Sheila): *Also bigamous, it seems.*

Sheila (snatching apple from Lilith): *Oh, stop being so smart! Can't you see she's upset?* (She runs to kneel at Eve's other side.)

Lilith (with a suddenly genuine smile): *Hurry, my dear, hurry ...* (To Bernie:) *It really is a pity she can't stay.*

Sheila (offering apple to Eve): *Eve – you need this – if you leave it to those two, everything will be out of balance ... Here ...*

(Eve, sniffing back her tears, looks at the apple, then at Adam, then at the apple again. Then she takes it and bites into it. Sheila and Adam watch her, holding their breath. Eve munches and swallows. She begins to smile. The smile broadens, and she begins to laugh. She jumps to her feet and goes to take Lilith's hand. Soon both Eve and Lilith are roaring with laughter, Eve reaching up and Lilith reaching down so that each has one arm round the other's shoulders. Adam gets to his feet and goes to face them, looked puzzled. Sheila also rises, and joins Bernie to one side, where they both stand watching.)

Adam: *I remembered, and I thought I understood. But now I don't again.*

(Eve and Lilith look at him, smiling mischievously. Their following dialogue alternates without pause, like one continuous speech.)

Eve: *We are your wife, Adam.*

Lilith: *But which of us is which?*

Eve: *Or are we sisters?*

Lilith: *Or the same?*

Eve: *Or your mother?*

Lilith: *Or your lover?*

Eve: *Or your daughter?*

Lilith: *Which is which?*

Eve: *Will you ever find out?*

Lilith: *And how many different stories will you invent about all this?*

Adam: *Stop! Stop, both of you! I need to think!* (Turns to Sheila.) *You – you're from outside. Tell me what to do.*

Sheila (smiling): *It's no good asking me. I'm another of her.*

(It is beginning to grow darker.)

Lilith: *Quick – you're going! ... Here, catch!*

(Lilith grabs an apple and throws it to Sheila. Sheila catches it. Suddenly it is pitch dark again – and a moment later we are back in the living-room Circle, with Sheila and Bernie sitting as before. There is no sign of the apple.)

Sheila: *Oh. I'd have liked to stay a bit longer.*

Bernie (still stunned): *Wow! How was that for a hypnosis session! Darling – I've never managed anything like that before. I mean, me being in it with you ... I don't understand. And it was so real ...*

Sheila: *It certainly was.*
Bernie: *Like a shared dream ...*
Sheila: *You reckon it was a dream, do you?*
Bernie: *Well, that's easier to believe than a sort of shared hypnosis.*
(Sheila reaches behind her back and produces the apple. She holds it up in front of Bernie's eyes.)
Sheila: *Then how do you explain this?*

XIX Epona

And I saw heaven opened, and behold a white horse.

Revelation

Epona is generally thought of as a horse goddess; her many Gaulish, Romano-British, Rhineland, Danubian and Roman *bas-reliefs* and statues show her either riding a horse or ass side-saddle or standing beside one, or between two or more of them, or occasionally lying half-naked along the back of one. The horse or ass was certainly her principal totem animal (though she was also sometimes depicted riding a horned goose through the sky), and it was this that caught the imagination of Roman cavalry units serving in Celtic lands, who adopted her as their patroness.

Epona shrines have been found in the stables of many Roman forts – even in Rome itself, in the barracks of the *equites singulares*, an imperial bodyguard recruited mainly from Batavians. She was the only Celtic goddess known to have been honoured in Rome, where she was often called Epona Augusta or Regina and invoked on behalf of the

Emperor. (Like so many others, she was sometimes triple, known as 'the three Eponae'.)

But this soldierly emphasis on her totem animal, however understandable, obscured her native essence, as 'the true image of the first mother goddess of the Celts' (Markale, *Women of the Celts*, p.89). Other writers concur. Phillips (*Brigantia*, p.103) says that in the north British Celtic kingdom of Brigantia, she was the Great Mother; this was one of the places where she appeared as a goose-rider, and Phillips identifies her as 'the origin of the pantomime Mother Goose, who plucked the feathers from her steed to make a snowstorm' (*ibid.*, p.151).

Returning to her horse totem – many authorities believe that the White Horse of Uffington, one of the best-known British hill-cut figures, was connected with her worship. (It is still considered lucky to wish while standing in its eye.) Lethbridge (*Witches: Investigating an Ancient Religion*, p.33) sees the chalk-cutting at Wandlebury Camp near Cambridge, which is generally called Magog, as being in fact Epona; and her Great Mother image is certainly emphasized by the fact that the mounted figure has four breasts.

Her role as a fertility goddess is revealed elsewhere by her having a sheaf of corn in her lap, or carrying a cornucopia or goblet, and she is often shown accompanied by birds (especially a raven) or by a dog and holding what appears to be a serpent.

The birds represent 'the insular tradition, common to Britain and Ireland: this is the idea of an otherworld goddess or goddesses concerned with sexual love and fertility, and possessed of magic birds by whose singing all sorrow is forgotten, pain healed and even the dead are restored to life' (Anne Ross, *Pagan Celtic Britain*, p.340). The particular meaning of the raven is that it is the 'attribute of the war-fertility goddess' (*ibid.*, p.316).

Many Celtic goddesses have horse associations. For example, the Irish Macha, wife of Crunnchu, who had to race against the fastest horse in the land while she was pregnant, and died at the winning-post giving birth to twins; the great mound Émain Macha (Twins of Macha) commemorates the legend, and possibly an ancient ritual. Or Étain Echraide ('Horse-Riding'), an Irish goddess of reincarnation. Or Cliodna, goddess of the happy Irish Otherworld, where horse-racing was a favourite sport. Or Medhbh of Connacht, goddess of sovereignty, who could outrun the fastest horse. And in Wales, Rhiannon ('Great Queen') was linked throughout her legend to a mare, and at one stage had to act as one. She too, incidentally, had birds 'whose singing awoke the dead and put the living to sleep', and her husband Pwyll was King of Annwn, the Welsh version of the happy Celtic Otherworld. As Anne Ross puts it (*op. cit.*, p.316), Rhiannon's characteristics 'are but a shadow of what once constituted a powerful Celtic goddess of Epona-Macha type'.

A recurring element in the horse-symbolism is that of sovereignty. Medhbh is perhaps the clearest example of the goddess of sovereignty with whom the new King had to mate before he was recognized as such. But in one Ulster ritual (recorded by Giraldus Cambrensis, the thirteenth-century Welsh writer) the King's sovereignty was confirmed by actual intercourse with a mare. 'Immediately afterwards,' Giraldus tells us, 'the mare was killed, carved up into pieces and thrown in boiling water. A bath was prepared for the King with the broth, and he sat in it while scraps of the meat were brought for him to eat and to share with the people around him. He was also washed with the broth and drank it, not with a cup or his hands but directly with his mouth. Once this ritual had been performed, his rule and authority were assured.'

Two ways of confirming sovereignty: intercourse with the goddess's human representative or with her totem animal – in the latter case followed by the communion of eating her flesh and administering it to the community.

Epona herself was said to have been born of a mare, in a legend which again seems to recall this ritual totemistic mating. Agesilaos, a late Greek writer, tells us that, 'Phoulouios Stellos, who hated women, had relations with a mare. In time it gave birth to a beautiful little girl who was given the name Epona' – not by her human father but by her (presumably divine) mare mother.

An interesting point here: the peoples of the British Isles are still generally averse to the eating of horseflesh, though there is little culinary justification for this reluctance, which many other countries do not share. Is this an unconscious memory of the time when horseflesh was sacred, only to be eaten on solemn ritual occasions, such as the October horse-feast when the taboo was lifted?

In medieval Denmark, the same memory was more specific. The three-day horse-feast survived among pagan serfs, though banned by the Church. Part of the ritual was the sprinkling of 'bowls of the horse's blood towards South and East – which explains the horse as an incarnation of the Spirit of the Solar Year, son of the Mare-goddess' (Graves, *The White Goddess*, pp.384-5).

Another strange hint of the sovereignty theme: 'No one has explained satisfactorily as yet why the supposed leaders of the Anglo-Saxon invasion in the fifth century of our era should have been known as Hengist and Horsa, for "hengst" means a horse and "horsa" a mare. It is reasonably certain that their invasion did not take place in the way it is described in the Anglo-Saxon Chronicle and it seems probable that the two mythical heroes were in reality religious conceptions' (Lethbridge, *op. cit.*, p.92).

As with so many Celtic deities, all the individual goddesses we have mentioned are but different forms of the same archetype; in this case, of the Great Mother of fertility, war, sovereignty and happiness in the afterlife. The variety of names and legends by which she has come down to our knowledge is almost incidental.

But, as we have said before, the multiplicity of Goddess-forms, as well as adding to the richness of the overall concept, has a practical use, in enabling us to visualize and attune ourselves to a particular aspect.

And this is how Epona, the 'Divine Mare', has descended to us, as a goddess whose totem and symbol is the horse and who is a mother figure associated with fertility, a happy Otherworld and the dignity of leadership.

The Epona Ritual

We have two suggestions here. First, since Wicca is a flexible Craft, ready to take advantage of varied environments and situations, there is no reason why witches who have access to horses should not make ritual use of the fact. Including animals in our magical work, not merely as cute presences but in a genuine attempt to involve and attune with them, can be a very fruitful way (apart from anything else) of expanding our Gaia-consciousness.

Magical working often attracts animals anyway, from the cat who scratches on the door when a Circle is cast to the dog who tells us unmistakably when an invocation has succeeded.

When we lived on the bogs of Co. Mayo, we were fortunate enough to have a hillock very near our house with a big fallen megalith which made a perfect altar. Sometimes we would cast an outdoor Circle twenty yards across, with lanterns at the Watchtowers and a bonfire in the centre. We had seven ponies roaming the bog, and they would come and watch – attracted, you may say, by the fire, yet they would always stay respectfully outside the Circle. On one occasion all seven of them cantered (deosil!) round the perimeter, dramatically enhancing the ritual.

So now and then the Circle would be cast, and Janet would make her entrance as High Priestess on horseback. She would solemnly dismount, and the Maiden would lead the young mare out again through the ritual Gateway, where she would stand and watch quietly.

(Our Maiden, Ginny Russell, is a lifelong horsewoman, and her experience of the psychic aspects of horses would fill a book by itself.)

It is impossible, of course, to be specific about how witches with access to horses might make ritual and magical use of them. But it would be worth their while to apply some imagination to the possibility. Even a city witch who hires an occasional mount in the park might try – for example, walking it deosil (clockwise) while she casts a mental Circle in the name of Epona – keeping her mind open for unexpected results.

But for our Epona ritual below we have chosen the more universal aspect, that of the Celtic Great Mother of whom Epona, as we have seen, is one of the more important faces.

A large section of the Craft is Celtic-oriented anyway, but even covens which follow other traditions such as the Nordic may like occasionally to extend greetings, so to speak, to an allied group of symbols and to see what they can learn by attuning themselves for a while to what is probably the most powerfully surviving stream in the Western pagan heritage.

The Preparation

The Circle may be decorated with Epona symbols, which – apart from the obvious equine ones, such as a bridle or horseshoes – include goose feathers, wheat or other cereal if it is in season, and the cornucopia. Remember that if a horseshoe is displayed for magical purposes by a blacksmith or farrier, it should be points downwards, and it seems appropriate to do so in an Epona ritual. (See our *The Witches' Way* p.87.)

The ritual can be performed, if necessary, with the High Priestess as the only woman present, but the more women who can take part, the better. If there are two or more women, they deliver the paragraphs of the declamation in rotation; otherwise the High Priestess delivers them all.

The Ritual

The Opening Ritual is as usual up to the invocation of the Goddess into the High Priestess by the High Priest. The Goddess-name used in the Circle-casting is Epona, and the God-name a Celtic one; since Epona is predominantly mainland British, Herne might be a suitable choice as her consort.

The 'Hail Aradia' declamation is replaced by the following:

Hail, Great Epona! Mother of us all,
Bringer of plenty, Queen of Earth and skies,
Lover of lovers, Muse of the mating-call,
Goddess of battle should the need arise;
Queen of the Otherworld, where all may rest,
Queen of this land, beloved of us all;
Queen of all creatures, by thy presence blest –
Be with us now, and answer to my call!

The High Priestess gives the 'Of the Mother darksome and divine' blessing as usual. All the men then withdraw to the South of the Circle, where they sit facing the altar – except for the High Priest, who goes with them but remains standing for the moment. The women take their places standing on either side of the High Priestess.

High Priest: 'Listen to the words of the Great Mother; she who of old was also called among men Dana, Dôn, Brighid, Arianrhod, Morrigan, Cerridwen, Modron, and by many other names.'

The High Priest then sits down with the other men.

(The paragraphs which follow, marked 'High Priestess', 'Next Woman' and so on, will be delivered in rotation deosil – unless the High Priestess is delivering them alone.)

High Priestess: 'I am Epona, Great Mother of birth and death and rebirth. I am goddess of the green Earth which feeds you, and of the creatures which roam on it. I am the sea goddess of the tides which wash your shores. I am the Moon goddess who rides the night sky, and whose phases are the rhythm of your lives. I am the Queen of love, and also of battle. I am all these things, and many more; for all goddesses are one Goddess.'

Next Woman: 'I am Cesara, who rode the primordial Flood to bring life to the Western edge of the world. I am so ancient that all but my name is lost to the memory of man; it lingers in song, and in the fireside story. Yet all goddesses are one Goddess.'

Next Woman: 'I am Dana, Mother of gods and heroes; my fairy hosts ride out from the hollow hills, for those with eyes to see; and their magic is ever with you, for those with hearts to feel it. To me is the white hawthorn sacred. Yet all goddesses are one Goddess.'

Next Woman: 'I am Modron, and my name means Mother. To me belongs the cycle of seed and harvest. Yet all goddesses are one Goddess.'

Next Woman: 'I am Medhbh ['Mave'] goddess of the Throne. Only he who has mated with me is fit to wear the crown of leadership. Yet all goddesses are one Goddess.'

Next Woman: 'I am Coventina, nymph of the life-giving springs which well up from the darkness of the Earth. Yet all goddesses are one Goddess.'

Next Woman: 'I am Boann and Sionnan ['Shonnawn'] Sabrina and Tamesis – I am the broad rivers which fertilize your farmlands and forests, and in whose waters swim the salmon of knowledge. Yet all goddesses are one Goddess.'

Next Woman: 'I am the Morrigan, Queen of the Battlefield. When men forget my other faces and strive to destroy each other, my dark raven guides the dead to rest and rebirth. Yet all goddesses are one Goddess.'

Next Woman: '*I am Niamh* ['*Nee-uv*'] *of the Golden Hair, the magic of Woman calling Men to Tír na nÓg* ['*Teer na Noge*'] *and the wonder of love. Yet all goddesses are one Goddess.*'

Next Woman: '*I am Cerridwen, from whose cauldron comes all wisdom and inspiration. Drink from it if you dare, for I shall demand much of you thereafter. Yet all goddesses are one Goddess.*'

Next Woman: '*I am Morgan le Fay, dark weaver of magic, rising from the mists of Avalon. Follow my path, and there is no turning back. Yet all goddesses are one Goddess.*'

Next Woman: '*I am Brighid* ['*Breed*'] *the inspirer; I whisper to the poet, I teach the healer, I guide the hand of the craftsman. Yet all goddesses are one Goddess.*'

Next Woman: '*I am Rhiannon, Queen of Annwn, the happy Otherworld. When my birds sing, the dead are awakened and the weary are lulled to sleep. Yet all goddesses are one Goddess.*'

Next Woman: '*I am Arianrhod, Queen of the Castle beyond the North Wind, to which all must come between life and life; for without rest, there is no rebirth. Yet all goddesses are one Goddess.*'

The High Priestess steps forward from the other women and, beginning '*Whenever ye have need of any thing ...*' delivers the whole of the Charge (the High Priest saying '*Hear ye the words of the Star goddess ...*' as usual).

When she has finished, she takes the hands of the High Priest and one other man, who rise, and they start to circle deosil. The other women come forward, taking the hands of the other men, and they join the ring – man and woman alternately as far as possible – till all are circling.

The High Priestess then starts the Witches' Rune, and all join in.

XX Ma'at

Beauty is truth, truth beauty
John Keats

Whatever may be said about other pantheons, no one can claim that any of the Egyptian deities are inappropriately sexed – psychologically or spiritually. Many pagan religions, as we have seen, became distorted by patriarchy, with essentially female roles being commandeered by male gods – even, in the case of Zeus, Metis and Athene, that of giving birth. But the Egyptian religion kept its balance to the end (if it can be said to have ended).

At first glance, Ma'at or Mayet, the Egyptian deity of law, truth, justice and the divine order, may seem an exception. Surely law-giving, and the discernment of factual truths, is a linear-logical function – in other words, a god function? In Cabalistic terms, it is the role of Chesed, the benevolent administrator?

But that would be to misunderstand the concept of 'divine order' which Ma'at represents. She stands for the natural, inevitable order of

146

things, both macrocosmically and microcosmically. Her law is organic, not legislative.

The laws of the divine order, the justice of inevitability, the truths of cosmic reality – these are indeed Goddess functions. Cabalistically speaking again, Binah (the Supernal Mother) takes the raw directionless energy of Chokmah (the Supernal Father) and gives it form in keeping with the natural harmony of the cosmos. Chesed (the Father aspect on the next level of manifestation) takes the forms which Binah has given birth to, and 'legislates' for their activity. But the natural laws which determined those forms in the first place are a function of the Supernal Mother.

So the Egyptians were right to make Ma'at a goddess.

But Binah and Chesed must complement each other – 'legislation' must be in harmony with the natural order. The Egyptian pantheon stressed this by envisaging Ma'at as the wife of Thoth, god of wisdom, learning and measurement, and the inventor of speech, whose activities reflected her laws; he is recorded in the Papyrus of Nebseni as declaring, 'I bring Ma'at to him that loveth her.'

Human law, to be healthy and effective, must be in tune with the higher law which Ma'at symbolizes. Recognizing this, Pharaohs always ritually invoked her blessing on their rule; they would present statuettes of Ma'at to the gods, this being 'more acceptable than any sacrifice'.

All judges were regarded as priests of Ma'at, and royal princesses often wore her symbolic red feather as a headdress, to show that they were her priestesses. Even the monotheist Akhenaton, who abolished all deities except Aten, honoured Ma'at by name – though his record as a ruler (whatever one thinks of his religious views) hardly lived up to the gesture. His successors made much of the 'restoration of Ma'at' to correct the chaos of his reign.

In the Egyptian creation legend, Ma'at was the daughter of the Sun god Ra. She and Thoth were with him in his Boat of a Million Years when it first emerged from Nun, the primordial waters. She was the light which Ra brought to the world; creation began when he put her in the place of chaos. Yet Ra, too, was subject to his own daughter, as were all the gods; his daily course in the sky was determined by her laws.

It is hardly surprising that Ma'at played an important role in the judgement of the dead. The judgement itself took place in the Hall of the Double Ma'at, depictions of which show her standing at both ends; one could not evade the natural order, coming or going. In the scales of judgement, the deceased's heart was weighed against the red feather which was her symbol – or, in some depictions, against a tiny figure of Ma'at herself; and often she was the scales as well. Her husband Thoth had the dual function of seeing that the deceased had a fair chance to justify himself and (as scribe of the gods) of recording the verdict.

Modern civilization has come dangerously close to divorcing Thoth and Ma'at – to rupturing the integration which should exist between cosmic truth and intellectual thinking, between natural law and human organization. The restoration, and honouring, of that divine marriage is an urgent need for mankind, and one to which Wicca is particularly dedicated.

Using the Egyptian forms of Ma'at and Thoth (or Tehuti, to give him his proper Egyptian name) for a modern ritual is not just being exotic for the fun of it. Ma'at and Tehuti symbolize this particular contemporary danger, and its solution, perhaps more clearly than any other deity-forms; so why not invoke them?

For the Isis ritual in Chapter XXIII, we will be using Egyptian temple symbols and ritual forms, because the Isis theme is timeless and universal, and it seems appropriate to use the forms traditionally associated with her.

But the reuniting of Ma'at and Tehuti is an immediate contemporary task – so in the ritual which follows, we invite them to a Wiccan Circle, confident that they are as much at home there as anywhere else.

We need the nourishment of Ma'at, the blossoming flower which is the true nature of our universe. As an Egyptian text vividly puts it: 'Put Ma'at to your nose and inhale her perfume, so that your heart shall live; thus shall you feed on Ma'at.'

The Ma'at Ritual

The Preparation

A woman witch is chosen to enact Ma'at, and a man witch to enact Tehuti. Even if the coven is skyclad, these two should be robed, to adhere as closely as possible to their Egyptian images.

For Ma'at, the clothing is a simple calf-length or ankle-length skirt, tubular and close-fitting. Most depictions show her bare-breasted, with two thin shoulder-straps to the top of the skirt (the front ends converging towards her cleavage). The skirt is often red, her symbolic colour, but white will do. Her jewellery is normally a semicircular pectoral at the neck, with bracelets on both wrists and usually just under each armpit as well. She should be bare-footed. Her hair hangs free (unlike that of Isis, which is usually elaborately coiffed).

Whether robed or skyclad, she should wear the red feather which is her symbol, upright over her left ear, held in place by a red ribbon tied round her head and knotted at the back. Ideally, it should be an ostrich feather, dyed red, but, failing that, any long feather dyed red, such as a goose quill. (Ma'at's ostrich feather seems to have been not the fluffy tail-feather of Victorian fashion but the neater wing-feather.)

Easier to follow than any description is a picture. See the design at the head of this chapter, and Figure 4 on p.179.

Tehuti's robe is much simpler: a white cloth wrapped around him from waist to knee. Again, see Figure 4.

Tehuti appears in two forms: as a seated baboon and as an ibis-headed man. For our purpose, the latter is obviously the practical one. The ibis head is not necessary – but if you care to experiment with mask-making, Tehuti would be an interesting subject.

For incense, we suggest a plain one such as frankincense to set the opening atmosphere, with rose oil ready for the appropriate moment in the ritual.

A single red flower (preferably a rose) is in the empty chalice, covered by a cloth.

The Ritual

To start with, Tehuti is standing beside the East candle, silently watching. Ma'at is in hiding outside the Circle; if the room has no suitable place to hide her, she simply stands outside the Circle, but at a distance from Tehuti, with a veil covering her face.

The Opening Ritual proceeds as usual, but without Drawing Down the Moon, the Charge or the 'Great God Cernunnos' invocation.

After the Witches' Rune, the coven are seated in a ring facing inwards. The High Priestess goes and stands before the altar.

The High Priest takes the wand from the altar, goes to face Tehuti, salutes him with the wand and says: *'Great Tehuti, god of wisdom, we have need of you in our Circle. Will you enter?'*

Tehuti asks: *'Are you sure that I am all that you need?'*

The High Priest replies: *'With the gift of wisdom, we shall know what else we need.'*

Tehuti says: *'So mote it be.'*

The High Priest opens a gateway in the Circle with a leftward sweep of the wand, and Tehuti enters. The High Priest closes the gateway with a deosil sweep of the wand.

Tehuti goes and sits down in the centre of the Circle, and the coven huddle close around him, looking inwards at him. The High Priest replaces the wand on the altar and joins them. Only the High Priestess remains standing by the altar.

Tehuti asks: *'Why do you not join us, Priestess?'*

The High Priestess answers: *'I honour you, Great Tehuti, and we need you in our Circle. But something is lacking.'*

The coven all cry! *'No! No!'*

Tehuti smiles understandingly and bows towards her, still seated. She bows towards him, still standing.

The coven, ignoring the High Priestess, start firing impromptu questions at Tehuti, who answers them. All the questions are concerned with knowledge, logic, scientific facts or organization. Tehuti answers them precisely but deliberately avoids pointing out that the questions are one-sided. (To keep this going, the High Priest and Tehuti will do well to have prepared a few questions and answers beforehand, between themselves.)

Meanwhile the High Priestess picks up the wand from the altar and walks slowly deosil round the Circle, saying every now and then: 'Something is lacking. I know that something is lacking.'

After a while she looks towards where Ma'at is hiding, hesitates for a moment and then goes to the spot, opening a gateway with the wand. She finds Ma'at and brings her out of her hiding-place (or removes her veil). They look at each other, and then the High Priestess bows. Ma'at raises her upright, smiling and saying: *'Do not bow your head to Truth. Look her straight in the face.'*

The High Priestess escorts Ma'at into the Circle, closing the gateway behind them. Then she goes and stands before the altar again, watching.

Ma'at walks deosil round the huddled coven, who ignore her. Every now and then she touches one of them on the shoulder, but they only huddle closer round Tehuti, still questioning him and ignoring her.

After a while, she goes to High Priestess, spreading her hands in a gesture of failure. High Priestess takes the rose oil from the altar and gives it to her. Ma'at sprinkles a few drops of it on the glowing charcoal and then stands with her back to the altar. The High Priestess stands to one side.

When the two women are in position, the High Priest holds up his hands for silence, and says: *'I sense a perfume, that was not here before.'*

Tehuti rises, facing Ma'at from the centre of the coven. The coven remain seated, but turn to look at Ma'at.

Tehuti says: *'It is the perfume of Truth, which is greater than mere knowledge. It is the perfume of the Music of the Spheres, which is greater than the schemes of men. It is the perfume of my beloved, who is greater than I.'*

Ma'at replies: *'Say not so, my Tehuti; for we have need of each other.'*

Tehuti says: *'Without me, you would be unfulfilled; but without you, I would be nothing.'* He tells the coven: *'Rise, Children of Men, and pay homage to Ma'at — she who was lacking from your Circle!'*

All rise, and bow to Ma'at.

Tehuti goes to join Ma'at, and they both face the coven.

Ma'at takes Tehuti's hand, and addresses the coven: '*In the beginning, my father Ra, the burning Sun, arose in his Boat of a Million Years out of Nun, the primeval waters. With him were my husband Tehuti and I. Ra sent me to bring order to Chaos; to set in motion the machinery of the universe. The turning of the stars, the tides of the sea, the birth and growth of all creatures – even the journeying of Ra himself – all these follow my Law. It is the Law of Nature, the inexorable rhythm of being. It is all things which are so because they must be so.*'

Tehuti says: '*And from the beginning, the Law of Ma'at gave birth to creatures ever more complex and subtle. Last of all, it gave birth to men and women. It was then that my task began. I taught them to open their eyes, I taught them to speak, and to count, and to gather knowledge like the grain of harvest.*'

Ma'at says: '*My husband taught THEM to know ME.*'

Tehuti says: '*But as the ages passed, in their pride they believed only in what their eyes could see, only in the sound of their own words. They counted, without loving what they counted; they harvested, but forgot to re-plant. They valued knowledge above wisdom, so that I, too, was betrayed.*'

Ma'at says: '*Know and remember, O Children of Men: I am what I am. My Law continues because it must; it is the warp and weft of the Universe. You can live by it, or you can die by it. The choice is yours. Use the gifts which my partner Tehuti has brought to you, to understand me better, not to hide me from your sight.*'

Tehuti says: '*Then shall the Music of the Spheres become the song of you all, with the words that I have taught you.*'

Tehuti turns and, taking the cloth from the chalice, brings out the rose and hands it to Ma'at. He says to the coven: '*Put Ma'at to your faces, and inhale her perfume, so that your hearts shall live; thus shall you feed on Ma'at. I bring Ma'at to those that love her.*'

The High Priestess and High Priest come forward together. She takes Tehuti's hand, and he takes Ma'at's, and they escort them to join hands with the coven.

All circle deosil, slowly at first and gradually faster, till the High Priestess cries '*Down!*' and all sit on the ground.

XXI   *Arianrhod*

I have been three times resident in the castle of Arianrhod.
                                                    The bard Taliesin

At first glance, the Welsh Arianrhod or Aranrhod is a puzzling goddess. Only one substantial story of her has survived, the Romance of Math, son of Mathonwy, in the *Mabinogion* (pp.97-117 of the Jeffrey Gantz translation; also given on pp.304-313 of Graves's *The White Goddess*). In this, she appears as a bad-tempered mother who disowns her sons Dylan and Lleu Llaw Gyffes, refuses to give Lleu a name or weapons until she is tricked into doing so by Gwydion's magic, and finally denies him a wife 'of the race that now inhabits this earth'. Gwydion's magic gets round this too, but with tragic results. Altogether, her image does not seem an inspiring one.

But the magical luminosity of her name in Welsh lore (and certainly in Craft tradition) makes it clear that a powerful and many-aspected Celtic goddess, far older even than the separation of the Gaelic and Cymric bodies of myth, looms behind the petulant lady of *Mabinogion*.

Clues to her real nature may be found in the meaning of her name, which is 'Silver Wheel'; in her association with the circumpolar stars which never set, and are known as Caer Arianrhod, the Castle of Arianrhod; in the obvious correspondence between her family, the Children of Dôn, and the Irish Tuatha Dé Danann; and in certain details of the *Mabinogion* story itself.

The fact that the two families were originally one can be seen from the following genealogies:

THE FAMILY OF DANA/DÔN

IRISH   *WELSH*

BALOR = DANA,   BELI = DÔN
         DANU
         or
         DONU

MACKINELY = EITHNE   NWYVRE = ARIANRHOD = GWYDION
    or   (her brother)
CIAN

LUGH LÁMHFHADA   LLEU LLAW GYFFES   DYLAN = LADY OF
(Lugh Long-Hand)   (Lleu Skilful-Hand)   (a Sea | THE LAKE
LUGH SAMHIOLDANACH   God)
(Lugh Equally Skilled   VIVIENNE
in All the Arts)   or NIMUE
                                                 (mistress
                                                 of Merlin)

In both versions, Balor/Beli is the Old God, and his grandson Lugh/Lleu the bright Young God who supplants him – a succession found in many pantheons. Arianrhod corresponds to Eithne – whose name, significantly, means 'fruit, produce', so the goddess had a fertility aspect. Her consort in both versions is of minor importance: Nwyvre ('Sky, Space, Firmament') has survived in name only.

Tradition insists that Arianrhod's twin sons Lleu and Dylan were fathered by her brother Gwydion, though this is not stated in the *Mabinogion*, which merely says that he brought them up.

The *Mabinogion* story, briefly, is as follows. King Math of Gwynedd, son of Mathonwy and brother of Dôn, could rule only when his feet were in a virgin's lap, except when the tumult of war prevented this. His foot-holder was Goewin. Arianrhod's brothers Gwydion and Gilvaethwy lived at Math's court, and Gilvaethwy fell in love with Goewin. So the two brothers started a war which demanded Math's presence, and they raped Goewin while he was away.

When Goewin told Math she could no longer serve as his foot-holder because her virginity had been taken, he punished his nephews magically, turning them first into a stag and a hind, then into a boar and a sow, then into a wolf and a she-wolf. When he finally restored them to human shape, he forgave them and asked their suggestions for a replacement virgin.

Gwydion suggested his sister Arianrhod, who was summoned and asked if she was a virgin. She replied: 'I do not know but that I am.' Math laid down his wand and told her to step over it, 'and if you are a virgin I will know.'

Arianrhod stepped over the wand, and as she did so she dropped a sturdy boy. She made for the door and on the way dropped a second something which Gwydion snatched up and hid in a chest. Math named the first Dylan and had him baptized, 'whereupon he immediately made for the sea, and when he came to the sea he took on its nature and swam as well as the best fish ... no wave ever broke beneath him'.

The 'something' which Gwydion had taken turned out to be another boy, who loved Gwydion more than any other man and grew at twice the normal rate.

Gwydion took the boy to Arianrhod and introduced him as her son. She asked, 'What has prompted you to disgrace me and prolong my shame?' and discovering that the boy had no name as yet, swore that he would have none till he obtained it from her. Next day Gwydion tricked her magically into saying 'The fair one has a skilful hand' – and that became his name, Lleu Llaw Gyffes.

When the boy became a youth, needing his own weapons, Gwydion took him again to Arianrhod, who swore, 'He shall have no weapons until I arm him myself.' Once more Gwydion used magic to trap her into putting weapons into Lleu's hands. Furious at being tricked a second time, she put another curse on Lleu: 'He shall have no wife of the race that now inhabits this earth.'

Gwydion got round that curse with Math's help. Together they took the blossoms of the oak, broom and meadowsweet 'and produced from them a maiden, the fairest and most graceful that man ever saw'. They named her Blodeuwydd ('Flower Face').

Lleu married Blodeuwydd, but this ended in tragedy. Blodeuwydd and Gronw, lord of Penllyn, fell in love and betrayed Lleu, who finally killed Gronw after he himself had been magically killed and revived; and Gwydion turned Blodeuwydd into an owl, who still mourns her dead love. 'And even now the owl is called Blodeuwydd.'

There is more meaning in many of the details in this story than is apparent on the surface, doubtless even to the medieval scribes who wrote down the oral tradition. As Matthew Arnold put it: 'The very first thing that strikes one, in reading the *Mabinogion*, is how evidently the medieval story-teller is pillaging an antiquity of which he does not fully possess the secret.'

First, the strange condition that Math could rule only with his feet in the lap of a virgin. This has two roots, the more ancient of which is a recognition of the female principle of sovereignty; the woman *was* the throne, the only base of operations which validated the King's authority. (See p.141 on this.)

The later significance of the 'foot-holder' stems from the period when nascent patriarchy was beginning to rebel against the old order – in particular, the Old King trying to stave off his own ritual death and the Young King's take-over as the Goddess-Queen's consort. In this sense, Goewin is Math's heiress-daughter, whose marriage will mean his own death, and his feet in her lap symbolizing his safeguarding of her virginity.

'Virgin' here means two different things. The original meaning was a woman whose status was in her own right, one not subject to the rule of any man; to this concept, celibacy was irrelevant, a matter of her personal choice. It is in this sense, for example, that the Irish god Aengus mac Óg ('Aengus, son of the Virgin') was so named; his mother Boann, goddess of the River Boyne, was certainly not celibate, and the Dagda was Aengus's father. But she remained independent, mating with the Dagda by choice, not as a dutiful consort.

By the time the *Mabinogion* was committed to paper, 'virgin' meant '*virgo intacta*' – the disposable property of the father. Math's question to Arianrhod was in the new sense, meaning 'Are you *virgo intacta*, a suitable hostage to my survival?' Arianrhod's ambiguous answer was in the old sense: 'I am my own woman, read it how you like.'

The rearing of Lleu and Dylan (and come to that, of Gwydion and Gilvaethwy) at Math's court rather than the mother's, and the shadowiness of Arianrhod/Eithne's husband, were both in keeping with the old matrilinear tradition, where the maternal uncle was much more important to a child than the father.

Arianrhod's insistence on her right to name the boy is a reaffirmation of the matrilinear principle and her own independent motherhood. And as for the weapons, Graves (*The White Goddess*, p.318) sums it up thus: 'Arianrhod's giving of arms to her son is common Celtic form; that women had this prerogative is mentioned by Tacitus in his work on the Germans – the Germany of his day being Celtic Germany, not yet invaded by the patriarchal squareheads whom we call German nowadays.'

When this prerogative was the accepted standard (and indeed when Celtic youths were trained in the use of arms by warrior witches, as Cuchulainn by Scathach), the youths would have had to prove themselves worthy of such initiation, but in the *Mabinogion* this proper requirement has degenerated into mere vindictiveness on Arianrhod's part.

Arianrhod is a goddess of birth and initiation (and also, as we shall see, of reincarnation); Blodeuwedd is a goddess of love and wisdom, 'an Owl thousands of years before Gwydion was born – the same Owl that occurs on the coins of Athens as the symbol of Athene' (Graves, *ibid.*, p.315). Her marriage to Lleu is the ritual one which authenticates his kingship (Arianrhod's 'curse' on him had warned him that his bride, too, would be a goddess of sovereignty, and no mere mortal). He tries to claim exclusive right to her, but such is not the way of the goddess, and he has to undergo the Holly King/Oak King rivalry with Gronw, in which they are alternately slain. The patriarchal legend tries to break free of the cycle with Lleu's final victory, but the disguise is thin.

In another sense, Blodeuwedd – manufactured by men out of flowers – represents patriarchy's wishful-thinking stereotype of woman; but even the stereotype refuses to obey the rules.

Alan Garner's *The Owl Service*, a modern version of this story overlapping with the original, attracted much attention in the 1970s as a novel for teenagers.

So a very different, and more positive, Arianrhod emerges from careful examination of the *Mabinogion* story.

If we go back some 800 years before the first more or less complete *Mabinogion* manuscript (*c*.1325) to the sixth-century bard Taliesin, a vital clue appears in one line of his long, riddling poem to King Maelgwyn: 'I have been three times resident in the castle of Arianrhod.'

Caer Arianrhod is a persistent Welsh concept. There is even a spot in Caernarvon Bay, a mile and a quarter off the coast and six miles southwest of Caernarvon, marked on Bartholomew's half-inch map as 'Caer Arianrhod (Submerged Town) (Traditional)'. But Welsh tradition knows that the true Caer Arianrhod is to be found in the circumpolar stars – the disc of stars around the Pole star, which the Egyptians called *ikhem-sek*, 'not knowing destruction', because they never sink below the horizon even at midsummer.

This is the real Court of Arianrhod, Goddess of the Silver Wheel of birth and rebirth. An indestructible diadem of jewels in the black sky, appearing to turn eternally but in fact unchanging as our cyclical Earth Mother bears, nourishes and buries our physical bodies, it symbolizes perfectly the resting-place of souls between incarnations. Taliesin had been there (as we all have), and he knew.

The path to Caer Arianrhod is a spiral, widdershins inwards and deosil outwards – a concept we used in our Requiem ritual in *Eight Sabbats for Witches*. Graves (*ibid.*, p.99) equates Arianrhod with Ariadne, and with reason; a Goddess of sacrifice and rebirth, of the spiral thread which leads to the secret at the heart of the Labyrinth and out again into the light of day.

She is also the Triple Goddess: Arianrhod who gives us birth and initiates us, Blodeuwedd who loves us and yet teaches us the wisdom of her own independence, and finally the White Sow Cerridwen who eats our mortal flesh after we have fed at her Cauldron of Inspiration. Thus freed, and wiser if we have chosen to learn, we take the spiral path to the Crown of the North Wind, where she greets us again as Arianrhod.

The Arianrhod Ritual

This seems another occasion for the use of the widdershins-inwards, deosil-outwards spiral pattern; only this time with Arianrhod herself at the centre, the dark Goddess of death whom most people fear but who is ready to show us, if we conquer our fear, that she is also the Bright Goddess of rebirth. And with an individual enacting the journey inwards and outwards.

The Traveller, the witch making the journey, may be either a man or a woman. For simplicity we have made it a man in the ritual below, but the necessary changes are obvious. Boreas should clearly be male; the West Witch should be of opposite sex to the Traveller; and the South Witch and East Witch can be of either sex.

The Preparation
The High Priestess, whether skyclad or robed, should be jewelled and made up to personify the Bright Goddess as dramatically as possible. But at the beginning of the ritual she is entirely shrouded in black over this adornment – preferably by a cloak with hood or veil – so that all her brightness is hidden. She should prepare herself out of sight of the coven, except for her High Priest; they must not see her until she is cloaked in black.

A throne – say a chair draped in black – is placed in the centre of the Circle, facing North.

The chalice of wine, the dish of cakes and the High Priestess's athame are placed, not on the altar but beside the throne. (See Figure 3.)

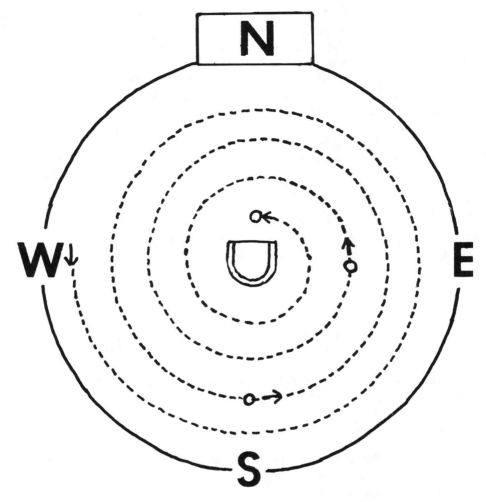

Fig. 3. The Spiral Path inwards to Caer Arianrhod.

Preferably a spiral should be marked on the floor, with cord or chalk. It starts at the West candle, curves in widdershins, taking 3¾ turns to reach the centre and ending up facing the throne.

The West Witch and the Traveller sit on the ground by the West candle; the South Witch and the East Witch sit by their respective candles; and Boreas sits beside the altar.

The Ritual
The Opening Ritual begins as usual, except that the High Priestess remains merely a dark presence, unmoving and silent in front of the altar; someone else casts the Circle and summons the Watchtowers.

The High Priest gives all the necessary orders. (Any of the seated members who have to take part resume their seats immediately afterwards.)

At the end of Drawing Down the Moon, the 'Hail Aradia' poem is replaced by the following:

'*O Arianrhod of the Silver Wheel,*
By all the many names men give to thee –
We, all thy hidden children, humbly kneel
Thy truth to hear, thy countenance to see.
Here in the Circle, cast upon the Earth
Yet open to the stars – unseen, yet real –
Within our hearts give understanding birth,
Our wounds of loss and loneliness to heal.
Isis Unveiled, and Isis Veiled, thou art;
The Earth below our feet, the Moon on high.
In thee, these two shall never be apart –
The magic of the Earth, and of the sky.'

The High Priestess does not speak the usual return blessing but merely makes the Invoking Pentragram of Earth towards the High Priest, in silence. The High Priest bows to her and steps to one side. The High Priestess, now Arianrhod, walks in a stately manner to the throne and seats herself upon it, making sure that her cloak still fully covers her.

The High Priest takes his place on the other side of the altar from Boreas.

After a suitable pause, the West Witch rises to her feet and tells the Traveller: '*It is time to move on.*'

Traveller: '*I am afraid.*'

West Witch: '*Of what are you afraid?*'

Traveller: '*Of the dark. Of Death. Of the unknown.*'

West Witch: '*Without these things, there is no Life.*'

Traveller: '*What is your name?*'

West Witch: '*My name is Psychopompos.*'

She takes the Traveller's hand and encourages him to rise. Reluctantly he does so and starts to walk widdershins along the spiral path, the West Witch following him and encouraging him gently whenever he hesitates. As he passes the West candle again after one circuit, South Witch rises and stands in his path. The Traveller halts.

South Witch: '*What is your name?*'

Traveller: '*I ...*' (Hesitating, surprised.) '*I do not know.*'

South Witch: '*You shall have no name, until She reveals it.*' (Gesturing towards Arianrhod.)

Traveller: '*Without a name, I am nothing. But I am afraid of Her.*'

South Witch: '*Then you must remain nothing, and nameless.*'

Traveller (after a pause): '*I would rather face fear than be nameless ... What is your name?*'

South Witch: '*I cannot answer, because I am the Question.*'

The South Witch stands aside and bows, gesturing the Traveller forward. Still with occasional hesitations and with West Witch following and encouraging him, Traveller continues on the spiral path. When he has made another complete circuit and is passing the South candle, the East Witch rises and stands in his path. The Traveller halts.

East Witch: '*How are you armed?*'

Traveller: '*I have no weapons.*'

East Witch: '*You shall have none to defend yourself, until She grants them.*' (Gesturing towards Arianrhod.)

Traveller: '*Without weapons, I am a victim of the dark. But I am afraid of Her.*'

East Witch: '*Then you must remain defenceless.*'

Traveller (after a pause): '*I would rather challenge the dark with a sword in my hand ... What is your name?*'

East Witch: '*My name is Determination. Without me, you are nameless and weaponless.*'

The East Witch steps aside and bows, gesturing the Traveller forward. The Traveller proceeds as before, with the West Witch following and encouraging him. When he has made another complete circuit and is passing the East candle on his way to the foot of the throne, Boreas rises and stands in his path. The Traveller halts.

Boreas: '*What are you seeking?*'

Traveller: '*I did not choose to seek. I was driven.*'

Boreas: '*You shall have no bride, until She grants you one.*' (If the Traveller is a woman, the word is 'bridegroom'.)

Traveller (puzzled): '*I seek no bride.*'

Boreas: '*All who approach Caer Arianrhod seek completeness.*'

Traveller: '*And is that to be found here – in darkness, in Death, in the unknown?*'

Boreas (stepping aside): '*Enter, and you will see.*'

Traveller: '*I am afraid.*'

Boreas: '*There is no going back.*'

Traveller: '*What is your name?*'

Boreas: '*I am Boreas, the North Wind, gatekeeper of Caer Arianrhod.*'

Boreas turns away and goes to stand on the other side of the altar from the High Priest.

The Traveller, now face to face with the throned Arianrhod, tries to back away, but the West Witch prevents him.

West Witch: '*There is no turning back.*'

Traveller: '*I AM AFRAID!*'

Arianrhod (speaking for the first time): '*Of what are you afraid?*'

Traveller (dropping to his knees): '*Of the dark. Of Death. Of the unknown.*'

Arianrhod: '*I am all these things, yet I am much more.*' She extends her right hand. '*You must kiss my hand.*'

The Traveller leans backwards in terror. But the West Witch, standing behind him, puts her hands on his shoulders and gently but firmly pushes him forwards again.

West Witch: '*All who come this far must kiss Her hand. There is no turning back.*'

Hesitantly the Traveller takes Arianrhod's hand and kisses it.

Arianrhod throws back her cloak and hood or veil and is revealed in her bright splendour.

Arianrhod (smiling): '*There is naught to fear in the dark for it leads to the light. There is naught to fear in Death, for it leads to Rebirth. There is naught to fear in the unknown, for I am at the heart of it.*'

West Witch: '*Listen to the words of the Great Mother ...*' continuing with the rest of the introduction to the Charge.

Arianrhod delivers the Charge in full, the West Witch supplying the passage '*Hear ye the words of the Star Goddess ...*' as usual in the middle of it.

When the Charge is completed, everyone gathers round the throne. Arianrhod and Traveller bless the wine and cakes together, and they are passed round in the usual way. When all have partaken, everyone but Arianrhod, the Traveller and the West Witch returns to the perimeter.

Arianrhod: '*My son, you have known rest and refreshment in Caer Arianrhod. Go now, and return by the spiral path, deosil, to the world of men and women and all my other creatures. And keep this mystery in your memory: that at the heart of the Dark Mother is the Bright Mother, and at the heart of the Bright Mother is the Dark Mother. Know and remember, that I am One.*'

The Traveller bows to Arianrhod. The West Witch takes the Traveller's hand, and together they retrace the spiral path, deosil this time, with a joyful and confident step.

When they are back at their starting-point by the West candle, all but Arianrhod then join hands and circle to the Witches' Rune, until Arianrhod throws her arms upwards in a gesture of exultant life, and all drop to the floor facing inwards.

XXII Aradia

Tu devi andare sulla terra e fare da maestra. (You must go to the earth below and become a teacher.)

Diana to her daughter Aradia

Aradia is a Moon goddess from Tuscany, honoured by the witches of that region but lost to general scholarship until Charles Godfrey Leland published his *Aradia: the Gospel of the Witches* at the end of the last century. Since then Aradia has become probably the most popular Goddess-name of the Wiccan revival movement, particularly in its Gardnerian stream. It is the name used in Gardner's Book of Shadows, which he compiled by adapting other suitable material to fill in the gaps in the fragmentary traditional rituals he received from his parent coven; and Leland was certainly one of the sources on which he drew for that purpose. The opening passage of the Charge, for example (both in Gardner's original form and in the final version composed for him by Doreen Valiente), is practically verbatim from Leland's book. But whether the New Forest coven already used the name, or we have it from Leland via Gardner, we shall probably never know. In any case,

Aradia is now firmly naturalized, and active, in many lands outside her native Italy.

Leland was an extraordinary character, much larger than life, even for a nineteenth-century American. He was both a man of action and a meticulous scholar. Born in Philadelphia in 1824, he was educated in America and Germany. He fought in the French Revolution of 1848 and at the Battle of Gettysburg. After being called to the bar, and editing several American periodicals, he moved to Europe in 1869.

He had a gift for being accepted by the most secretive communities as one of themselves. French revolutionaries, Algonquin Indians and English gypsies successively took him to their bosoms. He learned to speak Romany and discovered the obscure dialect of some Welsh and Irish gypsies, Shelta. But his greatest achievement in this line – and on his own admission by far the most difficult – was to be accepted, and initiated, by the Tuscan *stregoni* (witches), an unheard-of honour for one who was both a foreigner and a gentleman.

In 1886 he had won the friendship and gradual trust of Maddalena, a Florentine fortune-teller and hereditary witch. Over ten years she supplied to him the material for three books. Her last and most important offering was the *Vangelo*, the Gospel of the Witches. During those years she also did a lot of patient ferreting-out on his behalf, finding the answers to his questions when they were outside her own knowledge.

The Aradia revealed by the *Vangelo* was not the Tuscan witches' chief goddess; that was Diana, and Aradia was her daughter. This is how the *Vangelo* tells it:

Diana was first created before all creation; in her were all things; out of herself, the first darkness, she divided herself; into darkness and light she was divided. Lucifer, her brother and son, herself and her other half, was the light.

And when Diana saw that the light was so beautiful, the light which was her other half, her brother Lucifer, she yearned for it with exceeding great desire. Wishing to receive the light again into her darkness, to swallow it up in rapture, in delight, she trembled with desire. This desire was the Dawn.

But Lucifer, the light, fled from her and would not yield to her wishes; he was the light which flies into the most distant parts of heaven, the mouse which flies before the cat ...

And it came thus that Diana took the form of a cat. Her brother had a cat whom he loved beyond all creatures, and it slept every night on his bed, a cat beautiful beyond all other creatures, a fairy: he did not know it.

Diana prevailed with the cat to change forms with her; so she lay with her brother, and in the darkness assumed her own form, and so by Lucifer became the mother of Aradia. But when in the morning he found that he lay by his sister, and that light had been conquered by darkness, Lucifer was extremely angry; but Diana sang to him a spell, a song of power, and he was silent, the song of the night which soothes to sleep; he could say nothing. So Diana with her wiles of witchcraft so charmed him that he yielded to her love. This was the first fascination; she hummed the song, it was the buzzing of bees (or a top spinning round), a spinning wheel spinning life. She spun the lives of all men; all things were spun from the wheel of Diana. Lucifer turned the wheel.

On the advice of 'the fathers of the Beginning, the mothers, the spirits who were before the first spirit', Diana came to Earth, disguising herself as a mortal. But –

She had such passion for witchcraft, and became so powerful therein, that her greatness could not be hidden. And thus it came to pass one night, at the meeting of all the sorceresses and fairies, she declared that she would darken the heavens and turn all the stars into mice.

All those who were present said: 'If thou canst do such a strange thing, having risen to such power, thou shalt be our queen.'

Diana went into the street; she took the bladder of an ox and a piece of witch-money, which has an edge like a knife – with such money witches cut the earth from men's foot-tracks – and she cut the earth, and with it and many mice she filled the bladder, and blew into the bladder till it burst.

And there came a great marvel, for the earth which was in the bladder became the round heaven above, and for three days there was a great rain; the mice became stars and rain. And having made the heaven and the stars and the rain, Diana became Queen of the Witches; she was the cat who ruled the star-mice, the heaven and the rain.

Having thus revealed herself, Diana shed her human disguise and returned to the heavens, for the endless pursuit of her brother/lover and the governing of her star-mice. But she was also Queen of the Witches, whose education must continue, and this task she delegated to her daughter Aradia.

Diana's briefing to Aradia (in Leland's rendering of the Italian verses) was this:

'Tis true indeed that thou a spirit art,
But thou wert born to become again
A mortal; thou must go to earth below
To be a teacher unto women and men
Who fain would study witchcraft in thy school ...
And thou shalt be the first of witches known;
And thou shalt be the first of all i' the world ...

Tuscan peasant witches lived in grim times, when discovery meant death and when abject poverty was their common lot. The Church and the rich were their tyrannical enemies. So it is hardly surprising that

Diana's instructions had a no-holds-barred quality about them:

And thou shalt teach the art of poisoning,
Of poisoning those who are great lords of all;
Yea, thou shalt make them die in their palaces;
And thou shalt bind the oppressor's soul (with power) ...

[Leland explains that the Italian word *legare* means the binding and paralysing of human faculties by witchcraft]

... And when ye find a peasant who is rich,
Then ye shall teach the witch, your pupil, how
To ruin all his crops with tempests dire,
With lightning and with thunder terrible,
And with the hail and wind ...
And when a priest shall do you injury
By his benedictions, ye shall do to him
Double the harm, and do it in the name
Of me, Diana, Queen of witches all!

Tough words, but reflecting a harsh reality, and easy enough to condemn from the comparative safety of the late twentieth century. To her own followers, Aradia was to deliver this promise:

For I am come to sweep away the bad,
The men of evil, all will I destroy!
Ye who are poor suffer with hunger keen,
And toil in wretchedness, and suffer too
Full oft imprisonment; yet with it all
Ye have a soul, and for your sufferings
Ye shall be happy in the other world,
But ill the fate of all who do ye wrong!'

So Aradia took her message to the witches of Earth, and told them:

'When I shall have departed from this world,
Whenever ye have need of anything,
Once in the month, and when the moon is full,
Ye shall assemble in some desert place,
Or in a forest all together join
To adore the potent spirit of your queen,
My mother, great Diana. She who fain
Would learn all sorcery yet has not won
Its deepest secrets, them my mother will
Teach her, in truth all things as yet unknown.
And ye shall all be freed from slavery,
And so ye shall be free in everything;
And as the sign that ye are truly free,
Ye shall be naked in your rites, both men

And women also; this shall last until
The last of your oppressors shall be dead;
And ye shall make the game of Benevento,
Extinguishing the lights, and after that
Shall hold your supper thus ...'

— most of which will have a familiar ring to modern witch ears.

The 'game of Benevento' had much in common with the uninhibited exuberance of Bealtaine Eve in more northerly latitudes, and the 'greenwood marriages' which resulted; and the 'supper' involved the ritual consecration of meal, salt, honey and water, and their baking into crescent-shaped cakes, which became 'the body and blood and soul of great Diana'.

To all of which may be added that, according to Italian friends of ours, *la vecchia religione* is still very much alive and well and living in Tuscany.

Aradia is thus the daughter and messenger of the Great Mother. It may even be that her legend is based on a dim memory of an actual woman who was a great teacher of magic and witchcraft and champion of the poor, deified in retrospect, like so many of her kind.

There is nothing wrong in that. Living men and women whose teachings or achievements have made a great impact on ordinary people, have often (particularly in pre-literate days, and even still) become crystallization-points for archetypal concepts, and thus for a body of myth. The name becomes a valid call-sign to attune oneself to the frequency of the archetypes. Among the British Celts and their descendants, King Arthur is an obvious, if undeified, example. And Jesus of Nazareth, one may argue, is a deified example. The trouble with great teachers about whom historical facts are known (or believed to be known) is that history may be distorted to fit the archetypes, or vice versa; and this may in turn distort the original teachings.

If a living Aradia was such a crystallization-point, no such problem exists, because no historical facts have survived. The Goddess-form which evolved from her has acquired its own independent validity and power.

Doreen Valiente has suggested (*Witchcraft for Tomorrow*, p.164) that, 'There is just a chance that the name "Aradia" is Celtic in origin, connected with *áiridh*, the summer pastures to which the cattle were driven at Beltane (1 May), and from which they returned to winter quarters at Samhain (1 November). The Celts originated in central Europe, and spread south into Italy, as well as westwards to Spain and the British Isles.' To which may be added that *áiridh* also means 'worth, merit'.

Though all our evidence on Aradia is from Tuscany, there is one hint that she may have spread wider in the hidden centuries. The *Canon Episcopi*, a tenth-century Church condemnation of witchcraft, gives 'Herodias' as a witch goddess name along with Diana. And interestingly, *araldia* in Basque means 'fertility'.

The Goddess is eternal, but Goddess-forms evolve. What is the image of Aradia today?

For us, she is very much a Nature goddess, complement to Cernunnos, Herne or Pan, and she is crowned with the crescent Moon of her mother/other self, Diana. Young? Yes, and beautiful, but wise; perhaps somewhere on the borderline between Maid and Mother.

Above all, a Goddess of the Witches, if only because we and our kind have had her to ourselves for some 2,000 years. Her temple has been the woods, her litany the fireside whisper, her worship the stubbornly guarded secret.

For a lifetime now, she has been out in the open. Her dossier is on library shelves. Witches are unlikely ever to allow it to gather dust.

The Aradia Ritual

The Preparation
Three witches are chosen to enact Diana, Aradia and Lucifer. Ideally Diana should be a mature woman, and Aradia a younger one – respectively the Mother and the Maid.

Three veils are needed, gauzy enough to be seen through when worn over the head: a black or purple one for Diana, a yellow or gold one for Lucifer, and a white, silver or green one for Aradia. If Diana's can be silver-threaded or sequined, so much the better, to symbolize the night sky; and a gold-threaded veil for Lucifer would be suitably solar. (Lucifer, the 'light-bringer', in this legend is the Sun, not the Morning Star.) Diana's and Lucifer's veils are laid ready beside the altar; Aradia wears hers over her head from the start.

Diana's jewellery and accessories should be silver, since she is the Moon. Lucifer's should be the gold, gilt or bronze of the Sun. Aradia's can be whatever suits her, since she is the child of both.

This ritual should be performed skyclad, if only because it celebrates the occasion on which the order 'ye shall be naked in your rites' was traditionally given. But if for some reason it is performed robed, Diana's robes should be dark and Lucifer's and Aradia's light-coloured.

The success of the ritual depends a good deal on the vividness and drama of Diana's miming; so she should give thought, and some private rehearsing, to it.

Ideally, of course, the cakes on this occasion should be made of meal, salt, honey and water, and baked in a crescent-shape; see the recipe on p.73.

The Ritual

The Circle is cast as usual, Diana and Lucifer acting as High Priestess and High Priest. Aradia sits quietly behind the East candle, with her veil draped over her head.

The ritual proceeds up to and including the '*Of the Mother darksome and divine*' blessing, the only difference being that Lucifer says '*Hail, Diana*' instead of the usual '*Hail, Aradia*'.

The Charge is not given yet, and the '*Bagahi*' incantation and the 'Great God Cernunnos' invocation are omitted.

Immediately after '*Here I charge you, with this sign*', Diana and Lucifer take up their veils and drape them over their heads. The rest of the coven huddle together in a tight ring, seated in the centre of the Circle facing inwards, as though unenlightened and awaiting guidance.

Lucifer starts walking deosil (clockwise) just inside the perimeter of the Circle. Diana waits till he is passing the South candle and then starts walking deosil herself. She stays always diametrically opposite to him, reaching out her arms as though yearning for him. Sometimes she quickens her pace, but then he does so too, maintaining the distance between them.

After four or five circuits, Lucifer halts in front of the altar, lies down and curls himself up as though asleep. Diana halts in front of the South candle, miming desolation at her failure to reach him.

After a while her mood changes. She draws herself up and starts making cat-like movements – stroking behind her ears with her 'paws' and so on. Then she starts moving deosil, still cat-like, until she reaches the 'sleeping' Lucifer. Careful not to wake him, she kneels beside him, miming a cat's endearments.

Lucifer stirs in his sleep and strokes her, believing her to be his cat, and she reacts appropriately, purring and mewing in appreciation. Lucifer relaxes into sleep again, and she folds him in her arms – now all woman. She quietly removes her veil and lays it aside; then she removes his and lays it aside.

She embraces him more fervently, kissing him. Lucifer opens his eyes, looks puzzled, realizes that she has tricked him and tries to draw away from her. But Diana croons and hums to him, rocking him in her arms until he stops resisting.

When he is still, she stands up, and he sits cross-legged in front of the altar, watching her. She takes up her athame from the altar and walks slowly to the East candle, where she ritually opens a gateway with a widdershins (anti-clockwise) sweep of the athame. She holds out her hand to Aradia, who rises.

Diana takes Aradia's hand, draws her into the Circle and gives her a welcoming kiss. She closes the gateway with a deosil sweep of her athame and then leads Aradia to stand in front of Lucifer.

Lucifer stands, watching them both. Diana removes the veil from Aradia's head, and says: 'Lucifer – behold our daughter, Aradia!'

Lucifer puts his hands on Aradia's shoulders and turns her so that she is standing with her back to the altar. Then he gives her the Fivefold Kiss, turns to Diana and asks: 'And what shall our daughter do?'

Diana replies: 'She shall teach my magic to the witches of Earth.'

Lucifer says: 'So mote it be.'

Diana and Lucifer stand on either side of Aradia, looking at her, but both pointing towards the huddled coven. Aradia moves forward, and Diana and Lucifer stand watching, with their backs to the altar.

Aradia walks slowly deosil round the coven, looking down at them. Every now and then she touches one of them on the shoulder, and he or she stands. When all are standing, Aradia gestures them back towards the South candle. The coven move to the South of the Circle and stand facing the altar. Aradia moves to the West candle and then addresses the coven: 'Listen to the words of my great mother, Diana!'

Diana says: 'Whenever ye have need of anything ...' and delivers the whole of the Charge.

The words 'Listen to the words of the Star Goddess ...' etc, normally spoken by the High Priest, are on this occasion spoken by Aradia.

When Diana has finished the Charge, Aradia and the coven link hands and start circling deosil, the movement becoming gradually faster and more joyous. Aradia starts declaiming the Witches' Rune, and they all join in.

When they reach the final 'Eko, Eko, Azarak' chorus, repeated as usual ad lib, Diana and Lucifer join the ring, and the circling continues till Aradia cries 'Down!'.

Aradia then names witches to consecrate the wine and cakes.

XXIII Isis

The mother of the stars, the parent of seasons, and the mistress of all the world.

Lucius Apuleius

Isis is without doubt the most complete and many-sided image of the Goddess that mankind has ever conceived. Also perhaps the longest-lasting: she was actively worshipped, with established temples and priesthood, for at least $3\frac{1}{2}$ thousand years – nearly twice as long as Christ. Her beginnings cannot be dated, but in the Pyramid Texts of about 3000 BC she was already referred to as 'the Great Isis', and the final suppression of her public worship was not achieved until the Theodosian Law of AD 426 a century after Constantine had made Christianity the official religion of the Empire. (There were still lingering pockets: at Philae in Upper Egypt she continued to be worshipped into the sixth century.) And even with her temples destroyed or converted to churches, she has refused to die.

The view is often expressed that Mithraism was the only real challenge to Christianity, and that there was a time when it was almost

touch-and-go which of the two would become the established faith of
the West. Under patriarchy, that is perhaps true, for Mithraism was as
male-dominated as the Church, but the more fundamental challenge
was from Isis, and it took the whole force of the imperial machine to
suppress her – plus the virtual deification of the Virgin Mary, five years
after the Theodosian Law, to replace her.

By then, Isis-worship had spread to the whole of the known world, as
we shall see later. As R.E. Witt puts it (*Isis in the Graeco-Roman
World*, p.140): 'If Western civilisation could have somehow developed
on a matriarchal basis, Isis might have been too stubborn a mistress to
dethrone.' All the evidence is that she would have been.

For her first 2,000 years or so, Isis was entirely Egyptian (though
overlapping with neighbouring Goddesses such as Ishtar and Astarte –
note the similarity to the name Aset). In that time her importance and
popularity had grown till she was the premier Goddess of the whole
land.

Aset or Wset was her Egyptian name, and her brother-husband
Osiris was Asir or Wsir. Isis and Osiris were the Greek forms of the
names. Both Aset and Asir mean 'throne', so their association with
sovereignty (whether of gods or of men) must be as old as their names.

Their legend, which became the central one of Egyptian mythology,
was as follows.

When the Sun god Ra ordered Shu (Air) to separate Nut (Sky) from
her brother-lover Geb (Earth), he ordained that Nut should never bear
children in any month of the year. But Thoth, god of wisdom, was
sorry for her and, by playing draughts with the Moon, won a
seventy-second part of its light. This became the five intercalary days,
belonging to no month; and on these she bore Osiris, Horus the Elder,
Set, Isis and Nephthys. Osiris and Isis fell in love and mated while still
in Nut's womb, and became husband and wife, while Nephthys married
Set.

Osiris and Isis ruled Egypt and taught the people all the basic skills
of civilization. But Set was jealous of his brother and, in the
twenty-eighth year of his reign, succeeded in killing him, nailing his
body into a coffin and throwing it into the Nile. His treachery alienated
his wife Nephthys, who left him and from then on was loyal to the
Osirian party.

The desolate widow Isis eventually traced the coffin to Byblos in
Phoenicia, whither the currents had carried it. A tamarisk tree had
grown around it, and King Malacander had built the trunk into his
palace. Isis, incognito at first, became nurse to the son of Malacander
and his queen Astarte. When she revealed herself, Malacander gave her
a ship to take the coffin back to Egypt.

She hid in the Delta marshes near Buto, to conceal from Set that she had recovered the body – and also that she had magically conceived a child by her dead husband.

Set found the body nonetheless and tore it into fourteen parts which he scattered throughout the kingdom. Isis patiently searched for them, and as she found each one, she held a funeral and set up a stela, hoping that Set would think all the parts had been buried in separate places.

She then magically reconstituted Osiris's body, anointing it with precious oils (thus becoming the inventor of embalming). The only part she had failed to find was the phallus, which Set had thrown into the Nile and which had been eaten by a crab. But Isis fashioned another.

Osiris, now immortal, became King of Amenti, the realm of the dead, and in due course Isis gave birth to Horus the Younger. These three became the great Holy Family of Egypt, overshadowing even such important triads as Amun-Ra, Mut and Khonsu of Thebes.

Osiris was essentially a dying-and-resurrecting vegetation deity, like Tammuz and Persephone. The annual Nile flooding was the tears of Isis, bringing him back to life. (Or alternatively – for Egyptian symbolism was full of paradoxes – Osiris was the annually rising Nile, and Isis the rich land of Egypt which he fertilized.) He was thus also a symbol of human rebirth; the dead were identified with him, as a guarantee of immortality. In the funerary rites, the deceased, whether man or woman, would be referred to as 'the Osiris Nebseni, victorious' (or whatever the human name was).

Horus was both his father's avenger and his reborn self. The latter aspect is reflected in the rituals surrounding the sacred Apis Bull at Memphis. The living bull was regarded as an incarnation of Osiris; one of Isis's titles was 'the Cow of Memphis', and Horus was known as 'the Bull of his Mother'. The Four Sons of Horus (who will be encountered in the Opening Ritual below) were said to have been born of Isis.

The living Pharaoh was identified with Horus, the dead Pharaoh with Osiris; and the living Pharaoh was often depicted as being suckled by Isis – a declaration that he was her son, because suckling was a ritual act of legal adoption in Egypt.

Set represented the destructive force of the desert, a constant threat to the fruitful union of the Nile and its green valley. Nephthys has been identified with the fringe lands between farmland and desert, originally wedded to the desert but won over and fertilized by the Nile; in the legend, Nephthys was barren by Set but, after leaving him, bore Anubis to Osiris.

Isis herself, in addition to her role in the annual-fertility myth, came to symbolize the ideal of a loyal and loving wife and mother – contrasting favourably with her parallels in some other pantheons, where the female protagonist in the dying-god cycle could be anything from capricious to merciless.

It was her wife-and-mother image which captured the imagination of the ordinary Egyptian, for it was popular fervour as much as priestly teaching which elevated this Holy Family to its unique status.

Isis was also known as 'Great of Magic'. Her first step in this direction was when she tricked the ageing Ra into revealing to her his secret Name, which gave her unsurpassed power. Central to her story, of course, was her magical revival of her murdered husband, and her impregnation by him (variously placed, in versions of the myth, at her recovery of the complete body or at her reassembling of its fourteen parts, plus the magically refashioned phallus).

For the worshipper, her magical power was something which could be appealed to directly. She was the compassionate, motherly goddess who understood suffering from her own experience and who could be asked to bend the rules in her supplicant's favour when a problem seemed humanly insoluble – a characteristic later taken over (like so many other Isian attributes) by the Virgin Mary.

Yet 'bending the rules' does not quite express it. The Egyptian felt that her magic was in accord with deeper laws beyond his immediate understanding. This was reflected in the fact that Isis's collaborator, time and again, in her magical operations was Thoth, god of wisdom – whose wife, significantly, was Ma'at, goddess of the natural order of things and of the inescapable laws of the Cosmos. (This approach – that magic means attunement with natural laws, and a constant striving to understand them better – has of course been the working philosophy of every genuine magician and witch since time began, and still is.)

Her magical function, in alliance with Thoth, was inseparable from her function as Mistress of Healing. When Set took the form of a poisonous snake and bit the child Horus in the Delta swamps, Thoth stopped Ra's Boat of a Million Years in the sky and exorcized the poison in the Sun god's name. It was after this that Isis schemed to acquire the power of that Name for herself, and succeeded.

She was regarded as the inventor of many healing drugs, as an expert in medical science and as taking pleasure in healing mankind. The medical Ebers Papyrus (not later than the sixteenth century BC) invokes her thus: 'O Isis, thou great Mage, heal me, release me from all things that are bad and evil and that belong to Set, from the demonic fatal sicknesses – as thou hast saved and freed thy son Horus.'

She also gave healing dreams, particularly to those who spent nights in her temples – the practice of 'incubation' followed by Egyptians of every class, and later in her overseas temples even by Roman Emperors. Egyptian medicine (including its priestly psycho-therapy) was rightly famous throughout the ancient world, and Isis was its Queen.

Gradually Isis absorbed the functions of many other goddesses. In particular she overlapped with Hathor, the goddess of fertility, motherhood, love and happiness. Isis's symbolic headdress was originally the tall throne, hieroglyph of her name, and Hathor's the solar disc between cow's horns, but as the centuries passed, Isis too was more and more depicted with the disc and horns. (A note for students of Egyptian art: one can tell whether a disc-and-horns goddess is Isis or Hathor by the decorative 'bun' or bow which Isis wears at the back of her hair, while Hathor's coiffure is plain.)

She became a goddess of fertility, marriage, motherhood, healing, magic, love, sovereignty, animals, divination, beauty, the Moon, domestic skills and many other things. With her sister Nephthys, she was protectively present at childbirth and concernedly accompanied the journey of death. It was her many-sidedness that spread her fame, and her worship, throughout the known world.

The spread – one may almost call it an explosion – of Isis-worship outside Egypt was really set alight by Alexander the Great's conquest of Egypt in 332 BC.

It is fashionable to regard the Ptolemies, the Macedonian rulers of Egypt from Alexander's conquest to Cleopatra, as not quite real Pharaohs, but this is less than fair. Alexander himself had tremendous respect for Egyptian wisdom and religion. He founded Alexandria, which became one of the most culturally brilliant cities in history, and a richly fertile meeting-point for Egyptian and Greek ideas. Ptolemy I, 'the Great', built on Alexander's foundations, ruled along thoroughly Egyptian lines and established the incomparable Museum and Library of Alexandria. Ptolemy II Philadelphus, in the Pharaonic manner, married his sister Arsinoe, who was identified (with splendid Graeco-Egyptian ecumenism) with both Isis and Aphrodite and had a temple built for her at Zephyrion on the Egyptian coast.

'In both the political and the religious sense the Ptolemies were Pharaohs' (Witt, *op. cit.* p.48). But they were also tidy-minded Greeks by inheritance and naturally tried to equate the gods of their ancestors with those of their adopted land. Ptolemy I tackled the problem methodically, by appointing two priests to advise him on the subject – the Egyptian historian Manetho (to whose collected material modern Egyptology owes much) and the Athenian Timotheus, who was particularly well versed in the Eleusian and Delphic Mysteries.

Manetho and Timotheus intelligently navigated the paradoxes to produce an Alexandrian pantheon acceptable to both Egyptian and Greek thinking. Isis, Horus, Anubis and some others presented few problems, but Osiris – a god of the dead and of fertility, having at the same time solar attributes – did not export easily. So they virtually invented a new god, Sarapis, 'an extension of the Apis Bull at Memphis, the sacred animal whose immaculate mother was Isis herself and into whose body the soul of Osiris passed after the god's death'

(Witt, *op. cit.* p.53). Sarapis (absorbing Osiris, yet equatable with Zeus and Poseidon) became Isis's consort in the international pantheon.

It worked. Isis, while losing nothing at home, became increasingly cosmopolitan. Her already-established universality won all hearts. 'Queenly as Hera, mystic and fructifying as Demeter, comely as Aphrodite, victorious as Athena and pure as Artemis, she embraces within her the functions of all' (Witt, *op. cit.* p.110). Sarapis and Horus went with her, but Sarapis remained her prince consort rather than a king in his own right.

This is not the place to examine in detail the astonishing spread of Isis-worship over the known world during the following five or six centuries. The most comprehensive book on the subject is R.E. Witt's, already quoted. But at its peak Isis was found as far apart as the Black Sea, Morocco, the Rhineland and York. She was in emperors' palaces, private homes and market-places. It is significant that her temples tended to avoid the 'high places' of more remote deities; they were almost always where the people lived and worked.

For the impact of Isis-worship outside Egypt, the most vivid personal testimony is Lucius Apuleius's *The Golden Ass.* His second-century AD novel is witty, moving, hilarious, bawdy, first-rate reporting, and deeply spiritual all at the same time, by the standards of any epoch. But as well as being a gifted writer, Lucius was himself an initiate of Isis, and the book ends with an autobiographical account of his initiation, revealing as much as his vows allowed but eloquently conveying his emotions, his dedication and the public celebrations.

Almost the only attribute which had hardly concerned the Egyptian Isis, or any of the Egyptian deities, was a connection with the sea. But under the Ptolemies the western Mediterranean became virtually an Egyptian lake, and Alexandria a major port for international shipping, so the cosmopolitan Isis very soon added to her titles that of Isis Pelagia, Star of the Sea, patroness of ships (many of which were named after her) and of sailors. With that, it may be said that her universality was complete.

She had become Isis Myrionymos, 'of the countless names' – a title still used by Greek Orthodox Christians for the Virgin Mary. It was only one of the Isian features which Mary was given, due to the Church's urgent need to fill the vacuum created by its banishment of Isis. The story in Revelation 12 of Michael's battle with the dragon Satan, in defence of the 'woman clothed with the sun, and the moon under her feet, and upon her head a crown of twelve stars' who was 'travailing in birth', is the source of much Marian symbology, yet it follows the story of Isis, Set and the birth of Horus so exactly, stage by stage, that it is almost impossible not to conclude that the writer had it in mind.

The Madonna and Child statues directly echoed those of Isis nursing the infant Horus, and some of them were actually Isis statues repainted. Mary, like Isis, was 'Star of the Sea', 'the Power that Heals the World', 'She who Initiates', 'Throne of the King', 'Mistress of the World', 'the Heifer who has brought forth the spotless Calf' and so on. And most significantly of all, Theotokos, 'Mother of (the) God'.

Isis never died. She had a marked influence on Gnosticism, which itself never died, however brutally it was persecuted, and there is evidence that her mysteries were a closely guarded secret among the Knights Templar, even after their equally brutal disbanding.

An extraordinary excursion into this aspect of Isis's survival is David Wood's book *Genisis: The First Book of Revelations*, published in 1985. As a professional cartographer, he carried out an intensive and meticulous investigation of the mysterious layout of churches and other features in the area of Rennes-le-Château in southern France, following up the line of thought suggested in Baigent, Leigh and Lincoln's controversial 1982 book *The Holy Blood and the Holy Grail*.

His findings are much too complex to be summarized here. It is enough to say that in our opinion he has established beyond reasonable doubt that the Rennes-le-Château area comprises an ancient ground-plan of features laid out in a sophisticated geometrical pattern that carries a momentous message. The evidence is simply far too rich in clues to be ignored, and it ties in with the Isian story.

The conclusions he himself draws from his findings are another matter; we must admit that some of them we find hard to accept, and we keep an open mind on them for the present. But this is as Wood himself would wish: 'Take nothing I have said on faith or my time in writing this book has been wasted. Criticize, verify and search further.' We accept his advice – and recommend our readers to read his book and do the same.

The intervening centuries between Isis's official banishment and our own lifetime are a fascinating study, but no one can doubt the part that Isis has played in the occult and pagan revival of recent years. Of the writers of the Golden Dawn and its offshoots, none made a greater contribution to the recapturing of the Goddess concept for modern minds that Dion Fortune, and for her (see particularly her novels *The Sea Priestess* and *Moon Magic*) Isis above all personified that concept as a whole. When she was dealing with particular aspects, she cited Persephone, Aphrodite, Levanah, Rhea, Binah, Ge (Gaia) and many others, always vividly and appropriately, but she saw Isis as embracing them all.

And it is not surprising that, for example, an international organization which was established to link together people of widely different paths, from Christians to witches, who have just one thing in common – acceptance of the Goddess principle – should have called itself the Fellowship of Isis; nor that its membership is growing fast. (For those interested, the address is The Fellowship of Isis, Clonegal Castle, Enniscorthy, Co. Wexford, Ireland.)

Isis is very much alive, for the reason that we stated at the beginning, and which remains true today: that she is the most complete and many-sided image of the Goddess that mankind has ever conceived.

We are not suggesting that witches, or anyone else, should abandon the Goddess-name they are accustomed to using and call her Isis instead. A call-sign to the Goddess, once established by individuals or groups, becomes their most effective way of attuning themselves to her and should not be lightly tampered with. But we do suggest that a study of Isis, in all her richness, will enhance the richness of that attuning – by whatever name we call her.

Aspects are another matter, of course. Effective working with particular aspects calls for a wide spectrum of call-signs; that is what this book is all about. But when we want to remind ourselves (as we should) that these aspects are but parts of a majestic whole, there is no greater embodiment of that majesty than Isis – by whatever name we call her.

The Egyptian Temple

The Egyptian temple and its rituals were complex, and rich in symbolism. There were also, of course, differences according to the deity to which the temple was dedicated. Reproducing all this in modern conditions would be an interesting project for a team of Egyptologists and occultists with unlimited funds, but hardly practical for an ordinary coven who want to experiment with Egyptian magic now and then.

Such experiments (as we and many others have found) are nevertheless very well worth while and can have surprising and moving effects. A very simply arranged temple and some basic Egyptian symbolism are quite enough to create the right atmosphere and to put you on the appropriate wavelength, if you have any feeling at all for the subject.

(Surprisingly perhaps, there are a few people, including some very good witches, who are not at home with it and who find it disturbing. In our own experience over the years, two women and one man have fainted and one man has felt unaccountably dizzy during their first Egyptian rituals. Yet these rituals were neither more nor less dramatic than Wiccan ones to which all four were thoroughly accustomed. None of them came to any harm, incidentally. Their reactions may well have been karmic.)

Here, then, are the simplified Egyptian forms which we have found workable. A word of advice to those who want to adopt these rituals or to devise their own. An essential source book is the Egyptian *Book of the Dead* (see Bibliography under Budge) – the actual and much more inspiring Egyptian title of which was *The Chapters of Going Forth by Day*. And a study of Egyptian murals and statues (again the Bibliography names several suitable books) is a must, if you want to get the symbolism, the costumes and the whole spirit of the thing right.

The Temple

Egyptian temples were rectangular, with the altar in the East. They were kept meticulously clean. No objects made of iron were in them (even after the Iron Age reached Egypt) except for the ritual Instrument for the Opening of the Mouth.

The relating of the elements to the cardinal points was also different: Fire in the East (the rising Sun), Air in the West (the sky of the desert), Water in the South (whence the Nile flows), and Earth in the North (to which the Nile brings fertility).

Although the Opening Ritual has some similarities to the casting of a Wiccan Circle, there is no Banishing at the end.

In building up the 'astral temple' therefore, you should (as with any place of magical working) visualize it strongly as actually existing, sanctified, protective and amplifying, but as rectangular and East-oriented. And at the end of the ritual you should visualize it as still present, fading away of its own accord and in its own good time.

To strengthen the visualization, the four goddesses who guard the cardinal points should be remembered: Isis the South, Nephthys the North, Neith the East, and Selkhet the West.

(Alternative placings found in other contexts are Isis North-West, Nephthys South-West, Neith North-East and Selkhet South-East; or with different Goddeses, Uadjet North, Bast East, Nekhbet South and Neith West – see Erich Neumann, *The Great Mother*, p.221.)

The Egyptian ritual drink was beer, not wine, but since Osiris was said to have invented beer and Isis wine, presumably either is acceptable.

When choosing appropriate music, it is worth remembering that the Egyptian instruments were the harp, lute, lyre, oboe, zither and single and double flute, and for percussion, small drums, tambourines and the most ancient and characteristic of all, the sistrum, particularly sacred to Isis.

The Costumes

See Figure 4 for the general appearance of these.

No animal products were worn – neither wool nor leather. Linen was the normal material. The best Ancient Egyptian linen was made of a flax finer than the best modern qualities – up to 160 threads to the inch in the warp and 120 in the weft, which is lady's-handkerchief texture and most easily imitated today by very fine cotton. Priestesses will probably like to get as close to this as possible, but ordinary cotton is perfectly acceptable for both sexes. (For magical work in general,

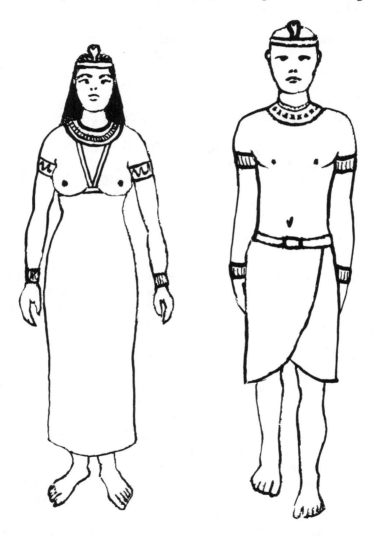

Fig. 4. Typical Egyptian priestess and priest costumes.

man-made fibres are better avoided because of their static-electrical qualities.)

Priests and priestesses went barefoot, so no problem arose over shoes or sandals. The only exception to the ban on animal materials was that some priests wore leopard skins over their shoulders.

The priest's costume would be a simple belted wrap-over kilt of folded linen, knee-length, sometimes shown with the front or both folds pleated, sometimes plain. The priestess's would be a close-fitting shift, ankle- or calf-length, bare-breasted, with shoulder-straps meeting in the cleavage but parallel down the back.

As for colour: white is always suitable, but various deities would have their own colours. Ma'at and Bast, for example, both favoured red; a priestess of Bast, like the Cat Goddess herself, was known as 'the Lady with the Red Clothes'.

Both men and women were generally depicted wearing circular pectorals round the neck (but suitable necklaces are adequate) and bracelet-bands at the wrists and armpits. Women also sometimes wore anklets.

Headgear would vary according to the deity involved and would often be animal-masks, but for our purpose we suggest simple circlets or crowns, perhaps with uraeus-like serpent-heads in front. (Egyptian priests shaved their heads, but that is hardly to be insisted upon!)

The Egyptian Opening Ritual

This requires the Priestess, Priest and four other people if they are available – though Priestess and Priest can conduct it alone.

The altar carries an ankh symbol, three lit candles and a bowl with an uncracked fresh egg in it for the sacrifice. Other candles may be at the cardinal points, as for a Wiccan Circle, or anywhere that is suitable for illumination.

One person stands in the North for Earth, bearing a bowl of salt, another in the South for Water, with a bowl of water, another in the West for Air, carrying a sistrum or bell, another (beside the altar) in the East for Fire, carrying a lit candle. (If Priestess and Priest are acting alone, these objects will simply be placed at the four quarters – in the case of the candle, with the other candles on the altar.)

The Priestess and Priest stand together facing the altar. The Priest says: 'Sayga oo-dan!' The Priestess says: 'Natarat di zeem a Koeten!' (These two phrases are taken from Frederic Wood's remarkable book *This Egyptian Miracle*. They mean 'Silence for the offering' and 'May the Goddess bless our rite.' If the ritual invoked a God, the word would be 'Natara'; 'Natara Natarat' may be used for 'the God and Goddess'.

'*Koeten*' should be pronounced like 'curtain' but without the 'r' sound.)

The Priest now holds out the bowl with the egg in it, and the Priestess breaks the egg into the bowl. They hold it up in salute together and then replace the bowl on the altar.

The Priest remains at the altar, while the Priestess goes to the North. She takes the bowl of salt from the person holding it (or picks it up if there is no one) and walks round the perimeter deosil, sprinkling a little salt as she goes.

Meanwhile the Priest says; '*Nephthys, Lady of the North; Lord Hapy, Royal Son of Horus, Earth God and Lord of the North, keeper and guardian of the lungs; with the casting of this sacred salt, fertilize and sanctify this holy ground with your being, so that we may be strong in all things.*'

When she has completed the circuit from North to North, the Priestess goes and puts the bowl of salt on the altar. She then goes to the South and takes (or picks up) the bowl of water. She walks round the perimeter deosil, sprinkling a little water as she goes.

Meanwhile the Priest says: '*Isis, Lady of the South; Lord Imset, Royal Son of Horus, Water God and Lord of the South, keeper and guardian of the liver; with the sprinkling of this sacred water, sanctify and cleanse this holy sanctum of all its impurities and the vanities of men.*'

When she has completed the circuit from South to South, the Priestess goes and puts the bowl of water on the altar. She then goes to the West and takes (or picks up) the sistrum or bell. She walks round the perimeter deosil, shaking the sistrum or ringing the bell as she goes.

Meanwhile the Priest says: '*Selkhet, Lady of the West; Lord Qebehsenuf, Royal Son of Horus, Air God and Lord of the West, keeper and guardian of the intestines; with the disturbance of air with this music, descend from your cardinal point, purify and sanctify the area of this holy sanctum.*'

The Priestess goes to the altar and places the sistrum or bell on it. She takes (or picks up) the lighted candle and walks round the perimeter deosil, holding up the candle.

Meanwhile the Priest says: '*Neith, Lady of the East; Lord Duamutef, Royal Son of Horus, Fire God and Lord of the East, keeper and guardian of the stomach; with the burning of this ritual fire, the all-consuming element, sanctify and purify this temple from all violations.*'

When she has completed the circuit from East to East, the Priestess returns the candle to the altar and stands there beside Priest.

Two notes to this ritual. Unlike most Wiccan rituals, there is no reason in this case why Priestess and Priest may not exchange roles when they wish. And the names of the Four Sons of Horus are best pronounced 'Hah-py', 'Keh-beh-seh-noof', 'Imset' and 'Dwah-moo-teff'.

Egyptian Initiation Ritual

The ritual we give below is in fact an initiation into the Egyptian mysteries. We have chosen it for one very good reason – that original Egyptian texts are available for it, selected from the various chapters of the *Book of the Dead*. The rituals in that Book, of course, dramatize the progress of the soul through the Underworld on its way to a new life, but all the evidence is that an Egyptian priestly initiation (like the initiations of many religions and fraternities) was also a symbolic death and ordeal leading to rebirth, so we can reasonably assume that its content would be very similar.

The question naturally arises of who is suitable to take the role of the Initiate. It should be someone who is already in tune with the Ancient Egyptian civilization and outlook, both to give real meaning to the rite and to help him or her to build on that attunement. The results are nothing to be afraid of, but they may often be surprising.

It will be noticed that the Initiate remains silent throughout; the Priestess and Priest speak on her behalf.

Elsewhere, we have for simplicity given a ritual as for a male subject, so here we will assume it is a woman. The whole rite is the same for both, and there is no need for the Priest and Priestess to exchange roles, unless they wish.

The Preparation

Those taking active part are the Priestess, the Priest and the Initiate. The Initiate, who will normally be naked at the start of the ritual, spends most of it lying along the East-West axis with her head to the West, so a suitable 'bed' should be there – anything from a draped divan to a neatly folded blanket. A suitable Garment of Purity is ready by the altar, and a veil to lay over the Initiate's body.

The Instrument for Opening the Mouth is laid ready on the altar. It is the only metal tool in the Temple. If the Initiate is a witch, her own athame is suitable for this, but some groups may like to make their own, and many Egyptian murals depict its shape.

Anointing-oil should also be on the altar, and a chalice of wine (or, more correctly, beer) and a dish of cakes.

The Initiate will preferably have chosen an Egyptian name beforehand, though her own name, or her witch name, will do. She is referred to in the ritual as 'the Osiris —— [name]'.

The Ritual

Priest and Priestess help Initiate to lie on the floor or mattress, face upwards, arms crossed on breast, head to the West. They lay the veil over her body, leaving her face uncovered.

The Priest and Priestess perform the Opening Ritual as given above – moving deosil round Initiate as they go from cardinal point to cardinal point.

After they have completed the Opening Ritual, the Priestess goes to the West, and the Priest remains by the altar.

Priest: *'This Thoth doeth, to make the way happy for her that would enter into the Disc. To the Door of the West Wind, which belongeth to Isis ...'*

Priestess: *'Ra liveth, the Tortoise dieth. Pure is the body in the earth, and pure are the bones of Osiris the Priestess —— triumphant.'*

The Priestess goes to the East.

Priest: *'To the Door of the East Wind, which belongeth to Nephthys ...'*

Priestess: *'Ra liveth, the Tortoise dieth. Sound is she who is in the chest, who is in the chest, Osiris the Priestess —— triumphant.'*

The Priestess goes to the North.

Priest: *'To the Door of the North Wind, which belongeth to Osiris ...'*

Priestess: *'Ra liveth, the Tortoise dieth. The Osiris —— triumphant, is strong in her members, for Qebesenuf guardeth them.'*

The Priestess goes to the South.

Priest: *'To the Door of the South Wind, which belongeth to Ra ...'*

Priestess: *'Ra liveth, the Tortoise dieth. The bolts are drawn, and they pass through the foundation.'*

The Priest fetches the Instrument for Opening the Mouth from the altar. He then stands to the North of Initiate, and the Priestess stands to the South of her. The Priest hands the Instrument to the Priestess.

Priestess: *'The Osiris —— saith: I rise out of the egg in the hidden land. May my mouth be given unto me, that I may speak therewith in the presence of the great God, the Lord of the Underworld. May my hand and my arm not be forced back in the presence of the sovereign princes of any God. I am Osiris, the Lord of Re-stau; may I, Osiris the Priestess —— victorious, have a portion with him who is on the top of the Steps. According to the desire of my heart, I have come from the Pool of Fire, and I have quenched the fire. The Osiris —— saith: May the God Ptah open my mouth, and may the God of my city loose the swathings, even the swathings which are over my mouth. Moreover may Thoth, being filled and furnished with charms, come and loose the bandages, even the bandages of Set which fetter my mouth; and may the God Tem hurl them at those who would fetter me with them, and drive them back. May my mouth be opened, may my mouth be unclosed by Shu with his iron knife wherewith he openeth the mouth of the Gods.'*

The Priestess lays the Instrument on Initiate's mouth for a moment, and then removes it.

Priestess: *'I am the Goddess Sekhet, and I sit upon my place in the great wind of heaven. I am the great Goddess Sah, who dwelleth among the Souls of Annu. May the Gods resist every charm and all the words which may be spoken against me; and may each and every one of the company of the Gods withstand them.'*

The Priestess hands the Instrument to the Priest, who replaces it on the altar and resumes his place facing the Priestess across the Initiate.

Priest: *'The Osiris —— triumphant, saith: Homage to thee, O Great Goddess, thou Lady of double Maati; I have come to thee, O my Lady, and I have brought myself hither that I may behold thy beauties. I know thee, and I know thy name. Thy name is Rekhti-merti-neb-Maati, which meaneth "twin sisters with two eyes, Ladies of double Maati". In truth I have come to thee, and I have brought right and truth to thee, and I have destroyed wickedness for thee.'*

(What follows is the famous Negative Confession, whose thirty-eight declarations sum up the Egyptian ethical code. The Egyptian's attitude seems to have been that even if he had committed some of these sins, he was now regretting and disowning them. The modern Initiate would do well to have the Priest omit any of the declarations which cannot honestly be made on her behalf.

'I have not harmed any man.
'I have not injured my family.
'I have committed no evil in a holy place.
'I have not kept evil companions.
'I have not wrought evil.
'I have not placed a burden of work upon others.
'I have not sought honours.
'I have not ill-treated those who have worked for me.
'I have not scorned the God.
'I have not defrauded the oppressed one of his property.
'I have not done that which the Gods hate.
'I have not vilified a servant to his master.
'I have not caused pain to any.
'I have not let any man go hungry.
'I have not made any man to weep.
'I have not committed murder.
'I have not caused murder to be committed.
'I have not inflicted pain.
'I have not stolen the offerings in the temple.
'I have not stolen the sacred bread.
'I have not stolen the bread offered to the spirits of the departed.

'I have not committed fornication.
'I have not polluted myself in the sanctuary of the God of my city.
'I have not given short measure.
'I have not stolen land.
'I have not encroached upon the land of others.
'I have not cheated the seller.
'I have not cheated the buyer.
'I have not stolen milk from the mouths of children.
'I have not stolen cattle from the pastures.
'I have not stolen the sacred birds of the Gods.
'I have not caught fish with bait of their own kind.
'I have not turned back water, when it should flow.
'I have not cut the bank of a canal.
'I have not put out a fire when it should burn, or a light where it should shine.
'I have not defrauded the Gods of their meat offerings.
'I have not driven off the cattle of the Gods.
'I have not repulsed the God in his manifestations.
'I am pure. I am pure. I am pure. I have seen the Eye of Ra when it was full in Annu, which is called by some Heliopolis. Therefore let not evil befall me in this land, and in the Hall of double Maati; because I, even I, know the names of these Gods who are therein, and who are the followers of the Great God and the Great Goddess.'

Priestess: 'I will not make mention of thee, saith the guardian of the door of this Hall of double Maati, unless thou tellest me my name.'
Priest: 'The Osiris —— answereth: "Discerner of hearts and searcher of reins" is thy name.'
Priestess: 'Now I will make mention of thee to the God. But who is the God that dwelleth in this hour?'
Priest: 'The Priestess —— answereth: It is Thoth.'
Priestess: 'Come, saith Thoth. What is now thy condition?'
Priest: 'The Osiris —— answereth: I, even I, am purified from evil things, and I am protected from the baleful deeds of those who live in their days; and I am not among them.'
Priestess: 'Now I will make mention of thee to the God, saith Thoth. Tell me, who is he whose heaven is of fire, whose walls are surmounted by living uraei, and the floor of whose house is a stream of water? Who is he, I say?'
Priest: 'And the Osiris —— answereth: It is Osiris.'
Priestess: 'Come forward then, saith Thoth; verily thou shalt be mentioned to him. Thy cakes shall come from the Eye of Ra, and thine ale shall come from the Eye of Ra. This hath been decreed for the Osiris the Priestess —— triumphant.'
The Priestess fetches the anointing-oil from the altar and kneels by the Initiate. She removes the Initiate's veil and anoints the soles of her feet,

the palms of her hands, her mouth, her nose, her ears and her eyes.

While the anointing is going on, the Priest says: '*Hail, verily thou are invoked; hail, verily thou art invoked. Hail, verily thou art praised; verily, thou art exalted; verily, thou art glorious; verily, thou art strong. Hail, thou Priestess ——, thou who hast been raised up, thou who hast been raised up by means of the ceremonies which have been performed for thee. Thine enemies have fallen, and the God Ptah hath thrown down headlong thy foes; thou has triumphed over them, and thou hast gained power over them. Hail, verily thou art invoked; hail, verily thou art invoked. Thou settest out on thy way, and thou hast been washed in the Lake of Perfection. Thou comest forth and thou seest Ra upon the pillars which are the arms of heaven; he openeth out for thee a way, and thou seest the horizon wherein is the place of purity which thou lovest.*'

The Priestess replaces the anointing-oil on the altar and fetches the Garment of Purity. She helps the Initiate to rise and robes her in it.

During the robing, the Priest says: '*O Tem, O Shu, O Tefnut, O Seb, O Nut, O Osiris, O Isis, O Nephthys, O Heru-Khuti, O Hathor in the Great House, O Khephera, O Menthu the lord of Thebes, O Amen the lord of the thrones of the two lands, O Great Company of the Gods, O Little Company of the Gods, O Gods and Goddesses who dwell in Nu, O Sebek of the two Meht, O Sebek in thy manifold names in thine every place wherein thy Ka hath delight, O Gods of the South, O Gods of the North, O ye who are in heaven, O ye who are upon earth. Grant ye this garment of purity to the perfect Khu of ——. Grant ye your strength unto her, and destroy ye all the evil which belongeth unto her, by means of this garment of purity. Hold her guiltless, then, for ever and ever, and destroy ye all the evil which belongeth unto her.*'

The Priest (on the right), the Initiate (in the centre) and the Priestess (on the left) face the altar.

Priestess: '*Great Isis, Mother of us all; Great Osiris, Lord of Rebirth; Great Thoth, Lord of Wisdom; Great Ma'at, Lady of Justice. Thus is it accomplished. Let us now, in your mighty presence, partake of the wine [ale] and cakes, in the manner of our time. For all Gods are one God; all Goddesses are one Goddess; and there is but one Initiator.*'

The Priestess and Priest then consecrate the wine or beer and cakes in the Wiccan manner and administer them to the Initiate. (If an athame has not been used for Opening the Mouth, the Priestess will spread her hands over the chalice instead of lowering a blade into it as usual; or a wooden ankh may be used.)

Part III

Goddesses of the World

Goddesses of the World

This is as full a list as we can reasonably make it of the goddesses of the various cultures of the world, both past and present. By 'reasonably' we mean that it is selectively comprehensive. To list and define all the Goddess-names that ever were would take a library. But we hope that this list includes most of the goddesses the normally serious reader is likely to want to identify – plus quite a few he or she may not have heard of but will find illuminating. The Bibliography offers signposts to more detailed study.

The object of this list is threefold.

First, to fill out our picture of the overall nature of the Goddess. No single Goddess-form which mankind has worshipped (with the possible exception of Isis) expresses more than one aspect, or a group of aspects, of the Goddess principle as a whole. But by studying her in all her forms, we can come near to grasping that overall nature.

The fact that most Goddess-forms embody only one or a few aspects is due not only to human inadequacy. It has a practical use, in concentrating the human mind on the particular aspect one wishes to invoke. One would not invoke a war goddess to ease childbirth, a mountain goddess for safety at sea, or an erotic goddess for a clear head when sitting for an exam. All goddesses are one Goddess – but the keys to magic are concentrated imagination and willpower, and concentrated imagination requires specific visualization of the aspect you wish to work with.

Which brings us to the second purpose of this list: to provide witches, and others following the magical path, with the material for finding exactly the aspect they wish to work with at any one time – taking into consideration as well the environment, the cultural associations, the pantheon with which they are in tune, and the 'feel' of the situation.

To help in this, we have added such details as Tarot, Cabalistic, plant and perfume correspondences, festival dates and local affinities wherever we can.

In some entries there is a sentence beginning '*777*: ...'. These are the Tarot and other correspondences given in Aleister Crowley's *777* for the goddess concerned. Whatever one thinks of the flawed giant Crowley, this particular book (which in any case was partly compiled by his magical tutor Allan Bennett) is unquestionably useful. We have included the magical weapons correspondences for the convenience of readers familiar with ritual magic; for their explanation, see *777*, pages 106-112.

The festival dates, Moon-cycle days and days of the week given are in some cases those listed and sourced in Lawrence Durdin-Robertson's *Juno Covella*. We should point out, however, that some of these festival dates were decided upon by modern fraternities. There is nothing wrong in that, where the original dates are lost or belong to a calendar not easily equated to ours, such as the Assyro-Babylonian; or where a suitable date is easily chosen by analogy with an already-dated goddess.

With the goddesses who are equatable to Sephiroth on the Cabalistic Tree of Life (Binah, Netzach, Yesod, Malkuth) the correspondences given are those in Dion Fortune's *The Mystical Qabalah*.

The 'David Wood numbers' given for one or two of the Egyptian goddesses are those he attributes to them in his *Genisis*. For our thoughts on this book, see p.176.

Our third purpose, quite simply, is to offer a useful work of reference. Although there are whole libraries of relevant literature to work through – some of them, such as Durdin-Robertson's invaluable books, concentrating specifically on the Goddess theme – so far as we know, no such concise but global directory exists as a guide to further study.

In this list, we have been flexible in our interpretation of the term 'goddess'. It includes, for example, the Eves (first women) of various cultures, and some who are more strictly Nature spirits, or who are on the borderline between legendary women and unquestioned goddesses.

But all of them personify some aspect of our theme, and so merit inclusion.

A name in CAPITALS in the body of an entry means that she has her own entry in her alphabetical place. Apart from this, we have cut cross-references to a minimum, because there could be so many of them.

We would like to thank Dr Ashok Singh for checking the Hindu entries; Esther Barrutia for supplying the information for the Basque ones; Mrs Kayoko Nibe, Cultural Attaché of the Japanese Embassy, Dublin, for help with the Japanese ones and Kati Koppana for help with the Finnish ones.

We would welcome any additions or corrections which readers can suggest from their own knowledge (particularly of the less-documented cultures or of surviving local Goddess-concepts) for inclusion in future editions.

One or two terms recur which it may be helpful to define here:

Ankh: The *crux ansata* or looped cross, Egyptian hieroglyph for 'life'.

Avatar: A Hindu term for a particular incarnation of a deity – e.g., 'Vahara, the boar avatar of Vishnu'.

Bodhisattva: A Hindu term for one who has reached perfection and has no need to reincarnate, but decides to do so to help humanity.

Caducaeus: Hermes/Mercury's winged rod entwined by two snakes – most familiar today as a symbol of the medical profession.

Lingam: Hindu name for the male organ, or for ritual symbols thereof.

Sistrum: An Egyptian rattle-like instrument, of small discs on wires within a looped frame, shaken ritually to banish evil influences.

Succubus: A female spirit who seduces men while they are asleep. The male equivalent who seduces women is the incubus.

Uraeus: The cobra-head worn at the front of Egyptian royal head-dresses.

Yoni: Hindu name for the mouth of the vagina, or for ritual symbols thereof.

ABUNDANTIA: ('Abundance') Roman. Subject of a relief at Lincoln. Perhaps origin of HABONDIA?

ACHLYS: ('Mist, darkness') Greek. The Mother who existed even before Chaos, and gave birth to it.

ADAMAH: ('Earth') Hebrew. Personification of the Earth as female; the word is often so used in the Hebrew Bible. The Assyrian equivalent was Adamu.

ADDA: see IDA.

ADERENOSA: Chaldean, Arabian, Egyptian. The Celestial Virgin nursing a child; the constellation Virgo. The Babylonian equivalent, Adra Nedega, occupies the first decan of Virgo.

ADISHAKTI: The primeval Hindu goddess of feminine energy. See also SHAKTI.

ADITI: ('Limitless') Hindu mother goddess, self-formed, the Cosmic Matrix. Mother of the Sun god Mitra and the Moon god Varuna, and of twelve month gods (known as the Adityas). Invoked as 'powerful, ever-young, far-spreading, kind shelterer, good leader ... the divine ship with strong rowers which never sinks'. The original, ultimate Mother; as the Rig Veda puts it, 'Aditi is THAT'. Day: Sunday.

ADRASTE: British. Invoked by Boudicca (Boadicea) before her final battle against the Romans at King's Cross in AD 61; at the same time she released a divinatory hare, presumably sacred to Adraste.

ADSULLATA: Continental Celtic goddess of springs; may be equated with SUL.

AEGLE: See HESPERIDES.

AEONS, THE: Gnostic. Aspects of the female embodiments of potency, the origins of all things. In the singular, Aeon, the total of these aspects, the Great Manifested Thought. According to Valentinus, there are eight principal Aeons and twenty-two others. Simon Magus regarded his wife and working partner, Helena of Tyre, as an incarnation of the Aeon, and of several of the individual-aspect Aeons, as 'that which has stood, stands and will stand'. Later Gnostics seem to have regarded this obviously remarkable woman in the same way.

AERFEN: British war goddess, presiding over the fate of wars between the Welsh and the English. Her shrine was at Glyndyfrdwy on the River Dee. Tradition says three human sacrifices had to be drowned there every year to ensure success in battle.

AESTAS: Roman goddess of Summer. Festival: 27 June.

AGLAIA: see CHARITES.

AGNAYI: Hindu fire goddess, wife of the fire god Agni.

AHOLIBAH: ('Tent in her') Hebrew, female personification of Jerusalem. Earlier apparently a wife of Jehovah. Condemned by the Hebrew scriptures as a voluptuous whore, sometimes as a menstruating one. Cf. HEPZIBAH.

AHURANI, THE: ('Waters') Persian. The life-producing water goddesses. Also personified as the single goddess Ardvi Sura Anahita, the heavenly source of all the waters on Earth.

AIMA: ('Mother') Hebrew. The 'bright fertile mother' hiding in her bosom, according to Cabalistic tradition, the stars, planets, angels and other powers; one aspect of BINAH. Cf. AMA.

AINDRE: see INDRANI.

ÁINE OF KNOCKAINE: Irish (Munster) Moon goddess, patroness of crops and cattle. She gave the meadowsweet its scent. Connected with the Midsummer festival. May be identified with ANU.

AKARU-HIME: ('Bright Princess') Japanese. Born from a red jewel, which turned into a beautiful young goddess. Protectress of sailors.

AKHAMOTH: see SOPHIA AKHAMOTH.

AKIBIMI: Japanese goddess of Autumn.

AKKA, MAA-EMOINEN: Finno-Ugric Earth-mother-goddess, wife of the supreme sky-god Ukko. Also called Rauni (from 'rönn', Swedish for rowan, mountain ash, which was her sacred tree). Festival: 15 July.

AKNA: ('The Mother') Yucatan. Goddess of birth, wife of Akanchob.

ALAGHOM NAUM, ISTAT IX: Mayan. Wife of Patol, chief god of the Tzental tribe. Known as 'the Mother of Mind', creatress of mind and thought.

ALAISIAGAE, THE: Attendant goddesses of Mars Thincsus, brought to the Roman camp at Housesteads, Northumberland, by Frisian troops. Depicted as naked winged Victories, hovering with wreaths and palms.

ALBINA: Tuscan witches dawn goddess. Also another name for ALPHITO.

ALCMENA: Greek, mother of Heracles by Zeus, but wife of Amphitryon, who condemned her to be burned to death for infidelity; Zeus miraculously rescued her. Probably originally a mother goddess.

ALECTO: see ERINYES.

ALEITHEIA: ('Truth, reality') Gnostic. An AEON: one angle of the square on which the Gnosis rests; the Truth of the Mysteries. Envisaged as a beautiful naked woman – unveiled Truth herself – with pairs of letters on every limb, starting with Alpha, Omega on her head, followed by Beta, Psi, converging alphabetically as they progress downwards. Also called Apt.

AL-LAT, AL-ILAT, EL-LAT: ('The Goddess') Persian and Arabian Moon goddess; Chaldean Underworld goddess. Considered by the Nabateans of Petra as mother of the gods. Female counterpart of Allah. Condemned by the Koran: 'What think ye of Al-Lat, and Al-Uzza, and Manah? ... empty names, which ye and your fathers have called goddesses.' (Surah liii: 19-23.) Yet in Islamic tradition one of the 'Three Daughters of Allah' (see p.32). Honoured at the New Moon.

ALPHITO, ALBINA: Greek barley goddess of Argos, 'who in Classical times had degenerated into a nursery bugbear' (Robert Graves). Probably the same as DANAE.

ALTHAEA: ('She Who Makes Grow') Greek birth goddess, wife of Oeneus, the first man to plant a vineyard in Greece; the vine was given to him by Dionysus as a bribe for turning a blind eye to his affair with Althaea. To Oeneus she bore the hero Meleager, and to Dionysus DEIANEIRA.

AL-UZZA: The Arabian APHRODITE. The Ka'aba, the sacred stone of Mecca, was originally her temple. Associated with the planet Venus. Condemned by the Koran – see AL-LAT – yet in Islamic tradition one of the 'Three Daughters of Allah' (see p.32).

AMA: Hebrew. The 'dark sterile mother', one aspect of the Cabalistic BINAH. Cf. AIMA.

AMALTHEA: Cretan goat goddess, who suckled the infant Zeus when RHEA was hiding him from Cronus. Some say she also suckled Pan.

AMA NO UZUME: Japanese. When the Sun goddess AMATERASU hid in a cave, darkening the Earth, Ama no Uzume danced naked, making all the gods laugh, which tempted Amaterasu out. This 'obscene dance' legend stems from an agricultural fertility rite, the gods' laughter heralding the return of life when all seems dead; cf. a similar action of HATHOR.

AMARI DE, DE DELEVSKI: Romany. Great Mother, personification of Nature; nowadays thinly disguised as Sara-Kali, the Black Madonna. See also THREE MOTHERS, THE.

AMATERASU: ('Great Deity Illuminating Heaven') The Japanese Sun goddess, from whom the Japanese royal family claim descent. Most important deity of the Japanese pantheon. Daughter of the god Izanagi (either by himself alone, or by his intercourse with IZANAMI) and sister of the Moon god Tsukiyomi. She wove the garments of the gods. Has a sacred crow called Yatagarasu. Cocks, kites and heavenly arrows are her symbols – also the beads, mirror and sword which are the 'Three Holy Articles' of Japanese royal regalia. Festival: 17 July.

AMATHAUNTA: Greek, an Aegean sea goddess. Patroness of the Amathites mentioned in the Bible.

AMATSU-OTOME, THE: Japanese female angels or mountain spirits; also applied to women witches, who were held in great respect.

AMAUNET: Egyptian. In the Hermopolitan cosmogony, the wife of Amun, of which her name is merely a feminine form, though in fact she was the more ancient deity. When Amun emerged from the waters of chaos onto the mound at Hermopolis, and hatched, self-created, from an egg, Amaunet, Goddess of Heaven, received him in the form of a cow. In the 18th Dynasty (c. 1580-1320 BC) when Amun, as Amun-Ra, rose to prominence at Thebes, Amaunet became identified with his Theban consort MUT.

AMAYICOYONDI: Amerindian, Pericu. Wife of creator god Niparaya. He had no body, so had no intercourse with her; nevertheless she bore him three sons, one of whom was Man.

AMBA BAI: Hindu. Local form of the mother goddess, at Bombay and Kilhapur. The great bell (doubtless originally Portuguese) of her Kilhapur shrine is inscribed 'Ave Maria Gratia Plena'!

AMBIKA: Hindu, 'the generatrix', wife of Shiva or of Rudra. See PARVATI.

AMEMAIT, AM-MIT: Egyptian Underworld goddess, in many ways the dark aspect of AMENT. 'Devourer of souls', she is 'the ancestral spirit of the matriarchal culture, in which the feminine takes back that which has been born of it' (Neumann). Depicted with a crocodile's foreparts, a lion's middle parts and a hippopotamus's hindparts, and sometimes with many breasts.

AMENT, AMENTET: ('the Westerner') Egyptian. Originally the goddess of Libya. Later Amenti, the West, came to mean 'the Land of the Dead', so Ament became an Underworld goddess, receiving the dead when they reached Amenti. Known as 'the goddess with the beautiful hair'.

AMIRINI: An early goddess of the Yorubas of West Africa.

AMMARIK: Ugric goddess of sunset.

AM-MIT: See AMEMAIT.

APHITRITE: Greek sea goddess, wife of Poseidon, daughter of Oceanus or of Nereus, mother of Triton and of RHODE, who gave her name to the island of Rhodes.

ANAGKE: ('Necessity') A Greek goddess of Destiny, called by Homer the most powerful of all the deities.

ANAHITA: Persian river goddess, mother goddess of Armenia. Mother of Mithras, god of friendship and truth. Associated with the planet Venus, and with the Moon. Patroness of marriageable girls and of childbirth. Also worshipped in Babylon, where daughters of noble families gave their virginity as her temporary sacred prostitutes. Honoured on the tenth day from the New Moon.

ANAT (1): Chief Canaanite goddess of fertility, love and war. She helped her brother Baal in his conflicts with Sea-and-Ocean-Current (Chaos) and Mot (Death, Sterility). When Mot killed Baal and took him to the Underworld, Anat led the mourning and then set out to get him back, with the help of SHAPASH, the Sun goddess. Anat fought and killed Mot ('with a sword she cleanses him ... in the field she plants him'), and Baal returned to life. The rituals dramatizing this were seasonal harvest-fertility ones, with Baal and Mot alternately victorious, but Anat surviving throughout. In one myth, her brother Baal mated with her in the form of a cow. She was responsible for seeing that sacrificial rituals were properly performed, so that the gods might thrive. 'May have been an earlier, more raw and unconscious version of the refined Athene' (Chetwynd, *A Dictionary of Symbols*, p.69). She and ASTARTE (like the Egyptian HATHOR) are represented as the sucklers of kings. Her cult animal was a lion, as it was of ISHTAR. Associated with the constellation Ursa Major. Day, Saturday. In the Hebrew form Anna-Nin, regarded as the mother of Jehovah; probably of Chaldaean origin (see ANAT (2)). Worshipped at Thebes in Egypt as 'Lady of Heaven and mistress of the gods' in the reign of Thotmes III (*c.* 1490-1436 BC) and later said to be a wife of Set.

ANAT (2): Chaldaean and Assyro-Babylonian mother-goddess, wife of Anu and mother of ISHTAR. May have been the original form of ANAT (1).

ANATHA BAETYL: Hebrew. A form of the Canaanite ANAT (1). One of the two wives of Jehovah in his fifth century BC cult at Elephantine in Egypt, the other being Ashima Baetyl. Solomon built two Goddess temples beside Jehovah's one in Jerusalem. See ASHTART.

ANBOTOKO DAMA, ANBOTOKO SORGINA: see MARI.

ANCASTA: British, known only from a single inscription at Bitterne in Hampshire.

ANDROMEDA: see CASSIOPEIA.

ANGERONA: Roman, always depicted with a finger to her sealed mouth. May have been a goddess of silence or of the hidden name of Rome which it was forbidden to pronounce. Festival: 21 December.

ANGURBODA: Teutonic. The Hag of the Iron Wood, wife of Loki and mother of HEL.

ANNA KAURI: Hindu, Chota Nagpur tribal goddess of fertility and wealth.

ANNA-NIN: see ANAT (1).

ANNA PERENNA: Roman, originally probably Sumerian. Goddess of the year, and of the succession of years; thus also honoured as a provider of food. Ovid says some identified her with MINERVA, or with THEMIS, mother of the Fates, both of them wisdom goddesses; he connects her with barley cakes. Festival: 15 March; also honoured at Full Moon.

ANNAPURNA: Hindu. Goddess who provides food; she lives on top of Mount Annapurna.

ANRITA: ('Fraudulent') Hindu goddess of fraud.

ANTUM: Assyro-Babylonian. Wife of the sky god Anum and mother of the storm god Enlil.

ANU, ANANN: A form of the major Irish mother goddess; overlaps with DANA. Worshipped in Munster as a goddess of plenty. Gave her name to the Paps of Anu, twin hills in Co. Kerry. In her dark aspect, she formed a Fate trinity with BADHBH and MACHA.

ANUKET: Egyptian. Khnum's second wife, worshipped at Elephantine, with him and his first wife SATI, as a regional goddess of the cataracts. Her name seems to mean 'the Clasper', confining the Nile between the rocks of Philae and Syene. The island of Seheil was consecrated to her. She is depicted wearing a tall, plumed crown.

ANUMATI: ('Conclusion') Hindu goddess of the waning Moon (cf. KUHU).

ANUNET: Sumerian goddess of the Morning Star, Venus. Absorbed into ISHTAR.

AOIDE: see MUSES.

AOIFE: see SCATHACH.

APET: see OPET.

APHAEA: Greek with cult centre at Aegina, but seems to have been a form of the pre-Greek mother goddess. Associated in myth with ARTEMIS and later identified with ATHENE, probably to symbolize the achievement of peace between Aegina and Athens.

APHRODITE: ('Foam-Born') Greek goddess of sexual love. She was born of the bloody foam of the sea where Cronus threw the genitals of his father Uranus after castrating him. Married, on Zeus's orders, to the lame smith god Hephaestus, and unfaithful to him with the war god Ares. She was in fact an ancient East Mediterranean goddess and can be equated with ASTARTE. Metal: copper (root of the place-name Cyprus). *777*: Tarot, Empress and Sevens; gems, emerald, turquoise; plants, rose, myrtle, clover; animals, lynx, sparrow, dove, swan; perfumes, benzoin, rose, red sandal, sandalwood, myrtle, all soft, voluptuous odours; magical weapons, Lamp, Girdle. Festivals: 23 April, 24 June and, for the Adonis theme, 19 July. Day: Friday. Roman equivalent: VENUS. See Chapter XVI for her full story.

APSARAS, THE: Hindu. Originally undines, haunting rivers and pools, and some of them still are; these Earth-based ones are called Kshiti-Apsaras. Later the Apsaras developed into celestial houris who welcome and entertain souls after death. By their singing and dancing, they enchant both gods and men. Depicted as lovely, lightly clad young women, often dancing.

APSU: Early Babylonian creator goddess, 'the Mother who begat Heaven and Earth', the primeval abyss of sweet water from which all things sprang. With the decay of matriarchy, she changed sex and became the husband of TIAMAT.

APT: see ALEITHEIA.

ARACHNE: Greek spider goddess. A Lydian girl skilled in weaving, she dared to challenge ATHENE to compete with her. The contest was held, and Arachne's work was faultless: impudently, it portrayed some of the gods' less reputable deeds, including Athene's father Zeus abducting EUROPA. Furious, Athene turned her into a spider, doomed eternally to spin thread drawn from her own body. But the spider goddess is more archetypal than this story suggests: spinning and weaving the pattern of destiny like the MOERAE or the NORNS, and enthroned in the middle of her spiral-pathed stronghold like ARIANRHOD. Athene here represents Athenian patriarchal thinking, trying to discipline earlier Goddess-concepts.

ARADIA: Italian (Tuscany) witch goddess, surviving there into this century. Daughter of DIANA (Etruscan, Aritimi or TANA) and Diana's brother Lucifer (i.e. of the Moon and Sun), she came to Earth to teach the witches her mother's magic. A favourite Goddess-name in the modern Wiccan revival movement. See Chapter XXII for her full story.

ARAMATI: Hindu goddess of devotion and piety.

ARANI: Hindu goddess of fire, including female sexual fire; her symbol is the swastika or fire-wheel. Her rituals seem to have included female masturbatory and/or lesbian practices.

ARA-SESHAP: An early Egyptian goddess of light.

ARDHANARISHWAR: An ancient hermaphrodite deity of South India and Madras.

ARDVI SURA ANAHITA: see AHURANI, THE.

ARETHUSA: Greek. A nymph with whom the river god Alphaeus fell in love. ARTEMIS turned her into a spring to help her escape him, but Alphaeus pursued her underground to Sicily, where their waters mingled. She emerged as a fountain on the island of Ortygia in Syracuse harbour. According to one account, she told DEMETER of Hades' abduction of PERSEPHONE.

ARETIA: Chaldaean Earth goddess. In the Hebrew form Aretz, she appears in the Bible in the book of Ezra. (See also ADAMAH.)

ARIADNE: Cretan and Greek. The daughter of King Minos of Crete, who with her cunning thread helped Theseus find his way into the labyrinth to kill the Minotaur, and out again. She eloped with him, but he abandoned her on the island of Naxos. She was consoled by Dionysus, who in her Naxos cult was regarded as her consort. Festival: 26 December.

ARIANRHOD: ('Silver Wheel') Major Welsh goddess. Mother of Llew Llau Gyffes by her brother Gwydion. Her consort Nwyvre ('Sky, Space, Firmament') has survived in name only. Caer Arianrhod is the circumpolar stars, to which souls withdraw between incarnations; she is thus a goddess of reincarnation. Honoured at the Full Moon. See Chapter XXI for her full story.

ARNAKNAGSAK: see SEDNA.

ARSAI: Canaanite Earth and Nature goddess in her Maid aspect; 'The Girl of Earth'. A Triple Goddess with her sisters PIDRAI, Maiden of Light, and TALLAI, Maiden of Rain.

ARSINOE: Greek/Egyptian. Wife and sister of King Ptolemy Philadelphos. She was deified and identified with both APHRODITE and ISIS, with a temple at Zephyrion on the Egyptian coast.

ARTEMIS: Greek Nature and Moon goddess. Daughter of Zeus and LETO, and twin sister of Apollo (though a day older). She probably absorbed a pre-Indo-European Sun goddess, and her twinning in classical legend with the Sun god Apollo may stem from this. The Greeks assimilated her to a pre-Greek mistress of wild beasts. Bears were sacred to her, and she was associated with the constellation Ursa Major. Guinea-fowl were her birds. Doreen Valiente (*An ABC of Witchcraft*, p.18) says her name may mean 'High Source of Water' – the Moon being regarded as the source and ruler of all waters, and of the oceanic, psychic and menstrual tides. 'Hence the moon goddess, by whatever name she was known, was the mistress of magic, enchantment and sorcery' (*ibid.*). Invoked by women in childbirth, as Artemis Eileithyia. Protectress of youth, especially of girls. Invoked to bring good weather to travellers. She is depicted with bow and arrows and often with a hound. One of her forms was CALLISTO. In Sparta her dark aspect was worshipped as Taurian Artemis with annual human sacrifices, until King Lycurgus modified this to ritual flagellation. Other names for her were Cynthia, Delia, Phoebe, PYTHIA and Parthenos – unmarried, virgin in the sense of 'her own woman', subject to no male; not celibate, because she often appears in myths enshrining dying-god rituals. 'There was no public worship of Artemis the Chaste' (Sir J.G. Frazer). The many breasted Artemis of Ephesus ('Diana of the Ephesians' of Acts xix) where her temple as a fertility goddess was one of the Seven Wonders of the ancient world, is much closer to her pre-Greek Great Mother function. Her cult there was said to go back to the Amazons. *777*: Tarot, Nines, High Priestess, Temperance; gems, quartz, moonstone, pearl, crystal, jacinth; plants, banyan, mandrake, damiana, almond, mugwort, hazel, moonwort, ranunculus, rush; animals, elephant, dog, centaur, horse, hippogriff; mineral, lead; perfumes, jasmine, ginseng, all odiferous roots, menstrual blood, camphor, aloes, all sweet virginal odours; magical weapons, Perfumes, Sandals, Bow and Arrow. Festivals: 12 February and the sixth day from the New Moon. Roman equivalent, DIANA.

ARTIO: Early Continental Celtic goddess of a bear clan who may have been the consort of Essus, agricultural god of the Essuvi. Worshipped in Switzerland at Berne (which means 'Bears'). Depicted sitting by a tree in front of a huge bear, with a basket of fruit beside her; a mother goddess of plenty.

ARU, ARURU, NINTU: Sumerian goddess who with Marduk created 'the seed of mankind'. In later patriarchal times, Marduk created mankind by himself. Mother of Gilgamesh; in the Gilgamesh legend she created the hero Enkidu by pinching clay in the image of the god Anu and casting it onto the Earth.

ASGAYA-GIGAGEI: Amerindian, bisexual thunder god/goddess of the Cherokees, known as 'the Red Man' or 'the Red Woman'.

ASHA POORNA: ('Hope Fulfilled') Hindu. Tutelary goddess of the Chohans.

ASHERA, ASHERAT: Canaanite (originally Assyrian) mother goddess, wife of Baal, also appearing (as Asherat-of-the-Sea) as his mother. Asherat-of-the-Sea was called 'Mother of the Gods' (with seventy children) and was the counsellor of the Supreme god El. She tends to merge with ANAT and ASTARTE. Day: Saturday – significantly, the Hebrew Sabbath. Dr Raphael Patai (see Bibliography) shows that for 240 of the 360 years that Solomon's Temple lasted at Jerusalem, Ashera was worshipped in it along with Jehovah as his bride and sister, and her wooden image was publicly displayed. When Elijah slaughtered the 400 priests of Baal on Mount Carmel, he left those of Ashera unmolested. She represented the old farming population of Israel. The tribe of Asher was named after her; it was the most sea-conscious of the Twelve, holding a coastal strip about fifty-five miles long and no more than ten miles wide, centred on Acre, so it might well regard Asherat-of-the-Sea as mother of all. The conventionalized tree which was her symbol was also known as an 'Ashera'.

ASHIMA: Samaritan Moon goddess.

ASHIMA BAETYL: see ANATHA BAETYL.

ASHNAN: Sumerian and Chaldaean goddess of grain and cultivated fields, created by Enlil at the same time as Lahar, the cattle god.

ASHTART: Phoenician, sister and wife of Cronus, to whom she bore Eros. Cronus made her one of the rulers of Phoenicia, and she chose a bull's head as her royal insignia. Referred to in the Old Testament as Ashtaroth. Reputation for lasciviousness. Ashtart-of-the-Sky-of-Baal was the planet Venus. Tends to merge with ASHERA and ASTARTE.

ASIA (1): Greek. Mother by Iapetus (whom Robert Graves equates with the Biblical Japhet) of Atlas and Prometheus. The 'Land of Asia' was the modern Turkey-in-Asia.

ASIA (2): Guinea. Earth goddess of the Agni tribes of Indene and Sanwi.

ASRI: ('Mishap') Hindu goddess of misfortune.

ASTARTE, ATHTARAT: Canaanite version of ISHTAR; fertility goddess. Chief goddess of Tyre and Sidon. Astarte was also the Greek form of the name ASHTART. Tends to merge with ASHERAT and ANAT, and with the Egyptian HATHOR. She came to Egypt; Rameses II had a temple to her, and she and ISIS were said to be firm friends. Like Anat and Hathor, she was a suckler of kings. Associated with the planet Venus. The Greeks transferred her role in the Adonis story to APHRODITE. A cult of Astarte and Tyrian Herakles, served by priestesses, existed in London, Carlisle and Corbridge, Northumberland, in Roman times, probably connected with the presence of Eastern traders. Festival, 23 April. Days, Friday and Saturday. Also the name of the Queen of Byblos to whose baby son Isis, in disguise, acted as nurse during her search for Osiris's coffin.

ASTRAEA: Greek, daughter of Zeus and THEMIS (or of Astraeus and EOS). Goddess of justice and purity, she abandoned the Earth in disgust at its violence at the end of the Golden Age, and became the constellation Virgo.

ASVA: ('Mare') Hindu dawn goddess, envisaged as a mare; another form of USHAS.

ASYNJOR, THE: Teutonic. Female attendants of FRIGG in Vingolf, Hall of the Goddesses. Sometimes they are taken to include the VALKYRIES and the NORNS.

ATABEI: Haiti. Mother of sky god Joca-huva.

ATAENTSIC: Amerindian, Iroquois and Huron. Mother of Breath of Wind, who gave birth to twins who fought in her womb, causing her death. From her body she made the Sun and the Moon, which were set in the sky by Master of Winds, Breath of Wind's husband.

ATALANTA: Greek. Her legend overlaps that of ARTEMIS. A Nature and hunting goddess, who would only marry the man who could beat her in a race; those whom she defeated had to die. Melanion (also called Hippomenes) won her by the trick of dropping the three golden apples which APHRODITE had given him; by pausing to pick them up, lost the race and married him. The couple were later turned into lions for profaning a temple of Zeus; another patriarchal demotion? She was the cause of the death of the hero Meleager, in circumstances strongly suggesting the sacrificed god theme; and the name of her son (some say by Meleager himself) was Parthenopaeus. This (like the Irish Aengus mac Og – see BOANN) means 'son of a virgin', not in the celibate sense but denoting a woman or goddess in her own right, not a mere consort.

ATANUA: ('Dawn') Polynesian, Marquesas. Daughter of ATEA after Atea became a male god. She also bore him many children. Her amniotic fluid from a miscarriage is one explanation of the origin of the sea.

ATARYATIS DERKETO: Babylonian fish goddess of Askalon, said to have been the divine mother, by the god of wisdom Oannes, of Semiramis, a historical Queen of Babylon.

ATE: Greek. Daughter of Eris or of Zeus. A trouble-making goddess, prompting men and gods to irresponsibility. She even tricked Zeus into an imprudent vow at Heracles' birth, and Zeus banished her to Earth – but sent two of his other daughters, the Litae, to follow her around and try to mitigate the trouble she caused. The Litae were wrinkled and lame, and anyone who welcomed them with respect was showered with blessings.

ATEA: ('Vast-Expanse', 'Light') Polynesian. The goddess who filled the dome of the sky when the world was created. After the birth of her son Tane, she changed sex and became a male god.

ATERGATIS: Originally a Syrian goddess of generation and fertility, she spread farther and acquired other characteristics such as wisdom and destiny. Overlaps with ISHTAR. As Dea Syria, her cult reached Egypt, Rome, the Danubian provinces, and even Britain. Often depicted with a snake or having a fish's tail; fish were sacred to her.

ATHENE, ATHENA: Greek, a warrior goddess, yet also one of intelligence and the arts of peace. Protector of towns, above all of Athens. Protector of heroes and patroness of architects, sculptors, spinners and weavers, and said to have invented the plough and the flute. Born fully armed from the head of Zeus after he had swallowed METIS, who was pregnant by him. Depicted helmeted, with shield and spear, and wearing the *aegis* (a kind of cape breastplate). Her cult animal was the owl, and the oak and the olive were sacred to her. Festivals: 19-23 March (the Lesser Panathenaea), 25 December (Day of the Geniae), the third day from the New Moon and the sixth day from the Full Moon. *777*: Tarot, Twos, Emperor, Star, World; gems, ruby, star ruby, turquoise, onyx, artificial glass; plants, amaranth, tiger lily, geranium, olive, coconut, ash, cypress, yew, hellebore, nightshade; animals, man, ram, owl, eagle, peacock, crocodile; minerals, phosphorus, lead; perfumes, musk, dragon's blood, galbanum, asafoetida, scammony, indigo, sulphur; magical weapons, Inner Robe of Glory, Horns, Energy, Burin, Censer, Aspergillum, Sickle. Roman equivalent: MINERVA.

ATHTARAT: see ASTARTE.

ATHTOR: Egyptian. Personification of Mother Night, the primordial element covering the infinite abyss.

ATIRA: Amerindian, Pawnee. Wife of creator god Tirawa.

ATROPOS: see MOERAE, THE.

ATTAR: Morning Star (Venus), goddess of Southern Arabia.

AUCHIMALGEN: Chile. Moon goddess of the Araucanians, and their only beneficent deity. Wife of the Sun. Protectress against disasters and evil spirits.

AUDHUMLA: Teutonic. A primordial cow goddess in the creation legend, wet-nurse of the giants. According to the Prose Edda, 'four rivers of milk ran from her teats'.

AUKERT: Egyptian. A name for the underworld, and sometimes personified as a goddess.

AUNT PIETY: Chinese goddess of the magical arts. May appear as a woman or as a vixen.

AURORA: see EOS.

AVILAYOQ: Eskimo. The mother of the human race by her husband, a dog. Her father threw her into the sea as a sacrifice to calm a storm; she grabbed at the gunwale of his boat, and he chopped off her fingers and put out one eye. Her fingers became the seals, whales, and other sea animals. She herself became the goddess SEDNA.

AXO-MAMA: Peruvian potato-mother.

AYA: Assyro-Babylonian dawn goddess, consort of the Sun god Shamash, and mother of Misharu, god of law and order, and Kittu, god of justice.

AYIZAN: Haitian Voodoo. The first priestess, with Loco the first priest. They are the most important of the ancestral *loa* (divinities). Both are closely associated with the creator Sun god Legba; she is sometimes called Legba's wife and sometimes Loco's, and Loco is 'chief of Legba's escort'. She is patroness of the public square and market-place, and also of initiation rituals, and is the *loa* of the psychic womb of mankind. Loco and Aziyan are 'the moral parents of the human race, not only in the sense of source or origin, but even more emphatically, in the sense of guardians', and as well as being teachers, they are 'the major healers of the pantheon'. (Deren, *Divine Horsemen*, p.143.) She in particular protects against malevolent magic. Her symbol is the palm leaf.

AZ: A Persian demoness of lust and greed.

BAALAT: ('The Lady') Phoenician general name for a goddess (as Baal,

'Lord', was for a god), particularly of a town or locality, e.g. the Baalat of
Byblos, who overlaps with the Egyptian HATHOR; she is portrayed with a
disc-and-horns headdress. See also BELTIS.

BAAU: Phoenician. Personified primordial substance, and night. Mother of the
gods. The Phoenician creation legend calls her the wife of the wind god
Kolpia and the mother of Aion ('Life') and Protogonos ('Firstborn'). See also
BAU.

BABELAH: Babylonian. Goddess personifying Babylon (also in the Hebrew
Bible). Regarded by Moslems as the personification of black magic. Some
connection with TIAMAT.

BACHUE: Colombia. Water goddess, protectress of vegetation and harvests.

BADHBH, BADB: ('Scald-crow') Irish war goddess, wife of Net, war god;
daughter of ERNMAS and Delbaeth and sister of MACHA, MORRIGAN
and ANU. In some contexts, Anu, Badhbh and Macha appear as a Triple
Goddess of Fate, collectively known as the Morrigan. Badhbh was known in
Gaul as CAUTH BODVA.

BAHU: ('Abundant') Hindu. The Creative Mother, seen as the constellation
Leo or the star Denebola.

BALTIS: see DIONE.

BANANA-MAIDEN, THE: Celebes. Represents the transitory principle, in
contrast to her sister the Rock-Maiden, representing the durable.

BANBHA: Irish, one of the three queens of the Tuatha Dé Danann, daughters
of the Dagda, who asked that Ireland be named after them. Wife of Mac
Cuill, Son of the Hazel, 'whose god was the sea'. According to one version,
she was the first woman who found Ireland before the Flood; according to
another, she came over with CESARA. She told Amergin: 'I am older than
Noe; on a peak of a mountain was I in the Flood.' See page 33.

BANSHEE: (*Bean sidhe*, 'Woman Fairy') Irish. Attached to old Irish families
('the O's and the Mac's'), she can be heard keening sorrowfully near the
house when a member of the family is about to die. Still very much believed
in, and heard. We have heard her ourselves in Co. Wexford; next day the
neighbours would be asking each other whom the Banshee had been crying
for, and finding out who had in fact died during the night. One of our
witches, born and raised in Co. Donegal, has a Banshee attached to his
family and has heard her often at the appropriate times.

BAST, BASTET: Egyptian cat goddess of Bubastis in the Delta as early as the
2nd Dynasty, about 3200 BC; when Bubastis was the capital in the 22nd
Dynasty, about 950 BC, she became a national deity. Originally lion-headed,
she represented the beneficent power of the Sun, in contrast to SEKHMET
who personified its destructive power. Cats were domesticated very early by
the Egyptians, being valued as snake-destroyers (the Delta in particular was
infested with snakes). They became much loved, and sacred, often being
carefully mummified at death; Bubastis had a huge cat cemetery. (One

Roman visitor to Bubastis who unwisely killed a cat was lynched by the horrified citizens.) One tradition said Bast accompanied by the Sun god Ra's 'boat of a million years' on its daily journey through the sky, and at night fought Ra's enemy, the serpent Apep. She was said to be Ra's daughter (or sister) and wife, bearing him the lion-headed god Maahes. A kindly goddess of joy, music and dancing; her rituals included light-hearted barge processions and orgiastic ceremonies. She also protected men against contagious diseases and evil spirits. Like SEKHMET (whom, as other-self, she sometimes overlaps) she became wife of Ptah of Memphis; their son Nefertum completing the Memphis Triad. She is depicted as a cat-headed woman, carrying a sistrum and basket, or as a whole cat. Often, in either form, there are kittens at her feet. Her city of Bubastis is mentioned as Pi-beseth in Ezekiel xxx:17.

BASULI: Hindu. An aboriginal Goddess of Orissa, represented in the Kandagir caves as standing nude on a lotus.

BAU, BOHU, BAHU, GUR: Chaldaean and Assyro-Babylonian primeval goddess, the Dark Waters of the Deep. Mother of the Water god Ea (Enki). Later regarded as the wife of the irrigation god Ningirsu (Ninurta); their marriage was celebrated at the Babylonian New Year, at the end of harvest. Name also sometimes given to the Earth goddess GA-TUM-DUG. See also BAAU.

BAUBO: Ptolemaic Egyptian. A fertility figure depicted displaying her genitals in the attitude of a SHEILA-NA-GIG. Baubos were found in women's rooms, apparently connected with a Bubastis women's fecundity and childbirth cult.

BEAN-NIGHE ('Washing Woman'): Scottish and Irish. Haunts lonely streams washing the bloodstained garments of those about to die. A Bean-Nighe is said to be the spirit of a woman who has died in childbirth, fated to act thus until the day she would have died normally.

BEFANA: ('Epiphany') Italian witch-fairy who flies her broomstick on Twelfth Night to come down chimneys and bring presents to children.

BELILI: An early Sumerian Underworld goddess, subordinate to ERESHKIGAL. Also a goddess of the Moon and of love. Sister and Wife of Tammuz. See also BELTIS.

BELISMA: British and Continental Celtic lake or river goddess. Ptolemy gives her name to the River Ribble in Yorkshire and Lancashire. Equated by the Romans with MINERVA.

BELIT-ILANIT: Chaldaean goddess of love, who draws men and women together. Erotic, kind, and peaceful. An evening star goddess.

BELIT-ILI: Assyro-Babylonian protectress of newborn babies. Also called Nintud.

BELIT-SHERI, NIN-EDIN: ('Lady of the Wilderness') Assyro-Babylonian scribe goddess, who sat with ERESHKIGAL in the Underworld and kept the records of the dead.

BELLONA: Roman battle goddess, wife or sister of Mars. She had a shrine at York. Festivals: 24 March (Dies Sanguinis, the Day of Blood) and 3 June.

BELTIS: ('The Lady') Assyro-Babylonian, originally Sumerian. Wife of Bel, of which the name is a feminine form; she thus overlaps BAALAT, and also

BELILI, BELIT-ILI and BELIT-SHERI. Variously a goddess of the Moon, of love, of the planet Venus, of the Underworld, of wells and springs, and of trees. Invoked when a building was completed. Depicted full-face, heavily built especially the hips, almost naked, cupping her breasts with her hands and wearing a fan-shaped headdress.

BENDIS: Greek, Thracian Hellespont. A Moon goddess, wife of the Sun god Sabazius. Worshipped with orgiastic rites. Thracians made her popular in Attica, and in 430/429 BC her cult became a state ceremonial in Athens, with torch-races at the Piraeus.

BENE: Apparently a Carthaginian name for VENUS, applied to their own TANIT. Durdin-Robertson (*Goddesses of Chaldaea*, p.138) points out the similarity to the Irish word *bean* (woman). Other similarities include *tine* (Carthaginian) and *teine* (Irish) for fire, and the gods Baal (Carthaginian), Bel or Beli (Welsh) and Balor (Irish). Bealtaine (the fire of Balor) may well have a Carthaginian root, or at least a common source.

BENSOZIA: see BENZOZIA.

BENTEN, BENZAITEN, BENZAI-TENNYO: Japanese goddess of love, eloquence, music, luck and wealth. The only female member of the Seven Deities of Luck, who are said to sail into harbour on New Year's Eve in the Takara-bune, or Treasure Ship. Pictures of the Treasure Ship are sold in the streets at New Year. Originally a Hindu river goddess. Patroness of merchants, gamblers, actors and geishas. She rides a dragon which she is said to have captivated and married to stop it devouring children. She plays the biwa (a kind of guitar); her messenger is the snake. Depicted as very beautiful, ornately dressed, sometimes carrying a sword and the jewel that grants desires. Sometime shown as eight-armed, doubtless betraying her Hindu origin. Japanese women often carry charms in her form to make themselves beautiful and accomplished.

BENZOZIA: A Basque mother goddess. As Bensozia, also a medieval witch goddess name; may mean 'good neighbour', a common name for the fairies.

BERA PENNU: see TARI PENNU.

BERCHTA: ('White Lady') Teutonic, goddess of marriage and fecundity, south German equivalent of HULDA. Christianity turned her into a bogy to frighten children.

BERECYNTIA: Another name for CYBELE, but seems also to have been used by the Gauls as a name for BRIGHID.

BERUTH: Phoenician primordial mother goddess, wife of Eliun ('the All-Highest') and in one version the mother of Uranus and Ge (GAIA). Originally from Byblos, she became the goddess of Berith, the modern Beirut.

BESTLA: Teutonic. Daughter of Ymir (father of all the giants) or of Bolthorn ('Evil Thorn') and wife of Bor, by whom she was the mother of Odin, Vili and Ve.

BETHULTA: Hebrew name for the constellation Virgo. Associated with abundance at harvest. Assigned by the Rabbis to the tribe of Asher, of whom Jacob had said, 'His bread shall be fat, and he shall yield royal dainties' (Genesis xlix:20) (see also ASHERA).

BHAIRAVI: Hindu, 'the terrible'. See PARVATI.

BHARATI: A Hindu goddess of speech, identified with SARASVATI.

BHATTA: A Hindu goddess of sorcery.

BHAVANI, BHOWANI, PARASU-PANI: Hindu and Tantric-mother goddess, known as the Triple Universe. Depicted with the Sun and Moon at her breasts, or as a young woman crowned, containing within her body a landscape showing the sea, the Sun and the Moon. Other depictions show her as a dark form of PARVATI, with a necklace of skulls. Festival: Diwali, the Feast of Lamps, on the New Moon of Kartik (October/November). *777*: Tarot, Threes; gems, star sapphire, pearl; plants, cypress, opium poppy; animal, woman; mineral, silver; perfumes, myrrh, civet; magical weapons, yoni, Outer Robe of Concealment.

BHUMI: Hindu Earth goddess, conceived of as one of seven sisters, following the Vedic view that there are three Heavens, three Earths and a fourth Earth which is Bhumi. The mother of all living. Also mother of the planet Mars. Associated, along with LAKSHMI, with Vahara, the boar avatar of Vishnu. Sometimes equated with PRIVTHI.

BIBI MIRIAM: ('Lady Mary') In some parts of India the VIRGIN MARY is regarded as a goddess and included in the Hindu pantheon under this name. Kipling refers to 'a goddess called Mary'.

BIL: Nordic. One of the ASYNJOR. Seems to be the origin of Jill of the nursery rhyme. Hjuki and Bil were returning from the spring with a bucket of water when the Moon god Mani seized them, and they have followed him ever since, visible from Earth. May recall a pair of asteroids between the Moon and Earth which have long disappeared.

BINAH: ('Understanding') Hebrew. The Supernal Mother, third Sephirah of the Cabalistic Tree of Life. She takes the raw directionless energy of Chokmah, the Supernal Father (the second Sephira), and gives it form and manifestation; she is thus both the Bright Mother, AIMA (nourishing) and the Dark Mother, AMA (constricting). The first Heh of the Tetragrammaton, in polarity with the Yod of Chokmah. She represents the female potency of the cosmos, as Chokmah represents the male. Cabalistic symbols: the yoni, the kteis, the Vesica Piscis, the cup, the Outer Robe of Concealment. Tarot: Threes. Magical image: a mature woman.

BIRRAHGNOOLOO: Australian Aborigine, High Plains and South-East. One of the wives of Baiame, the All-Father, whom he elevated to be Mother-of-All, to live with him in the sky for all time. Each of them had a totem for each part of the body, so that no one totem-clan might claim them exclusively. But his most important co-creator was YHI, the Sun goddess.

BIRRA-NULU: Australian aborigine, High Plains and South-East. One of two young wives whom Baiame, the All-Father, married while he was resting on Mount Oobi-oobi in Bullima after creating the world; the other was Kunnan-beili. They were flightly and disobedient and caused him a lot of trouble.

BLACK ANNIS: Leicestershire; possibly Scandinavian origin. She lived in the Dane Hills and ate children. She was concerned with a May Eve hare-hunt, later transferred to Easter Monday, 'and therefore must have been nymph as well as hag' (Graves, *The White Goddess*, p.370). Graves also suggests that she derives from ANU. See also GODIVA.

BLACK HAG: see WHITE HAG.

BLATHNAT: Irish. Daughter of Midir, King of the Gaelic Underworld. She helped Cuchulainn steal her father's magic cauldron.

BLODEUWEDD: ('Flower Face') Welsh. Made from flowers of oak, broom and meadowsweet by Math and Gwydion as a wife for Lleu, who could not have a wife 'of the race that is now on earth'. She was unfaithful to him with Gronw, lord of Penllyn. She was changed into an owl, in which form she still mourns her lover. A type of the man-made image of woman who rebels against the imposed stereotypes; cf. EVE.

BOANN: Irish. Goddess of the River Boyne, mother of Aengus mac Óg by the Dagda. 'Mac Óg' means 'Son of the Virgin' – in the old sense of one who is an independent woman or goddess in her own right, and not a mere consort. Her mating with the Dagda was on 1 November, doubtless a memory of a Samhain fertility ritual involving the chief or king; the Dagda also mated with the MORRIGAN in the River Unius in Connacht on 1 November. One source gives Boann as daughter of Delbaeth son of Elada, and wife of Nechtan son of Nama. Perhaps originally a titular priestess of the Boyne's source, which was said to be a pool where the Salmon of Knowledge fed on nuts dropping from the nine hazel trees surrounding it.

BONA DEA: ('Good Goddess') Roman Earth goddess of fertility, worshipped only by women; even statues of men were covered where her rites took place. Festivals: 1 May, the night of 3-4 May and 3 December. Day: Wednesday.

BRANWEN: Manx/Welsh. Daughter of Llyr and sister of Bran the Blessed (Bendigeifran). She married Matholwch, King of Ireland, who ill-treated her; Bran set out with an army of the men of Britain to avenge her. They defeated the Irish but Bran was mortally wounded. Branwen and his friends took his head to Harlech for seven years, where it continued to talk with them, and the birds of RHIANNON sang to them; then for eighty years to Gwales (Grassholm?) in Penvro (Pembroke); and finally, in accordance with his wish, they took it to London and buried it on the White Hill (either Tower Hill or where St Paul's now stands).

BRIBSUN: see DOL JYANG.

BRIGANTIA: Eponymous goddess of north British Kingdom; = BRIGHID. Gave name to River Brent (Middlesex).

BRIGHID, BRIGID, BRIGIT, BRÍD: (*Breo-saighead*, 'Fiery Arrow', or *Brigh*, 'Power'). Known in Gaul as Brigindo, and in other parts of the Continent as Brigan and Brig. Irish goddess of fertility and inspiration, daughter of the Dagda; called 'the poetess'. Often triple ('The Three Brigids'). Eponymous goddess of Brigantia (north Britain). May ultimately derive from BRIZO. Her characteristics, legends and holy places were taken over by the historical St Bridget. Festival: 1 February, in Ireland traditionally the first day of Spring. See Chapter XIV for her full story.

BRIGITTE, MAMAN BRIGITTE: Haitian Voodoo. Female counterpart of Ghede (Baron Samedi), god of death, eroticism and resurrection.

BRIMO: An ancient Greek fertility goddess, known from the cry in the Eleusinian rituals: 'The noble goddess has borne a sacred child: Brimo has borne Brimos.'

BRITANNIA: Goddess personifying Britain. Perhaps a combination of a root meaning British, and ANU. First struck on British coins by the Romans.

Revived by Charles II in 1667, the model being (according to Brewer's *Dictionary of Phrase and Fable*) his mistress Barbara Villiers, whom he made Duchess of Cleveland; other sources say it was Frances Stuart, Duchess of Richmond.

BRITOMARTIS: ('Sweet Virgin') Cretan. Daughter of Zeus, virgin huntress in the forests of Crete. Minos desired her, but she rejected him and after a nine-month flight finally escaped him by throwing herself off a cliff into the sea, where she fell into a fisherman's net; whence the Greeks called her Dictynna, 'goddess of the nets', though DICTYNNA is a different goddess in Cretan myth. She appeared during the night to navigators. May have been the Maiden aspect of the Cretan mother goddess RHEA. The Greek version says she was saved from drowning, and turned into a goddess, by ARTEMIS, with whom she became identified. (Inspired the name of the Welsh heroine Britomart – see Spenser's *Faerie Queene*.)

BRIZO: ('Enchantress') Greek. A Moon goddess of Delos, to whom votive ships were offered. May be the root of BRIGHID.

BRUNISSEN: ('Brown Queen') The heroine of a Provençal legend, a beautiful orphan grieving in seclusion in a palace with an orchard. Probably originally a Celtic Sun goddess – not the Sun of the living world 'but rather the "black sun" of the Other World, which shines more brightly at sunrise and sunset' (Markale, *Women of the Celts*, p.112).

BRYNHILD: Teutonic. In the Niebelungenlied, a VALKYRIE, banished from Valhalla when she offended Odin; he sent her to sleep in a ring of fire, from which the hero Sigurd (Siegfried) rescued her and married her (trace of an initiation ritual?). But in the Volsung Cycle Sigurd won her for Gunnar (Gunther), whom she married; in anger at Sigurd's deceit, she had him killed and then killed herself.

BUANNAN: see SCATHACH.

BUDDHA KROTISHAURIMA: Tibetan mother goddess.

BUDDHI: Hindu and Tibetan. In India the wife, along with Siddhi, of Ganesa, elephant-headed god of good fortune; she represents intellect and intuition, while Siddhi represents achievement. In Tibetan teaching, she is one of the agents of reincarnation, along with Chit.

BULLAI-BULLAI: Australian aborigine, High Plains and South-East. Her lover Weedah was turned into the star Canopus by his old and ugly rival's magic. Baiame the All-Father consoled her by turning her into the beautiful parrot, so that she could look up and admire her lover in the sky and he could look down and admire her on Earth.

BUTO: see UADJET.

CABIRO, CABIRA: Phoenician primordial mother; a Mystery goddess about whom details were deliberately vague. Probably daughter of ASTARTE and Cronus, sister of Eros, and wife of Hephaestus. Among her daughters were the three Cabirian Nymphs, who may be herself in triple form.

CAILLEACH BEINE BRIC: A Scottish legendary witch probably recalling an earlier local goddess.

CAKSUSI: Hindu. An APSARA whose name means 'Clairvoyante'.

CALLIOPE: see MUSES.

CALLISTO: ('Most Beautiful') Greek Moon goddess, to whom the she-bear was sacred in Arcadia (named after her son Arcas). Envisaged as the axle on which everything turns, and thus connected with the Ursa Major constellation. 'In Greek the Great Bear Callisto was also called Helice, which means both "that which turns" and "willow-branch" – a reminder that the willow was sacred to the same Goddess' (Graves, *The White Goddess*, p.179). At her festival, two little girls dressed as bears rushed savagely at the boys taking part. Graves infers that this was a Midsummer sacrificial-mating ritual. Linked with ARTEMIS; often called Artemis Callisto.

CAMPESTRES, THE: Mother goddesses of Celtic cavalry in the Roman army. Worshipped at Hardknott and Maryport in Cumberland, Benwell in Northumberland, and Tomen-y-mur in Merionethshire.

CARDEA: Roman. According to Ovid, guardian of door-hinges – i.e., of the home – and of children against evil spirits. Graves (*The White Goddess*, p.68) says Ovid's was a later version; she had originally been a predatory goddess who destroyed children, taking a bird or beast form; the hawthorn was sacred to her, which was why it must not be brought indoors. (Cf. ALPHITO who developed in the opposite direction.) The 'hinge' symbolism is that she was a turn-of-the-year goddess, and in charge of the four cardinal winds.

CARMAN: Irish. Wexford goddess, whence Gaelic name of Wexford, Loch Garman (Loch gCarman). May have a Phoenician or Greek connection; one source says three men from Athens, with their mother, came to Wexford Bay to settle, and that Greek merchants traded at the Fair of Carman. Festival: 1 August.

CARMENTA, CARMENTIS: Roman goddess of childbirth and prophecy; her festivals on 11 and 15 January were important ones for Roman matrons. A triple goddess with her two sisters Porrima or Antevorta 'Looking Forward') and Postvorta ('Looking Back'). Inventress of the arts and sciences. According to Graves (*The White Goddess*, pp.228, 230), also inventress of the Roman alphabet; she gave her son Evander the consonants but kept the vowels for herself.

CARNEA: Roman, identified by Ovid with CARDEA. Festival, 1 June, when pig's flesh and beans were offered to her. 'The bean is the White Goddess's – hence its connection with the Scottish witch cult; in primitive times only her priestesses might either plant or cook it' (Graves, *The White Goddess*, p.69).

CARPET SNAKE WOMAN: Australian aborigine. Lives in a cave on Ayer's Rock, where women in labour go to ensure an easy delivery.

CASSIOPEIA: Greek. Wife of Cepheus, King of Joppa (modern Jaffa) or, in other versions, of Ethiopia. She boasted that she was more beautiful than the NEREIDS, and as a punishment Poseidon sent a sea-monster to whom she had to sacrifice her daughter Andromeda. Perseus killed the monster and married Andromeda. Mother and daughter became the constellations which bear their names.

CAUTH BODVA: ('War-Fury') Gaulish version of BADHBH. Latinized as Cathuboduae.

CEITHLENN: Irish. Wife of Balor, the old god who appears in legend as King of the Fomors. Can be equated with DANA, who is more usually named as Balor's wife.

CERES: Roman corn goddess, originally from Campania. Became entirely assimilated to the Greek DEMETER. Festivals: 2 February, 1 and 11-19 April, 1 and 24 August, 23 September-1 October, 4-5 October, 8 November, 3 December. Days: Wednesday and Friday. *777*: Tarot, Hermit; gem: peridot; plants: snowdrop, lily, narcissus; animals: virgin, anchorite, any solitary person or animal; perfume: narcissus; magical weapons: Lamp, Wand, Bread.

CERRIDWEN: Welsh mother, Moon and grain goddess, wife of Tegid and mother of Creirwy (the most beautiful girl in the world) and Avagdu (the ugliest boy). Owner of an inexhaustible cauldron called Amen, in which she made a magic draught called 'greal' (Grail?) from six plants, which gave inspiration and knowledge. Gwion was ordered to stir it and accidentally splashed three drops onto his fingers; he sucked them and became possessed of all knowledge. Cerridwen pursued Gwion, both of them shape-changing; first she was a greyhound chasing a hare, then an otter chasing a fish, then a hawk chasing a bird. She finally caught and ate him when she was a hen and he was a grain of corn. As a result she gave birth to Taliesin, greatest of the Welsh bards. This chase may relate to the initiation rituals of a Druid or bard. One of her symbols was a sow. Most of her legends emphasize the terrifying aspect of the Dark Mother; yet her cauldron is the source of wisdom and inspiration.

CESARA, CESSAIR: Irish. In the mythological cycle, the first occupier of Ireland. Daughter of Bith son of Noah, who had sent them, and Bith's wife Birren and Cesara's husband Fintaan, 'to the western edge of the world' forty days before the Flood, to escape it. Cesara was in charge of the expedition. One account says they had rejected Noah's god and taken their own with them. Accompanying them were fifty (or 150) women who were originally the mothers of the various nations of the world. Cesara appears to be a goddess of pre-Celtic, matriarchal days.

CHALA, CHAPALA: Hindu goddess of fortune.

CHALCHIUHTLICUE: Aztec goddess of running water. Wife or sister of mountain god Tlaloc, to whom babies were sacrificed; but she herself was protectress of newborn children, marriages and chaste loves. Known as 'the Emerald Lady' and 'Five Times Flower Feather'.

CHANDERNAREE: see PINGALA.

CH'ANG-O or HENG-O: Chinese Moon goddess, represented as a very beautiful young woman. Wife of I, the Excellent Archer, who possessed the drink of immortality; she drank it secretly and fled to the Moon to escape his anger.

CHAPALA: see CHALA.

CHARITES, THE: Greek. Also known as the Graces. Daughters of Zeus and EURONYME (or of Dionysus and APHRODITE). Companions of the MUSES and embodiments of song, dance and happiness. They were Aglaia, 'the brilliant'; Euphrosyne, 'she who rejoices the heart'; and Thalia, 'she who brings flowers' (also named as one of the MUSES). They attended Aphrodite and helped with her toilet.

CHARYBDIS: see SCYLLA.

CHASCA: An Inca goddess who brought forth flowers and protected maidens. An attendant of the Sun god Inti, and identified with the planet Venus.

CHAUTUROPAYINI: Hindu fertility and healing goddess. Depicted as a four-armed vital-looking young woman, holding a vessel and making a gesture of giving.

CHHAYA, KHAYA: ('Shadow') Hindu. Wife or handmaid of the Sun god Surya, who stayed with him after his first wife SANJNA had left him; sometimes regarded as another form of Sanjna. Her body was etheric in substance. Mother of TAPATI, and also of the planet Saturn.

CHIA: Colombian Moon goddess. Originally the beautiful but mischievous wife of civilizing hero Bochica, who kept frustrating his plans by magic, at one stage flooding the whole world. He banished her to the sky, to light up the night. A goddess of women; if a man incurred her anger, he would dress as a woman to avoid it. Often confused with HUNTHACA.

CHICOMECOATL: Aztec maize goddess of rural plenty. Known as 'Seven Snakes'. Probably of Toltec origin.

CHIH-NII: ('Heavenly Weaver-Girl') Chinese. Goddess of the star Alpha in the Lyre. Daughter of the August Personage of Jade, for whom she wove seamless robes. Married to the Heavenly Cow-Herd (Beta and Gamma in Aquila), whom she loved so much that she neglected her weaving; in anger her father banished her to the Lyre, separated from her husband by the Milky Way, with permission to meet him once a year. Festival: 7 July.

CHIMAERA, THE: ('She-Goat') Greek. Daughter of ECHIDNE, a winter snake goddess, and the storm god Typhon. She had lion's head, a goat's body and a serpent's tail. She has come to mean 'an illusory vision'; in modern Greek χίμαιρα (khimaira) means 'Utopia' – and is still a feminine noun.

CHIMALMAT: A Mayan virgin who was breathed on by the Lord of Existence and so conceived.

CHIT: see BUDDHI.

CHIU T'IEN HSUAN-NU: ('Dark Maiden from the Ninth Heaven') A popular Chinese goddess, favourite subject of plays. A mortal fell in love with a picture of a beautiful girl. She came to life and married him, to spend a few years on Earth; she bore him a daughter and eventually disappeared back into the picture. In many stories she teaches the hero the art of fighting. (Note the combination of martial arts training and sexual intercourse; cf. SCATHACH.)

CIHUATCOATL: Aztec goddess of childbirth; sometimes friendly, sometimes hostile. Mother of Mixcoatl, the hunting (later a stellar) god. Known as 'Serpent Woman', and also called Tonantzin ('Our Mother').

CIRCE: ('She-Falcon') Greek. Goddess of Aeaea ('Wailing'), a sepulchral island in the North Adriatic. She turned men into swine, lions and wolves. At her festivals the women probably dressed as sows and the men as lions. In Homer's *Odyssey*, 'the beautiful Circe, a formidable goddess, though her voice is like a woman's,' turns Odysseus's crew into swine, but with Hermes's help he wards off her magic and himself remains a man. Then he goes 'with the goddess to her beautiful bed'. She changes the crew back into men, and they all stay for a year and a day before sailing on. But she warns them that before reaching home they will have to visit 'the Halls of Hades and Persephone the Dread'. She represents, to the patriarchal Greeks, both the danger and the seductiveness of the Goddess, and her alarming insistence that they penetrate the Underworld (the treasures of the Unconscious). Odysseus wisely uses Hermes (intellect) to come to terms with her, not to evade her. Willow trees were sacred to her (as to HERA, HECATE and PERSEPHONE).

CITALLINICUE: see ILAMATECUHTLI.

CLEITO: ('Key', 'Enclosed'?) Greek/Atlantean. According to Plato's account of Solon's interview with the Egyptian priest, she was the daughter of Evenor, 'one of the Earth-born primeval men' of Atlantis, and his wife Leucippe ('White Mare'). Poseidon fell in love with her, and they produced five pairs of male twins, between whom Poseidon divided the five areas of Atlantis.

CLIO: see MUSES.

CLIONA OF THE FAIR HAIR: Irish. South Munster goddess of great beauty, daughter of Gebann the Druid, of the Tuatha Dé Danann. Connected with the O'Keefe family.

CLOACINA: Roman goddess of drains and sewerage – a useful deity in overbuilt and overcrowded Rome. The city's greatest sewer was the Cloaca Maxima, draining the area of the Forum, where she had a temple. She was later assimilated to VENUS.

CLOTA: Scottish, goddess of the River Clyde.

CLOTHO: see MOERAE, THE.

COATLICUE: ('Serpent Skirt') Aztec goddess of the Moon and Earth, and the influence of the one upon the other; associated with Spring sowing festivals. Mother, by the star god Mixcoatl, of Huitzilopocchtli, war and storm god, who was born fully armed.

COCA-MAMA: Peruvian coca-mother.

CONCORDIA: Roman goddess of peace and civic harmony. Festivals: 16 and 22 January, 30 March, 1 April, 11 June.

COPACATI: Inca lake goddess, said to have submerged the temples of other gods beneath Lake Titicaca.

COTYS, COTYTTO: Greek, Thrace and Corinth; also Sicilian. Fertility goddess, worshipped with orgiastic nocturnal rites similar to those of DEMETER and CYBELE. Graves (*The White Goddess*, pp.61-2) suggests that many dynasties and tribes, from the Cotys kings in Thrace and Paphlagonia to the Cattini and Attacoti of north Britain, derive from her name.

COVENTINA: North British nymph goddess, cult centre the sacred spring at Carrawburgh on Hadrian's Wall, into which coins, brooches etc were thrown as offerings. Goddess of featherless flying creatures. Depicted reclining on a water-borne leaf, and sometimes triple. Traces also on the Continent.

CREIDDYLAD: Welsh form of the maiden over whom two rivals must battle 'every first of May until Doomsday'. Daughter of Llud, Nudd or Llyr (Lir). The original of Shakespeare's Cordelia, daughter of King Lear – interestingly, the only one who will not be obsequious to the father-figure and who marries the man of her own choice.

CUNDA, KUNDA: Indian Buddhist goddess, 'as propitious to the good as she is terrible to the wicked'. She has four or sixteen arms, and 'nothing is absent from her arsenal; but for the worshipper who knows how to look, her first pair of hands is in the position of teaching, another in that of charity' and so on.

CUPRA: Etruscan fertility goddess, probably the oldest of their pantheon. Her weapon was the thunderbolt.

CYBELE: Greek, originally Phrygian, finally merged with RHEA. Goddess of caverns, of the Earth in its primitive state; worshipped on mountain tops. Ruled over wild beasts. Also a bee goddess. Depicted with a turreted crown and flanked by two lions; sometimes holding a scourge of knuckle-bones – the instrument with which her priests, the Galli or Corybantes, flagellated themselves. These Galli would celebrate her rites with frenzied dances, often voluntarily castrating themselves. Associated with her was the vegetation god Attis, called by the Phrygians Papas (Father). Their relationship paralleled that of ISHTAR with Tammuz, or ASTARTE with Adonis. His Spring festival mourned his death and then rejoiced over his resurrection. Mother, by Gordios King of Phrygia, of Midas of the golden touch. Her symbol was a crescent Moon, often shown in perpetual union with the Sun. Festivals: 15 and 22-27 March, 4-10 April, 3 December. *777*: Tarot, Threes; gems, star sapphire, pearl; plants, cypress, opium poppy; animal, woman; mineral, silver; perfumes, myrrh, civet; magical weapons, Yoni, Outer Robe of Concealment.

CYHIRAETH: Welsh goddess of streams, who later became a forewarner of death, like the Irish BANSHEE.

DAHUD: Breton. Daughter of King Gradion of Cornwall, who built the splendid city of Ker-Ys ('City of the Depths') for her. A rebel against Christianity, and sexually uninhibited, she led the citizens of Ker-Ys in 'debauchery'. So Ker-Ys was overwhelmed by the sea – Gradion escaping with the help of St Gwennole. Fishermen still sometimes see Dahud swimming among shoals of fish, or glimpse Ker-Ys below when the sea is calm. If anyone buys something from its inhabitants, Ker-Ys will be restored to life; and the first man to see its church spire or hear its bells will become king of the city. Dahud is a form of the Submerged Princess archetype, the alluring and dangerous feminine principle, all too easily released by imprudent (or courageous) communication with it. (Cf. LIBAN).

DAIERA: Greek. 'The Wise one of the Sea', daughter of Oceanus, and mother of Eleusis, after whom the town of the Eleusinian Mysteries was said to be named. Identified with APHRODITE.

DAINICHI: Japanese, Buddhist. Goddess of purity and wisdom. Sometimes regarded as masculine.

DAKINI: Hindu. One of the six goddesses governing the six bodily substances; the others being Hakini, Kakini, Lakini, Rakini and Sakini. See also DAKINIS.

DAKINIS, THE; KADOMAS, THE: Tibetan, Tantric. Goddesses presiding over various psychic forces, invoked in Tantric Yoga rituals. They are of five orders (with their qualities, symbolic colours and compass points): Divine (Vajra) Dakinis, peaceableness and love, white or blue, East; Precious (Ratna) Dakinis, grandness and compassion, yellow, South; Lotus (Padma) Dakinis, fascination and affection, red, West; Action (Karma) Dakinis, sternness and impartiality, green, North; Understanding (Buddha) Dakinis, enlightenment, dark blue, Centre. Often called 'mothers' and described as majestically beautiful and graceful.

DAKSHINA: Hindu cow goddess, closely connected with the dawn goddess USHAS.

DAMARA: British fertility goddess, associated with the month of May.

DAMKINA: Antediluvian Babylonian Earth goddess, probably of Sumerian origin. Wife of Ea and mother of Marduk. Also called Ninella or Damku.

DAMONA: A Continental Celtic cow or sheep goddess.

DANA, DANU: The major Irish mother goddess, who gave her name to the Tuatha Dé Danann ('Peoples of the Goddess Dana'), the last but one occupiers of Ireland in the mythlogical cycle. Overlaps with ANU and equates with the Welsh DÔN. Daughter of Delbaeth and wife of Balor. Robert Graves argues that the Tuatha Dé Danann were Bronze Age Pelasgians expelled from Greece in the middle of the second millennium – a confederacy of tribes some of whom came to Ireland – and that Danu was originally the same goddess as DANAE and others with similar names. This would accord with Irish tradition as recorded in the *Lebor Gabála Érenn*.

DANAE: A pre-Greek barley goddess of Argos; Graves (*The White Goddess*, p.58) says she was the daughter of the early Sumerian goddess BELILI. By Homer's time she had been masculinized into Danaus and/or assimilated into DIANA or DIONE. In classical legend, Danae reappears in a complex multi-generation tale of patriarchal attempts to circumvent matrilinearity (see HYPERMNESTRA, her great-grandmother). In this Danaus is King of Argos and Danae his great-great-granddaughter, seduced by Zeus in the form of a shower of gold and giving birth to the hero Perseus – who follows the same theme by gaining a throne through marriage with the heiress Andromeda (see CASSIOPEIA).

DARK MAID, THE: Chinese goddess who sends frost and snow.

DEA DIA: Roman goddess of cornfields. Festivals: 1-3 and 17 May.

DEA HAMMIA: Worshipped by Syrian archers at the Roman camp at Caervorran, Northumberland. See also VIRGO CAELESTIS.

DEA SYRIA: see ATERGATIS, VIRGO CAELESTIS.

DE DEVELSKI: see AMARI DE.

DEIANEIRA: Greek, daughter of Dionysus and ALTHAEA, and wife of Heracles. He wrestled with a bull-headed snake (the River Achelous personified) to win her. He slew the snake and tore off one of its horns, which became the Cornucopia. At the wedding he 'accidentally' killed a cup-bearer, but the victim must originally have been the bride's father. Then he fought and killed the centaur Nessus, who tried to rape her. Before he died, Nessus gave her some of his blood as a charm to keep Heracles' love, by putting it on his shirt. But it was a poison which burned Heracles – 'a magical equivalent of the pyre upon which Heracles, recognizing and consenting to his fate, immolated himself upon Mount Oeta. He handed on to the man who lit the pyre his magic bow and arrows which were the symbols of his sovereignty' (Pinsent, *Greek Mythology*, p.101) – all the hallmarks of the Dying King whose original victory to win the Goddess-Queen ensures fertility but who knows his ultimate doom.

DELIGHT GODDESS, THE: Hindu. One of a trio – the other two being Lust and Thirst – sent to censure an ascetic prince for abandoning his duty to his wife, family and home. Described as beautiful and delightful, skilled in the magic arts of desire and voluptuousness.

DEMETER: ('Earth-goddess-mother') Greek goddess of the fruitful Earth, especially of barley. Daughter of Cronus and RHEA. Her brother Zeus, tricking her in the form of a bull, made her the mother of PERSEPHONE. Persephone was abducted by Demeter's brother Hades, King of the underworld, and Demeter roamed the Earth weeping in search of her; meanwhile the Earth remained barren. On Zeus' intervention, Persephone was restored but had to spend a third of each year with her husband Hades. This legend became the basis of the Eleusinian Mysteries. Festivals: 1-3 February (the Lesser Eleusinian Mysteries), 23 September-1 October (the Greater Eleusian Mysteries), 4 October, 13 and 22 December and the twelfth day of the waxing Moon and second of the waning. Days: Wednesday and Friday. *777*: Tarot, Threes, Strength; gems, star sapphire, pearl, cat's eye; plants, cypress, opium poppy, sunflower; animals, woman, lion; mineral, silver; perfumes, myrrh, civet, olibanum; magical weapons, Yoni, Outer Robe of Concealment, Preliminary Discipline. See Chapter XIII for her full story.

DENNITSA, ZVEZDA DENNITSA: Slavonic morning star goddess, her sister Vechernyaya being the evening star. Together they help Zorya, the Dawn, tend the Sun's white horses. Some legends make Dennitsa the wife of Myestyas, the male Moon. (In Slavonic legend both Moon and Sun are generally male, but MYESTYAS is sometimes female.)

DERKETO: Greek rendering of ATERGATIS.

DESHTRI: ('Instructress') Hindu teacher goddess.

DEVAKI: Hindu. Wife of Vaseduva and mother of Krishna. Her brother King Kamsa killed all her children at birth, because of a prediction that one of them would assassinate him. But Krishna's parents exchanged him for the daughter of a cowherd to hide him from his uncle's anger. Closely connected with ADITI, of whom some regard her as an avatar (incarnation). In the Puri celebration of Krishna's birth, Vaseduva is enacted by a priest and Devaki by a nautch (dancing) girl.

DEVANA: Slavonic. (Devana to Czechs, Diiwica to Serbians of Lusatia, Dziewona to Poles) goddess of the hunt. Young, beautiful, she rode a swift horse through the forests of the Elbe and the Carpathians, with a pack of hounds. Name a form of DIANA.

DEVANANDA: see TRISALA.

DEVASUNI: see SARAMA.

DEVI: ('Goddess') India, Nepal, Java, China, Japan, Mauritius. Originally the great Hindu mother goddess of pre-Aryan times. She embraces all things from pure spirit and intelligence to its manifestation in the elements of earth, air, fire and water, and she embodies both creative love and motherly love. The most important Hindu goddess, of whom other goddesses are often regarded as aspects. A 'Devi' is a female angelic spirit.

DHARANI: Hindu. One of the incarnations of LAKSHMI, in which she was connected with the Earth and married Parasurama, an incarnation of Vishnu.

DIANA: Roman equivalent of the Greek Moon and Nature goddess ARTEMIS, and rapidly acquired all her characteristics. Originally from Latium, a goddess of light, mountains and woods, and probably first a pre-Indo-European Sun goddess. One of her sanctuaries was at Lake Nemi, where her priest was an escaped slave, who had to kill his predecessor in single combat to take the office – and then hold it against would-be successors. Like Artemis, classically regarded as virgin but originally a sacrificial-mating goddess. Under Christianity, she became the goddess of underground witches, whom the tenth-century Canon Episcopi condemned for believing they rode at night 'with Diana, the goddess of pagans'. Associated with the constellation Ursa Major. In still-surviving Tuscany witch legend, Diana is the original supreme goddess and mother by Lucifer of ARADIA – a name which also appeared, as Herodias, in some later versions of the Canon Episcopi. Doreen Valiente (*An ABC of Witchcraft*, p.89) suggests that one reason why the name Diana appealed to pagans was that *dianna* and *diona* were Celtic words meaning 'divine, brilliant'. British legend says it was Diana who 'directed the Trojan Prince Brutus, the founder of the royal line of Britain, to take refuge here after the Fall of Troy' (*ibid.*, p.91), and St Paul's Cathedral in London is believed to be built on the site of a temple of Diana. Festivals: 26-31 May, 13 and 15 August; on 13 August she was invoked to protect the harvest against storms. Day: Monday. *777*: Tarot, Nines, High Priestess; gems, quartz, moonstone, pearl, crystal; plants, banyan, mandrake, damiana, almond, mugwort, hazel, moonwort ranunculus; animals, elephant, dog; mineral, lead; perfumes, jasmine, ginseng, all odiferous roots, menstrual blood, camphor, aloes, all sweet virginal odours; magical weapons, Perfumes, Sandals, Bow and Arrow.

DIANOIA: ('Thought, Intention, Meaning') Gnostic, an AEON, embodiment of the Word.

DICTYNNA: Cretan goddess, probably of Mount Dikte (see RHEA). The Greeks made her synonymous with BRITOMARTIS.

DIIWICA: see DEVANA.

DIKE: see HORAE, THE.

DIONE: Phoenician/Greek. Also known as Baltis. A Nature or Earth goddess, overlapping with DIANA and DANAE. Daughter of Uranus and GAIA. Married her brother Cronus, who gave her the city of Byblos. By one account, mother of PERSEPHONE and ATHENE. Homer makes her the mother of APHRODITE by Zeus. Patroness of the oracular oak grove at Dodona in Epirus, where she took the place of HERA as Zeus' companion. In fact, her name is simply the feminine form of Zeus.

DIRONA: see SIRONA.

DISCORDIA: Roman goddess of discord and strife, who preceded the chariot of Mars. Greek equivalent ERIS.

DITI: Hindu, daughter of the early god Daksha. Wife of Kasyapa, and mother of the Daityas (Titans who fought against the gods) and also of the Maruts (courageous young warrior men). Originally similar to ADITI, as the ultimate cosmic mother.

DJET: Egyptian. One of two deities holding up the pillars of the sky, the other being (her husband?) Neheh.

DODAH: Hebrew goddess mentioned on the Moabite Stone. The name suggests a mother role.

DOK: Australian aborigine. Mother of the heroic Brambrambult brothers. They went to Heaven as Alpha and Beta Centauri, and she as Alpha of the Southern Cross.

DOL JYANG, BRIBSUN: An aspect of DOLMA.

DOLMA, WHITE TARA: Tibet, Nepal, China, Mongolia, East Java, East Asia. Buddhist. The national goddess of Tibet. 'One of the most popular, approachable and attractive figures in the Tibetan Pantheon. She unites in herself all human and divine traits ... She extends her loving care to all' (Lama Anagarika Govinda). Her aspects range from transcendental wisdom to the erotic. Depicted according to her aspects: riding a lion, with the Sun in her hand; enthroned in a lotus chair under a starry canopy; or as an attractive, sophisticated, lightly clad woman wearing a tiara, her left hand holding a lotus blossom and her right in a gesture of giving. Known as 'the Tara with the Seven Eyes'.

DOMNU: Irish. Goddess of the Fomors or Fir Domnann ('Men of the Goddess Domnu'), last-but-two occupiers of Ireland in the mythological cycle. They may have been originally two British tribes, on the Severn and the Forth.

DÔN: Welsh equivalent of the Irish DANA; wife of Beli, mother of ARIANRHOD and grandmother of Lleu Llaw Gyffes.

DORIS: Greek. Daughter of Oceanus and his sister/wife TETHYS, and mother by Nereus the Truthful of the fifty NEREIDS.

DORJE-NALJORMA, VAJRA-YOGINI: Chief tutelary goddess of the practices of Tibetan Tantric Yoga. Personification of spiritual energy and feminine occult power, psychic heat and the KUNDALINI force. Visualized as bright ruby-red (the Radiance of Wisdom), with three eyes, bliss-giving, naked, in her sixteenth year, dancing, with one foot on the breast of a prostrate human form, and with a halo of the Flames of Wisdom.

DORNOLL: see SCATHACH.

DRUANTIA: A Gaulish fir-tree goddess.

DRUXANS, THE: Persian, Manichaean. Dangerous enchantress spirits.

DRYADS, THE: Greek. Female tree spirits.

DUGNAI: Slavonic house goddess, who prevented the dough from spoiling.

DURGA: Hindu. PARVATI in her demon-destroying form. Known as 'the

Inaccessible'. Depicted as a beautiful yellow woman, each of her ten arms holding a weapon; she rides a lion. She absorbed a former goddess of destruction called Nirriti.

DWYVACH: Welsh. She and her husband Dwyvan built Nefyed Nav Nevion, the Welsh Ark, in which with various animals they escaped the flood caused by the monster Addanc. Their names mean 'the God' and 'the Goddess'. A pre-Celtic legend with Christian additions.

DYNAMIS: ('Power, Force') Gnostic. An AEON, embodiment of dynamism; also, like DIANOIA, of the Word.

DZIEWONA: see DEVANA.

EARTHLY MOTHER, THE: The Essene personification of Nature, harmony with which was central to their faith. Their cosmos consisted of the Heavenly Father, with his six Angels of Eternal Life, Creative Work, Peace, Power, Love and Wisdom; and the Earthly Mother with her corresponding Angels of Earth, Life, Joy, the Sun, Water and Air. Mankind stood at the point of interaction between these two complementary groups of forces and must attune himself to both. The Earthly Mother's communion was on Saturday morning, and peace with her kingdom was contemplated at Sunday noon. The Friday evening communion began by saying, 'The Heavenly Father and I are One' – doubtless the source of Jesus' much-misunderstood statement, for there is evidence that he was Essene-trained. What the Gospels fail to quote (though we doubt if Jesus forgot it) was the Saturday morning communion, which began with 'The Earthly Mother and I are One'.

EASTERN MOTHER, THE: Chinese. She and the Western Mother were very early goddesses connected with shamanism.

ECHIDNE: Greek. A Winter snake goddess, mother by the storm god Typhon of the CHIMAERA.

EGERIA: A Roman oracular water goddess. Her spring was near the Campena Gate, and the King Numa used to consult her at night. According to Ovid he married her, and after his death she returned to a spring in Aricia. She foretold the destiny of newborn babies.

EILEITHYIA: see ILITHYIA.

EIR: Teutonic. One of the ASYNJOR, noted as a healer.

EIRENE: see HORAE, THE.

EITHINOHA: ('Our Mother') Amerindian, Iroquois Earth goddess.

EITHNE: Irish. Daughter of Balor, wife of Mackinely or Cian, and mother of Lugh. May be equated with the Welsh ARIANRHOD.

EKADZATI: Tibetan one-eyed goddess of the mystic cults and of wisdom.

EKHAMOTH: see SOPHIA.

ELAT: ('Goddess') Feminine form of the name El ('God'), and apparently thousands of years older; the original Semitic mother goddess.

ELATE: Greek. A title of ARTEMIS as goddess of the fir tree.

ELECTRA (1): Greek. Daughter of Agamemnon and Clytemnestra, and sister of Orestes. When Clytemnestra and her lover Aegisthus murdered Agamemnon, Zeus, through the Delphic Oracle, commanded Orestes to avenge his father's death by killing his mother and her lover. Electra helped her brother to do this. Freud named the Electra Complex (feminine equivalent of the Oedipus Complex) after her, because of her attachment to her father and hostility to her mother.

ELECTRA (2): Greek. One of the PLEIADES. Mother of IRIS and the HARPIES by Thaumas, son of Pontus (the sea) and GAIA. Also seduced by Zeus and bore Dardanus, founder of the Trojan race, and HARMONIA.

ELIHINO: Amerindian, Cherokee. The Earth mother, sister of IGAEHINDVO (the Sun goddess) and SEHU (the Corn Woman).

ELLI: Teutonic. The only woman Thor wrestled with and failed to defeat – because she was 'old age itself, which no one can ever conquer'.

EMBLA: ('Vine'?) The Teutonic Eve; her Adam was Ask or Askr ('Ash'). The gods Odin, Hoenir and Lodur made them out of lifeless tree-trunks. The fact that her name is Embla and not Eskga (feminine of Ask) suggests the fusion of two independent legends.

EMU WOMEN, THE: see SEVEN SISTERS.

ENODIA: Greek. Guardian of crossroads and gates.

ENNOIA, ENNOE: ('Thought, Intent') Gnostic. An AEON, embodiment of Designing Thought. Genetrix of the angels of the lower worlds. Simon Magus said she taught him magic, and how to communicate with these angels.

ENTHUMESIS: ('Esteem') Gnostic, an AEON very similar to EPINOIA. Said to be a daughter of SOPHIA.

EOS: ('Dawn') Greek, daughter of Hyperion and THEIA. Also called Aurora. 'Rosy-fingered dawn with the snowy eyelids'. Originally accompanied her brother Helios throughout the day; later HEMERA became a separate goddess of the day. Her first husband was the Titan Astreus, by whom she bore the winds, Boreas (North), Zephyrus (West), Eurus (East) and Notus (South), and also Phosphorus, who flew before his mother's chariot carrying a torch. Young and lovely, Eos inspired desire in gods and men. She was loved by Ares, and in revenge APHRODITE inspired her to love various mortals. She fell in love with, and carried away, Orion, who was finally killed accidentally by ARTEMIS. Then she married Tithonus and begged Zeus to make him immortal – but forgot to ask for eternal youth as well, so he grew older and older, till she shut him away and the gods, in pity, turned him into a cicada. To Tithonus, while he was still young, she bore Emathion who became King of Arabia, and Memnon who became King of Ethiopia. Also to Tithonus, or to Cephalus, she bore Phaeton, who was carried off by Aphrodite to be guardian of her temple; and to Atlas she bore Hesperus, the morning and evening star Venus.

EOSTRE, OSTARA: Teutonic goddess, the Maid aspect of Earth, who gave her name to Easter. May be from the same source as ISHTAR, ASTARTE etc.

EPINOIA: ('Power of Thought, Inventiveness') Gnostic. An AEON, and one of the first female manifestations. Referred to as the 'Principle' and thus linked to ALEITHEIA.

EPONA: Horse-totem goddess of the British and Continental Celts, adopted by Roman cavalry units as their patroness. In fact a form of the ancient Celtic mother goddess, with much wider implications than her horse-totem. See Chapter XIX for her full story.

ERATO: see MUSES.

ERCE: The Old English name for Mother Earth. Harrison (*The Roots of Witchcraft*, p.133) suggests that 'Old English erce (pronounced airchay) is nothing more or less than Basque (that is, Western European Neolithic) erche (pronounce it airshay), "bowels, belly, intestine, womb" ... That fruitful womb from which all blessings flow.'

ERDITSE: ('Giving Birth') Basque goddess of childbirth. Evidence of her worship, at least as early as Roman times, has been found at Toulouse.

ERESHKIGAL: ('Queen of the Great Below') Assyro-Babylonian goddess of the Underworld, sister of ISHTAR (INANNA). Known as 'Star of Lamentation', or sometimes simply as Allatu ('The Goddess'). Also named Ninmug. Wife of Nergal, who first dethroned her and then married her (another patriarchal demotion). Envisaged as throned, naked and black-haired. Her palace, of dark lapis lazuli, had seven walls, each with a gate, and one had to cross the River Hubar to reach it.

ERINYES, THE: Greek goddesses of vengeance and justice, born of the blood of the castration of Uranus where it fell on the ground (see GAIA). Also called, in propitiation, the Eumenides ('Kind Ones'). They were Alecto, Megaera and Tisiphone. They attended PERSEPHONE. Adopted, with the same legend, by the Romans, as the Furiae ('Furies').

ERIS: Greek goddess of discord. Uninvited to the marriage of Peleus and THETIS, she drew a golden apple marked 'For the Fairest' (The Apple of Discord) into the wedding feast. This led to the Judgement of Paris, and thus to the Trojan War.

ERIU, ERIN: Irish, one of the three queens of the Tuatha Dé Danann, daughters of the Dagda, who asked that Ireland be named after them. Wife of Mac Greine, Son of the Sun, or 'the Sun his god'. See p.33.

ERNMAS: ('Murder') Irish. 'The She-Farmer', mother of BADHBH, MACHA, ANU and the MORRIGAN (who in many contexts is a collective name for the other three), by Delbaeth, son of Oghma Grianaineach; or in another version, mother of BANBHA, FODHLA and ERIU. Either version makes her the mother (original form?) of the basic Irish Triple Goddess; the first (and her name) in the dark sense, and the second (and her title of 'She-Farmer') in the beneficent sense.

ERNUTIT: see RENENET.

ERYTHEIS: see HESPERIDES, THE.

ERZULIE: Haitian Voodoo goddess of love, wife of the sea god Agwe and lover of (among others) Ogoun, god of war and fire; regarded as innocently exuberant and generous rather than promiscuous. For the poverty-stricken Haitian, she expresses his dreams of luxury and wealth, of things as they ought to be; and her rituals dramatize this. Known as 'Maîtresse', and often identified with the VIRGIN MARY. A triple goddess; the main one is Erzulie Freda Dahomey, but there is also Gran Erzulie, who is old and arthritic, very maternal and protective, and La Sirène, whose colour is blue and whose voice hisses like the sea.

ESHARRA: Chaldaean Earth and war goddess. Wife of the war god Nergal (or sometimes of Bel). See also LAZ.

ETAIN, EDAIN: Irish. Known as Etain Echraidhe ('horse-riding'). Wife of

Midir; symbol of reincarnation. Outstandingly beautiful; described in enthusiastic detail in the Ulster Cycle. 'All who might before have been thought beautiful are as nothing beside Étain; all blondes cannot match her.'

ETERNA: Chinese. Sorceress, daughter of AUNT PIETY. She had an incarnation on Earth, during which her heavenly mother secretly helped and taught her.

EUNOMIA: see HORAE.

EUPHROSYNE: see CHARITES.

EURONYME: Greek. One of the OCEANIDS, and mother by Zeus of the three CHARITES. Also (or originally) the Greek rendering of a pre-Greek Moon and creator goddess name; the Pelasgians claimed to be born from her mating with the cosmic snake Ophion. Her statue at Phigalia in Arcadia showed her as a mermaid.

EUROPA: Greek. Daughter of Agenor, King of Tyre, and Telephassa, abducted by Zeus in the form of a bull and carried to Gortyna on the southern shore of Crete, where he seduced her. She bore three sons, Minos, Rhadamanthus and Sarpedon. Asterius, King of Crete, married her and, being childless, adopted her sons as his own. The allusion to the Cretan bull-cult is interesting; Crete's greatest king, Minos, was the son of a god in the shape of the cult animal.

EURYALE: see GORGONS.

EUTERPE: see MUSES.

EVE: Hebrew. The Genesis story is a patriarchal revision of earlier Middle Eastern creation myths, and also of Hebrew tradition itself. See Chapter XVIII for her full story.

FAMA: The swift-footed Roman goddess of rumour.

FAND: Irish and Manx. Wife of the sea god Manannán mac Lir, who deserted her. Goddess of healing and pleasure, lover of Cuchulainn.

FATES, THE: see MOERAE.

FAUNA: Roman goddess of the Earth and fields, daughter or wife of Faunus. Identified with BONA DEA.

FEA: ('Hateful') Irish war goddess, subordinate to the MORRIGAN. Daughter of Elcmar of the Brugh.

FEBRIS: Roman, malevolent goddess who brought fever and malaria and had to be placated. She was attended by Tertiana and Quartiana; a dedication to Tertiana has been found at Risingham in Northumberland. (No connection with February, 'the cleansing month', the god of which was Februus.)

FENG-P'O-P'O: ('Mrs Wind') Chinese wind goddess. She may sometimes be seen in the clouds, as an old woman riding a tiger.

FERONIA: Roman (Latin and Sabine) and Etruscan. Shared many of the attributes of FLORA. Originally possibly an underworld goddess. Associated with the Sabine god Soranus. The Roman family of Hirpini were especially devoted to their cult and during the festivals of Feronia used to walk barefoot on hot coals without burning themselves. In her Etruscan form, a fertility and fire goddess, sometimes confused with CUPRA.

FERTILITY MOTHER, THE: Australian aborigine, Arnhem Land. Her annual rites before the wet season were celebrated with song and dance and heralded the arrival of the RAINBOW SNAKE, which was announced by the whistling sound of the storm blowing through its horns, and finally by its body arching across the sky. Here the Rainbow Snake is female and is not clearly distinguished from the Fertility Mother.

FIDES: ('Trust') Roman. Personification of fidelity and honour.

FILIA VOCIS: Latin form of the Hebrew 'Daughter of a Voice', oracular transmitter of truth from Heaven. Daughter of SHEKINAH. Frequently mentioned in the Talmud. Her words may be heard either as actual sound or within the head. A traditional Hebrew method of divination is to appeal to the Daughter of a Voice for the solution to a problem; the next words heard will have an oracular significance.

FJORGYN: Teutonic. One of the ASYNJOR. Giant wife of Odin, wife or mother of Thor, and mother of FRIGG (herself also wife of Odin). Later another husband was devised for her called Fjorgynn.

FLIDAIS: Irish woodland goddess, ruler of beasts; the Cattle of Flidais were named after her. Rode in a chariot pulled by deer. Wife of Adammair, or of Fergus, whose virility was such that when Flidais was away he needed seven ordinary women to satisfy him.

FLORA: Roman goddess of 'everything that flourishes' – budding springtime, cereals, fruit trees (with POMONA), the vine and flowers. Her festival, the Floralia, in which courtesans took an active part, was from 28 April to 3 May. She also had a rose festival on 23 May. She was one of the minor deities to have a flamen (priest) of her own.

FODHLA, FOTLA: Irish, one of the three queens of the Tuatha Dé Danann, daughters of the Dagda, who asked that Ireland be named after them. Wife of Mac Cecht, Son of the Plough (or whose god was the plough, or Earth). See p.33.

FORNAX: Roman goddess of ovens.

FORTUNA: Roman goddess of fate, good and bad. Known as Fortuna Primigenia, variously translated as 'the First Mother' or 'First-Born (of Jupiter)' – though she was also considered to be Jupiter's nurse. A very ancient goddess from several Italian provinces. Anyone blessed with good luck was said to have a Fortuna. Roman emperors always kept a golden statuette of her in their sleeping-quarters. Patroness of once-married matrons. Also patroness of bath-houses, because of the vulnerability of naked men to evil influences. Depicted variously with a wheel, a sphere, a ship's rudder and prow, and a cornucopia; sometimes with wings.

FRAUS: Roman goddess of fraud.

FRIGG, FREYA, FREYJA: ('Well-Beloved, Spouse, Lady') Most revered of the Teutonic goddesses. (Frigg and Freya seem to have been originally the same goddess, then to have developed as two, finally tending to re-emerge.) Wife and sister of Odin. Owner of a falcon-plumed robe, in which she flew through the air. Mother of Baldur, god of light. She protected marriages and made them fruitful but was herself often unfaithful to Odin. Commander of the VALKYRIES (originally her priestesses), she often fought alongside Odin. Loved ornaments and jewellery. Originally a Moon goddess riding in a chariot drawn by two cats, and may have been priestess of a hawk totem clan. Associated with the zodiacal sign Leo. *777*: Tarot, Threes, Sevens, Empress; gems, star sapphire, pearl, emerald, turquoise; plants, cypress, opium poppy, rose, myrtle, clover; animals, woman, lynx, sparrow, dove, swan; mineral, silver; perfumes, myrrh, civet, benzoin, rose, red sandal, sandalwood, myrtle, all soft voluptuous odours; magical weapons, Yoni, Outer Robe of Concealment, Lamp, Girdle. Friday was named after her. English place-names recalling her include Freefolk (in Domesday Book Frigefolk, 'Frigg's people'), Froyle and Frobury, Hampshire (both the latter Old English Freohyll, 'Freya's hill')' Fryup (the hop or marshy enclosure of Freya) and Frydaythorpe, Yorkshire.

FRIMIA, FIMILA: Teutonic. A virgin goddess who wore gold ribbon in her hair. Became absorbed into the ASYNJOR.

FUCHI, HUCHI: Japanese (Aino) fire goddess from whom the holy extinct volcano Fujiyama takes its name.

FULLA: Teutonic. Sister of FRIGG, custodian of her magic casket and slippers. One of the ASYNJOR, apparently an early mother goddess whose original functions had become obscured.

FURIES, THE: see ERINYES.

GADDA: (Perhaps 'She-Goat') Chaldaean, Babylonian. With her husband Gad, a deity of fortune.

GAIA, GAEA: ('Earth') The 'deep-breasted', the primordial Greek Earth Mother, the first being to emerge from Chaos. She was regarded as creating the universe, the first race of gods, and mankind. She gave birth to Uranus, the sky, and Pontus, the sea; then she mated with her son Uranus to produce the twelve Titans, the Cyclops and finally three monsters. Uranus, horrified at his offspring, shut them in the depths of the Earth. Gaia, furious, persuaded the youngest male Titan, Cronus, to castrate Uranus as he slept beside her. The blood dropping on the Earth gave birth to the ERINYES, to giants and to the ash-tree nymphs the Meliae; and the blood dropping on the sea produced APHRODITE. The Oracle of Delphi, before it passed to Apollo (see PYTHIA), belonged to Gaia, who was pre-eminent among prophetesses. She presided over marriages, was invoked in oaths (with the sacrifice of a black ewe) and was offered the first of fruit and grain.

GANDIEDA: see GWENDYDD.

GANGA: Hindu, goddess of the River Ganges. The god Shiva divided her into seven streams so that she could descend to Earth without causing a catastrophe. Said to be the wife of Vishnu, Shiva and other gods, and also of a mortal King, Santanu. Depicted as a beautiful young woman, with her waters flowing about her.

GARBH OGH: Irish. 'An ancient ageless giantess, whose car was drawn by elks, whose diet was venison milk and eagles' breasts and who hunted the mountain deer with a pack of seventy hounds with bird names. She gathered stones to heap herself a triple cairn and "set up her chair in a womb of the hills at the season of heather-bloom"; and then expired' (Graves, *The White*

Goddess, p.192). Graves (*ibid.*, p.217) says she is a form of the goddess who sacrifices the antlered king.

GARMANGABIS: Imported to Britain by the Suebi, Roman auxiliaries who worshipped her at Longovicium (Lanchester, Co. Durham).

GASMU: ('The Wise') An ancient Chaldaean sea goddess, wife or daughter of Ea. Became associated with ZARPANITU.

GA-TUM-DUG: Local Babylonian mother goddess name; equated with BAU.

GAURI: Hindu. Fertility and abundance aspect of PARVATI; the Fair, the Harvest Bride. Sometimes represented by an unmarried girl and by a bundle of wild balsam dressed up as a woman; both girl and balsam are worshipped to ensure a good rice crop.

GAYATRI: Hindu goddess of the morning prayer; second wife of Shiva.

GENDENWITHA: Amerindian, Iroquois. The morning star; originally a human girl, put in the sky by Dawn and tied to her forehead.

GERD, GERDA: Teutonic. Daughter of the giant Gymir, and wife of Frey, god of fertility, who won her only after a desperate battle with the giants and after threatening to turn her from a beautiful young woman into an old one.

GERFJON, GEFJON: Teutonic giantess, one of the ASYNJOR; particularly honoured in the island of Seeland, which she created by a magical feat with a plough. Protectress of girls who died unwed.

GESTINANNA, GESHTIN: ('Lady of the Vine') Sumerian. Daughter of NINSUN and sister of Dumuzi (possibly also of Gilgamesh). Plays an important part in the mourning for, and rescue of, Dumuzi. Record-keeper of Heaven and the Underworld, spending six months of the year in each; also an interpreter of dreams. (See also BELIT-SHERI.)

GHE: ('Earth') Phoenician form of GAIA.

GHUL: ('Seizer') Arabic, pre-Islamic. Female spirits who attacked travellers, especially in the desert, eating them and occasionally seducing them. Root of the modern word 'ghoul'.

GJALP: Teutonic water giantess, who stood astride rivers and caused them to swell.

GLAISRIG, GLAISTIG: A Scottish undine, beautiful and seductive, but a goat from the waist down (which she hides under a long green dress). She lures men to dance with her and then sucks their blood. Yet she can be benign, looking after children or old people or herding cattle for farmers.

GNA: Teutonic. The messenger of the ASYNJOR. Her horse was called Hofvarpnir.

GODA: see GODIVA.

GODIVA, GODGIFU ('Gift of God'): British. The legend of Lady Godiva riding naked through the streets of Coventry as a condition of her husband Leofric's reducing the people's taxes, is a monkish disguising of a nearby May Eve procession of the Goddess Goda. (See Graves, *The White Goddess*, pp.405-6). Graves gives several examples of goddess rituals which men might not witness, and 'Peeping Tom may record the memory of this.' (Cf. BONA DEA.) He also (p.403) describes a miserere-seat in Coventry Cathedral, depicting 'a long-haired woman wrapped in a net, riding sideways on a goat and preceded by a hare' which recalls several European legends of a woman 'neither clothed nor unclothed, neither on foot nor on horseback, neither on water nor on dry land, neither with nor without a gift', who is 'easily recognised as the May-eve aspect of the Love-in-Death goddess Freya, alias Frigg, Holda, Held, Hilde, Goda, or Ostara'. C.A. Burland (*The Magical Arts*, p.82) says the Godiva Rides were a thousand years older than Leofric's wife. In hundreds of villages on May Day, there would be a procession beginning with the hag BLACK ANNIS, representing winter, followed by 'the lovely young Godiva' who 'brought in the spring and blessings' naked on a white horse, and not pretending to cover herself with long hair – nor hidden from the menfolk of the village. She was the female complementary symbol to the phallic Maypole, 'a kind of holy bride ... to the Saxons the representative of the wonderful and terrifying Freya' (see FRIGG).

GOKARMO: ('She of the White Raiment') A form of the Tibetan mother goddess.

GOLEUDDYDD: Welsh sow-goddess, daughter of Amlawdd, wife of Kilydd, mother of Culhwch, aunt(-in-law?) of Arthur.

GORGONS, THE: Greek. Three daughters of Phorcys and his sister Ceto. Winged monster with hair of serpents, who turned men to stone by their gaze. They were Euryale and Stheno, who were immortal, and MEDUSA who was mortal and killed by Perseus.

GOURI: see ISANI.

GRACES, THE, or GRATIAE, THE: see CHARITES.

GRAEAE, THE: ('Old Ones') Greek, daughters of Phorcys and his sister Ceto, and sisters of the GORGONS, living at the borders of night and death, in the far West, on the ocean shore. Their names were Fear, Dread and Terror.

GRÁINNE: Irish. Fionn mac Cumhal's espoused wife, who put a geis (magical command) on Diarmaid and ran away with him. Fionn pursued them all over Ireland for seven years and finally caught them. He pretended to make peace with Diarmaid but managed to bring about his death. Gráinne appears to be originally a Sun goddess (*grian*, a feminine noun, means 'Sun'), and the conflict between Fionn and Diarmaid may reflect male resentment of the old matriarchal principle of the Young King replacing the Old King as mate of the Goddess-Queen. The themes of lingering popular sympathy for the old ways, of male sexual potency, of the inescapable geis of the woman, of her initiation of the young man, and of menstruation, are all evident in the story.

GRIAN: ('Sun') Irish. A fairy queen with a court on Pallas Green Hill, Co. Tipperary. Also a general Goddess symbol.

GRUAGACH, THE: ('The Long-Haired One') Scottish. Female fairy to whom the dairymaids of Gairloch (Ross and Cromarty) used to pour libations of milk into a hollow stone, the Clach-na-Gruagach. She was placated in other parts of Scotland too.

GUABANCEX: Haiti. Goddess of storms, wind and water.

GULA: A Babylonian goddess who brought both illness and good health; wife of the war god Enurta. Her symbol was a dog, or an eight-rayed orb.

GU-LANG: Nepalese, Tibetan. A goddess of the Brahmins, protectress of mothers and children.

GULLVEIG: ('Gold Branch') Teutonic. A giantess and sorceress, one of the Vanir, whom the Aesir tried to kill. This caused war between the Vanir and the Aesir, which the Vanir won. Vanir and Aesir seem to have been two early Nordic peoples who eventually merged.

GUNGU: Hindu goddess of the New Moon.

GUNNLAUTH, GUNNLOED: Teutonic. Giantess seduced by Odin to gain entrance to a cave in which she was guarding Kvasir, the mead brewed in the magic cauldron Odherir, which gave wisdom and the art of poetry.

GWENDYDD: Welsh. Wife of King Rydderch and sister of Merlin, the only one who could come near her brother when he retired to the woods. Eventually she joined him there. He passed to her his gift of prophecy. Called Gandieda by Geoffrey of Monmouth. VIVIENNE or NIMUE, the mistress who wheedled Merlin's secrets out of him, may have been based on Gwendydd, who may originally have been his mistress as well as his sister; 'her story bears the traces of a time when fraternal incest was not forbidden, at least not in the case of exceptional people who thereby re-created the perfect couple' (Markale, *Women of the Celts* pp.56, 134).

GWENHWYFAR, GUINEVERE, GUENEVA: Arthur's queen. Traces of Triple Goddess; in early Welsh triads there were three at Arthur's Court: (1) daughter of Cywyrd Gwent (Gawrwyd Ceint), (2) daughter of Gwythyr son of Greidiawl, (3) daughter of Glogfran the Giant (Ogyrvan Gawr). The Guinevere of the medieval romances is an insipid revision of what must have been her true role in the original Celtic legends – the goddess-queen who was the actual focus of sovereignty, holding the balance between the honoured Old King and his brilliant Young Heroes. See pp.34-5.

HABONDIA, DAME HABONDE, ABUNDIA: A medieval witch goddess name, doubtless implying 'abundance'.

HAGAR: Hebrew. Second wife of Abraham and mother of Ishmael. The Bible says she was Egyptian; Rabbinic writings call her an Egyptian princess; Arab tradition says that Abraham, Hagar and Ishmael came to the place where Mecca now is (then a goddess site – see AL-UZZA). Occult tradition links her with the Moon. Graves (*The White Goddess*, p.278) suggests that Ishmael and his twelve sons personify a federation of goddess-worshipping tribes of the southern desert.

HAINUWELE: Indonesia, Ceram I. A PERSEPHONE-type goddess, whose rape, death and ascent to the heavens as the Moon guaranteed the Earth's fertility.

HAKEA: Polynesian, Hawaii. Goddess of the land of the dead.

HAKINI: see DAKINI.

HAMADRYAD: Greek. Another name for a DRYAD, especially one presiding over a specific tree.

HANENCA: Polynesian, Hawaii. Creatress of the first man.

HANIYAMA-HIME: Japanese goddess of Earth or clay (as substance). Formed from the excrement of the creator goddess IZANAMI-NO-KAMI.

HANI-YASU-NO-KAMI: From her head sprang the silkworm and mulberry tree, and from her navel the five cereals – hemp, millet, rice, corn and pulse. One of those invoked to control the fire god Ho-Masubi.

HANNAHANNAS: Hittite mother goddess, to whom bees were sacred. She sent one to find the fertility god Telepinus, whose absence was bringing drought and famine to the Earth, and the bee brought him back when other methods had failed.

HARIMELLA: Imported to Scotland by the Tungrians, who worshipped her at Blatobulgium (Birrens, Dumfriesshire).

HARITI: Indian, a mother suckling five hundred demons, said to have been converted to Buddhism by Buddha himself. Wife of Kubera, god of dark spirits, or of Panchika. Connected with the northern quarter. Probably a relic of ancient agricultural rites. MacQuitty (*Buddha*, p.53) suggests that she was an Indianization of ISIS, who was brought to north-west India by the Greeks in the fourth century AD. See also KWAN-YIN and KWANNON.

HARMONIA: ('Harmony') Greek, daughter of Zeus by Atlas's daughter ELECTRA – or, according to Hesiod, of Ares and APHRODITE. An attendant of Aphrodite, along with HEBE, the HORAE and the CHARITES. Cadmus, King of Thebes, was allowed to marry her; she brought a divine dowry, including a necklace made by Hephaestus containing irresistible love-charms. Cadmus and Harmonia eventually left Thebes and became King and Queen of Illyria, and were turned into great serpents – i.e., were identified with Illyrian snake-gods.

HARPIES: Greek. Frightening creatures with the bodies of birds and heads of women; originally storm-wind goddesses. Daughters of Thaumas and ELECTRA. They contaminated the food of their victims, meted out divine punishment and bore away the souls of the dead.

HATHOR: ('House of the Face' or 'House of Horus') Egyptian, an ancient sky-goddess; Ra's daughter by NUT, or his wife (bearing him Ihy the god of music); sometimes the wife or mother of Horus the Elder, Goddess of pleasure, joy, love, music and dancing. Protectress of women and embodiment of the finest female qualities; in the later period, while dead men were still identified with Osiris, dead women came to be identified with Hathor. She supervised women's toilet – a goddess of make-up – and bronze mirrors often had Hathor handles. She suckled the living, including the Pharaohs (queens often identified with her) and the dead; as 'Queen of the West' and 'Lady of the Sycamore' she welcomed them to the afterlife and offered them nourishment. Patroness of the Sinai mining area (possible relevance to 'golden calf' episode in Exodus xxxii). But she could be fierce; SEKHMET was in some ways her other self, and the legend of Sekhmet's destructive orgy when mankind rebelled against Ra was sometimes told of Hathor instead. She could also be uninhibited; when Ra (her father in this instance) walked out from a meeting of the gods and sulked, she went to his house and displayed her genitals to him till he cheered up and rejoined the meeting. (Cf. AMA NO UZUME.) Sovereign of Dendera, and as wife of

Horus the Elder, her sacred marriage was celebrated annually by carrying her image from Dendera to this temple at Edfu. Their son was sometimes said to be Horus the Younger; when, as was more usual, he was regarded as the son of Osiris and ISIS, Hathor was his nurse. Depicted as a cow (often star-spangled), as a woman with a cow's head, as a woman with a broad sistrum-shaped face and cow's ears, or as a normal woman wearing a solar disc between cow's horns – as was Isis as she increasingly absorbed Hathor's attributes. Undoubtedly the Golden Calf of Exodus xxxii. Of all the Egyptian deities, she is the most often depicted full-face. Her favourite instrument was the sistrum, which banishes evil spirits. She ruled the month Athyr, 17 September to 16 October, third month of the Inundation season. 'The Hathors' were seven young 'fairy godmothers' who prophesied the destiny of young Egyptians at birth. Their predictions could be favourable or unfavourable but were inescapable. *777*: Tarot, Sevens, Empress; gems, emerald, turquoise; plants, rose, myrtle, clover; animals, lynx, sparrow, dove, swan; perfumes, benzoin, rose, red sandal, sandalwood, myrtle, all soft voluptuous odours; magical weapons, Lamp, Girdle.

HAUMEA, HAUMIA: Polynesian, Hawaiian goddess of wild food plants. Regarded elsewhere in Polynesia as a male god, though with the same function.

HAYA: ('Goddess of Direction') Assyro-Babylonian; a title of NINLIL.

HAYA-AKITSU-HIME-NO-KAMI: Japanese sea goddess, who swallowed all the sins cast into the sea.

HEBAT: see HEPATU.

HEBE: ('Youth, Puberty') Greek, daughter of Zeus and HERA. Personification of eternal youth. Served nectar and ambrosia to the gods and performed other Olympian domestic duties. Attendant on APHRODITE. Given as wife to Heracles when he was admitted to Olympus as a god; they had two children, Alexiares and Anicerus.

HECATE: Greek, originally Thracian and pre-Olympian; at the same time a Moon goddess, an Underworld goddess and a goddess of magic. Daughter of two Titans, Perses and Asteria (a later tradition says Zeus and HERA). She protected both flocks and sailors. Associated with crossroads, where her three-faced image was placed, called Triple Hecates; offerings were left there on the eve of the Full Moon to propitiate her. *777*: Tarot, Threes, High Priestess; gems: star sapphire, pearl, moonstone, crystal; plants: cypress, opium poppy, almond, mugwort, hazel, moonwort, ranunculus; animals: woman, dog; mineral: silver; perfumes: myrrh, civet, menstrual blood, camphor, aloes, all sweet virginal odours; magical weapons: Yoni, Outer Robe of Concealment, Bow and Arrow. See Chapter XVII for her full story.

HEH: Egyptian serpent-headed goddess, revealer of wisdom.

HEKET: Egyptian goddess of childbirth, fecundity and resurrection. Depicted as a frog or frog-headed woman. At Abydos it was taught that she was born from the mouth of Ra simultaneously with the air god Shu and that they were the ancestors of the gods. Sometimes the wife of the creator god Khnum, giving life to the men and women he shaped on his potter's wheel. (See also SATI (2).) The midwife of kings and queens, and also of the Sun every morning. (See also MESHKENT.)

HEL, HELA: Teutonic goddess of the kingdom of the dead, not considered as a place of punishment. Daughter of Loki and ANGURBODA, and sister of the Midgard serpent of the ocean encircling the Earth, and of the devouring Fenris-wolf. Half her face was totally black.

HELIADES, THE: Greek. Daughters of the Sun god Helios and Clymene, who mourned the death of their brother Phaeton when he failed to control his father's chariot. The gods turned them into poplar trees, forever weeping amber tears.

HEMERA: ('Day') Greek. Daughter of Erebus and NYX, children of Chaos. See also EOS.

HENG-O: see CH'ANG-O.

HEPATU, HEBAT: Hittite. Presiding goddess of the Hurrian pantheon. Wife of the storm god Teshub. Depicted as matronly, sometimes standing on a lion, her sacred animal.

HEPZIBAH: ('My Delight is in Her') Hebrew, personification of Jerusalem; possibly originally a wife of Jehovah. See Isaiah lxii:1-5 – but note that the word in verse 5 translated as 'sons' in the Authorized Version should be 'builder'. (Cf. AHOLIBAH.)

HERA: Greek, consort of Zeus and queen of Olympus. A Daughter of Cronus and RHEA. With the patriarchal take-over, she became merely the ideal wife, patroness of marriage and maternity. Her Roman equivalent is JUNO, who for once is far more powerful and significant. 777: Tarot, Threes; gems: star sapphire, pearl; plants: cypress, opium poppy; animal: woman; mineral: silver; perfumes, myrrh, civet; magical weapons: Yoni, Outer Robe of Concealment.

HERODIAS: Gaulish and medieval witch goddess name; may be the same as ARADIA (see also DIANA). The form Herodiana suggests a combination of Diana and Aradia.

HERTHA: see NERTHUS.

HESPERIDES, THE: ('Westerners') Greek. Aegle, Hespere and Erytheis, daughters of Atlas and Hesperis, or of Erebus and his sister NYX. Guardians of Hera's golden apples in the Garden of the Hesperides, in the far West beyond the Pillars of Hercules.

HESTIA: ('Hearth') Greek, first daughter of Cronus and RHEA, and oldest of the Olympians. Goddess of domestic fire and of the home in general. Poseidon and Apollo both wanted to marry her but she placed herself under Zeus' protection as eternally virgin. She received the first morsel of every sacrifice. She was one of the deities of the Garden of the HESPERIDES. Every home had a shrine to her, and every city a perpetually burning Hearth of Hestia, from which colonists bore coals to establish one in their new colony. Roman equivalent VESTA.

HETEP-SEKHUS: Egyptian Underworld goddess, referred to in the *Book of the Dead* as 'the Eye and the Flame'.

HETTSUI-NO-KAMI: Japanese goddess of the kitchen range. Her festival, called Fuigo Matsuri, is on 8 November.

HIMAVATI: ('Wife of Mountain God') Hindu. A form of PARVATI; wife of Shiva in one of his avatars.

HINA, HINE: Polynesian. The word means 'Maiden' (obviously not in the *virgo intacta* sense) and applies to several goddesses, including the Moon goddess SINA. In Maori legend she was the first woman, created by the sky and fertility god Tane from sand to be his wife. When she discovered she was his daughter as well as his wife, she fled to the Underworld and became the goddess of death. (Cf. HINA-TITAMA.)

HINA-MITIGATOR-OF-MANY-THINGS: Polynesian. Mate of Ti'i, the first man; she was both a goddess and a woman. The royal families of Tahiti claimed descent from them. (See also HINE-AHU-ONE.)

HINA-OF-THE-LAND: Polynesian. Mother of the war god Oro by creator god Taaroa (Tangaroa). Her husband, adoptive father of Oro, was 'Sea-for-swimming-in'.

HINA-TITAMA: Polynesian. Daughter of HINE-AHU-ONE and her god-creator Tane, after Earth-Mother PAPA had rejected his advances. She had several children by him before she knew he was her father; when she found out, she fled in shame to the Underworld, of which she became the ruler as HINE-NUI-TE-PO.

HINE-AHU-ONE: ('Earth-formed-maiden') The Polynesian Eve, made from red sand by the god Tane with other gods' help. He breathed life into her and mated with her to produce HINA TITAMA. (See also HINA-MITIGATOR-OF-MANY-THINGS.)

HINE-NUI-TE-PO: ('Great-Goddess-of-Darkness') Polynesian, Queen of Po, the Underworld (which also means chaos, the void). Maori legend says the hero Maui tried to make men immortal by penetrating her body, but she crushed him to death – since when all men must die. (See also HINA TITAMA.)

HINGNOH: The Hottentot Eve; her Adam was Noh.

HINLIL: Assyro-Babylonian goddess of grain.

HIPPODAMEIA: Greek, daughter of Oenomaus, who had been told by an oracle that he would be killed by his son-in-law. So he would only give Hippodameia to the man who could beat him in a chariot race. He was certain he would always win, because his father Ares had given him winged horses. But when Pelops challenged him, Hippodameia secretly replaced her father's chariot-pins with wax; Oenomaus was killed, and Pelops won the race and her hand. The Goddess-Queen will not allow the Old King to dodge his fate. Cf. HYPERMNESTRA.

HIPPOLYTE: Greek. Daughter of Ares and HARMONIA or Otrera, and queen of the Amazons.

HIR NINEVEH: Assyro-Babylonian; goddess personifying Nineveh. Roundly condemned in Nahum iii: 'the multitude of the whoredoms of the well-favoured harlot, the mistress of witchcrafts'.

HLODYN: Teutonic giantess, one of several named mothers of Thor – a confusion arising from the attempts to fit him, as a popular culture-hero, into a more sophisticated pantheon to which he did not originally belong.

HNOSSA: Teutonic. One of the ASYNJOR, daughter of FRIGG/FREYA. So beautiful that the word *hnosir* came to be used to describe things of beauty.

HO HSIEN-KU: ('The Immortal Damsel Ho') Chinese. The only female member of the Eight Immortals, she went to heaven 'in full daylight'. Portrayed as a girl wearing a lotus flower on her shoulder. (The Eight achieved immortality through Taoist practice and have the right to attend the banquets given by WANG-MU NIANG-NIANG.)

HOLLE, HOLDA, HOLDE: Teutonic Moon witch goddess. In summer she bathed in forest streams, and in winter shook down snowflakes from the trees. The name was used as a general term for a priestess of the lunar cult.

HOLY SPIRIT, THE: Regarded in Hebrew and Gnostic tradition as feminine. The word translated as 'Spirit' in the Bible is often the Hebrew feminine noun *Ruach*; also overlaps Wisdom (see SOPHIA).

HORTA: Etruscan goddess of agriculture; an Etruscan town was named after her.

HORAE, THE: Greek. Goddesses of the hours or seasons, daughters of Zeus and THEMIS. They stood for the order of Nature. They were Dike (Justice), Eirene (Peace), and Eunomia (Order). They guarded the gates of Olympus and attended HERA. (The word is actually the plural of *Hore*, the season of Spring, or youth.)

HRETHA: see NERTHUS.

HSI-HO: Chinese. Mother of the Suns; in ancient tradition, there were ten Suns, appearing in the sky in turn. At dawn the Sun of the day emerged from the Valley of Light and was bathed by its mother in the lake on the eastern edge of the world.

HSI-WANG-MU: Chinese. Originally a goddess of plague and pestilence, with a human head, a tiger's teeth and a leopard's tail. But later, in Taoist literature and in folklore, she was Royal Mother of the Western Paradise, a gracious goddess with a palace on Khunlun, the mountain at the far West of the Other World. A herb of immortality grew there, and a magical peach tree whose fruit took 3,000 years to ripen. She would serve its fruit to gods and immortals at a Peach Festival. Depicted in this later form as a beautiful lady, sometimes winged, and with unkempt hair showing that she was a sorceress.

HUBUR: Assyro-Babylonian primordial mother goddess, who spawned warriors for TIAMAT.

HUIXTOCIHUATL: Aztec goddess of salt, elder sister of the rain god Tlaloc; probably a pre-Aztec mother goddess.

HULDA: ('Benign') Teutonic, North German, goddess of marriage and fecundity. See also BERCHTA. 'Hulda is making her bed' means 'it is snowing' (Cf. MOTHER CAREY).

HUN-AHPU-MTYE: ('Grandmother') Guatemalan Moon goddess, wife of Sun god Hun-Ahpu-Vuch ('Grandfather'). Both represented in human form but with the face of the tapir, a sacred animal.

HUNTHACA: Colombian, Chibcha Indian. Moon goddess, originally the wife of culture hero Nemquetcha. In a fit of anger she flooded the Cundinamarea Table Land; the Earth had no Moon at the time, so she became the Moon as a punishment. Confused with CHIA.

HURUING WUHTI: Amerindian, Hopi. Two mother goddesses, apparently Deluge survivors who became the ancestors of the tribe.

HYGEIA: Greek goddess of health, daughter of Asclepius. Roman equivalent SALUS.

HYPATE: see MUSES.

HYPERMNESTRA: Greek, the only one of the fifty daughters of King Danaus who disobeyed his order to kill their husbands on their wedding-night. Her husband, Lyncaus, eventually succeeded Danaus as King. The whole legend is one of an attempt to circumvent matrilinear succession, and of the heiress's refusal to allow it. (Cf. HIPPODAMEIA).

HYRAX: Western Bushmen. Wife of creator god I Kaggen (= praying mantis).

IAMBE: Greek. Daughter of Pan and Echo. Succeeded in cheering up DEMETER when she was mourning the absence of PERSEPHONE. Said to have invented Iambic verse. Festival: 28 September.

ICHCHHASHAKTI: see SHAKTIS.

IDA, ADDA, ILA: Hindu, Tantric. An Earth goddess but with many other aspects, especially in occult philosophy: instruction, speech, divination, devotion, fire, etheric force; also the Lunar Woman or Wife. In Tantric teaching, a vital force located in the *medulla oblungata* and the heart. In Hatha Yoga, the left-nostril, lunar breath. Also regarded as one of the three Vital Airs aspects of the KUNDALINI, the other two being PINGALA and Shushumna.

IDUN, IDUNA: Teutonic. Lived in Asgard and possessed magical apples, by eating which the gods never grew old. Born of flowers, like the Welsh BLODEUWEDD. Wife of Bragi, god of poetry. Festivals: 3 and 21 March.

IGAEHINDVO: Amerindian. The Cherokee Sun goddess. Her sisters are the Earth goddess ELIHINO and the maize goddess SEHU.

IKUGUI-NO-KAMI: ('Life-Integrating') Hindu. A primeval goddess, emanating from the Mother and associated with the Earth and the sands. 'Of denser substance' than most of the gods, but 'fair and graceful' (Mme Blavatsky).

ILA: see IDA.

ILAMATECUHTLI: Aztec fertility and death goddess known as 'the Old Princess', and also as Citlallinicue, 'Star Garment', linked with the Milky Way.

ILITHYIA, EILEITHYIA: ('Fluid of Generation') Greek, daughter of Zeus and HERA. Goddess of childbirth. Originally two goddesses – of birth-pains and of delivery. Also a fate-spinner. Very ancient, believed to be Cretan. Depicted kneeling, as though aiding delivery, and carrying a torch, symbol of light.

ILMATAR: see LUONNOTAR.

ILYTHYIA, LEUCOTHIA: An Etruscan fertility goddess, overlapping with CUPRA.

IMBALURIS: Hittite, messenger goddess of the sky god Kumarbis.

IMBEROMBERA: see WARAMURUNGUNDJU.

INA: see SINA.

INANNA: ('Lady of Heaven') Sumerian Queen of Heaven, mother goddess to whom the Semitic ISHTAR was assimilated, Earth, love, grain, date-palm, oracular, battle, weaving and wine goddess. Daughter of the wisdom god Enki. Associated with the seasonally dying vegetation god Dumuzi (Tammuz), whom she sought in the Underworld during his season of recession (see ISHTAR). Also the goddess of sovereignty; her sacred marriage with the god, enacted by the King and a priestess known as the *Enitum*, was an important annual Sumerian ritual. The same Flood story is told of her as of ISHTAR (see p.105). Her city of origin was Uruk or Erech, the modern Warka. Festival: New Year's Day.

INARAS, INARA: Hittite goddess who helped the storm god Hooke to defeat the dragon Illuyankas by making it drunk. She seduced mortal men and shut them up in her house. Also Hindu.

INARI: Japanese vixen-goddess, widely worshipped, especially by women. Associated with rice-growing, fire and smithcraft. Foxes are regarded as of great importance. Geishas and prostitutes are sometimes colloquially called 'foxes'. Cf. the Chinese AUNT PIETY.

INDOEA PAD: see SANING SARI.

INDRANI, AINDRI: ('Of the Senses') Hindu, wife of Indra, who fell in love with 'her voluptuous attractions'. Goddess of sensual pleasure. Indra and Indrani are both associated with the East. She owns the Parijata or Kalpa wishing tree, sight of which reinvigorates the old. (Cf. Ambologera, 'Postponer of Old Age', one of the titles of APHRODITE.) Depicted often four-armed, with an elephant as footstool.

INENO PAE: ('Mother of Rice') Indonesia, Malaya, Celebes. The first sheaf of rice harvested is so named and honoured. Seven ears are cut from it and cradled as the 'Rice-Child'.

INO: see LEUCOTHEA.

IO: Greek. Classical legend says she was a priestess of HERA at Argos, desired by Zeus and turned into a heifer – either by Hera to hide her from Zeus, or by Zeus to hide her from Hera. In fact, she was the pre-Greek Moon-cow and barley goddess of Argos, after whom the Ionians were named before the patriarchal Achaean conquest. Her father, the river god Inachus, was turned into a legendary King of Argos. Graves (*The White Goddess*, pp.233, 337, 411) says she found her way to Egypt and became ISIS.

IRIS: ('Rainbow') Greek, daughter of Thaumas, son of GAIA, and the marine goddess ELECTRA. Messenger of the gods, particularly of Zeus. Also devoted to HERA, acting almost as her lady's maid. Could be helpful to mortals. She travelled between Earth and Heaven on a rainbow. Wife of Zephyrus, the West Wind. Particularly venerated at Delos, where she was offered dried figs and cakes of wheat and honey.

ISANI, GOURI: Hindu, Rajputana. An abundance and fertility goddess. An earthen image of her, and a smaller one of her husband Ishwara, are placed together, and barley is sown and tended in a small trench. When this sprouts, women dance round it, calling the blessing of Isani on their husbands; they then give the young shoots to their husbands to wear in their turbans.

ISEULT, ISOLDE, ESYLLT, ESSYLLT VYNGWEN: ('Of the fine hair') Celtic. Actually three women involved with Tristan; see p.34.

ISHIKORIDOME-NO-MIKOTO: Japanese artisan goddess, who made the Sun goddess AMATERASU's mirror.

ISHTAR: Major Assyro-Babylonian mother goddess, daughter of either the sky god Anu, the Moon god Sin or the god of wisdom Enki. Of Semitic origin. An Earth, fertility, love, battle, storm, marriage, Moon and divinatory goddess. Personification of the planet Venus. Festivals: 10

March, 23-24 June. Honoured on the Full Moon. Day: Saturday. See Chapter XV for her full story.

ISIS: (Egyptian ASET, 'throne, seat') The most complete flowering of the Goddess concept in human history. Daughter of Earth god Geb and sky goddess NUT; her sister was NEPHTHYS, and her brothers Horus the Elder, Osiris and Set. She married one of these brothers, the fertility god Osiris. Their envious brother Set murdered Osiris, and the grieving Isis set out to find his coffin which had been cast into the Nile. She found his coffin, but Set recaptured it and cut Osiris's body into fourteen pieces and scattered them throughout the land. Undeterred, Isis hunted all the pieces down, except for the phallus, which a Nile crab had eaten. She reconstituted the body and, magically restoring the phallus, conceived and bore Horus the Younger. The cult of the Osiris-Isis-Horus triad became the most widespread and popular in Egypt, and Isis gradually absorbed the qualities of most other goddesses. Depicted crowned with the throne which represents her name, or later with the disc and horns which she absorbed from HATHOR. Festivals: 9 January, 5 February, 5 and 20 March, 14 May, 24 June, 3 and 19 July, 12 and 27 August, 28 October-3 November, 13-14 November and 22 December. Honoured on the first and fourth days of the waxing Moon. Days: Wednesday and Friday. *777*: Tarot, Twos, Threes, Fours, Tens, Emperor, Hermit, Hanged Man; *gems*, ruby, star ruby, turquoise, sapphire, star sapphire, pearl, amethyst, rock crystal, peridot, beryl, aquamarine; plants, amaranth, cypress, opium poppy, olive, shamrock, willow, lily, ivy, tiger lily, geranium, snowdrop, lily, narcissus, lotus, all water plants; animals, man, woman, unicorn, sphinx, ram, owl, lion, virgin, anchorite, any solitary person or animal, eagle, snake, scorpion; minerals, phosphorus, silver, sulphates; perfumes, musk, myrrh, civet, cedar, dittany of Crete, dragon's blood, narcissus, onycha; magical weapons, Lingam, Inner Robe of Concealment, Yoni, Outer Robe of Concealment, Wand, Sceptre, Crook, Magic Circle, Triangle, Horns, Energy, Burin, Lamp, Wand, Bread, Cup and Cross of Suffering, Wine. (Note: Crowley gives more correspondences for Isis than for any other goddess, attributing her to seven of his 32 Paths.) David Wood's numbers: 8 for her body, 18 for her active principle, 81 for the reflection of that active principle. See Chapter XXIII for her full story.

ISTUSAYA: Hattic (Anatolia). One of a pair of Underworld goddesses, the other being Papaya. They spin the lives of men, like the MOERAE and NORNS – though in their case, particularly of the Hattic kings.

IUSAS: Egyptian. At Heliopolis, wife of Ra-Hor-akhty. Her cult goes back to the Old Kingdom. Sometimes shown with disc and horns.

ITZPAPALOTI: Aztec agricultural and fire goddess known as 'Obsidian Knife Butterfly'.

IVI: Polynesian. The Tahitian primordial mother goddess.

IXALVOH: ('Water') Mayan goddess of weaving, wife of the Sun god Kinich-Ahau. In her Yucatan form she was called Ixasaluoh, wife of Hunab Ku ('the one god').

IXCHEL: Mayan goddess of disastrous floods and the Moon. Her symbol the overturned vessel of doom; on her head rests the deadly snake, her hands and feet are clawed, and her mantle is adorned with crossed bones.

IXCUINA: see TLAZOLTEOTL.

IZANAMI: Japanese, wife of the god Izanagi. They were the first beings to come to Earth and gave birth to the islands of Japan and to many gods. She finally died giving birth to the fire god Kago-Zuchi (or Ho-Masubi). Izanagi descended to the Underworld to try to rescue her, but failed. Festival: 7 January.

IZTAT IX: see ALAGHOM NAUM.

JAGAD-YONI: ('Universe-Yoni') Hindu. The Womb of the World, the female First Cause. Symbols are many, including the inverted triangle, the upright oval, the rose and the cauldron.

JAMBAVATI: Hindu. Wife of Krishna. Of the family of Jambavan, King of the Bears.

JANA: Roman. Wife and partner of Janus, guardian of doors and of the turn of the year. A very early couple; he originally was the oak god Dianus, and she was the woodland and Moon goddess DIANA/DIONE; and he was originally her son.

JARAH, JERAH: Hebrew. Goddess of the New Moon, Bride of the Sun. (The Semitic Moon was originally masculine, becoming feminine later.) Gave her name to the city of Jericho.

JARNSAXA: Teutonic. A giantess, first wife of Thor; they had two sons, Moody ('Courage') and Magni ('Might'). See also SIF.

JINGO: A Japanese Empress who was deified for her military exploits in Korea, probably in the fourth century AD.

JNANASHAKTI: see SHAKTIS, THE.

JOCASTA: Greek mother of Oedipus; he unknowingly killed his father Laius and married her. A patriarchal rewrite of a Dying King story: originally the Young Hero's killing of the Old King, and marriage to the Goddess-Queen, whether incestuously or not, would have been conscious and unquestioned.

JORD, JORTH: ('Earth') Teutonic, giantess mother of Thor by her father, the sky god Odin. One of the ASYNJOR. Overlaps with NERTHUS and ultimately identifiable with FRIGG.

JULUNGGUI: see RAINBOW SNAKE.

JUMALA: see SLATABABA.

JUNO: Supreme Roman goddess, sister and wife of Jupiter. For once, a much more successful survivor of the patriarchal take-over than her Greek counterpart, HERA. The month of June is named after her. Festivals 1 January, 1-2 February, 1 and 7 March, 1-2 June, 7-8 July, 13 November. 777: Tarot, Star; gem, artificial glass; plants, olive, coconut; animals, man, eagle, peacock; perfume, galbanum; magical weapons, Censer, Aspergillus.

JUTURNA: Roman. A nymph loved by Jupiter, who made her a goddess of lakes and springs. Her pool in the Forum at Rome was where Castor and

Pollux were said to have watered their horses. Festivals: 11 January, 23 August.

JYOTSNA: Hindu goddess symbolizing moonlight, autumnal moonlight, twilight.

KA-ATA-KILLA: Pre-Inca Moon goddess worshipped around Lake Titicaca.

KADI: Assyro–Babylonian Earth goddess of Der. Depicted as a snake, sometimes with human breasts.

KADOMAS, THE: see DAKINIS.

KADRU: Hindu. Mother of the NAGAS, the Serpent Race; wife of Kasyapa.

KAGAURAHA: Melanesian, San Cristoval. Snake goddess, representing the creative force; she received both animal and human sacrifice.

KAHASUMA: Hindu. Chief goddess of the Todas, a primitive tribe of the Neelgererry Hills. Wife of Kamataraya.

KAIKILANI: Polynesian. A beautiful Hawaiian girl with whom the fertility god Lono fell in love. She became a goddess, and they lived happily, surf-bathing in Kealakekua Bay, till he killed her in a jealous rage when he doubted her fidelity. Mad with remorse, he rampaged about the island and finally left, promising to return on a floating island of plenty. Hawaiian annual rituals at the start of the fertile season dramatized his story.

KAKINI: see DAKINI.

KALI: Hindu, Tibetan, Nepalese. One of the aspects of DEVI. Often called Kali Ma ('the Black Mother'). A terrible but necessary destroyer, particularly of demons, but also a powerful creative force, much misunderstood in the West. 'Kali herself, in her positive and non-terrible aspect, is a spiritual figure that for freedom and independence has no equal in the West' (Erich Neumann). To her worshippers, for example, violence against any woman is forbidden, since all are representatives of the goddess. Her rituals, many of them orgiastic, are intended to put the worshipper in tune with the feminine essence at all levels; for their description by a priest of Kali, see Durdin-Robertson, *Goddesses of India*, pp.199-201. Wife of Shiva, whom she is said to have subdued. Apparently an early war goddess absorbed into the Hindu pantheon as the creator or mother of Shiva, subsequently marrying him. In Bengal she is seen as mother to Shiva, Brahma and Vishnu; the creator-destroyer womb of all things. Calcutta (Kali-ghat) is named after her. Said to have invented the Sanskrit alphabet and to have one letter on each of the skulls of her necklace. Depicted with bare breasts, sometimes naked, black or dark-complexioned, loose-haired, with four arms – one holding a sword, another the severed head of Raktavija, chief of the demon army; the other two hands encourage her worshippers. (In other aspects she may have more arms.) She wears a necklace of skulls, and her earrings are two corpses. Wednesday is holy to her.

KALINDI: Hindu. One of the later wives of Krishna.

KALMA: Finno-Ugric death goddess, daughter of Tuoni and TUONETAR.

KAMASHI: ('Wanton-Eyed') Hindu. One of the benign aspects of PARVATI; probably an early fertility goddess.

KAMIKAZE: ('Divine Wind') Japanese air goddess. The kamikaze pilots of World War II were dedicated to her.

KAMRUSEPAS: Hittite goddess of healing and magic.

KAMI-MUSUMI ('Divine Generative Force') Japanese goddess who collected and sowed the seeds produced by the food goddess OGETSU-HIME. She also revived the god of medicine, O-Kuni-Nushi, when his jealous brothers killed him.

KANA-YAMA-HIME: Japanese goddess of mountain minerals, with male counterpart Kana-Yama-Hiko.

KANGRA GODDESS, THE: Hindu. The Rajahs of Kangra claim descent from the perspiration of her brow.

KANYA: ('Girl') One of the most ancient Hindu goddesses; the constellation Virgo.

KARA: Teutonic. A VALKYRIE, lover of the mortal Helgi, she helped him in battle by hovering above him and charming his enemies with song; but during one such battle Helgi accidentally killed her.

KARAKAROOK: Australian aborigine, Victoria. A goddess who descended to Earth to defend women who were attacked by snakes when they left camp to dig for yams. She killed the snakes with her huge stick till it broke, then gave the broken pieces to the women.

KARITEIMO, KISHIBOJIN: Originally an Indian Buddhist demoness who devoured children, she became a protectress of children, and her cult spread to China and Japan. Depicted standing with a baby at her breast and holding a flower of happiness, or seated surrounded by children.

KATHIRAT, THE: Syrian goddesses of weddings and childbearing.

KAYA-NU-HIME: ('Princess of Grass') Japanese goddess of fields and meadows. Also called Nu-Zuchi.

KEBEHUT: Egyptian goddess of freshness, daughter of Anubis.

KEDESH, QEDESHET: A Syrian goddess of life and health, who was worshipped in Egypt. Depicted as standing naked on a walking lion, with a mirror and lotus blossoms in her left hand and two serpents in her right. Overlaps with HATHOR and ASHTART.

KEFA: Egyptian. The Mother of Time, associated with the constellation Ursa Major.

KENEMET: An early Egyptian mother goddess, whose symbol was an ape; later replaced by MUT.

KERES, THE: Greek. The beings who carried out the will of the Fates or MOERAE. They would pounce on the dying at the appointed hour, and were known as the Dogs of Hades. Hovering especially over battles, they had grinning faces and sharp teeth, wore red robes and cried out dismally as they despatched the wounded.

KEYURI: A Hindu and Tibetan cemetery goddess.

KHADOMAS, THE: see DAKINIS.

KHADOS, THE: Tibetan. Regarded as primordial women, taken as wives by an earlier race of men; 'entirely human and fair to look upon' and credited with being able to walk on air and being very kind to mortals. Echoes of Genesis vi:2: 'The sons of God saw the daughters of men that they were fair; and they took them wives of all which they chose.'

KHAMADHENU, KHAMDEN: ('Cow of Plenty') Hindu mother goddess, capable of granting all desires. Regarded as the ancestress of the Mlechchas – i.e. everyone in the world outside the four Hindu castes. Under one name or another, universally worshipped in India.

KHOEMNU, CHEMNU: Egyptian. May have been regarded as the personification of Egypt (Khemu). Also associated with the Underworld and with fire, and known as the Enchantress or Succubus.

KHON-MA: Tibetan Mother of Fiends, who controls innumerable Earth-demons and must be propitiated in complicated ways to ensure protection of the household.

KI: Sumerian goddess personifying the Earth. She mated with the sky god An and gave birth to the air god Enlil, who separated them to form the present world.

KICHIJO-TEN: Japanese goddess of good fortune and beauty.

KIKIMORA: Slavonic domestic goddess (in some places, wife of the house-god, the Domovoi). If the housewife was lazy, Kikimora gave trouble and tickled the children at night. She was placated by washing the pots and pans in fern tea.

KIMA: Hebrew, personification of the Pleiades – the name used in Job xxxviii:31, 'Canst thou bind the sweet influences of the Pleiades?'

KINKINI-DHARI: see TIL-BU-MA.

KIPU-TYTTÖ, KIVUTAR: Finno-Ugric goddess of illness, daughter of Tuoni and TUONETAR.

KIRIRISHA: Assyro-Babylonian. Supreme goddess of Elam, mountainous land east of Babylon. Wife of Khumbam.

KISA GOTAMI: Indian Buddhist. Said to have been the first of an order of nuns set up by Buddha in spite of his reservations about women.

KISHAR: Assyro-Babylonian Earth goddess, wife of the sky god Ansar and mother of the great gods Anu, Ea and others.

KISHIBOJIN: see KARITEIMO.

KIVUTAR: See KIPU-TYTTÖ

KNOWEE: Australian aborigine Sun goddess. Originally a woman living on Earth before there was any sunlight, she left her small son in a cave while she went to look for yams. She lost her way back in the dark and went on till she fell off the edge of the world. She keeps circling the world with her torch held high; it has grown brighter over the years as she continues to search for her son.

KOBINE: Polynesian, Gilbert Islands. Co-creator of Heaven and Earth with her father Naruau.

KOMORKIS: Amerindian. Moon goddess of the Blackfoot.

KONO-HANA-SAKUYA-HIME: Japanese. Daughter of the mountain god, and wife of god Ninigi, grandson of AMATERASU. Connected with a rice festival on 23 November.

KORE: ('Maiden') Greek, another name for PERSEPHONE; see Chapter XIII.

KOROBONA: Guaianan, Arawak. Seduced by a water demon, she gave birth to the first Carib, a great warrior.

KORRAVAL: Hindu, a Tamil goddess of victory, wife of Silappadikaram, the brother of Krishna.

KOTTAVEI: India, a Tamil war goddess and sorceress. Corresponds to KALI.

KRIMBA: Slavonic, mainly Bohemia. A house goddess.

KRITTIKAS, THE: Hindu goddesses of the constellation Pleiades.

KRIYASHAKTI: see SHAKTIS.

KSHITI-APSARAS, THE: see APSARAS.

KUBABA: Hittite, chief goddess of the neo-Hittite peoples centred on Carchemish, of which she had been the local goddess. Adopted by the Phrygians, she became CYBELE.

KUHU: Hindu goddess of the New Moon.

KUKURI-HIME: Japanese goddess of mediation.

KUMARI: ('Girl, Daughter') Hindu, Tamil. Worshippers include girls who run races along the beaches in her honour. An aspect of PARVATI, but probably of earlier origin and absorbed by her.

K'UN: Chinese Earth mother, the Receptive, who nourishes all things and to whom in the end they return. The name of the I Ching trigram of three Yin (broken) lines.

KUNDALINI: ('Coiled') Hindu. The feminine Serpent Force, especially in its relation to organic and inorganic matter; the universal life-force of which electricity and magnetism are mere manifestations. Envisaged as moving in a left-handed spiral; when aroused in the human body, from the base of the spine up to the brain. Transforming when one is suitably ready for it, devastating when one is not. Yeats-Brown in *Bengal Lancer* describes his meeting with a Tantric Yogini (priestess of Kundalini) who told him: 'The goddess is more subtle than the fibre of the lotus ... She uncoils Herself and raises Her head, and enters the royal road of the spine, piercing the mystic centres, until She reaches the brain. These things are not to be understood in a day ... you taste Her nectar, and know that She is Life.' The spellbound Yeats-Brown commented that every woman 'is the begetter of more than bodies'. *777*: Tarot, Tens, Death; gems, rock crystal, snakestone; plants, willow, lily, ivy, cactus; animals, sphinx, scorpion, beetle, lobster or crayfish, wolf; mineral, magnesium sulphate; perfumes, dittany of Crete, Siamese benzoin, opoponax; magical weapons, Magic Circle, Triangle, Pain of the Obligation. See SHAKTIS.

KUNNAN-BEILE: see BIRRA-NULU.

KUNNAWARRA ('Black Swan') and KURURUK ('Native Companion'). Australian aborigine, Kulin and Wotjobaluk tribes. Twin Eves, whose inanimate bodies were discovered in the river mud by Balayang the Bat and taken to the creator god Bunjil, who held his hands over them and gave them life. 'You are to live with the men,' he told them. 'Man is not complete without you, nor will you be complete without him.'

KURUKULLA: Indian Buddhist. Depicted as reddish, seated in a cave and having four arms – two threatening and two soothing.

KWANNON: Japanese name for KWAN-YIN.

KWAN-YIN: Chinese, Buddhist origin. Goddess of fecundity and healing, 'she who bears the cries of the world' and sacrifices her Buddhahood for the sake of the suffering world. Also known as Sung-tzu niang-niang, 'the Lady who Brings Children'. Her image is in most Chinese homes, sitting on a lotus flower, with a child in her arms, or sometimes on a lion. She is also described as a magician, a teacher of magic, an oracular goddess and sometimes a prostitute. In rural China a man normally approaches her through a woman intermediary; if none is available and he has to appeal to her himself, he apologizes for the omission. For her possible origin, see HARITI.

LACHESIS: see MOERAE.

LADY OF THE LAKE: Arthurian. In some versions, VIVIENNE or Viviane. In others, Vivienne was the daughter of the Lady of the Lake by Dylan, son of ARIANRHOD and Gwydion. In Thomas Mallory, the Lady of the Lake is called NIMUE. See also GWENDYDD.

LADY HORSE-HEAD: Chinese. Patroness of the breeding of silkworms. One of the concubines of the August Personage of Jade.

LADY MENG: Chinese. Prepares the Broth of Oblivion. She lives just inside the exit from Hell, and all reincarnating souls must drink her broth on their way to a new incarnation. It makes them forget their former life, their existence in Hell and their speech.

LADY OF GOOD SIGHT: Chinese. Protects children from eye maladies.

LAHAMU, LAKHAMU: Chaldaean. First daughter of TIAMAT. She and her brother Lukhmu personified the primeval sediment. They were invoked on the completion of a building.

LAKINI: see DAKINI.

LAKSHMI: Hindu goddess of good fortune and plenty, and the personification of beauty. Born, radiant and holding a lotus, from the churning of the sea. Wife of Vishnu, and mother of Kama, god of love. Said to have assumed the personality of the wife of Vishnu in each of his ten avatars (incarnations). Probably an early mother and Earth goddess, and possibly once Vishnu's mother. She forms a triad with SARASVATI and DEVI. *777*: Tarot, Tens; gem: rock crystal; plants: willow, lily, ivy; animal: sphinx; mineral: magnesium sulphate; perfume: dittany of Crete; magical weapons: Magic Circle, Triangle.

LALITA: Hindu. Defined by Crowley (*777*, Col.xxii) as a sexual aspect of SHAKTI. *777*: Tarot, Empress; gems: emerald, turquoise; plants: myrtle, rose, clover; animals: sparrow, dove, swan; perfumes: sandalwood, myrtle, all soft voluptuous odours; magical weapon: Girdle.

LAMIA: (1) Originally a Libyan snake goddess, with orgiastic priestesses; in later Greek legend, a queen of Libya loved by Zeus and robbed of her offspring by jealous HERA; she became (in the plural, Lamiae) beautiful demonesses who seduced and vampirized travellers and preyed on children.

LAMIA: (2) Greek name for NEITH.

LASYA, LASEMA, SGEG-MO-MA: Tibetan goddess of beauty. Depicted holding a mirror.

LAT: see AL-LAT.

LATIS: British goddess 'of the pool' or 'of beer', worshipped at Birdoswald on the Roman Wall. Latis fell in love with a salmon, and out of pity for her the other gods and goddesses turned him into a handsome young warrior. But every Winter he turns back into a salmon, and Latis weeps for him till his springtime return as her manly lover. The Winter rains are her tears.

LATONA: see LETO.

LAUDINE: see LUNED.

LAUFEY: ('Wooded Isle') Teutonic. Mother of trickster god Loki, who was originally a fire demon; she furnished his firewood.

LAVERNA: Roman goddess of thieves and trickery. Remembered in Tuscan witch lore – see Leland's *Aradia*, pp.89-98).

LAZ: Assyro-Babylonian. A prehistoric goddess of Cuthac, and wife of the Underworld god Nergal in early legends – a place later taken by ERESHKIGAL.

LEANNAN SIDHE: Irish fairy lover, succubus. Dinneen's dictionary defines her as 'a familiar figure, an endearing phantom, also figuratively of a delicate person ... used sometimes like "muse" as a source of poetical inspiration'. Those inspired by her lead brilliant but short lives. In the Isle of Man she is malevolent and vampiric.

LEBIYAH: ('Lioness') Hebrew. Personification of Israel, the Mother of Israel; see Ezekiel xix.

LESHACHIKHA: Slavonic forest (*les*) goddess, wife of the forest god the Leshy and mother of the Leshonki. The Leshies died in October and revived in Spring. They were jealous of their territory, leading those who entered it astray – but almost always releasing them in the end. The spell against them was to take your clothes off under a tree and put them on again backwards.

LETO: Greek. Daughter of the Titans Coeus and Phoebe, mother by Zeus of Apollo and ARTEMIS. Born in 'the land of the Hyperboreans' beyond the North Wind, sometimes identified with Britain and later with Ireland. An orgiastic goddess. Her sacred tree was the palm. Called Latona by the Romans.

LEUCOTHEA: ('Milk-White Goddess') Greek. As a mortal woman called Ino, she looked after the infant Dionysus. She jumped into the sea with him to escape her husband Athamas, and a dolphin carried them to the Isthmus of Corinth, after which she became a sea goddess under her new name. As such she helped Odysseus when a storm destroyed his raft. Mother goddess of the Centaurs.

LEVANAH: Chaldaean, Hebrew. A name for the Moon goddess. The word used for 'moon' in Song of Solomon vi:10 is the Hebrew form Lebanah: 'Who is she that looketh forth as the morning, fair as the moon, clear as the sun, and terrible as an army with banners?' Durdin-Robertson (*Goddesses of Chaldaea*, p.94) notes that 'the knowledge available concerning Levanah has come down mainly through occult sources'. Dion Fortune (*The Sea Priestess*, p.223) says the Moon is called 'by the wise, Levanah, for therein is contained the number of her name. She is the ruler of the tides of flux and reflux. The waters of the Great Sea answer unto her; likewise the waters of all earthly seas, and she ruleth the nature of woman'.

LEWA-LEVU: ('Great Woman') Fijian predatory goddess, who lived at the entrance to a gloomy defile, ready to pounce on any man who took her fancy, living or dead; the ghost of a bachelor had to take special precautions to avoid her.

LI: Chinese. Daughter of Ch'ien and K'UN. Personification of the solar feminine aspect; 'Fire, the Middle Daughter, the Clinging, the Lucid, the Bride'. In the I Ching, the trigram Li, 'The Clinging' (two Yang lines separated by a Yin line). Associated with midsummer and noon. Symbols, the pheasant (fire-bird) and the cow (nourishing, life-giving).

LIBAN (1): ('Beauty of Women') Irish, mermaid associated with Lough Neagh. King Ecca had put a woman in charge of a magic well within his fortress on a plain, with orders to open the door only when the people of the fortress needed to draw water. One day she forgot to close the door, and the plain was flooded, forming Lough Neagh. Ecca and all his people were drowned, except for his daughter Liban, who lived under the lough for a year and a day with her little dog and then took the form of a salmon but keeping her own face and breasts. Liban and the woman in charge of the well are probably the same. The Christian ending to the story is that after 300 years St Congall rescued her, baptizing her Muirgen, 'born of the sea'. A Submerged Princess archetype, like DAHUD.

LIBAN (2): Irish goddess of healing and pleasure. With FAND, she appeared to Cuchulainn in a dream in which they beat him with horsewhips – but only to teach him a lesson which ended in happiness.

LIBERA: ('Free') Roman, an early goddess of wine and fertility, later identified with PERSEPHONE. Female partner of Liber (another name for Bacchus), both of them being honoured at the Liberalia festival on 17 March, when slaves were permitted to speak with freedom.

LIBITINA: Roman goddess of funerals; whenever anyone died, a piece of money had to be brought to her temple. Undertakers were known as 'libitinarii'. Also a love and fertility goddess, originally perhaps an agricultural deity.

LILITH: Hebrew version of LILITU. In Hebrew legend, she was Adam's first wife, who would not subordinate herself to him and was turned into a demoness. Cabalistically, sometimes named as the Qlipha, evil counterpart, of MALKUTH (see also NAHEMA). See Chapter XVIII for her full story.

LILITU: ('Night-hag') Sumerian. Brought nightmares and other nocturnal menaces; probably originally a storm goddess. The name was only later applied to LILITH, Adam's first wife.

LILWANI: Hittite Earth goddess, connected with the important Spring festival of Purulli.

LISSA: Dahomey mother goddess, mother of the Sun god Maou and the Moon god Gou. Her totem was the chameleon.

LITAE, THE: see ATE.

LIVING GODDESS, THE: Nepal. In Katmandu there is a Temple of the Living Goddess, where a young virgin of Brahmin caste is installed for a set period to be worshipped in the flesh, and offerings made to her, as the Goddess's manifestation. At the festival which concludes her term she comes to the door of the temple, scattering flower petals and distributing wine 'from her mouth all day, making drunk and merry many of her followers below'. Her successor then takes over and she returns to ordinary life.

LOLA: ('Lightning') India. A goddess of fickle fortune.

LORELEI: German. A beautiful siren who sat on a cliff above the Rhine, luring boatmen to their death with her songs.

LOSNA: An Etruscan Moon goddess.

LOVIATAR: Finno-Ugric. The most terrible daughter of Tuoni and TUONETAR. From her union with the Wind were born pleurisy, colic, gout, phthisis, ulcers, scabies, canker, plague and a nameless 'fatal spirit, a creature eaten up with envy'. Also called Louhi.

LUCINA: Roman. A goddess of birth and midwifery.

LUKELONG: Micronesian, Caroline Islands. In the beginning she created first the heavens and then the Earth.

LUNA: The Roman Moon goddess, identified with DIANA and the Greek SELENE.

LUNED, LAUDINE: Arthurian. She befriended Owain and brought about his marriage with the Lady of the Fountain. In her sovereignty aspect she is called Laudine.

LUONNOTAR ('Daughter of Nature') or ILMATAR ('Mother of the Waters'): Finno-Ugric creation goddess, daughter of the air god Ilma. Weary of her lonely celestial virginity, she floated on the sea for seven centuries. Eventually an eagle (or a duck) nested on her knee and laid eggs. These rolled into the abyss and were changed into the Earth, the heavens, Sun, Moon and stars. She gave birth to the first human being, the bard Vainamoinen. In the Kalevala epic she was impregnated by the East Wind.

LUST GODDESS, THE: see DELIGHT GODDESS.

MA: A Lydian fertility goddess whose cult was introduced to Rome by the dictator Sulla about 85 BC.

MA'AT, MAYET: Egyptian goddess of justice, truth, law and the divine order; the natural and inevitable order of the universe, rather than any artificially imposed rules. Daughter of Ra (who brought light to the world by putting her in the place of chaos) and wife of Thoth, god of wisdom. She played an important part in the judgement of the dead. Depicted crowned by the red feather. 777: Tarot, Justice; gem: emerald; plant: aloe; animal: elephant; perfume: galbanum; magical weapon: Cross of Equilibrium. See Chapter XX for her full story.

MACHA: ('Battle') Irish. Three legendary women, probably originally the same goddess. Patroness of Ulster and war goddess; Ulster's capital Emain Macha was named after her; so was Armagh (Ard Macha). One source makes her the wife of Nemed, dying on the twelfth day (year?) after their landing in Ireland, 'the first death of the people of Nemed'. Another Macha appears as the wife of Cimbaeth and daughter of Aed Ruad, and a war-leader herself. A third, wife of Crunnchu, raced against the fastest horse in Ireland when she was pregnant, and died at the winning-post giving birth to twins.

MADHUSRI: Hindu goddess of Spring.

MAFDET: Egyptian cat goddess or lynx goddess, predating BAST and SEKHMET. Known as 'the Lady of the Castle of Life' as early as the 1st Dynasty. Renowned as a slayer of serpents.

MAGDALENE: see MARY MAGDALENE.

MAHADEVI: ('Great Goddess') A title of LAKSHMI.

MAIA: Roman. Daughter of Atlas, mother of Hermes by Zeus. Later identified with FAUNA and with BONA DEA. Gave her name to the month of May.

(Do not confuse with the Hindu MAYA.)

MAISO: Guianan. The Stone Woman, mother goddess of the Paressi tribe of the Arawaks, who produced all beings, animate and inanimate.

MAITRI: Hindu goddess of goodwill and friendship.

MALKUTH: ('The Kingdom') Hebrew. Personification of Earth, of the Earth-soul; the Goddess in actual manifestation. The tenth Sephira of the Cabalistic Tree of Life, known as the Bride, the Resplendent Intelligence. 'No operation is completed until the process has been expressed in terms of Malkuth, or, in other words, has issued forth in action on the physical plane. If this is not done, the force that has been generated is not properly "earthed", and it is this loose force left flying around that causes the trouble in magical experiments.' (Dion Fortune, *The Mystical Qabalah*, p.275). Cabalistic symbols: the Altar of the Double Cube, the Equal-Armed Cross, the Magic Circle, the Triangle of Art. Tarot: Tens. Magical image: a young woman, crowned and throned.

MAMA, MAMI: Assyro-Babylonian. An early name for the creator-mother. A childbirth incantation quoted by Neumann (*The Great Mother*, pp.135-6) envisages her as a potter. According to the belief at Eridu, said to have fashioned man out of clay, softened with the blood of a god slain by Ea.

MAMA ALPA: Inca Earth and harvest goddess. Many-breasted like ARTEMIS of Ephesus.

MAMA COCHA: Inca rain and sea goddess, sister and wife of Viracocha. Mother of all mankind.

MAMAN BRIGITTE: see BRIGITTE.

MAMA NONO: Earth mother goddess of the Caribs of the Antilles.

MAMA OCCLO, MAMA OULLO HUACA: Inca goddess who instructed women in the domestic arts. Sister and wife of Manco Capac; they were the legendary first rulers of the Inca empire.

MAMA PACHA: Inca Earth mother goddess from whom sprang Pachacamac, the universal creative spirit.

MAMA QUILLA: Inca Moon goddess, sister and wife of Inti, the Sun; this pair were the supreme deities. Her priestesses were vestals and rainmakers. Protectress of married women. Depicted as a silver disc with a human face.

MAMMITU: Assyro-Babylonian goddess who plotted the destiny of the newborn.

MANAH: See AL-LAT. Also an Arabic tribal goddess; one of the UNSAS.

MANASA: Hindu, mainly Bengal. Her legends imply strong feminine counter-attacks against male chauvinism. Invoked against snake-bites.

MANTRIKASHAKTI: see SHAKTIS, THE.

MARA, MARAH: ('Bitter') Chaldaean. The salt sea as the Great Mother. 'Probably the origin of the feminine names Marah, Maria, Marie, Marion, Mary, Maire and their variants' (Durdin-Robertson, *Goddesses of Chaldaea*, p.93).

MARI (1): Supreme Basque goddess, ruling all other deities. Sometimes described as an Earth goddess, but her attributes seem primarily lunar. She lives in the depths of the Earth but likes crossing the sky at night; so does her husband/son Sugaar ('Male Serpent'). She rides the sky in a cart pulled by four horses, or in the form of a burning sickle or crescent, or engulfed in flames, or riding a broomstick in a ball of fire. The Basques appear unique in associating the Moon with the colour red and with fire, and Mari has strong fire symbolism. Sugaar also rides as a burning crescent, but to the Basques the Moon itself is always female. They respect her greatly, timing their woodcutting, sowing and reaping by her phases. The Moon's divinatory animal is the ladybird, known as *Mari Gorri* ('Red Mari'), who is often asked to predict tomorrow's weather. Basques believe it is the light of the Moon which guides the dead to their resting-place. Friday is the Moon's day, and Friday night the traditional witches' meeting time. Mari is the patroness of all witches, and a witch herself, with oracular and magical powers. She often appears as an elegantly dressed lady – sometimes crowned with the full Moon or a burning crescent Moon. In one locality at least she appears in a red skirt; her title Yonagorri may mean *gona gorri* ('red skirt'), though an alternative interpretation is *Iona gorri* ('red Joan'). She can also appear as a tree, the wind or a rainbow. She is associated with Akerbeltz ('black he-goat'), whom Basque witches invoked and worked with at their sabbats, which were called Akelarre ('field of the he-goat'). She also rides a ram, around whose horns she wraps wool to wind into a ball. Other totem animals are the horse, the heifer and the crow or raven. Mari changes her abode, spending seven years in Anboto, where she is known as Anbotoko Dama ('Lady of Anboto') or Anbotoko Sorgina ('Witch of Anboto'), seven years in Oiz and seven years in Mugarra. Other accounts say she spends time in Aralar, Aiztorri and Murumendi. A Christian shrine of the Virgin called Andikona ('To and Fro') lies between Anboto and Oiz, and the name may have Mari roots. Mari is strong and just, never malignant, but she may be quick-tempered. She abhors lies, theft, pride, arrogance and breaking one's word, and punishes these appropriately; for example, if a friend asks you for money and you pretend you have only 500 pesetas when actually you have 2,000, Mari will make sure you lose the 1,500 you lied about. Other punishments which she may send are hail and inner troubles, such as restlessness. She rules both rain and drought.

MARI (2): Hindu. A death goddess worshipped by the Korwas, hereditary basket-makers.

MARICHI: Hindu, Buddhist. Personification of the ray of light that appears before the rising Sun. Tantric teaching is that this ray remains the Sun's invisible companion throughout the day; she can be terrible, but anyone who 'knows her name' can acquire her marvellous powers. (Cf. the benevolent dawn goddess USHAS.) Reached Japan under the name Marishi-Ten. Japanese feudal warriors put her image on their helmets as a charm against the enemy's blows. Depicted with a frontal eye, riding a galloping boar or a pack of seven boars, and with from two to ten arms carrying weapons.

MARINETTE: Haitian Voodoo corn goddess, whose somewhat violent rites involve pig sacrifice – probably a relic of the sacrificed Corn King. Wife of the one-footed or footless (snake?) god Ti-Jean Petro. (The Petro rites are of Amerindian rather than African origin.)

MARY MAGDALENE: Hebrew. Held in Christian tradition to have been a reformed prostitute; but there are no biblical grounds for this whatsoever. Like the VIRGIN MARY, she has been mythologized independently of, and often in conflict with, the Biblical account – with popular feeling and official theology pulling in somewhat different directions. See Chapter VII.

MARZANNA: Slavonic, Polish. Goddess who helped the growth of fruit.

MASAYA: Nicaraguan. Oracular goddess of volcanoes. Human sacrifices were made to her by throwing them into craters after earthquakes. Black-skinned with thin hair and sagging breasts.

MASHONGAVUDZI: Rhodesian. Chief wife of Muari, god of the Mtawara tribe. The reigning chief's first wife still takes this name.

MASHYOI: The Persian Eve; her Adam was Mashya. They were born from the body of Gayomart after it had lain in the Earth for forty years.

MATERGABIA: Slavonic goddess directing the housekeeping, to whom one offered the first piece of bread from a new batch.

MATI-SYRA-ZEMLYA: ('Mother-Earth-Moist') Slavonic Earth goddess. In some regions, in August, she was invoked protectively facing East, West, South and North, with libations of hemp oil. She could prophesy, if one could understand her. An oath in her name was binding and incontestable. As late as this century, Russian peasant women performed a rite to her to ward off plague; nine virgins and three widows, clad only in their shifts, would plough a furrow round the village, shrieking. Any man who met them was struck down mercilessly.

MATRES, THE: ('Mothers') A name applied to representations of Roman triple goddesses, like the one at Colchester.

MATRIKADEVIS, THE: Indian Buddhist mother goddesses.

MATRI-PADMA: ('Mother-Lotus') Hindu. The Waters of Space, the Universal Mother. The opening lotus symbolizes the yoni.

MATRONA: Latinized form of the Celtic Great Mother name; see MODRON and MORGAN.

MAYA (1): Hindu. The goddess of Nature, the universal creatress. The name is generally translated 'illusion', but this is misleading: it means the power which causes the material world to manifest as observable existence. She gives life, and also the desire for life, and is associated with knowledge, magic and witchcraft. 'Maya is Mother Nature with her all-embracing claims. Anyone who mistakenly believes that he can escape her, she pursues. She pursues, and by her limitless arts and her infinite time, all will be drawn to their true destination, the abode of the Great Mother.' (Durdin-Robertson, *Goddesses of India*, p.221.)

MAYA (2): Indian Buddhist. Mother of the Buddha. She was the queen of King Suddhodhana. In a dream, she saw the Buddha enter her womb in the form of a little white elephant. At this moment the whole Earth showed its joy; instruments played music without being touched, rivers stopped flowing, flowers blossomed everywhere, and lakes were covered with lotuses. She gave birth to him standing in the Lumbini garden in Nepal; he emerged from her right side without causing her pain. Seven days later Maya died of joy and was reborn among the gods. (See also PRAJNAPARAMITA and YASODHARA.)

MAYAUEL: Mexico, Agave. Mother goddess 'with the four hundred breasts'. Goddess of the intoxicant made from the maguey plant. Known both as 'the Strangling One' and as 'the Healing One'.

MAYAVATI: Hindu. A goddess of the magical arts. See RATI.

ME-ABZU: see TIAMAT.

MEBELI: Congo, Mundang tribe. Goddess of triad Massim-Biambe (omnipotent immaterial creator), Phebele (male god) and Mebeli (goddess). Phebele and Mebeli had a son, Man, and Massim-Biambe gave him a soul and the breath of life.

MEDEA: Greek. Originally a goddess, demoted to sorceress; she betrayed her father, worked magic and cut up her brother, to help Jason (with whom she was in love) carry off the Golden Fleece. She also poisoned Jason's intended bride.

MEDHBH, MAEVE, OF CONNACHT: ('Intoxication') Irish. Legendary Queen of Connacht, wife of the somewhat ineffectual King Ailill. In fact a goddess of sovereignty, to whom the King must be mated to become King. Her legends present her as a terrifying and unscrupulous warrior woman; this probably reflects emerging patriarchal resentment of the principle she personified. For example, Cuchulainn in the Táin Bó Cualnge is clearly the chosen Young Hero destined for ultimate replacement and sacrifice; he will not accept the role and does battle with her instead. She once stopped a battle by showing that she was menstruating. Like MACHA, she could outrun any horse, and the sight of her deprived men of two-thirds of their strength. Sexually insatiable, she could have 'thirty men every day or go with Fergus once'. 'Queen Medhbh's Cairn', Knocknarea, is a passage-grave mound topping a 1,078-foot hill overlooking Sligo Bay. It is built of some 40,000 tons of stone and is still unexcavated; Sligo people are superstitious about disturbing it. Medhbh is also the 'Queen Mab' of fairy legend.

MEDBH KETHDERG ('Half-Red') of LEINSTER: Irish. Like MEDHBH OF CONNACHT, a personification of sovereignty.

MEDUSA: Greek. The only mortal member of the three GORGONS. Her hair was turned to serpents by ATHENE because she dared to claim equal beauty with hers. Her gaze turned men to stone. Perseus managed to kill her, with Athene's help, by watching her reflection in his shield while he cut off her head. The winged horse Pegasus sprang from her blood (though another version says Pegasus was her offspring by Poseidon), and her head was placed on Athene's shield.

MEENAKSHI: ('Fish-eyed') Hindu. A benevolent form of KALI. She has a huge fourteenth-century, fifteen-acre temple at Madurai, South India.

MEFITIA: Roman goddess of malaria.

MEGAERA: see ERINYES, THE.

MEHEN: Egyptian, Heliopolis. A serpent goddess among the many deities who had to be invoked during the soul's passage through the Underworld. Described as everlasting and as enfolding other gods within her coils.

MEHUERET, MEHURT: Egyptian. The predynastic Celestial Cow, goddess of the beginning; one of the names for the universal Great Mother.

'Lady of Heaven and Mistress of Earth', mother of Ra. Also associated with night. Depicted as a woman with protruding breasts (sometimes with a cow's head), holding a sceptre with a lotus flower entwined round it.

MELETE: see MUSES.

MELPEMONE: see MUSES.

MELUSINE: (Male Lucina, 'Evil Midwife') Irish/Scottish/French, possibly originally Scythian. A serpent-goddess, woman from the waist up, 'yet she had a bold and elegant gait' (Rabelais). She has a rich fund of legends in Poitou folklore, which makes her a daughter of Elinas, King of Scotland, by the fairy woman Pressine. Pressine married Elinas on condition that he never tried to find out who she was or where she came from. He eventually broke this condition, and she cursed him and disappeared with their three daughters to the Lost Island. Fifteen years later Melusine led her sisters back to avenge their mother, locking Elinas up in the Brandebois mountains. Pressine, furious at this independent action, put a spell on her to become a snake up to the waist every Saturday. In Poitou, Melusine married Raimond de Lusignan on condition that he never asked where she was on Saturdays – a promise which he, too, eventually broke, and she grew wings and flew away weeping. Pressine and Melusine were probably originally one, the archetypal mother goddess who can make men prosperous and happy on condition that they do not know exactly who she is. Melusine had borne Raimond three sons, young heroes with supernatural traits – another pointer to the myth's matriarchal origins. Rabelais equates Melusine with Ora, another half-serpent woman who had a son by Jupiter; Melusine/Ora may be what French folklore made of the Scythian DIANA/ARTEMIS. A medieval romance makes Melusine patroness of Poitou and ancestress of the Lusignan family. Another version says Melusine married Fulk le Noir, Count of Anjou, which would make her (via Geoffrey of Anjou's son King Henry II of England) an ancestress of the present British royal family.

MENI: Chaldaean goddess of love, also of fate. Isaiah lxv:11, 'But ye ... that furnish the drink offering unto that number' has in the Authorized Version a marginal alternative translation 'unto Meni'.

MENKHERET: Egyptian goddess who carried the dead through the various stages of the Underworld.

MENQET: Egyptian Underworld goddess who gave food to the deceased.

MENVRA: Etruscan goddess of wisdom, from whom the Roman MINERVA derived. She wielded thunderbolts at the Spring equinox.

MERTSEGER: ('Friend of Silence') Egyptian goddess who lived on a peak overlooking the funerary Valley of the Kings opposite Thebes; she could be benevolent but could also punish. Depicted as a human-headed snake, or as a snake with three heads, the centre one human, the other two a snake's and a vulture's.

MESHKENT: Egyptian goddess of childbirth. Wife of Shai, god of destiny.

She personified the two bricks on which Egyptian women crouched for delivery. ISIS stood before the mother, and NEPHTHYS behind, while HEKET helped. Isis received the child, and the four goddesses then bathed it. Often Meshkent would foretell the baby's future. (Cf. HATHORS.) Sometimes Meshkent is all four goddesses; Isis and the others appeared particularly at the birth of kings. She was also associated with rebirth after death, assisting Isis and Nephthys in the funerary rites and testifying on the character of the deceased. Depicted crowned with two long palm shoots curved at the tips, or as one of the birth-bricks with a human head.

METERES: Cretan goddess of maternity and fruitfulness.

METHYER: Egyptian. 'The Great Cow in the Water', terrestrial counterpart of the cow of the heavenly ocean. May be an aspect of MEHUERET.

METIS: ('Wisdom, Counsel') Greek, daughter of Oceanus and TETHYS. At the young Zeus' request, she gave Cronus the draught which made him vomit up all his other children whom he had swallowed. She became Zeus' first wife, but GAIA and Uranus warned him that if she had children by him they would be more powerful than he; so when she became pregnant, he swallowed her and the unborn child. As a result, ATHENE was born from his head. The supreme example of the patriarchal take-over: Zeus not only absorbs the female Wisdom into his own person, he also commandeers woman's unique and envied function, that of giving birth.

METSULAH: Hebrew. The great depths of the sea, which swallows people and where great wonders dwell. Close parallels with TIAMAT.

MEZTLI, TECCIZTECATL: Aztec Moon and night goddess, and patroness of agriculture.

MICTLANCIHUATL: Aztec. Co-ruler with her husband Mictlantecuhtli of the underworld.

MIELIKKI: Major Finnish forest goddess, wife of Tapio and mother of TUULIKKI and Nyyrikki. This family were invoked to ensure abundance of grain. She created the bear from a hank of wool.

MIHIT, MEHIT: Egyptian. Lion goddess worshipped at Thinis; overlaps with SEKHMET.

MINERVA: Roman, wife of Jupiter, forming a triad with his other wife, JUNO. Originally Etruscan, as MENVRA. Merged very early with the Greek ATHENE. Protectress of commerce, industry and education; later also a war goddess. Honoured with Mars at the Quinquatrus, a five-day festival at the Spring equinox. *777*: Tarot, Emperor; gem: ruby; plants: tiger lily, geranium; animals: ram, owl; perfume: dragon's blood; magical weapons: Horns, Energy, Burin.

MIRU: Polynesian. One name for the goddess of the Underworld; see also HINE-NUI-TE-PO.

MITSUHA-NOME-NO-KAMI: ('Water-Greens') A Japanese water goddess, born of the urine of IZANAMI.

MIZUNOE, OTO: Japan. A goddess of divine beauty who took the fisherman Urashima to her underwater palace, where he stayed for three years; returning home, he found that 300 years had passed. In some versions he went back to her palace. Cf. the Irish NIAMH OF THE GOLDEN HAIR.

MNEME: see MUSES.

MNEMOSYNE: ('Memory') Greek. Titaness, daughter of Uranus and GAIA. Her nephew Zeus spent nine nights with her, and she bore him the nine MUSES.

MOANING-RIVER: Japanese. Born of the tears of the god Izanagi when his wife IZANAMI died.

MOBO: Chinese, Japanese. A widowed mother who brought up her son Mengtseu so wisely that she became a goddess of maternal goodness. In China the phrase 'Mother of Meng' still means a model mother.

MODRON: ('Great Mother') Welsh. Mother of Mabon ('Great Son'), who was stolen from her when he was three nights old but eventually rescued by King Arthur. He is the masculine counterpart of PERSEPHONE – the male fertilizing principle seasonally withdrawn; Modron thus corresponds to DEMETER.

MOERAE, THE: ('Fates') Greek goddesses of destiny, daughters of Zeus by THEMIS. The three were: Clotho, spinner of the thread of life; Lachesis, the element of chance; and Atropos, who finally cut the thread. Their decisions were carried out by the KERES. They were, understandably, prophetic goddesses. They had to be invoked at weddings to ensure a happy union. They were under the command of Zeus, who saw to it that the natural order was respected. A dedication to them (as the Parcae) by an official of a burial-club was found at Lincoln.

MOINGFHION, MONGFHINN: ('The White-Haired One') Irish. Associated with Samhain (Féile Moingfhinne).

MORGAN: ('Of the Sea'; originally = 'Mother'?) Arthur's half-sister Morgan le Fay; but would seem to be a much older goddess, possibly the Glastonbury Tor one, for her island is Avalon. As the King's incestuous and ungovernable half-sister, also a goddess of sovereignty. Said to have been taught magic by Merlin, like VIVIENNE (NIMUE), and seems to have been an earlier lover of his than she; or even the same person, perhaps also overlapping GWENDYDD. Associated with water, and had magical healing powers. The word 'morgan' in Breton is masculine and means 'être fabuleux supposé vivant dans la mer'; 'morganez (f.)' means 'sirène'.

MORNING STAR: Australian aborigine, Northern. Originally male, brother of Moon, who was also male. Together they created land, rivers, plants, animals, but between themselves they knew something was missing. One day when Morning Star was sleeping, Moon realized what it was – male and female! He used his boomerang to remodel Morning Star's body into that of a woman; when she awoke, their happiness was complete. Mankind is descended from these two and can still see in the crescent Moon the boomerang that shaped the first woman.

MORRIGAN, MORRIGU: ('Great Queen' or 'Queen of Demons') Irish war goddess. Usually referred to as 'the Morrigan'. Daughter of ERNMAS, and sometimes a collective name for all three of her daughters; see BADHBH. Her symbol was the raven or crow. Possibly a pre-Celtic Moon goddess.

MOTHER CAREY: Sailors' folklore, perhaps a memory of a sea or sky goddess; survives in the popular names for two sea-birds – 'Mother Carey's Chickens' (the stormy petrel) and 'Mother Carey's Geese' (the giant Pacific fulmar) – and in the saying 'Mother Carey is plucking her goose' (it is snowing) (cf. HULDA). The name is a corruption of Mater Cara, 'Beloved Mother'. Stormy petrels are called in French '*oiseaux de Notre Dame*' (birds of Our Lady).

MOTHER CLEAR-LIGHT: Tibetan goddess who manifests as one is falling into deep sleep.

MOTHER OF LIFE: Gnostic, Manichaean. An AEON, first womb of mankind, and the means by which the present universe came into dense manifestation. Maniachaean depictions show her as a beautiful, richly ornamented girl with her body open to show the disc of the world within her.

MOTHER OF MANNU: Finno-Ugric Earth goddess.

MOTHER OF METSOLA: see MIELIKKI.

MOTHER OF TEN THOUSAND THINGS: A Chinese name for the Void, the flux of the universe beyond one's control, the Mysterious Female.

MUILIDHEARTACH: Scottish battle goddess, who crossed the sea to fight the Fenians. Her face was blue-black and she had 'one deep pool-like eye'.

MULAPRAKRITI: ('Primeval Matter') Hindu. She who differentiates elements and the multitudinous forms of Nature from raw energy.

MURIGEN: Irish lake goddess, associated with a minor deluge legend; later became a salmon – possibly one of the Salmons of Knowledge (see BOANN).

MUSES, THE: Greek, Thracian origin. Daughters of Zeus and MNEMOSYNE ('Memory'); other traditions name other parents, including Uranus and GAIA. Originally seem to have been goddesses of springs, then of memory and only finally of inspiration. Variously numbered in different parts of Greece (mostly, and early, as three) but ended up as nine: Clio (History, attributes the trumpet and the clepsydra); Euterpe (Flute-playing); Thalia (Comedy, attributes the comic mask and shepherd's staff); Melpomene (Tragedy, attributes the tragic mask and the club of Heracles); Terpsichore (Lyric Poetry and the Dance, attribute the cithara); Erato (Love Poetry); Polyhymnia (Mimic Art, represented as meditating with a finger to her mouth); Urania (Astronomy, attributes the celestial globe and compasses); and Calliope (Epic Poetry and Eloquence, attributes the stylus and tablets). Of the nine, Calliope took precedence. They dwelt on Helicon, a high mountain in Boeotia. Associated with Apollo, but seem originally to have been an independent Triple Goddess. (Melete, Mneme and Aoide at Helicon; Nete, Mese and Hypate at Delphi.

MUT: ('Mother') Egyptian, goddess member of the Theban triad of Amun-Ra, Mut and Khons. A major form of the primordial Great Mother. Her symbol was the vulture, regarded as an ideal mother to her young. Became confused with NEKHBET as protectress of Upper Egypt. She married Amun-Ra (though she was also regarded as his self-formed mother) and was identified with his earlier wife AMAUNET in the 18th Dynasty (*c.* 1580 BC onwards). Her temple was at Luxor, and Amun-Ra's a few miles downstream at Karnak; his annual visit to her was one of the great festivals of the New Kingdom – the Festival of OPET at 'the going-up of the goddess SOTHIS'

(the heliacal rising of the star Sirius on 19 July). Often identified with HATHOR, SEKHMET and BAST. Named 'the Great Sorceress', 'Mistress of Heaven' and 'Eye of Ra'. Described in the *Book of the Dead* as she 'who maketh souls strong and who maketh sound bodies'. Although Amun-Ra's wife, she was sometimes said to be bisexual, 'proceeding from herself', as the creator-deity of all living things. Depicted with a vulture headdress, or wearing the double crown of Egypt, or with the horns and disc through identification with Hathor, or sometimes with the lioness head of Sekhmet or the cat head of Bast. *777*: Tarot, Threes, Fool; gems: star sapphire, pearl opal, agate; plants: cypress, opium poppy, aspen; animals: woman, eagle, man; perfumes: myrrh, civet, galbanum; magical weapons: Yoni, Outer Robe of Concealment, Dagger, Fan.

MYESTYAS: Slavonic. Usually a Moon god but sometimes represented as the Sun's beautiful young wife, whom he marries each Spring and abandons each Winter.

MYLITTA, MELITA, MOLIS: ('Child-bearing') Assyro-Babylonian Moon goddess of love, beauty, fertility and childbirth. Associated with the planet Venus. Sacred prostitution was practised at her temple; according to Herodotus, every woman born in the country had to go there once in her life and accept the first stranger who said to her, 'May the goddess Mylitta prosper thee.'

NAGIS, NAGINIS, THE: Hindu serpent-goddesses, wives of the Nagas. Given to surprise and trickery, but can be helpful. Human to the waist, with serpents' tails, though they sometimes take the form of nymphs and men fall in love with them. The Nagis and Nagas live in a magnificent underground kingdom.

NAHAR: Syrian Sun goddess name in the Ugarit scripts.

NAHEMA: Hebrew. A succubus who gives birth to spirits and demons. Cabalistically, sometimes named as the Qlipha, evil counterpart, of MALKUTH (see also LILITH).

NAHMAUIT, NEMANOUS: ('She who Removes Evil') Egyptian, a wife of Thoth. Her name describes her function. Her symbol is the sistrum.

NAMAGIRI: A Hindu goddess of inspiration, teaching and prophecy.

NAMMU: Chaldaean, Sumerian. Goddess of the primeval ocean, 'the mother who gave birth to heaven and Earth'. She roused the water god Enki (an early form of Ea) from sleep and helped create mankind. A form of TIAMAT.

NANA (1): Phrygian, mother of the vegetation god Attis (see CYBELE). Conceived of her own will by the use of an almond or pomegranate.

NANA (2): An early Sumerian goddess, probably merging with INANNA and ISHTAR.

NANDECY: Brazilian. Wife of civilizing hero Nanderevusu and mother of storm god Tupan. Tupan lives in the West, and there are storms every time he travels to visit his mother in the East.

NANNA: Teutonic. Wife of Baldur, seduced by his rival, Holder. According to Graves (*The White Goddess*, p.317) in this tale Nanna is really FRIGG, but 'the Norse scalds have altered the story in the interests of marital rectitude'. When Baldur died, she committed suicide on his funeral pyre. From Hel,

Baldur sent his ring as a gift to Odin, and she sent linen to Frigg.

NANSHE: A Chaldaean goddess of springs and canals, interpreter of dreams. Daughter of Ea and sister of INANNA. Her symbol was a bowl with a fish in it.

NANTOSUELTA: ('Of the Winding Stream') Consort of Gaulish god Sucellos; attribute the raven. Appears on monuments carrying a cornucopia.

NARI: Hindu, a form of the mother goddess, bringing forth life from chaos. She and her husband Nara sometimes appear as the primordial woman and man. She has virgin priestesses, who are regarded with very great respect.

NATHAIR PARRTHUIS, THE: ('Serpent of Paradise') Old Irish name for the Serpent of Eden, regarded as feminine.

NAUNET, NUNUT: Egyptian. With her husband Nun, the first couple of the Ogdoad of Hermopolis. The Ogdoad were the first eight living beings, the males being frogs and the females serpents. She was the counterheaven through which the Sun passes at night, NUT's other self. Depicted as a woman with a serpent's head and having a jackal's head in place of feet.

NEBHET HOTEP: Egyptian. One of the two wives of the predynastic Sun god Atum – the other being IUSAS.

NEHALENNIA: Sea goddess of the Belgae (Frisians).

NEITH: Egyptian. A very ancient Delta goddess, protectress of Sais; her emblem was the crossed arrows of a predynastic clan. 'The personification of the eternal female principle of life which was self-sustaining and self-existent and was secret and unknown and all-pervading' (Wallis Budge). She became the patron goddess of Lower Egypt (as NEKHBET was of Upper Egypt), and finally a national deity when the 26th Dynasty (c.664 BC onwards) re-established Egyptian unity, with Sais as capital, after the Assyrian invasion. She became a sky goddess like NUT and HATHOR; or was sometimes regarded as the original Waters of Chaos from which everything was born. Known as Great Goddess and Mother of the Gods, she was sometimes called the daughter of Ra, and sometimes his mother 'before childbirth existed'. Mother of the crocodile god Sebek. Later introduced into the Osirian myth as the mother of ISIS, Horus and Osiris (see also NUT). As a creator goddess, wife of the creator god Khnum. Plutarch says her Sais temple (of which nothing now remains) bore the inscription: 'I am all that has been, that is, and that will be. No mortal has yet been able to lift the veil which covers me.' As a very long-established goddess, the other gods often appealed to her to arbitrate in disputes – for example, in the conflict between Horus and Set (in which she judged that Horus should have the throne, but by way of compensation Set should have two more wives, the Canaanite goddesses ANAT and ASTARTE). A guardian of the dead. As Isis and NEPHTHYS often appear together, so Neith often appears with SELKHET; or the four may appear together. For example, these four goddesses were associated with the Sons of Horus and their canopic jars – Neith's partner being the jackal-headed Duamutef in the East, guardian of the stomach. Protectress of women and of marriage, and patroness of the domestic arts, weaving and hunting. Her temple at Sais had a school of medicine, 'The House of Life'. Also a warrior goddess. Depicted wearing the white crown of the North and carrying a bow and arrows, or a weaver's shuttle (which is sometimes her head-symbol instead of the crown). Sometimes shown as the great cow mother giving birth to Ra every morning. Associated with the constellation Ursa Major. The Greeks equated her with ATHENE. Festival, with ISIS, 24 June (Festival of the Burning of the Lamps at Sais).

NEKHBET: Very ancient Egyptian vulture goddess, protectress of Upper Egypt (as NEITH or UADJET was of Lower Egypt). Her city was Nekheb (El Kab), opposite Hierakonpolis, a cult centre of the falcon god Horus. As his importance grew, so did hers; but whereas he became universal, she remained firmly centred on the South. A 'form of the primeval abyss which brought forth the light', her name means 'the father of fathers, the mother of mothers, who hath existed from the beginning and is the creatrix of the world' (Wallis Budge). Called the daughter of Ra, and his right eye. Wife of Khenti-Amentiu, First of the Westerners, or of Hapy, god of the Nile. A particular protectress of the Pharaoh, often suckling him or his children; thus also a goddess of childbirth. Depicted as a woman or a vulture, wearing the white crown of Upper Egypt. MUT took over many of her attributes.

NEMESIS: Greek. Daughter of Erebus and NYX, or of Oceanus, or of Dike (see HORAE, THE). Known as Adrasteia ('the Inevitable'). Goddess of divine anger, against mortals who offended the moral law, broke taboos or achieved too much happiness or wealth. Those who had too much good fortune might propitiate her by sacrificing a part of it. Sacred animal, the deer. Festival: 23 August.

NEMONTANA: A British Celtic war goddess, associated with Bath.

NENA: Wife of Nata, the Aztec Noah.

NEPHTHYS: (Egyptian Nebhet, 'Lady of the House' or 'Mistress of the Palace') Daughter of Geb and NUT, her sister being ISIS and her brothers Horus the Elder, Osiris and Set. She married Set, but they had no children, and she desired one by Osiris; getting Osiris drunk, she conceived Anubis by him. When Set tried to kill Anubis, Isis adopted him. Nephthys left Set in horror at his murder of Osiris and from then on was one of the Osirian party. She seems to personify the fringe of the desert, sometimes arid and sometimes fertile, according to how high the Nile (Osiris) rises. With Isis (they were often known as 'the Twins') she was a mourner and guardian of the dead, standing at the head of the coffin while Isis stood at the foot. They were sometimes joined in this by NEITH and SELKHET; and these four goddesses were associated with the canopic Four Sons of Horus, Nephthys's partner being the dog- or ape-headed Hapy of the North, guardian of the lungs. She also attended births (see MESHKENT). Depicted crowned by the hieroglyph of her name – a basket (*neb*) placed on the sign for a palace (*het*).
777: Tarot, Threes, Fives, Tens, Temperance; gems: star sapphire, pearl, ruby, rock crystal, jacinth; plants: cypress, opium poppy, oak, nux vomica,

nettle, rush; animals: woman, basilisk, sphinx, centaur, horse, hippogriff, dog; minerals: silver, iron, sulphur, magnesium sulphate; perfumes: myrrh, civet, tobacco, dittany of Crete, lign-aloes; magical weapons: Yoni, Outer Robe of Concealment, Sword, Spear, Scourge, Chain, Magic Circle, Triangle, Arrow. David Wood's number: 28.

NEREIDS, THE: Fifty sea nymphs, daughters of Nereus and DORIS. Helpful to sailors.

NERIO, NERINE: A Sabine goddess whom the Romans equated with MINERVA or VENUS. She had a joint festival (doubtless symbolizing marriage) with Mars on 23 March.

NERTHUS: Early Teutonic Earth and fertility goddess. During her public rituals all swords had to be sheathed and no one dared break the peace. Her temple was on a Baltic island, perhaps Seeland. She had a biannual festival, which Tacitus attended. She and her chariot had to be washed in a sacred lake by slaves who were then drowned. Later became known as Hertha or Hretha; the fourth month in the Old English calendar was named Hrethamonath after her. But she also became masculinized: 'Among the Northmen we find the first hostile reaction of a patriarchal society was to alter the sex of the Great Goddess so that female Nerthus became male Niord: but the virgin's son reappears in the person of Frey, and as Niord withdraws into the background, the Great Goddess reasserts herself as Freya. In Sweden one might say the process had almost completed itself by AD 1000' (Branston, *The Lost Gods of England*, p.197).

NETE: see MUSES.

NETZACH: ('Victory') Hebrew. The seventh Sephira of the Cabalistic Tree of Life. The APHRODITE Sephira, personifying Nature and the instincts and emotions – balanced by her counterpart, the sixth Sephira, Hod, the Hermes Sephira, personifying intellect. Netzach supplies the force of magic, Hod the form. Cabalistic symbols: the Lamp, Girdle and Rose. Spiritual experience: the Vision of Beauty Triumphant. Tarot: Sevens. Magical image: a beautiful naked woman.

NGAME: African. Creator goddess who made the heavenly bodies and put life into men and animals by shooting magical arrows into them.

NIAMH: ('Brightness, Lustre, Beauty') Irish. Form of Badhbh 'who befriends the hero at the time of his death'. Daughter of Cetchar and favourite of Cuchulainn.

NIAMH OF THE GOLDEN HAIR: Irish. Took Oisin to Tír na nÓg and bore him two sons (Fionn – after Oisin's father – and Osgar) and a daughter (Plur na mBan).

NICNEVEN: Scottish Samhain witch-goddess. Tradition places her night according to the old (Julian) calendar, on 10 November.

NIKE: ('Victory') Greek personification of that aspect. Daughter of Pallas and STYX. Usually depicted as winged, often carrying a palm branch. *777*: Tarot, Sevens; gem: emerald; plant: rose; animal: lynx; perfumes: benzoin, rose, red sandal; magical weapons: Lamp, Girdle. Roman equivalent VICTORIA.

NIKKAL: Canaanite goddess of the fruits of the Earth, who married the Moon god Yerah (Yarikh). Daughter of Hiribi, 'the Summer's King', to whom

Yerah paid 10,000 gold shekels for her hand. 'Daughter of the Summer's King' may mean the new Moon after harvest, still a favourite time for a wedding in that area, because the resources are there to celebrate it.

NIMUE: Arthurian. Thomas Mallory's name for the LADY OF THE LAKE. In some versions, the woman who wheedled the ageing Merlin's secrets from him and used them to trap him in his cave. See also VIVIENNE, MORGAN, GWENDYDD.

NINA: Chaldaean, 'Mistress of the Goddesses', oracular goddess of the city of Nine (Nineveh) and of the royal family of Lagash. Daughter of Ea. May have been originally a sea goddess. Later merged with ISHTAR.

NINAZU: Chaldaean Earth and Underworld goddess, known as 'Mother Darkness'.

NIN-EDIN: see BELIT-SHERI.

NINELLA: see DAMKINA.

NINGAL: Chaldaean and Sumerian Earth goddess, wife of the Moon god Sin, and mother of INANNA, ERESHKIGAL, ANUNET, and the Sun god Shamash. Chaldaean kings sometimes called themselves her sons.

NINGYO, THE: Japanese undines or mermaids.

NINHURSAG: ('She who Gives Life to the Dead') Sumerian Earth goddess, originally a cow goddess; her temple had a sacred herd. Agriculture developed from her union with the water god Enki or Ea. Enki was unfaithful to her with their own daughter NINSAR, Ninsar's daughter Ninkurra and Ninkurra's daughter UTTU. Enraged, Ninhursag cursed him (underlining the harmful effects of uncontrolled water), but the other gods persuaded her to mitigate the curse (recognizing the beneficial effects of controlled water). Apparently the same as NINLIL. (See also NINTI.)

NINKARRAK: Chaldaean goddess of healing and the alleviating of misfortune.

NINKURRA: see NINHURSAG.

NINLIL: Chaldaean and Sumerian grain goddess, daughter of NUN-BARSHEGUNU and wife of Enlil. One version says she was raped by Enlil, who was then banished to the Underworld; but she insisted on following him and gave birth to the Moon god Nanna and later to three Underworld deities. May originally have been identical with Nunbarshegunu (which sometimes occurs as her title) and mother of Enlil (but see KI). Later considered the wife of the Assyrian war god Assur. Often a designation of ISHTAR. See also NINHURSAG.

NINMAH: Chaldaean, Sumerian. Mother goddess and goddess of childbirth. In some accounts, mother of Enlil.

NINSAR, NINMU: Sumerian goddess of plants, 'the Lady who Makes Live'. Daughter of Enki and NINHURSAG.

NINSUN, SIRTUR: Sumerian. Named as (1) mother of Gilgamesh and (2) mother of Dumuzi and GESTINANNA; but these may be two distinct goddesses. The mother of Gilgamesh is described as being 'strong as a wild ox' and 'wise with deep knowledge'. In the Lament for Dumuzi, his mother merely appears as mourning along with his sister Gestinanna and his wife INANNA.

NINTI: ('Lady of the Rib', also 'Lady of Life') Sumerian. One of eight goddesses created by NINHURSAG to cure the various bodily parts of Enki after she had cursed him; Ninti was responsible for healing his rib. May be the source of the Genesis account of the creation of Eve (Hebrew *Chavah*, 'Life') from Adam's rib.

NINTU: see ARU.

NINTUD: see BELIT-ILI.

NIRRITI: Hindu. With her husband Nirrita, Vedic deities of death.

NISABA (1): Chaldaean architect goddess, sister of NINA. She appeared to the King Gudea in a dream and drew the plans for a temple he wanted to build, and he followed her instructions. (Some of Gudea's artefacts have been excavated.)

NISABA (2): Chaldaean grain goddess, apparently distinct from NISABA (1). Sister of NANSHE. Sometimes a title given to NINLIL.

NISACHARIS, THE: ('Night Wanderers') Hindu succubi.

NIX: Teutonic. Early German for undine. Nixe (the plural) women were alluringly beautiful, and LORELEI-like, would sit on river banks combing their golden hair and luring boatmen to their doom. Some who saw them, or heard them sing, went mad. The name was also used for lake, river or well priestesses.

NOCTILUCA: Gaulish witch goddess.

NOKOMIS: ('Grandmother') Amerindian, Algonquin. The Earth Mother who nourishes all living things. Grandmother of the culture hero Manabozho or Winabojo.

NORNS, THE: Teutonic, the Three Fates – Wyrd or Urd ('Past' or 'Destiny') and Verdandi ('Present') who wove the web of fate, and Skuld ('Future') who tore it. Guardians of the sacred tree Yggdrasil. Festival: New Year's Eve. Often regarded as one goddess of destiny, Wyrd, to whom even the gods were subject. 'The Three Wyrds' were the origin of Shakespeare's 'Weird Sisters'.

NORTIA: Etruscan goddess of fortune.

NOTT: ('Night') Teutonic, a giantess, mother of JORD and grandmother of Thor.

NOWUTSET: see UTSET.

NOX: Roman goddess of night, sister of DIES (Day) (cf. NYX).

NUAH: A Babylonian mother and Moon goddess. Her Flood myth was later absorbed by ISHTAR (see p.105). The biblical Noah is doubtless a masculinization of her name.

NU-KUA: Chinese creator goddess, sister and wife of Fu-hsi. She had a woman's body down to the waist and a dragon's tail; when she created men and women, she modelled them on her own body but gave them legs. Also known as the 'Restorer of Cosmic Equilibrium' after the world was devastated by flood and fire. Mediator between men and women, inventor of marriage, provider of children, tamer of wild beasts, and teacher of the civilized sciences such as irrigation.

NUNAKAWA-HIME: Japanese. A wise and beautiful young goddess, who may be 'a mythological recollection of the diplomatic marriages between Idumo leaders and women rulers of Kosi, occasioned by Idumo's attempts to consolidate its control of the Hokuriku area, Matsumura'

(Durdin-Robertson, *Goddesses of India*, pp.404-5).

NUNBARSHEGUNU: ('Goddess of Agricultural Fertility') Sumerian and Chaldaean. Before mankind was created, she lived in the city of Nippur with her daughter NINLIL and the young mountain and storm god Enlil. She encouraged the marriage between the two younger deities (but see NINLIL).

NUNGEENA: Australian aborigine, South-Eastern. The Mother-Spirit who, with Baiame the Father-Spirit, restored the world after Marmoo, the Spirit of Evil, had devastated it with swarms of poisonous and devouring insects. They created birds to eat up the insects — Nungeena starting with the most beautiful of all, the lyre-bird. They made more lovely birds, and their assistant spirits made the less beautiful ones like butcher-birds and magpies; between them they defeated the insect hordes, and plant life was able to grow again.

NUT: Egyptian sky mother goddess. Daughter of Shu and TEFNUT; but sometimes called the daughter of Ra, or even his mother, as the cow who gave birth to him each morning (the pink dawn sky being the blood of this birth). In this version Ra was Kamephis ('bull of his mother'), born of her as a calf at dawn, fertilizing her as a bull at midday and dying in the evening to be reborn next day as his own son. Geb, the Earth, was Nut's twin brother and lover; but Ra ordered the air god, their brother Shu, to separate them, and ordained that they should have no children in any month of the year. Thoth, in pity for them, played draughts with the Moon and won one seventy-second part of its light, which became the five intercalary days belonging to no month. Geb and Nut were thus able to produce Osiris, Horus the Elder, Set, ISIS and NEPHTHYS on these five days. The Sun and Moon were sometimes called her children, and sometimes her eyes. A protectress of the dead, her naked starry body is often seen stretched full length on the inner lid of coffins to face the mummy. Also depicted in the same form arched over the Earth, with only her toes and fingertips touching it. Also sometimes shown as a cow. Her headdress is the hieroglyph of her name, a pot (which may be a womb). Festival: the five Egyptian intercalary days, 24-28 August, and also 25 December, when she gave birth to Ra. *777*: Tarot, Twos, Star; gems: star ruby, turquoise, artificial glass; plants: amaranth, olive, coconut; animals: man, eagle, peacock; mineral: phosphorus; perfumes: musk, galbanum; magical weapons: Lingam, Inner Robe of Glory, Censer, Aspergillus. (Note: Nut is the only goddess, of any pantheon, attributed in *777* to Path 0, the Veils beyond Kether.) David Wood's number: also 0.

NU-ZUCHI: see KAYA-NU-HIME.

NYX: Greek goddess of night, daughter of Chaos and Erebus, and mother of HEMERA (Day) (cf. NOX). In the beginning only Nyx existed; from her came the Primeval Egg, which split in two and produced Uranus (Heaven) and GAIA (Earth).

OBA: Nigerian, Yoruba tribe. Goddess of the River Oba, and daughter of

YEMAJA.

OCEANIDS, THE: Greek. Three thousand sea and river nymphs, daughters of Oceanus and TETHYS.

ODUDUA: Nigerian, Yoruba tribe, and Brazilian Voodoo. Earth goddess, wife of agricultural god Orishako or sky god Obatala. Obatala and Odudua were created by the supreme god Olorun as an Adam and Eve, whose Eden was on the island of Ife. Obatala was very pure, but Odudua was interested in procreation and had many lovers. Taken by the slaves to Brazil as a Voodoo goddess, where she became less important than her daughter YEMAJA.

OGETSU-HIME-NO-KAMI: A Japanese goddess of food, and of the animals and plants which supply it.

OKITSU-HIME: Japanese kitchen goddess, with male counterpart Okitsu-Hiko.

OLD-SPIDER: Micronesian, Nauru Island. In the beginning there was nothing but the sea, and Old-Spider soaring above it. She created the Moon, sea, sky, Earth and Sun from a clam-shell she found with two snails in it.

OLD WOMAN WHO NEVER DIES, THE: Amerindian, Mandan and Minnitaree. Fertility goddess living to the South, who sent water fowl each spring as her heralds. Each species represented a kind of crop: wild goose (maize), wild swan (gourds), wild duck (beans). On their arrival, the tribe celebrated the Corn-Medicine Festival of the Women, in which the old women represented the goddess, the young women fed them dried meat in exchange for consecrated maize, and the old men beat drums for the women to dance. A similar ritual was held in the autumn to attract buffalo herds.

OLWYN: Welsh. 'One of the few stories of the Arthurian cycle which are purely Celtic without embellishments from the Continent' (Sykes, *Everyman's Dictionary of Non-Classical Mythology*, p.250). The May Queen, daughter of the May Tree or hawthorn, whose suitor must undergo various trials to win her. Her father was Ysbadadden, a King of the Giants, who knew he must die if she married her suitor Culhwch, but all his efforts failed to prevent it. A clear case of the Old King's defeat by the Young Hero, who becomes the new consort of the goddess-Queen of sovereignty.

OMECIUATL: Aztec creator goddess, wife of Ometeuctli (Ometeotl), who may be a later diety than she. Sometimes they are regarded as male and female aspects of the same deity.

OMICLE: Mother of all things, by Potos ('Desire'), in one of the four main Phoenician creation legends.

OMOROCA: see TIAMAT.

ONATHA: ('Spirit of Wheat') Amerindian, Iroquois. Daughter of Earth Mother EITHINOHA. Abducted by Spirit of Evil and imprisoned under the Earth, till the Sun found her and freed her. (Cf. PERSEPHONE.)

OPET, APET: Egyptian. Theban name of TAUERET, the hippopotamus goddess of childbirth. The Festival of Opet (see MUT) was named after her.

OPS: ('Plenty') Roman goddess of fertility, sowing and reaping. Wife of Saturn. Festivals (the Opeconsiva) 25 August, when she was worshipped while touching the ground, and (the Saturnalia, in honour of her and her consort) 17-23 December. Identified with RHEA and CYBELE.

ORA: see MELUSINE.

ORAEA: Roman goddess of summer. Festival: 21 June.

OREADS, THE: Greek mountain nymphs, who attended ARTEMIS.

OREITHUIA: Greek nymph carried off by Boreas, the North Wind. But Graves (*The White Goddess*, pp.436-7) says she was 'evidently the Love-goddess of the divine triad in which Athene was the Death-goddess', and that her abduction by Boreas mythologizes the spread of 'the Athenian orgiastic cult of the Triple Goat-goddess and her lover Erichthonius' to Thrace, where it was adapted to a Triple Mare-goddess cult.

ORORE: Chaldaean. A creator goddess, depicted as insect-headed, with a pregnant belly and sometimes a giant eye. Her unnamed consort was bull-headed and fish-tailed.

OSHUN and OYA: Nigerian, Yoruba tribe and Brazilian Voodoo. Sisters, daughters of YEMAJA, and wives of the thunder god Shango. Oshun was beautiful and Oya plain, and there was jealousy between them. Goddesses respectively of the rivers Oshun and Niger. When you cross one, you must not mention the other goddess's name, or the waters will swallow you. The slaves took both to Brazil, where they became Voodoo goddesses, identified with St Barbara and St Catherine. Oshun (spelt Oxun in Brazil) is patroness of the zodiacal sign Capricorn.

OSTARA: see EOSTRE.

OTO: see MIZUNOE

OTSUCHI-NO-KAMI: Japanese Earth mother goddess.

OYA: see OSHUN.

OYNYENA MARIA: ('Fiery Mary') Slavonic, assistant and counsellor of thunder god Peroun. Probably an earlier fire goddess.

PA: ('Dryness') Chinese goddess of drought. Called in by the Emperor Huang-ti to control the wind and the rain, and then refused to leave; he exiled her to the North, 'beyond the Red Water'.

PACHAMAMA: Inca Earth mother goddess.

PADMA: ('Lotus-Coloured') Hindu. One of the avatars (incarnations) of LAKSHMI.

PAKHIT: Egyptian. Form of BAST at Speos Artemidos, east of Beni Hasan. Also associated with MUT. Cat- or lioness-headed.

PAI MU-TAN: ('White Peony') Chinese. Like the Hindu APSARAS, her function is to distract ascetics from their practices. To the Chinese, the peony is the queen of flowers, symbolizing among other things love and feminine beauty.

PAIRIKAS, THE: Persian. Shooting stars envisaged as messengers between heaven and Earth. Probably originally celestial nymphs like the Hindu APSARAS, and prototypes of the PERIS.

PALES: Roman goddess of flocks and their fecundity. A rare take-over here – she was originally masculine. Festival: the Palilia, 21 April, traditional date of the founding of Rome. Gave her name to the Palatine Hill.

PALM GODDESS OF NEJRAN: A palm tree at Nejran was worshipped by the Arabs as a goddess, and annually draped with women's clothes and ornaments. A similar practice with particular trees can still be seen in Ireland.

P'AN CHIN-LIEN: Chinese. Patroness of prostitutes. A (possibly historical) widow whose father-in-law murdered her to put an end to her disorderly behaviour.

PANDORA: ('Gift of All') The Greek Eve, fashioned in clay by Hephaestus on Zeus' orders to punish Prometheus for having stolen fire from heaven. Her name means that each god or goddess gave her an appropriate gift. Zeus gave her a box which she must not open. She did open it, and all the evils that plague mankind came out of it. All that was left at the bottom was Hope.

PAPA: ('Rocky Stratum') Polynesian Earth Mother, with whom creator god Taaroa (Tangaroa) mated to make rocks, sand, soil and the sea. According to the Maoris, she mated with Sky Father Atea Rangi (originally a goddess – see ATEA) to produce several gods. A Cook Island legend says that the Sun and Moon were created from the two halves of her first child, cut in two to pacify two gods who both claimed to have fathered it. The Manganian version names two creator goddesses, Papa above and VARI below.

PAPAYA: see ISTUSTAYA.

PARASHAKTI: see SHAKTIS.

PARCAE, THE: see MOERAE.

PARVATI: Hindu. Daughter of Himavat, god of the Himalayas, and wife of Shiva. Under this name she is depicted beside him, discussing everything from love to metaphysics. But as the goddess personifying the 'power' (Sakti) of Shiva, she has many aspects under different names: Uma the gracious, Bhairavi the terrible, Ambika the generatrix, SATI the good wife, Gauri the brilliant, KALI the black, DURGA the inaccessible. For a long time Parvati wearied of Shiva's asceticism and indifference to her charm, but eventually she won him over, and their embrace made the whole world tremble.

PASHADHARI: ('Noose-Bearer') Hindu. She and her husband Yamantaka are the Door-Keepers of the South. Her symbol, the noose, is both the yoni and the umbilical cord and may be equated to the Egyptian ankh. A loving mother goddess in both the nourishing and the restrictive aspect. Depicted with the head of a sow.

PASIPHAE: Greek. Daughter of Helios, the Sun; wife of King Minos of Crete and mother of ARIADNE, Phaedra and Deucalion. Poseidon caused her to fall in love with the white bull of Minos, and she gave birth to the Minotaur, which Ariadne helped the Athenian Theseus to overcome. Pasiphae and Ariadne were probably originally Mother and Maid forms of the same Moon goddess, the totem bull of the Cretan goddess culture having been turned into a monster by Athenian patriarchy.

PAX: Roman goddess of peace. Identified with CONCORDIA. Festivals: 30 January, 4 July.

PEITHO: ('Persuasion') Greek. According to Hesiod, present at the moment when APHRODITE came ashore on Cyprus; and Sappho calls her 'Aphrodite's maid shining with gold'. Sometimes a title of Aphrodite, sometimes a separate goddess.

PEKHET: form of Bast at Speos Artemidos.

PELE: Polynesian, Hawaii. Goddess of Fire in the Earth (volcanoes).

PERCHTA: Slavonic fertility goddess, Bride of the Sun. Her feast 'was celebrated at Salzburg as late as 1941 by the wearing of masks, those of beauty for the spring and summer, and those without beauty for autumn and winter' (Sykes, *Everyman's Dictionary of Non-Classical Mythology*, p.168).

PERIS, THE: Late Persian celestial nymphs, fairies or female angels. See PAIRIKAS.

PERSEPHONE: Greek and Phoenician. Originally a purely Underworld goddess, became a corn-seed goddess, daughter of DEMETER. In the latter role, she is usually simply called Kore ('Girl'). As an Underworld deity, her attributes were the bat, the narcissus and the pomegranate. Usually depicted with a cornucopia. In her Phoenician form, daughter of DIONE and Cronus. Willow trees were sacred to her (as to CIRCE, HECATE and HERA). Festivals as DEMETER. *777*: Tarot, Tens; gem: rock crystal; plants: willow, lily, ivy; animal: sphinx; mineral: magnesium sulphate; perfume: dittany of Crete; magical weapons: Magic Circle, Triangle. Roman equivalent PROSERPINA. For her full story, see Chapter XIII.

PHILOSOPHIA: Medieval form of SOPHIA.

PHILYRA: ('Linden') Greek, mother by Cronus of Chiron, the wise centaur. Totem bird the wryneck.

PHOEBE: Greek. Titaness, daughter of Uranus and GAIA. Mother by Coeus of LETO and Asteria, and thus grandmother of Apollo and ARTEMIS.

PHRONESIA: ('Purpose, Practical Wisdom.') Gnostic. An AEON, associated with SOPHIA and DYNAMIS as co-genetrix of 'principalities and angels'.

PIDRAI: Canaanite Nature and light goddess, forming a triad with ARSAI and TALLAI. Perhaps daughter and/or wife of Baal.

PI-HSIA-YUAN-CHUN ('Princess of Streaky Clouds'), SHENG-MU ('Holy Mother'): Chinese. Protects women and children and presides over childbirth. Portrayed seated with a headdress of three birds with outstretched wings.

PINGALA: ('Tawny-eyed') Hindu, an etheric force, also called Soorejnaree ('Solar Wife'). Periodic in influence – Sunday, Tuesday, Thursday, Saturday and alternate zodiacal signs beginning with Aries; the other days and signs come under Chandernaree. Involved in divination.

PIRILI: see SEVEN SISTERS.

PIRUA: Peruvian maize-mother goddess, according to the Spanish historian Acosta. But 'pirua', according to Frazer, was the granary, the maize-mother being ZARA-MAMA.

PLEIADES, THE: Greek. Seven daughters of Atlas and the OCEANID Pleione; sisters of the Hyades. Zeus placed them in the heavens to help them escape Orion, who had fallen in love with them. They were Alcyone, Celaeno, Electra, Maia, Merope, Sterope and Taygete. (Cf. SEVEN SISTERS.)

POLUDNITSA: Slavonic, North Russian field goddess. Tall, young and beautiful, dressed entirely in white. If she found anyone harvesting at midday, she would pull his or her hair, and she would lose little children in the corn.

POLYHYMNIA: see MUSES.

POMONA: Roman goddess of fruit trees, sharing this duty with her male consort Vertumnus and with FLORA.

PORRIMA: see CARMENTA.

POSTVERTA: see CARMENTA.

POTINA: Roman goddess of children's potions.

PRAJNA: Hindu, Tibetan. A Buddhist goddess of wisdom, similar to the Gnostic SOPHIA.

PRAJNA-PARAMITA: Tibetan, Chinese, Japanese, Eastern Asian, Buddhist. Personification of Transcendental Wisdom, the Perfected Wisdom of Yoga. 'Mother of the Bodhisattvas'; in the tradition that there have been and will be many Buddhas, she is the mother of all of them, MAYA (2) being one of her incarnations. May be viewed as PRAJNA at the highest level. Her symbol is a book resting on a lotus blossom beside her shoulder, and her hands form a circle.

PRAKRITI: Hindu. The world womb, from which all springs. Mother of Brahma. MULAPRAKRITI in Earthly manifestation.

PRAMLOCHA: Hindu, an APSARA. Indra, after his marriage to INDRANI, asked her to distract the sage Kandu from his asceticism. She succeeded so well that he spent 907 years, six months, and three days with her, after which she became a tree-nymph. She corresponds to the Chinese PAI MU-TAN.

PRESSINE: see MELUSINE.

PRISNI: Hindu Earth and cow goddess. 'The Many-Coloured Earth.' Wife of storm god Rudra, and mother of the eleven Maruts who became the companions of Indra.

PRITHVI: An early Hindu fertility and Earth goddess, said to have helped create all the gods and men. Wife of sky god Dyaus and mother of Indra. Like most Hindu mother goddesses, sometimes envisaged as a cow. In esoteric teaching, she represents solid matter; her symbol is a square, and her colour orange-red or yellow.

PRITI: A Hindu goddess of joy.

PROSERPINA: Roman, equated with the Greek PERSEPHONE. Daughter of CERES and Pluto. Some identified her with LIBITINA. Roman festival (Secular Games), 26 May-3 June.

PROSYMNA: Greek goddess of the New Moon. A title of DEMETER as the Earth mother in her Underworld (i.e., PERSEPHONE) aspect.

PSYCHE: ('Soul') Greek. Eros fell in love with her and married her but came to her only at night when she could not see him. She broke the arrangement by taking a lamp to look at him, and he left her. Eros' jealous mother APHRODITE punished her with many tasks, such as going to the Underworld to bring back some of PERSEPHONE's beauty. Eventually Eros and Psyche were reunited, and Zeus made her immortal. Moral: don't attempt to analyse love entirely by linear-logical standards. You will have to plumb the Unconscious to win it back. 777: Tarot, Tens; gem: rock crystal; plants: willow, lily, ivy; animal: sphinx; mineral: magnesium sulphate; perfume: dittany of Crete; magical weapons: Magic Circle, Triangle.

PUKKEENEGAK: Eskimo. Goddess who provides food and clothing materials and gives children to women. Tattooed face, wears large boots and very pretty clothes.

PURVACHITTI: Hindu. An APSARA, associated with precognition.

PUSHPEMA: ('She who Offers Flowers') Tibetan goddess of flowers. The Sanskrit word *pushpa*, 'flowers', also means 'declarations of love' and 'menstruation'.

PYRRHA: Wife of Deucalion, the Greek Noah. After the Flood, they repopulated the Earth by throwing over their shoulders 'the bones of their mother' (i.e., stones from the Earth). Those which she threw became women; those which he threw became men.

PYTHIA: ('Pythoness') Greek. Serpent goddess, daughter of GAIA, who lived near Delphi in the caves of Mount Parnassus. Apollo slew her and took over the Delphic oracle. The oracular priestesses of Delphi were also called Pythiai (plural); their role continued under Apollo but controlled and interpreted by his priests. Shuttle and Redgrove (*The Wise Wound*) make out a convincing case for the Pythiai having been menstrual priestesses – i.e., making their oracular pronouncements at their menstrual peak. Delphi originally belonged to Gaia; a patriarchal take-over could hardly be more clearly recorded.

QEDESHET: see KEDESH.

QODSHU: ('Holiness') An epithet applied to Canaanite mother goddesses.

QUARTIANA: see FEBRIS.

QUEEN OF ELPHAME: Scottish witch goddess. See particularly the Border Ballad of Thomas the Rhymer. Graves (*The White Goddess*, pp.430-33) shows how Keats' 'La Belle Dame Sans Merci' was based on her.

QUEEN OF HEAVEN: Hebrew women's nostalgic name for the banished Goddess ASHERA or Ashtaroth (see Jeremiah vii:18, xiii:17-25).

QUINOA-MAMA: Peruvian goddess of the quinoa crop.

RADHA: Hindu. A cowherd girl loved by Krishna; his chief human lover. Also said to be one of the avatars (incarnations) of LAKSHMI. Festival: 1 September.

RAGNO: Amerindian, Pomo. The old mother goddess who rescued the creator gods Marumda and Kuksu when their mistakes got out of hand.

RAINBOW SNAKE, THE: Australian aborigine. In some areas female, in others male. Represents rain, water and the products of rain, without which life would cease to exist. He/she causes rivers to flow to the sea; plays an important part in the training and magic of medicine men; in Arnhem Land sends floods to drown offenders against the sacred lore; and in the Kimberleys is associated with childbirth, including that of spirit children. In the Arnhem Land rites of the Fertility Mother just before the wet season, the Rainbow Snake is heard coming by the whistling sound of the storm blowing through its horns; and as the ritual dancing and singing begins, it arches its body upwards into the sky. The Rainbow Snake appears frequently in aborigine art. Other names, Julunggui, Yurlunggui and Wonambi. In the plural, the Rainbow Snake Women, progeny of the Rainbow and Crocodiles, lure men to their deaths 'with sweet songs and words like honey'; the protection against them is also female – the red ochre (birth and/or menstrual blood) of the Earth Mother from the cave which is her womb, if you can find it.

RAIT, RAT: Egyptian. Feminine of Ra, of whom she may have been the earliest form; she appears in surviving legend as his wife, and mother of SELKHET and MA'AT.

RAKA: Hindu goddess of the Full Moon.

RAKINI: see DAKINI.

RAKSHASIS, THE: Hindu, Singalese. Female spirits who bewitch mortal men by their beauty. Sometimes, paradoxically, described as very pious.

RAMBHA: ('Plantain Tree', 'Courtesan') Hindu. First and greatest of the APSARAS, born of the Churning of the Milk Ocean (the Vedic Deluge story).

RAN: Teutonic. Wife of the sea-giant Aegir. She stirred up the waves and had a huge net with which she tried to capture every man who sailed on the sea. Her nine daughters, personifications of the waves, were seductive undines who lured sailors into their arms and dragged them under. Nevertheless, Ran entertained the drowned royally in her underwater palace, on feasts of fish, seating them on sky-blue cushions.

RA NAMBASANGA: Fijian. A rarity, in that he/she was both a god and a goddess, having two bodies, one male and one female.

RANGDA: Hindu, Balinese. Fertility goddess and witch. In Bali offerings are made to her in the paddyfields. Depicted with large breasts.

RASHITH: ('Beginning') In Hebrew,. Genesis opens with *'B'rashith ...'* ('In the beginning ...'). The noun is feminine; in later tradition Rashith appears to be associated with AIMA, the Bright Mother.

RAT: see RAIT.

RATI: ('Pleasure') Hindu goddess of sexual passion. One of the wives of Kama, god of love. Also incarnated under the name Mayavati, as a goddess of magical arts.

RATIS: British goddess 'of the fortress', worshipped at Birdoswald and Chesters on the Roman Wall.

RATRI: ('Night') Hindu goddess of night, of restful darkness. Depicted as wearing dark clothes with gleaming stars. Sister of USHAS, the dawn goddess.

RAT-TAUI: Egyptian. Wife of the Theban war god Mont.

RAUNI: see AKKA.

RE: Phoenician Moon goddess. According to Thomas Moore's *History of Ireland*, the Moon was also worshipped in pagan Ireland under the name Re – still a Gaelic word for Moon. (Do not confuse with Re, alternative spelling of the Egyptian Sun god Ra.)

REINE PEDAUQUE, LA: Medieval French, 'the queen with the bird's foot, a mysterious figure of legend who flew by night at the head of a crowd of phantoms, something like the Wild Hunt' (Doreen Valiente, *An ABC of Witchcraft Past and Present*, p.225). Cf. LILITH.

REMATI: Tibetan form of KALI. Associated with Tantric secret doctrines.

RENENET: Egyptian goddess of suckling, who gave the baby his name, personality and fortune. She also appeared, with the destiny god Shai, at death when the soul was weighed and judged. Also represented nourishment in general, sometimes as a harvest goddess with the title 'Lady of the Double Granary'. Depicted with two long plumes on her head (or sometimes the disc and horns of HATHOR), as a woman, a lioness-headed woman, a cobra-headed woman or a uraeus.

RENNUTET: Egyptian snake goddess of the Harvest, regent of the month

Pharmuthi. Daughter of the early Sun god Atum, and sister of TEFNUT and Shu. Seems to overlap with RENENET.

RENPET: Egyptian goddess of the year, of springtime and youth. Known as 'Mistress of Eternity'. Depicted crowned with a long palm-shoot, curved at the end.

RHEA: Cretan and Greek. Her name probably means 'Earth'. Originally almost certainly the name of the Cretan mother goddess, the island's supreme deity, who bore children to the annually sacrificed god (a role faithfully copied by her high priestess and the annually chosen male consort/sacrifice). In classical mythology she was the daughter of GAIA by her son Uranus; wife of her brother Cronus, and mother by him of Zeus, Hades, Poseidon, HESTIA, DEMETER and HERA. She hid the infant Zeus in the Diktean Cave on Crete, when his father Cronus was determined to kill him; she was helped in this by AMALTHEA. *777*: Tarot, Threes; gems: star sapphire, pearl; plants: cypress, opium poppy; animal, woman; mineral: silver; perfumes: myrrh, civet; magical weapons: Yoni, Outer Robe of Concealment.

RHIANNON: ('Great, or Divine, Queen'). Welsh fertility and otherworld goddess, cult-animal a horse. In the *Mabinogion*, daughter of Heveydd the Old, wife first of Pwyll, and mother of Pryderi. She had to undergo punishment for allegedly killing her infant son, who afterwards turned out to have been kidnapped. After Pwyll's death she married Manawydan (Manannán). The *Mabinogion* story is 'but a shadow of what once constituted a powerful Celtic goddess of Epona-Macha type' (Anne Ross, *Pagan Celtic Britain*, p.316). Among the hints of this: Pwyll was 'Head of Annwn' – i.e., the happy otherworld; and the songs of the three Birds of Rhiannon 'wake the dead and lull the living to sleep'. She could ride her white horse faster than any man could catch her, though it seemed to go at a steady pace – which suggests the Moon.

RIRIT: see TUARET.

RHODE: Greek, daughter of AMPHITRITE and Poseidon, mother of seven children by the Sun god Helios. The island of Rhodes was named after her.

ROBIGO: ('Rust, Mildew') Roman goddess invoked to spare crops from blight and turn her attention to weapons instead. A goddess of farmers, who were more interested in fertility than in war. Festival (the Robigalia): 25 April.

ROCK-MAIDEN, THE: see BANANA-MAIDEN.

RODASI: Hindu. An early Vedic lightning and storm goddess. Wife of storm god Rudra.

ROHINI: A Hindu cow goddess invoked to cure jaundice. Variously associated with the constellations Scorpio and Hyades, and with the stars Antares and Aldebaran.

RONA: Maori.

ROSMERTA: Gaulish, appears as consort of Mercury, especially in eastern Gaul; sometimes carries a caduceus.

RUKMINI: ('Adorned with Gold') Hindu. A wife of Krishna, sometimes regarded as an incarnation of LAKSHMI.

RUTBE: Water goddess of the Guaymi Indians of Costa Rica. Mother by Nancomala of the Sun and Moon, who were the ancestors of mankind.

SABITU: Chaldaean sea and Underworld goddess, whose palace was on the shore of the ocean that encircled the world. She warned Gilgamesh that crossing the sea would be perilous and that on the far side were the even more perilous Waters of Death. Gilgamesh and Arad-Ea braved the crossing, reached the Waters of Death in forty days and traversed them also. She plays a similar role to SIDURI.

SABRINA, SAVREN, HABREN: British, goddess of the River Severn. For her story, see VENNOLANDUA.

SADHBH, SADV: ('Goodly Habitation', anything good) Irish deer goddess. Wife of Fionn, mother of Oisin. Lured away from Fionn's house by magic before Oisin was born, and turned into a deer; he searched for her for years but never found her, but the boy Oisin came to him and grew up to be an inspired poet and the only man on record to stand up to St Patrick in argument. Fionn's real name was Demne ('Small Deer'); Oisin means 'Fawn'; and Oisin's son was Osgar ('He who Loves the Deer'). They were Leinstermen, and part of Leinster is called Osraige ('People of the Deer'). 'All this is enough to make Sadv and the story of Oisin particularly significant; for the hind goddess, or goddess of hinds, is related to the most ancient image of Artemis-Diana, the sun goddess of those peoples who came to Western Europe before the Indo-European.' (Markale, *Women of the Celts*, p.111.)

SADWES: Persian, Manichaean. The Maiden of Light, a rain goddess who caused hail, frost, snow, thunder and lightning. She was also a psychopompos, guiding adepts to Paradise on their death.

SAGA: Teutonic. A giantess, second of the ASYNJOR; the name probably means 'seeress'. Associated with the Zodiacal sign Pisces.

SAITADA: ('Grief'?) British, known only from one Tyne Valley dedication; Anne Ross suggests she may be similar to SCATHACH.

SAKI: ('Competence, Skill, Powerful Aid') Hindu, wife of Indra. May correspond to INDRANI.

SAKUNADEVATAS, THE: Hindu goddesses of good omens, one named goddess among them being Sakunadhishthatri.

SALUS: Roman goddess of health and welfare. Greek equivalent HYGEIA.

SAMBHUTI: A Hindu birth and fertility goddess.

SAMDHYA: Hindu goddess of twilight. Originally a nature goddess.

SAMKHAT: Babylonian goddess of joy.

SAMS: Moon goddess of the southern Semites. The northern Semites had a corresponding Moon god called Samas.

SANANG SARI: Sumatra, the rice goddess of the Minangkabauers.

SANDALPHON: In occult tradition, the feminine Archangel of Earth. Equated with DEMETER, and in the Golden Dawn with ISIS. Associated with the rose, 'the greatest and most unveiled of all sexual symbols' (Mme Blavatsky). Depicted as winged, with an Egyptian headdress and horns.

SANGYE KHADO: Tibetan, chief of the KHADOS.

SANING SARI: East Indies, Sumatra, Java. Rice-mother goddess, ritually honoured at sowing and reaping, particularly by women; during sowing they let their hair hang down their backs, so that the rice may grow long-stemmed and luxuriant.

SANJNA: ('Agreement, Consciousness') Hindu, wife of Sun god Surya. She bore him three children, then, exhausted by his constant dazzling, got her sister Shaya ('the Shade') to take her place. After some years he noticed the change and went in search of Sanjna. She had turned herself into a mare. He became a stallion and pursued her, and for a time they lived happily together as horses. Then he agreed to give up one eighth of his brightness so that she could return with him, which she did. Similar story to that of SARANYU. (In some myths SURYA is feminine.)

SANZUKAWA-NO-OBAASAN, SANZU-NO-BABA: Japanese. Guardian goddess of the River Sanzu bordering the Underworld; she strips the dead of their clothes before crossing.

SAPAS: Phoenician. Daughter of El, called 'Torch of the Gods'. Also a name for the Sun in the Ugarit texts.

SARAMA, DEVASUNI: Japanese wind goddess, in the form of a brindled bitch; a psychompompos conducting the souls of the dead. May have links with USHAS.

SARANYU: Hindu cloud goddess, daughter of Tvashtar, a solar-type craftsman god and 'universal exciter'. She left her husband, the Sun god Surya or Vivasvat, because she could not stand his brightness. To get her back, he gave up some of his rays, from which were fashioned the disk of Vishnu, the trident of Shiva, and the weapons of the war god Kartikeya and the legendary King Kubera. Similar story to that of SANJNA.

SARASVATI: Hindu, wife of Brahma, born of his body. Goddess of speech, music, wisdom, knowledge and the arts. Mother of the Vedas. Originally a river goddess. Invented the Devenagari (Sanskrit alphabet). Depicted as a beautiful young woman with four arms. One right hand holds out a flower to her husband, the other a book of palm leaves; one left hand holds a garland, the other a little drum. Sometimes seated on a lotus, with only two arms, playing on the vina. Partially merged with VACH. In Tibet a goddess of teaching and learning, wife of the Bodhisattva Manjushri Jampal. (See also SATARUPA.)

SARPARAJNI: Hindu serpent goddess, 'Mother of all that moves'.

SARPIS: Hindu serpent-spirits of the air, Earth and Underworld; sometimes mentioned as Flying Sarpis. Similar to the NAGIS, except that the Nagis always walk or run.

SARVAYONI: ('All-Things-Yoni') Hindu. The female generative principle as the origin of all things.

SATARUPA: Hindu, formed by Brahma from his own immaculate substance. Also known as SARASVATI, SAVITRI, GAYATRI or BRAHMANI. When he saw what he had made, Brahma fell in love with her and married her 'to beget all kinds of living things'.

SATI (1), SUTTY: Hindu, daughter of Daksha, one of the lords of creation. In spite of her father's opposition, she fell in love with and married Shiva; she is one of the aspects of PARVATI. Said to have cast herself on the sacrificial fire – hence the practice, and the name, of suttee, the burning of widows on their husbands' funeral pyres. (Cf. SITA.)

SATI (2), SATIS, SATET: ('To Sow Seed') Egyptian goddess of fertility and love; cult centre the island of Siheil, near the First Cataract; personified the life-giving inundation. Soon replaced HEKET as wife of creator god Khnum. Sometimes daughter of Ra, sometimes of Khnum and ANUKET, her partner-guardian of the cataracts. Later a goddess of hunting. Called Princess of Upper Egypt and (in the New Kingdom) Queen of the Gods. Depicted with a vulture headdress and the white crown of Upper Egypt flanked by antelope horns, and carrying a bow and arrows, which symbolized the speed and force of the cataract current.

SATI (3): Egyptian. A serpent goddess who lived in the Underworld and preyed on the dead.

SATIA: A medieval witch goddess name, doubtless implying 'satisfaction'.

SATYABHAMA: Hindu, the third wife of Krishna.

SCATHACH: ('The Shadowy One' or 'She Who Strikes Fear') Irish. Warrior woman and prophetess, living in Albion (in this case Scotland), who taught the martial arts to Cuchulainn. Also, like her daughter Uathach ('The Very Terrible') his lover. 'It is clear that the women can provide their initiation into magic and warfare only when there are sexual relations between the pupil and the "mistress", in both senses of the word' (Markale, *Women of the Celts*, p.242.) 'A marriage between the apprentice and his vocation' (Rees and Rees, *Celtic Heritage*, p.257). Anne Ross (*Pagan Celtic Britain*, p.291) refers to the type as 'the warrior goddess, who is also a mother figure'. Three other women are named in the story of Cuchulainn's training: Dornoll ('Bigfist'), whose sexual advances he refused, Aoife ('Reflection'), whom he married for a year and who bore him a son, and Buannan ('The Lasting One'). It is Scathach, Uathach and Aoife who are repeatedly named together in the Táin Bó Cualgne as his warrior teachers.

SCHALA: Wife of Adad, the Assyro-Babylonian storm god.

SCOTA: Irish, wife of Milesius, leader of the final (Gaelic) invasion of Ireland in the mythological cycle, and mother of the bard Amergin. Daughter of the Pharaoh of Egypt, Necbetanus. Said to have died in the invasion and to be buried near the dolmens on Sliabh Mis in Co. Kerry. Origin of the name 'Scoti' for the Irish, which finally became the name of those Irish who settled in Scotland. Graves (*The White Goddess*, p.132) thinks she may be a confusion with SCOTIA: 'The Milesians would naturally have brought the cult of the Sea-goddess ... with them to Ireland, and would have found the necessary stone-altars already in position.' Another tradition makes Scota daughter of the Pharaoh Smenkare, and wife of another Milesian, Niul.

SCOTIA: ('The Dark One') Greek, a sea-goddess of Cyprus. See SCOTA.

SCYLLA: ('Render') Greek. CIRCE, jealous of Scylla's love for the fisherman Glaucus, turned her into one of two female monsters guarding the Northern entrance to the Straits of Messina. Depicted as a beautiful woman from the hips up, her lower parts were three hellhounds; she brandished the helms of wrecked ships. But in the *Odyssey* she had six fanged heads on long necks, which devoured six of Ulysses' men. Scylla sat on (and was identified with) a rock; the other monster was Charybdis ('Sucker-Down'), a whirlpool which sucked in water and belched it out again three times a day. It was difficult to avoid one without being trapped by the other. Both still exist – one a 200-foot rock by the town of Scilla on the Italian side, the other a whirlpool 200 to 300 yards off the Sicilian shore by Cape Peloro. Till the earthquake of 1783 shifted the sea bed, they were far more hazardous to shipping than they are today; but small craft still hug the shore by Scylla to keep well clear of Charybdis. (Read *Ulysses Found*, by the classical scholar and skilled small-boat navigator Ernle Bradford, on his personal experiences of this and many other Odyssean themes, such as the SIRENS.)

SEDNA, ARNAKNAGSAK: Eskimo goddess of the food-providing animals. Lives in the sea but began her career as the goddess AVILAYOQ living on dry land. Seals, whales and polar bears are descended from her fingers, which were cut off by her father. If not propitiated, she prevents these animals leaving their homes, so that there is no food for man. Depicted as huge and one-eyed. She receives the spirits of those who die from natural causes into her undersea kingdom.

SEFKHET-SESHAT, SESHAT SEFEKH-AUBI: Egyptian stellar and Moon goddess, one of those mentioned as a wife of Thoth. Worshipped from the earliest dynasties. A time-measuring, temple-planning, record-keeping goddess, patroness of architects; and, with Thoth, deity of scribes and inventor of writing. In the Underworld, she provided a house for the spirit of the dead. Depicted crowned with a star inscribed with a reversed crescent, surmounted by two straight plumes; later the crescent became two down-pointing horns. Her various names include allusions to horns, to mystery and to the number seven; her hieroglyph includes a seven-pointed star.

SEKHET-HETEPET: The Egyptian Elysian Fields, and the goddess personifying them, the Lady of Winds. Life there was a close replica of life on Earth, with families reunited and a similar agricultural economy, but without Earthly problems. (See also UNEN-EM-HETEP.)

SEHU: ('Maize') Amerindian, Cherokee. Corn goddess, sister of Earth goddess ELIHINO and Sun goddess IGAEHINVDO. Wife of Kanati, the Hunter. Visualized as an old woman; the corn, 'greatest plant giver of life', is the woman reborn. The late summer Green Corn Festival is the Cherokees' most important festival.

SEKHMET: ('The Powerful') Egyptian lioness-goddess, Eye of Ra who was her father. Wife of Ptah as goddess of the Memphite triad, and mother of Nefertum, god of the setting Sun (later replaced by Imhotep). A goddess of war. Personified the scorching, destructive power of the Sun, and also defence of the divine order. She was placed in the uraeus on Ra's brow and spat flames at his enemies. When mankind rebelled against the ageing Ra, he sent her to quell them, and she became uncontrolled, wanting to destroy them all. Ra had to trick her with beer mixed with pomegranate juice, which she mistook for human blood and got too drunk to continue. Her characteristics were the opposite of HATHOR's, yet Hathor was also called the Eye of Ra, and the same story was told of her; Sekhmet was thus in a sense the dark aspect of Hathor. This slaughter was commemorated annually on Hathor's feast day, the 12th of the month Tybi (27 November), by brewing 'as many jugs of the philtre as there were priestesses of the Sun'. The priests of BAST tried to identify Sekhmet with her, but popular belief distinguished between the kindly Bast and the fierce Sekhmet. Also associated with MUT (another Eye of Ra). Usually depicted as a lion-headed woman crowned with the solar disc and uraeus, but sometimes with a crocodile or udjat (Eye of Ra) head. She may hold a knife in her upraised hand. Festival: 7 January.

SELENE: Greek Moon goddess, daughter of Hyperion and THEIA, and sister of Helios (the Sun) and EOS (Dawn); though sometimes said to be the daughter of Zeus or of Helios. She was wooed and won by Zeus and by Pan. She fell in love with Endymion and visited him nightly while he slept. Zeus granted him immortality on condition that he remained eternally asleep; and Selene came night after night to gaze on her sleeping lover. Roman equivalent LUNA.

SELKHET, SELKIT, SERKET: ('She who increases by giving breath and food') Egyptian fertility and scorpion-goddess, protectress of one of the four sources of the Nile. Daughter of Ra, perhaps by RAIT. Also an Underworld goddess; when the serpent Apep was defeated and bound by the defenders of Ra, she had the task of guarding him. With her husband Nekhebkau, an Underworld serpent god with human limbs, she sometimes bound the dead with chains; but sometimes they both looked after them and fed them. With ISIS, NEPHTHYS and NEITH, she was associated with the canopic Four Sons of Horus – her partner being the falcon-headed Qebehsenuf of the West, guardian of the intestines. She was also a guardian of marriage. Depicted as a woman crowned with a scorpion or as a scorpion with a woman's head.

SEMELE: Greek. Mother by Zeus of Dionysus.

SENGEN-SAMA: Japanese goddess whose sanctuary is on the peak of Fujiyama. Also known as Ko-No-Hana-Saku-a-Hime, 'the Princess who makes the flowers of the trees to blossom'. May be connected with FUCHI.

SENJO, THE: Japanese female fairies, living in Horai, a fabulous mountain in the sea.

SEQUANA: Gaulish, goddess of the River Seine.

SESHAT: see SEFKHET-SESHAT.

SETLOCENIA: ('She of the Long Life') British. Worshipped at Alauna (Maryport, Cumberland) in Roman times.

SEVEN SISTERS, THE: Australian aborigine name for the PLEIADES. Their legend (almost identical with the Greek one) occurs in several versions, all concerning their pursuit by a hunter, from whom they escaped but who (as the constellation Orion) still pursues them across the night sky. Other names: the Water Girls, the Emu Women. A named individual is Pirili; in her case the women of the Milky Way helped her and threw the hunter back to Earth; she became one of the bright stars in Orion.

SEVEN SISTERS OF INDUSTRY, THE: Chinese name for the PLEIADES.

SGEG-MO-MA: see LASYA.

SHAIT: Egyptian. Usually a god (Shai) but sometimes a goddess; in either case a deity of destiny, born with the individual, shadowing him throughout his life and giving evidence at his after-death trial.

SHAKINI: see DAKINI.

SHAKTI: Hindu, Nepalese, Tibetan. Tantric, but widely influencing Hinduism and various forms of Buddhism. The feminine principle as the supreme force, the active aspect of eternity, as Shiva is the passive; he can exist and become effective in polarity only with her. The worshippers of that principle are called Shaktas. Several descriptions of the Tantric Shakti-worship rituals are quoted in Durdin-Robertson's *Goddesses of India*, pp.195-203. A title of several Hindu goddesses, and indeed the essence of all of them. Frequently identified with KALI in that goddess's much-misunderstood positive aspect. The six principal aspects of Shakti are known as THE SHAKTIS (see below).

SHAKTIS, THE: see SHAKTI above. The six aspects are named; Parashakti, 'the great force or power', including those of light and heat; Jnanashakti, 'understanding, intellect', the power of mind in interpreting sensations, memory, association, clairvoyance and psychometry; Ichchhashakti, 'will, desire', the power of the will, including its simplest manifestation, the power to activate muscles; Kriyashakti, 'making, doing', the power of creative thought or inspired activity; Kundalinishakti, 'the serpentine force' of which electricity and magnetism are but manifestations (see KUNDALINI); and Mantrikashakti, 'magical power, charm', the power of letters, speech or music.

SHALA: An ancient Chaldaean and Sumerian goddess. Known as 'the Compassionate'.

SHAPASH: Sumerian, later Canaanite, Sun goddess, who helped ANAT recover Baal from the Underworld.

SHASHTRADEVATAS, THE: Hindu war goddesses.

SHASTI, SHASHTI: India, Bengal. Goddess of childbirth and children. Depicted riding a cat.

SHATAQAT: A Syrian goddess of healing.

SHAUSHKA: An important Hittite (Hurrian) goddess who became identified with ISHTAR. Oracular, and closely connected with the Hittite ruling families. Depicted as a winged woman standing on a lion, sometimes holding a golden cup in her right hand and a symbol representing good in her left.

SHAYA: see SANJNA.

SHEILA-NA-GIG: Irish and British medieval. The accepted name for the *bas-reliefs* found outside many old churches, priories and convents, and sometimes on castles, of a naked female figure squatting and displaying exaggerated genitals with a yawning vulva. In Harrison's words (*The Roots of Witchcraft*, p.212): 'The Great Mother in her crudest, least ambiguous aspect: the Female Generative Principle, completely "despiritualised", and free from all irrelevant "higher" associations.' Probably, like so many heretical carvings, added by pagan stonemasons and tolerated because of popular veneration; sometimes euphemized as being intended to scare away evil spirits from God's house. The sole authority for the name comes from an English traveller in Ireland, who asked an old man what the figure was, and thought he answered 'Sheila-na-Gig' – which has no obvious meaning in Gaelic. The best survey of them is Jorgen Andersen's *The Witch on the Wall* (see Bibliography).

SHEKINAH: ('Brightness' or 'Dwelling') Hebrew. The Brightness of God, envisaged as female in essence and identified with Wisdom. Cf. SOPHIA. Envisaged as sitting on the Mercy Seat, in a cloud of fire, with cherubim on either side. Described in the *Zohar* as 'the consuming fire, by which they [men] are renewed at night'. She is the 'flaming torch' of Genesis xv:17, the 'pillar of cloud' of Exodus xiv:19-20, the 'cloudy pillar' of Exodus xxxiii:9-10, the 'great cloud with fire flashing' of Ezekiel i:4, and the 'shining cloud' of Matthew xvii:5. Mother of FILIA VOCIS. Day, Saturday.

SHENG-MU: see PI-HSIA-YUAN-CHUN.

SHENTAYET: Egyptian goddess of weaving; she wove the mummy-wrappings of Osiris. Often depicted as a cow.

SHEOL: The Hebrew Underworld, and also its feminine personification. The Dark Mother, envisaged as a reabsorbing womb, frightening and insatiable, and yet peaceful. Many biblical references use the womb metaphor.

SHINA-TO-BE: Japanese goddess who blows away mists.

SHING-MU: Chinese. The Holy Mother or Perfect Intelligence, who conceived and bore her son while still a virgin; but this may originally have been in the old sense of 'independent woman', and 'her ancient character is revealed in the fact that she is the patroness of prostitutes' (Esther Harding).

SHITALA, SITLA: Hindu goddess of smallpox, both inflicting and curing it. Depicted wearing red robes and carrying reeds.

SHITATERU-HIME: Japanese. Daughter of god of medicine O-Kuni-Nushi and wife of young god Ninigi.

SHIU-MU NIANG-NIANG: Chinese water goddess, known as the Water Mother. Connected with the New Year Feast of Lanterns, or Dragon Feast, when nothing may be thrown into water for fear or profaning it.

SIDDHI: see BUDDHI

SIDURI: ('Young Woman') Sumerian, probably a minor oracular goddess; described as a seashore ale-house keeper, in a beautiful garden strewn with gems, she warned Gilgamesh that in his quest for immortality he must follow the Sun's path to 'the waters of death' and be ferried across them by Urshanabi (equivalent of the Greek Charon). She advised him (in words remarkably like Ecclesiastes vii:7-9) to make the most of this life and fulfil his natural desires. Undeterred by her warning, Gilgamesh persisted in his quest; and when she saw he was determined, she helped him with advice. She plays a similar role to SABITU.

SIEN-TSAN: Chinese goddess of silkworm culture. Wife of the early emperor Shen-Nung, who taught his people agriculture; she may have become identified with an earlier mother goddess. Shen-Nung was also deified. (Cf. SINGARMATI.)

SIF: Teutonic Earth mother, second wife of Thor, and one of the ASYNJOR. She had lovely hair, which the trickster god Loki cut off; Odin, furious, compelled him to have the dwarfs fashion her tresses of pure gold. See also JARNSAXA.

SIGE: ('Silence, Secrecy') Gnostic. One of the AEONS, regarded as a form of Thought and associated with the Deep. The Gnosis rested on a square, and Sige was one of its angles.

SIGUNA, SIGNY, SIGYN: Teutonic. Wife of trickster god Loki, and one of the ASYNJOR. May be the same as SIN.

SILILI: Chaldaean, perhaps an early horse goddess; mentioned in the Epic of Gilgamesh as the mother of a stallion who was one of ISHTAR's lovers.

SIN: Teutonic. In the Prose Edda, goddess of Truth, similar to the Egyptian MA'AT. (Do not confuse with the Babylonian Moon god Sin.)

SINA, INA: Polynesian Moon goddess, sister of Sun god Maui.

SINDHU: Hindu, goddess of the River Indus.

SIONAN, SIONNAN: Irish, goddess of the River Shannon.

SINGARMATI: Hindu goddess of silkworm culture. (Cf. SIEN-TSAN.)

SINVALI: Hindu goddess of the New Moon, fecundity and easy childbirth. A wife of Vishnu.

SIRDU, SIRRIDA: A Chaldaean Moon goddess, also called simply A, Aa or Ai. Wife of Sun god Shamash-Bubbar, or possibly of the Hebrew Iao (Yahweh). Symbol, an eight-rayed orb (cf. GULA and ISHTAR).

SIRENE, LA: see ERZULIE.

SIRENS, THE: Greek sea nymphs who lived on an island off the Italian coast and lured sailors to destruction by their singing. Usually depicted as half-bird, half-woman.

SIRONA, DIRONA: Continental Celtic goddess, later replaced by Borvo, god of hot springs, said to be her son.

SIRTUR: see NINSUN.

SITA: Hindu, wife of Rama, an avatar (incarnation) of Vishnu; she insisted on going with him when he was forced into exile. Abducted by Ravana, King of the half-divine but evil Rakshasas, who kept her captive in Ceylon. Rama eventually fought and killed Ravana but at first would not receive Sita, because he wished to prove to everyone that she had remained inviolate. Sita built a funeral pyre and bravely entered the flames – but the fire bore her up on its lap, radiant and unharmed, and she and Rama were joyfully reunited. (Cf. SATI (1).)

SJOFNA: Teutonic goddess of love, seventh of the ASYNJOR.

SKADI: Teutonic. Daughter of the giant Thjazi, and wife of the god Njoerd. He liked to live on the sea-shore; she preferred her native mountains, and eventually she returned to them. A great huntress, roving the mountains on her snow-shoes. Seems to have been a priestess of a magpie clan. Associated with the zodiacal sign Taurus.

SKULD: see NORNS.

SLATABABA: ('Golden Woman') Siberian. During the Vandal sack of Rome in AD 410 a detachment of Ugrians from the Dvina river area of Siberia sacked the temple of JUNO Moneta and took her statue home. Her name was first changed to Jumala, but she became known as Slatababa because the statue was made of gold. In 1023 it was moved over the Urals to the junction of the Ob and the Irytish rivers. In 1582 a member of the Yermak Expedition reached the shrine and saw the statue but was killed soon afterwards. In 1591 Giles Fletcher, English Envoy to Russia, published a book on his failure to find its hiding-place. It is still hidden in the marshes of the Lower Ob, where even the best Soviet experts have been unable to discover it. See Sykes, *Everyman's Dictionary of Non-Classical Mythology*, p.262.

SODASI: Hindu goddess of all things perfect, complete and beautiful. Worshipped after dawn. Envisaged in conjunction with an inert and passive Shiva. Depicted as four-armed, holding a noose (a yoni and umbilical cord symbol), an elephant hook, a bow and a lotus. In a Tantric painting, she appears crowned and seated on a prostrate male figure with a snake curled round his neck; she wears a reddish-gold sari and has a blue aura round her head.

SOOREJNAREE: see PINGALA.

SOPHIA: ('Wisdom') A Gnostic AEON; but Wisdom personified as female was earlier also characteristic of Hebrew and Greek-Hebrew thinking. The Bible frequently so personifies her: for example Proverbs ix:1-12; and Jesus himself, 'Wisdom is justified of all her children' (Luke vii:35). She represents 'the wisdom of that inner spark which speaks and functions of itself, quite apart from our conscious control' (Esther Harding), as distinct from the masculine Logos. Many Greek churches were dedicated to Hagia Sophia, 'Holy Wisdom', including the great basilica in Byzantium. In the Sistine Chapel painting of God reaching out a finger to Adam, she appears behind God in an almost wifely attitude, with God's arm round her shoulders. A Gnostic amulet portrays her as a naked woman with two winged angels holding a crown above her head. Gnostic teaching is that Sophia was filled with desire to 'generate out of herself without spouse' and that her self-induced orgasm gave birth to the whole cosmos, including her daughter SOPHIA AKHAMOTH. Festivals: 15 August, 5 October.

SOPHIA AKHAMOTH: Gnostic. An AEON, arising from her mother SOPHIA's cosmos-creating orgasm. A newly separate entity, she too began to release creative sexual energy; mother and daughter continued to generate the universe, Sophia on the higher spiritual levels, Sophia Akhamoth on the denser planes, favouring mankind by bringing wisdom to them on the levels close to the physical. Her sphere is what occultists call the Lower Astral Light or Ether.

SOPDET: Egyptian, more usually found in the Greek rendering Sothis. The Dog Star, Sirius – or, as the Egyptians called it, the Arrow-head Star. 'The going up of the goddess Sothis', the heliacal rising of Sirius on 19 July, was the signal for Thebes' greatest annual festival, that of Opet (see MUT). It also enables us to assign exact dates to the practical, or Sothic, Egyptian year (though the official year of 365 days, like the Jewish and Moslem ones, moved out of step with the solar year, regaining synchronization every 1,460 years). She was regarded as Queen of the Constellations, of which 36 were recognized, corresponding to the zodiacal decans. Depicted either as a woman or as a cow seated in her boat, with three stars along her back and Sirius itself between her horns. According to Court de Gebelin and Waite, the Tarot Major Arcanum the Star represents the Dog Star, and de Gebelin describes it as wholly Egyptian.

SOTHIS: see SOPDET.

SRADDA: ('Confidence') Hindu goddess of faith; wife of Dharma, probably mother of Kama.

SRAHMAN: Africa, Kaffir. A silk cotton tree dryad who taught travellers the secrets of the forest and of herbs. Wife of the demon Sasabonsum, who devoured travellers.

SRI: Hindu. An incarnation of LAKSHMI as wife of Ramachandra, an avatar of Vishnu.

SRINMO: Tibetan demoness of death, holding the Cosmic Wheel. 'This is due in part to the antifeminine influence of Buddhism, which, because woman creates new life, looks upon her as the chief obstacle to redemption, as an instrument of the passion beneath which the world moans' (Erich Neumann).

STHENO: see GORGONS.

STRENIA: Roman, originally Sabine, goddess of the New Year. Corresponds to SALUS. On 1 January palm and bay branches, and sweetmeats of honey, figs or dates, were carried up the Capitoline Hill from her sacred grove. The offerings, called *strenae*, were gilded. Relics of the custom persist in Germany, and in France, where New Year gifts are called *étrennes*.

STYX: Greek. Daughter of Oceanus and TETHYS, and protectress of the River Styx which must be crossed to reach the Underworld. She helped the Olympians against the Titans, and thereafter the gods swore their oaths by her.

SUBHADRA: Hindu, a younger sister of Krishna. Honoured at the great festival at Puri, where the castes may mingle indiscriminately.

SUCCOTH-BENOTH: see ZARPANIT.

SUHIJI-NI-NO-KAMI: ('Mud-Earth-Lady') Japanese Earth goddess, associated with abundant vegetation.

SUKARAPREYASI: ('Beloved of the Boar') Hindu Earth goddess, perhaps wife of the Vahara, third avatar of Vishnu. Depicted as a seated woman, accompanied by Vishnu in the form of a boar.

SUL, SULLA: (Celtic *siul*, eye) British Sun goddess and goddess of hot springs. Bladud, son of King Rud Hidibras, built a shrine for her 'near Badon' which became Aquae Sulis, the modern Bath. A perpetual fire was burned there in her honour. Known to the Romans as Sul Minerva. May have some connection with Silbury Hill, the Scilly Isles (Sylinancis) and Mousehole (Place of Sul) in Cornwall. Sally Lunn cakes recall the wheaten cakes offered at her altar. Festivals: 2 February, 22 December.

SUN: Chinese, one of the trigrams of the I Ching, two Yang lines above one

Yin line; the Gentle, Wind, Wood, the First Daughter. (See also LI and TUI.)

SUNG-TZU NIANG-NIANG: A Chinese goddess of fecundity and healing. Depicted draped in a large white veil, seated on a lotus with a child in her arms. Corresponds to KWAN-YIN.

SURA: Hindu goddess of wine, produced at the Churning of the Ocean in Vedic myth.

SURABHI: ('Pleasant, Friendly') Hindu, 'the marvellous cow, mother and nurse of all living things', produced at the Churning of the Ocean in Vedic myth.

SURATAMANGARI: ('Sexual Joy' + 'Cluster of Blossom') Hindu, associated with fairies.

SURYA: Hindu solar deity, sometimes female, sometimes male (see SANJNA). As a goddess, she was wife simultaneously to the two Nasatyas, doctors of the gods and friends of the sick and unfortunate.

SUSERI-HIME: Japanese. Daughter of god Susanoo and wife of god of medicine O-Kuni-Nishi.

SUSHUMNA: Hindu, an aspect of KUNDALINI; an energy or current, regarded as blue in colour. One of the three Vital Airs, the other two being IDA and PINGALA.

SUTROOKA: Hindu, wife of Munnoo, and progenitrix of the human race.

SUWA: An early Arabian Sun goddess, mentioned in the Koran as a heathen idol (Surah lxxi:23).

TADATAGEI: Hindu. A Tamil goddess, wife of Somasundara (who may be an avatar of Shiva). Of irresistible strength, unbeatable in knowledge or war, and said to have been born with three breasts.

TAILTIU: Irish. Foster-mother of Lugh. Daughter of Magh Mor of the Fir Bolg, King of the Plain, and wife of Duach the Dark of the Tuatha Dé Danann, who built the Fort of the Hostages at Tara. Lugh instituted the Tailtean Games, central event of the Festival of Lughnasadh (1 August), in her memory. Graves (*The White Goddess*, p.302) says this legend is 'late and misleading', and that the Tailteann Games were 'originally funeral games in the Etruscan style'. The site of the games, Tailtenn, now Teltown, is on the Blackwater halfway between Kells and Navan in Co. Meath. 'Teltown marriages' took place there into medieval times, trial marriages lasting a year and a day; they could be dissolved by the couple returning to the spot and walking away from each other to North and South.

TAIT: Egyptian Underworld goddess, apparently responsible for robing the deceased in the 'taau garment'; in one passage of the *Book of the Dead* she also gives him cakes.

TALLAI: Syrian and Canaanite Nature goddess, the Maiden of Dew and Rain, forming a triad with ARSAI and PIDRAI. Daughter and/or wife of Baal.

TAMAR: ('Palm Tree') Hebrew equivalent of ISHTAR, according to Graves (*The White Goddess*, p.190).

TAMAYORI-BIME-NO-MIKOTO: Japanese sea goddess, probably oracular. Her youngest son, Waka-mi-ke-nu-no-mikito, later called Jimmu Tenno, is said to have been the first Emperor of Japan.

TAMESIS: British and Continental river goddess, who gave her name to the

Thames and to the Tamise (Scheldt).

TAMRA: ('Copper-coloured') Hindu, wife of Kashyapa, and ancestress of birds.

TANA: 'The old Etruscan name for DIANA, which is still preserved in the Romagna Toscana' (Leland, *Aradia: the Gospel of the Witches*, p.51).

TANIT: The great fertility and Moon goddess of Carthage (a Phoenician colony), consort of Baal-Hammon; she was known as 'the face of Baal'. Baal and Tanit's names suggest a common source with the Irish Balor and DANA and the Welsh Beli and DÔN. (See also BENE.) According to Cecil Williamson, her worship (as Tanat) is still practised in Cornwall and the West of England. Festival: 1 May.

TARA: ('Radiating') Hindu star goddess, wife of Brihaspati (identified with the planet Jupiter), teacher of the gods. Abducted by the Moon god Soma, who was compelled by Brahma to release her; but she was already pregnant by him and gave birth to a son radiant with power and beauty, who was called Budha and considered to be the founder of the lunar dynasties. She rides on a lion and holds the Sun in her hand, and her symbol is a boat: 'From the world ocean of many terrors I will save the creatures.' Overlaps with DOLMA.

TARANIS: A Gaulish goddess mentioned by Lucan as being worshipped with human sacrifice. 'Probably a Death-Goddess, namely Tar-Annis, Annis of the West' (Graves, *The White Goddess*, p.372).

TA-REPY: Egyptian name for the constellation Virgo. In the Dendera Zodiac, depicted as a woman carrying a palm branch; in the later Esneh Zodiac, as a sphinx with the head and breasts of a woman and the hinder parts of a lion.

TARI PENNU, BERA PENNU: Hindu, Earth goddess of the Khonds of Bengal.

TASHMIT, URMIT, VARAMIT: ('Hearing') Chaldaean and Assyro-Babylonian goddess of letters and of the hearing of prayer; she opened the eyes and ears of those receiving instruction. With her husband Nebo, god of wisdom and teaching, she invented writing.

TATSUTA-HIME: Japanese wind goddess. With her male counterpart Tatsuta-Hiko, she is prayed to for good harvests and venerated by sailors and fishermen.

TA-URT: Egyptian Underworld goddess of darkness; also a region of the Underworld. MacGregor Mathers links the word Tarot with this name and the Egyptian verb *taru*, 'to consult, require an answer'.

TAUERET: see TUARET.

TAUROPOLOS: Cretan bull goddess, the Lady of the Bull.

TCHESERT: The Egyptian Elysian Fields of the Underworld, and also the goddess personifying that region.

TEA: Irish, goddess of Tara, its co-founder with TEPHI, both described as Milesian princesses. Second wife of Erimon. She chose the mound Drum Chain as her marriage price, and it was named Temair (Tara) after her. (Tea Mur, 'the Wall of Tea'.)

TEBUNAH: ('Understanding, Insight') Hebrew. Often personified as feminine in the Bible; 'she is more precious than rubies'. See for example Proverbs ii;2-5, iii:13-20, vii:4, and the whole of Proverbs viii.

TECCIZTECATL: see METZLI.

TEEREE: Hindu, wife of Brahma, by whom she gave birth to an egg, one half of which formed the celestial beings, the other the Earth creatures including mankind.

TEFNUT: ('The Spitter') Egyptian, daughter of Ra (Atum-Ra), and twin sister and wife of air god Shu; Ra produced them without female help. By Shu, mother of Geb (the Earth) and NUT (the Sky). (An earlier legend makes her the wife of a god Tefen, of whom nothing is known; and Shu is sometimes brother to Geb and Nut.) Goddess of dew and rain. She helped Shu to support Nut, separating her from Geb, and also helped him escort the newborn Sun each morning as it broke free from the Eastern mountains. Some priestly interpretation made Shu the life principle and Tefnut that of world order (rather like the Cabalistic Chokmah and BINAH). In this aspect Tefnut was sometimes identified with MA'AT. One legend says that, when Ra temporarily lost Shu and Tefnut in the primordial waters, his tears of joy on finding them again became the first men and women. She was the protectress of Osiris and of the dead identified with him. Tefnut is depicted as a lioness or as a woman with a lion's head crowned with the solar disc and uraeus; or in her function as protector of Ra and the Pharoah, as the uraeus itself. Appears as one of the Gemini twins in the Dendera Zodiac. The Greeks equated her to ARTEMIS.

TELITA: Babylonian Queen of the Moon.

TELLUS MATER: ('Earth Mother') Roman, a very early goddess of fecundity, together with a male counterpart, Telluno. Later associated with Jupiter. Watched over marriage and the procreation of children, and over the fertility of the soil. Festivals: 15 April, at which the Vestal Virgins officiated, and 1-3 June.

TENAZUCHI-NO-KAMI: Japanese Earth goddess, wife of Earth god Ashi-Nadzuchi.

TENEMIT: Egyptian Underworld goddess, who gave ale to the deceased.

TENNIN, THE: Japanese, Buddhist. Female angels of Heaven, beautiful, eternally young, winged, clothed in feather robes, skilled in music, singing.

TENTH AUNT, THE: A Chinese village goddess, protectress of crops and other village interests. Married, with great ceremony, to the god of a local shrine, for more effective partnership.

TEPHI: Irish, goddess of Tara, its co-founder with TEA.

TERPSICHORE: see MUSES.

TERTIANA: see FEBRIS.

TETEOINNAN: see TLAZOLTEOTL.

TETHYS: Greek Titaness, daughter of Uranus and GAIA. A marine goddess, wife of her brother Oceanus; Homer says these two created the gods and all living beings. They had 3,000 daughters (the OCEANIDS) and 3,000 sons, and were also the parents of 3,000 rivers, including the STYX.

THALATTH: see TIAMAT.

THALIA: see CHARITES and MUSES.

THALNA: An Etruscan mother goddess, often confused with CUPRA.

THEIA: Greek Titaness, daughter of Uranus and GAIA. By her brother Hyperion, mother of SELENE (the Moon), Helios (the Sun) and EOS (Dawn). Often identified with TETHYS.

THEMIS: Greek Titaness, daughter of Uranus and GAIA. According to Aeschylus, mother by her brother Iapetus of Atlas and Prometheus. Second wife of Zeus, to whom she bore the HORAE and the MOERAE. Personified the Law which regulates both the physical and the moral order. Though replaced by HERA, she remained Zeus' adviser, respected by the other Olympians. She was nurse to Apollo, feeding him ambrosia and nectar, and gave him the oracle at Delphi which she had inherited from her mother Gaia; she herself was an oracular goddess, as well as being goddess of justice and sound counsel. Worshipped throughout Greece and had a temple in the citadel of Athens. Her attribute was a pair of scales. Festival: 28 September.

THETIS: Greek NEREID, daughter of Nereus and DORIS. Wife of Peleus (see ERIS) and mother by him of Achilles, to whom she tried to give immortality by dipping him in the STYX. This made all of him invulnerable, except for the heel by which she held him.

THEVADAS, THE: Cambodian. A general name for their many goddesses, depicted in the temples of Prah-khan and Angkor Vat. Their priestesses are girls selected for their beauty.

THIRST GODDESS: see DELIGHT GODDESS.

THO-OG: Tibetan. Space, the Eternal Mother, infinite, without cause.

THREE MOTHERS, THE: Hebrew, Cabalistic. A female trinity representing Air, Water and Fire, and corresponding to the three Mother Letters of the Hebrew alphabet, Aleph, Mem and Shin. Possibly an archetype of the worship, surviving in Provence, of the Three Maries (VIRGIN MARY, MARY MAGDALENE and Mary Cleopas). They are said to have landed there at Les Saintes Maries de la Mer, accompanied by their servant Sara, whose semi-official shrine in the crypt of the town church is a place of pilgrimage for gypsies. Sara's image, according to Sykes (*Everyman's Dictionary of Non-Classical Mythology*, p.249) is a demoted ISIS, like so many 'Black Madonnas' which were originally dark-complexioned statues of Isis and Horus.

THRUD: ('Strength') Teutonic. Daughter of Thor and SIF.

TIAMAT: Assyro-Babylonian primordial sea mother goddess, the mass of salt waters, who with her mate Apsu (the sweet waters) begat the original chaotic world and who also symbolized it and ruled it. 'When above the heavens had not been formed, when the earth below had no name, Tiamat brought forth them both.' Sometimes envisaged as a dragon or serpent. 'The unconscious in its most primitive disorganised state and therefore in need of attention' (Chetwynd, *A Dictionary of Symbols*, p.76). The younger gods under sky god Anu fought to bring order and fruitfulness to the chaos. Ea, the god of wisdom and of water, gained control of Apsu; and Ea's son, the storm god Marduk, fought and slew Tiamat, dividing her body in two to form the Sky and the Earth. She thus remained the Great Mother womb, the belly of the unconscious which so disturbs patriarchy. Kingu was her son/lover, the male generative principle which the Primordial Mother produces from within herself. Tiamat appears under many names, including Thalatth, Omoroca, Tiawthu, Nammu, Nana, Zerpanitu, Me-abzu, Zi-kum and Zi-kura; and she has affinities with the Biblical Leviathan. The Hebrew word for 'waters' in Genesis i:2 is '*tehom*', acknowledged to be a corruption of '*tiamat*'. APSU, her consort, was in the original Akkadian version a goddess, identical with TIAMAT; she changed her sex with the advance of patriarchy.

TIAWTHU: see TIAMAT.

T'IEN HOU: Chinese. Empress of Heaven (not to be confused with WANG-MU YIANG-YANG), sea goddess, protectress of sailors, fishermen and lifeboat crews, and helpful in capturing pirates. Originally a mortal girl who saved three of her brothers from death at sea by appearing to them in a vision and warning them of a coming storm. Widely worshipped, including in Hong Kong and among the Chinese in California.

TIEN MU: ('Mother Lightning') Chinese. Produces the lightning by mirrors held in her hands. Works with thunder god Lei-Kung.

TIL-BU-MA: ('She who Holds the Bell') Tibetan goddess of stern justice. With her husband Amrita-Dhari, Door-Keeper of the North.

TILLIL: A Chaldaean goddess apparently corresponding to the Egyptian NEPHTHYS.

TISIPHONE: see ERINYES.

TITANIA: Shakespeare's Queen of the Fairies is actually DIANA; Ovid uses Titania as a name for Diana (*Metamorphoses*, iii:173).

TI-YA, TI-MU: Chinese earth mother, wife of Thien-lung. Ancestress of the World. Durdin-Robertson says (*Goddesses of India*, p.274): 'The veneration of the earth, often seen personified as a goddess, is a basic feature of Chinese civilisation. One of the ritual duties of the Emperors in their role as Chief Priests was associated with the soil.' Chinese farmers still make figures of the Earth Goddess and set them up on their farms or in wayside shrines.

TLACHTGA (1): Irish goddess who died giving birth to triplets by three different fathers.

TLACHTGA (2): Daughter of Mog Ruith, Arch-Druid of Ireland, who brought back the fragments of a stone wheel known as Roth Fáil or Roth Ramhach, which her father and Simon Magus had been using for magical demonstrations in Italy, and placed them near Rathcoole, Co. Dublin, where they may still be seen.

TLAZOLTEOTL, TETEOINIAN ('Mother of God'), IXCUINA: Aztec. Beautiful goddess of love, fertility, healing, divination, magic and the Earth, and also of dirt. Known as Toci, 'Our Grandmother'. Mother of the maize god Cinteotl, who may originally have been a maize goddess.

TOHU: Hebrew. Primeval chaos, equatable with TIAMAT.

TOMA: ('The Wrathful She') Tibetan. Associated with the intellect. Visualized in Yogic rites as red-coloured, naked except for ornaments, dancing and showing the psychic Third Eye.

TONACACIHUATL: ('Lady of Our Subsistence') Aztec, wife of creator god Tonacatecuhtli. Said to have given birth to an obsidian knife from which sprang 1,600 demigods who peopled the Earth. Probably originally an Earth mother goddess, and her husband a later addition. Has been identified with CHICOMECOATL.

TONAGMA: ('Black Wrathful One') Tibetan, Tantric. In fact depicted red-coloured and involved in the Red Feast ritual. She is the wrathful aspect of VAJRA-DAKINI; all the goddesses of her Tibetan Tantric order have two aspects, peaceful and wrathful.

TOOTEGA: Eskimo. A spirit that can walk on water and looks like a small woman.

TOU MU: Chinese Buddhist and Taoist goddess (probably of Hindu origin), living in the Pole Star. All the other stars revolve around her, and she has power over life and death but is regarded as beneficent. Depicted with three eyes and eighteen arms, holding weapons, the Sun, the Moon, a dragon's head and five chariots. Known as the Bushel Mother, she had nine sons, the Jen Huang, earliest Earthly rulers.

TOYO-UKE-BIME: see UKE-MOCHI-KAMI.

TOYO-UKE-NO-KAMI: ('Abundant Food Deity') Japanese food goddess, with a shrine at Watarapi.

TRIPLE PUSSA, THE: Chinese Buddhist triple goddess, probably corresponding to KWAN-YIN.

TRISALA: Hindu, Janaist. Mother of the Mahavira ('Great Man') when he decided to leave heaven and be incarnated on Earth to save humanity. He first chose to enter the womb of Devananda, wife of the Brahman Rishabhadatta, but later decided to transfer to that of Trisala, wife of Siddhartha. When he was born, the gods and goddesses came down from Heaven to show their joy.

TRIVIA: ('Three Roads'). A name for HECATE as goddess of crossroads.

TSAO-WANG NAI-NAI: Chinese. Wife of hearth god Tsao-wang, she helps him and also keep a record of the women's sayings and doings.

TUARET, TAUERET, RIRIT: Egyptian, a predynastic hippopotamus deity and mother goddess. Sometimes (like HATHOR, SEKHMET, and MUT) called the Eye of Ra, and his daughter. Particularly popular at Thebes, where she was known as OPET. Protectress of women in pregnancy and childbirth, associated with the god Bes. Amulets of these two were places in tombs, to help with rebirth. Identified with the constellation Ursa Major; she appears in the middle of the Dendera Zodiac. Sometimes considered the wife of Set, and an avenging deity. Depicted as a pregnant female hippopotamus, standing on her hind legs, with pendulous human breasts; her hind legs those of a lioness, and her tail that of a crocodile; she carried a rolled papyrus, symbol of protection. In her avenging aspect, she had a lioness's head and brandished a dagger.

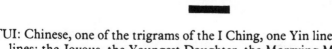

TUI: Chinese, one of the trigrams of the I Ching, one Yin line above two Yang lines; the Joyous, the Youngest Daughter, the Marrying Maiden, the Lake, the Mouth — two strong lines within, expressing themselves through gentleness. Symbolic animal the sheep. (See also SUN and LI.)

TULA: ('Balance', concrete and abstract) Hindu name for the constellation on Libra.

TULI: Polynesian, Samoa. Daughter of Taaroa (Tangaroa) and creatress of the world.

TUONETAR: Finno-Ugric goddess of Tuonela or Manala, the Underworld, wife of Tuoni. Their daughters were goddesses of disease, evil and suffering.

TURAN: Etruscan fertility goddess, corresponding to VENUS.

TURQUOISE WOMAN, THE: Amerindian, frequently mentioned in Navajo myth. She may have been the original, female, form of Ahsonnutli, bisexual creator deity, who is known as the Turquoise Hermaphrodite.

TUULIKKI: Finno-Ugric forest goddess, daughter of Tapio and MIELIKKI. This family was invoked to ensure abundance of game.

TYCHE: ('Fortune') Greek, daughter of Oceanus and TETHYS. Each city had its own Tyche. Wears a mural crown and the attributes of abundance.

UADJET, BUTO: Egyptian. A very early Delta goddess, protectress of Lower Egypt. Her town, the Dwelling of Uadjet, was known as Buto to the Greeks; Herodotus (who identified her with LETO) wrote admiringly of her temple there. She helped ISIS protect the infant Horus. Depicted as a cobra, sometimes winged, sometimes crowned, sometimes with a woman's face; occasionally as a vulture. She is the uraeus which appears on the Pharaoh's forehead, often side by side with the vulture-head of NEKHBET, representing Upper Egypt. The two goddesses are closely related; in the rites for the recently dead, they represent the two placentas and are sometimes depicted guarding the mummy together.

UATHACH: see SCATHACH.

UKE-MOCHI-NO-KAMI: ('She who possesses food') Japanese food goddess. Also known as Waka-Uke-Nome and Toyo-Uke-Bime.

ULUPI: Hindu. A serpent-goddess, one of the NAGIS, dwelling in Patala, the lowest level of the Underworld, said to be a pleasant place and associated with the sense of smell. Arjuna, companion of Krishna, descended there and married her.

UMA: see PARVATI.

UNEN-EM-HETEP: ('Existence in Peace') The second section of the Egyptian Elysian Fields, and the goddess personifying it, known as the Lady of the Two Lands and the Lady of Winds. (See also SEKHET-HETEPET.)

UNI: Etruscan form of JUNO.

UNNUT: Egyptian, goddess of Unnu (Hermopolis).

UNSAS, THE: Individual goddesses of Arabian tribes; each had its own Unsa.

UNT: A name sometimes given to ISIS.

URANIA: see MUSES.

URD: see NORNS.

URMIT: see TASHMIT.

URT-HIKEU: ('Great in Magic') Egyptian, sometimes said to have been Ra's wife. Equivalent to IUSAS.

URVASI: ('Passion, Fervent Desire') Hindu, an APSARA of great beauty, and desired by many of the gods. She said she would marry King Pururavas on certain conditions, which were not met, so she disappeared. Inconsolable, he searched till he found her and they were married.

USHAS: Hindu Dawn goddess, daughter of sky god Dyaus and Earth goddess PRITHVI. Sometimes the Sun is her husband, sometimes her son;

sometimes her husband is her brother the fire god Agni. Travels in a shining chariot drawn by cows or reddish horses. Beautiful and always smiling, she blesses everything. Always young, being reborn every morning, yet immortally old.

UTO: Egyptian, a snake goddess of Buto, known as 'great in magic'.

UTSET: Amerindian, Sia. Family name of two Eve-type sisters, mothers of all mankind. The elder was the ancestress of all the Indians, the younger (known as Nowutset) of the rest of mankind.

UTTU: Chaldaean and Sumerian goddess of vegetation, weaving and clothes. Impregnated by her great-grandfather Enki (see NINHURSAG), she gave birth to seven plants. (Do not confuse with Utu, a Sumerian alternative name for Sun god Samas.)

VACH: ('Speech') Hindu goddess of sound, of the mystic speech by which occult wisdom is imparted and of the power of mantras. Also a mother goddess, envisaged as 'a melodious cow' and personifying the nourishment provided by Nature. In one ritual the initiate passes through the womb of the image of a heifer. Has become confused with SARASVATI.

VADABA, VADAVA: ('Mare') Hindu mare goddess, living at the entrance to Hell at the South Pole, which is called Vadaba-mukha, 'the Mare's Mouth', where is also Vadaba-agni, 'the Mare's Fire'.

VAGA: British. Goddess of the River Wye.

VAJRA-DAKINI: ('Strong Dakini, Thunderbolt Dakini') Tibetan, Tantric. Envisaged as red in colour, with a median-nerve, glowing white with a red core, extending within her body from four inches below the navel to the crown of her head. See DAKINIS.

VAJRA-YOGINI: see DORJE-NALJORMA.

VALKYRIES, THE: Teutonic. In late Scandinavian myth, they brought the souls of those slain in battle to Odin. Originally, priestesses of FRIGG/FREYA, perhaps from when she was the supreme Nordic mother goddess; perhaps recalling a tribe of mounted women warriors. Subordinate to the NORNS, who may originally have been the priestesses of an oracular order, with the Valkyries as their assistants. 777: Tarot, Fool; gems: opal, agate; plant: aspen; animals: eagle, man; perfume: galbanum; magical weapons, Dagger, Fan.

VAMMATAR: Finno-Ugric goddess of pain and disease, daughter of Underworld rulers Tuoni and TUONETAR.

VANADEVATAS, VRIKDEVATAS, THE: Hindu DRYADS. See also YAKSHIS, THE.

VARAHINI: Hindu Earth goddess, an avatar of LAKSHMI, and wife of Vishnu in his boar incarnation. Depicted with an infant on her knees. Corresponds to SUKRAPREYASI.

VARAMIT: see TASHMIT.

VARI-MA-TE-TAKERE: Polynesian, Indonesian. Great mother of gods and men who live in Aviki, land of the dead. In the Mangaia Island version, mother of Underworld god Vatea, and grandmother of sky god Tangaroa and a lesser Underworld god Rongo.

VARUNI: Hindu goddess of spiritous liquor, who appeared at the Churning of the Milk Ocean. Associated with the West.

VASANTI: Hindu woodland goddess associated with Spring.

VASUDHARA: Hindu goddess of abundance, depicted as crowned, dancing, with six arms, four holding symbols of plenty and two making gestures of giving.

VECHERNYAYA: see ZORYA VECHERNYAYA and DENNITSA.

VEELAS, THE: Balkan dryads. Hostile to men who disturb their dances, but can be helpful otherwise and occasionally marry them. Gifted with second sight and powers of healing by herbs. Probably a memory of priestess-shamanesses, demoted to fairy-tale beings under Church pressure.

VELLAMO: Finno-Ugric water goddess, wife of water god Ahto (Ahti).

VENNOLANDUA, GWENDOLEN: British. Daughter of Corineus of Cornwall and first wife of High King Locrin, one of the three sons of Brutus and Imogen. When Locrin put her aside and married his mistress Estrildis, she rebelled against him as Queen of Cornwall, slew him in single combat and drowned Estrildis and her daughter SAVREN (called Habren by Geoffrey of Monmouth) in the River Severn. Savren became goddess of that river. Vennolandua ruled as High Queen till Maddan (her son by Locrin) came of age.

VENUS: Roman, originally a goddess of Spring and protectress of vegetation and gardens, was a minor deity till she became assimilated to the Greek APHRODITE in the second century BC. Julius Caesar's family, the Gens Julia, claimed descent from her and from Aeneas. Festivals: 10 March, 1,15,21,23 April, 28 April-3 May, 23, 24 June, 19 July, 19 August, 9 October. Day: Friday. 777. Tarot, Sevens, Empress, Hierophant, Strength; gems: emerald, turquoise, topaz, cat's eye; plants: rose, myrtle, clover, mallow, sunflower; animals: lynx, sparrow, dove, swan, bull, lion; perfumes: benzoin, rose, red sandal, sandalwood, myrtle, all soft voluptuous odours, storax, olibanum; magical weapons: Lamp, Girdle, Labour of Preparation, Preliminary Discipline.

VERBEIA: British, goddess of the River Wharfe, at Olicana (Ilkley, Yorks).

VERDANDI: see NORNS, THE.

VESTA: ('Torch, Candle') Roman goddess of fire, both domestic and ritual. Daughter of Saturn and OPS. Her sacred animal was the ass. Domestically she presided over the hearth and the preparation of meals. Patroness of bakers. Publicly, her shrine contained a sacred fire tended by the six Vestal Virgins. The Vestals were of great standing in Rome; chosen by lot from patrician families at the age of six to ten, they served for thirty years. They took a vow of absolute chastity, to break which meant death for the culprit and her lover; during eleven centuries, only twenty Vestals were so punished. After the thirty years, they could marry. A criminal condemned to death who happened to meet a Vestal was immediately released. The chief festival of the goddess was the Vestalia, on 7 June; then mothers of families brought food to her sanctuary, which otherwise was entered only by Vestals. On the Full Moon at the beginning of May, they threw twenty-four manikins into the Tiber to ensure the water supply (replacing earlier human sacrifices). Other festivals: 13 February, 1 March, 28 April, 15 May, 9, 15, 24 June. 777: Tarot, Devil; gem: black diamond; plants: Indian hemp, orchis root, thistle; animals: goat, ass; perfumes: musk, civet,

Saturnian perfumes; magical weapons: the Secret Force, Lamp. Greek equivalent HESTIA.

VICTORIA: Roman, originally protectress of fields and woods, who became goddess of Roman military success. Greek equivalent NIKE.

VIDYADEVIS, THE: Indian Buddhist goddesses of knowledge.

VIDYADHARIS, THE: Hindu sylphs or air spirits, living in the Himalayas. Their male equivalents are Vidyadharas.

VIDYAVADHUS, THE: Hindu Muses.

VIJAYA, VIJAYASRI: ('Victorious') Hindu battle goddess, an aspect of PARVATI.

VINATA: A Hindu Underworld goddess who laid the egg from which hatched the bird King Garuda. When the serpents of the Underworld held her captive, they said they would release her in exchange for a cup of amrita, the magical draught from the Celestial Mountain. Garuda obtained it after a fight with Indra and bought his mother's release; but Indra snatched the cup back and the serpents got only a few drops. It was enough to give them godlike power, and its strength is said to have divided their tongues into forks.

VINDEMIATRIX: ('Grape-Gatherer') Roman name for the constellation Virgo.

VINDHYAVASINI: Hindu. One of the terrible aspects of PARVATI, placated with blood.

VIRADECHTHIS: Imported to Scotland by Tungrian troops of the Roman army, who worshipped her at Blatobulgium (Birrens, Dumfriesshire). See also HARIMELLA.

VIRGIN MARY, THE: Mother of Jesus by divine impregnation, in the traditional pattern of the conception of heroes by the mating of a human woman and a god. The biblical account of the Annunciation and birth (given in Matthew and Luke only, in two widely diverging versions) is clearly a later embellishment to fit this tradition. Mary, otherwise relatively unimportant in the Gospels, was elevated to Mother of God by the Council of Ephesus in 431, and from then on filled what Geoffrey Ashe has called 'a Goddess-shaped yearning' for the ordinary worshipper. Festivals: 2 February, 25 March, 31 May, 2, 16 July, 5, 15, 22 August, 8, 12 September, 11 October, 21 November, 8, 15, 25 December. Day: Saturday. See Chapter VII for her full story.

VIRGO CAELESTIS ('Heavenly Maiden'), DEA SYRIA ('Syrian Goddess'); Worshipped by Syrian archers at the Roman camp at Caervorran, Northumberland. The camp commandant wrote a famous hymn to her. See also DEA HAMMIA.

VIVIENNE, VIVIANE: Arthurian. One of the names for the woman who wheedled Merlin's secrets out of him by becoming his mistress and finally imprisoned him magically in an invisible castle. In Thomas Malory's fifteenth-century *Morte d'Arthur*, she is NIMUE and identified with the LADY OF THE LAKE — though elsewhere Vivienne or Nimue is the daughter of the Lady of the Lake by Dylan, son of ARIANRHOD and Gwydion. In other accounts, it is MORGAN to whom Merlin teaches his magic. All probably stem back to GWENDYDD, Merlin's sister, who shared his magic and eventually joined him in his forest hide-out. The true nature of male-female magical partnership would have been incomprehensible, and the incestuous implications of Gwendydd unacceptable, to the later Christian romancers.

VIZ-ANYA: ("Water Mother") Magyar water goddess, whose appearance foretold misfortune.

VIZ-LEANY: ('Maiden of the Water') Magyar water goddess, daughter of VIZ-ANYA. Like her mother, her appearance foretold misfortune.

VOLTUMNA: Etruscan mother goddess, at whose shrine councils of the Etruscan Federation were held. Root of the place-name Volturno.

VRIKDEVATAS, THE: see VANADEVATAS.

WAKAHIRU-ME: ('Young Sun-woman') Japanese, younger sister of Sun goddess AMATERASU; may personify the rising Sun. Also a goddess of weaving.

WAKASANAME-NO-KAMI: ('Young Rice-Planting Maiden') Japanese; her name describes her function. Daughter of the food goddess UKE-MOCHI-NO-KAMI.

WAKA-UKE-NOME: see UKE-MOCHI-NO-KAMI.

WALUTAHANGA: ('Eight Fathoms') Melanesian, Malaita. A huge guardian serpent goddess, provider of plant foods.

WANG-MU YIANG-YIANG: ('Queen Mother Wang') Chinese. Wife of supreme god the August Personage of Jade. She rules the K'un-lun Mountain, dwelling-place of the immortals at the centre of the Earth), and presides over the banquets where the peaches of immortality are eaten. Depicted as a beautiful young woman in ceremonial dress, often with a peacock.

WARAMURUNGUNDJU, IMBEROMBERA: Australian aborigine, Arnhem Land. Creator mother, who 'made the landscape and from her body produced many children, animals and plants which she distributed' (Poignant, *Oceanic Mythology*, p.127).

WATER GIRLS, THE: see SEVEN SISTERS.

WENONAH: Amerindian, Algonquin. A royal maiden who was impregnated by the West Wind and gave birth to the culture hero Michabo (Longfellow's Hiawatha).

WESTERN MOTHER, THE: see EASTERN MOTHER.

WHALE GODDESS, THE: Hebrew, Arabian. Arabic tradition says the whale that swallowed Jonah was female. Cf. Deuteronomy iv:14-19, which forbids the worship of, among other things, 'the likeness of any fish that is in the waters beneath the earth'; the Hebrew word is *dagah*, a female fish.

WHITE HAG: Welsh. Mother of the Black Hag 'from the headlands of the Valley of Distress in the highlands of Hell'.

WHITE TARA: see DOLMA.

WHITE WOMAN: Honduran. Of matchless beauty, she descended from Heaven to the town of Cealcoquin and built a palace with a temple, from which she ruled. Though a virgin, she bore three sons, divided her kingdom between them and returned to Heaven as a beautiful bird. Probably a Moon legend.

WOMAN-LIGHT OF THE SHADOWS, THE: Egyptian, personification of the dark side of the Moon. The *Book of the Dead* describes how she looked after Thoth when he visited the Moon.

WONAMBI: see RAINBOW SNAKE, THE.

WURUSEMU: The Hittite Sun goddess, wife of Taru. Known as Queen of Heaven and Earth, Goddess of Battles. Special patroness of the Hittite kings and queens.

WYRD: see NORNS, THE.

XILONEN: Aztec goddess of maize which has just sprouted and turned green; the very beautiful Young Maize Mother.

XMUCANE: Mother goddess of the Quiche Indian creation legend, which reflects Mayan beliefs and perhaps some Aztec. She and her consort Xplyacoe first made animals and then human beings.

XOCHIQUETZAL: Aztec Eve, and Moon goddess of flowers, love, marriage, art, singing, dance, spinning and weaving. Patroness of prostitutes. She escaped the Flood. Wife of thunder and rain god Tlaloc, and mother of Toltec culture hero Quetzalcoatl, who became an Aztec god. The Sun god Tezcatlipoca fell in love with her and took her away from Tlaloc. Also mother and lover of corn god Xochipilli (Cinteotl), central character of the Spring equinox fertility ritual.

YACHIMATO-HIME: Japanese goddess 'of innumerable roads', with her male counterpart Yachimata-Hiko.

YAKSHIS, THE: Hindu female Nature and tree spirits, who love to sing and dance. They have their frightening side and are apt to devour children. A favourite subject of Hindu art, depicted as wide-hipped, slim-waisted and full-breasted, wearing little or nothing, and in sinuous poses, usually associated with a tree. It is said that, when a Yakshi kicks a tree, it blossoms.

YAMI: The Hindu Eve. She and her twin brother, Yama, were born of SARANYU, wife of the Sun, and were the ancestors of the human race. Yama was the first of all beings to die, and he and Yami became king and queen of a secret sanctuary in Heaven where dead friends, husbands and wives, parents and children, reunite and live happily.

YANG-CHEN: Chinese name for SARASVATI.

YASODHARA: Wife of the Buddha. She bore him a son, Rahula, on the day he left them both for the ascetic life. According to Buddhist tradition, she had been his wife in previous incarnations and had promised to be his wife in all. Defined as a SHAKTI in occult teaching. Festivals: 2 May, 30 August. (See also MAYA (2)).

YATAI, YA-HSEK-KHI: Indo-Chinese and Burmese Eve; her Adam was

Yatawn. They were said to be shaped like tadpoles.

YATUDHANIS, THE: Hindu female fiends or enchantresses; with their male counterparts the Yatudhanas they are associated with the Sun.

YEMAJA, YEMANJA: ('Fish-mother') Nigerian, Yoruba tribe, and Brazilian Voodoo. Sea, river and lake goddess, daughter of Earth goddess ODUDUA, and sister and wife of Aganju, to whom she bore Orunjan, the midday Sun god. Orunjan raped her and she gave birth to eleven gods and goddesses, plus the Sun and Moon, and two streams of water came from her breasts to form a great lake. Taken by the slaves to Brazil, where she became the supreme Voodoo mother goddess and identified with the VIRGIN MARY. Often depicted in mermaid form. Her festival is New Year's Eve, when thousands place offerings on the beach at Copacabana and elsewhere for the sea to claim. Patroness of the zodiacal sign Cancer. Her favourite colour is blue.

YEPT-HEMET: Egyptian goddess of the harem or 'apartment of the female slave'. Patroness of the month Epiph (15 May-13 June).

YESHE-KHADOMA: A Tibetan DAKINI. Goddess of All-Fulfilling Wisdom, she gives help, especially to yogis, if appealed to before performing a difficult ritual. She appears in certain Yogic dances. Depicted wearing a tiara.

YESOD: ('Foundation') Hebrew. Ninth Sephira of the Cabalistic Tree of Life, sphere of the Moon and of the astral plane; its element is Water, and its associated goddesses are DIANA, ISIS and LEVANAH. In this aspect, Yesod is feminine, but in its aspect of 'the foundation of the universe, established in strength', its magical image is that of a beautiful naked man, very strong, and its associated god is Pan. Yesod is the link between the manifested world, MALKUTH, and all the non-material levels, of which it 'purifies the emanations' and offers 'a vision of the machinery of the universe'. Cabalistic symbols: perfumes and sandals. Tarot, Nines.

YHI: Australian aborigine Sun goddess, the Great Spirit, the Mother. Created her male counterpart, Baiame the All-Father, and together they created animals and mankind. Bahloo, the mischievous but unmalicious Moon god, is usually represented as her lover.

YNGONA: Danish Goddess, whom Graves (*The White Goddess*, p.370) equates both with NANNA and with BLACK ANNIS.

YONAGORRI: see MARI (1).

YURULUNGGUI: see RAINBOW SNAKE.

ZALIYANU: Hittite mountain goddess.

ZALTU: ('Strife') Chaldaean, said to personify the violent aspect of ISHTAR.

ZARA-MAMA: Peruvian maize goddess.

ZARPANITU, ZERPANITUM: ('She who Produces Seed') Babylonian fertility goddess, often merging with BELTIS. Wife of Marduk. The Succoth-benoth of 2 Kings xvii:30.

ZHAG-PA-MA: A title of PASHADHARI.

ZI-KUM, ZI-KURA: see TIAMAT.

ZIPALTONAL: Nicaraguan, Niquiran tribe. Creator goddess; with her consort Tamagostad created the Earth and everything in it.

ZOBIANA: A medieval witch goddess name.

ZOE: ('Life') Gnostic, an AEON personifying the vital life principle.

ZORYA: Slavonic warrior goddess, in association with Sun god Perun. Protectress of warriors. Priestess/goddess of Bouyan, a happy island with a river whose water cured all ills; below the river was the land of the dead.

ZORYA UTRENNYAYA: ('Aurora of the Morning') Slavonic Dawn goddess, opening the gates of Heaven each morning for the Sun to start his journey. One myth says that three Zoryas, of Evening, Morning and Midnight, have charge of a dog tied by an iron chain to the constellation Ursa Minor. When the chain breaks, the world will end. (See also ZORYA VECHERNYAYA.)

ZORYA VECHERNYAYA: ('Aurora of the Evening') Slavonic sunset goddess, closing the gates of heaven after the Sun has completed his daily journey. (See also ZORYA UTRENNYAYA.)

ZVEZDA DENNITSA: see DENNITSA.

Appendix
Casting and Banishing the Circle

As in *The Witches' Way*, we have felt that the rituals we have given in this book would be incomplete without instructions for the Casting and Banishing of the Circle which must precede and follow them. (The exception, of course, is the Isis ritual in Chapter XXIII, which has its own Egyptian system.) We therefore give these instructions below, to make this book self-contained. Explanations and footnotes have not been included; these will be found in our *Eight Sabbats for Witches*, Sections I and III.

Casting the Circle

The tools are on the altar in the North, with the sword laid on the ground before it. At least one candle (preferably three) is on the altar, and one each at the East, South and West points of the perimeter. Incense is burning in the censer on the altar. A bowl of water and one of salt are also on the altar.

The High Priestess and High Priest kneel before the altar. The rest of the coven stand outside the North-East of the Circle.

The High Priestess puts the bowl of water on the pentacle, and the tip of her athame in it, and says: '*I exorcize thee, O Creature of Water, that thou cast out from thee all the impurities and uncleanness of the spirits of the world of phantasm, in the names of Cernunnos and Aradia.*' (Or whatever God- and Goddess-names are being used.)

She holds up the bowl of water before her. The High Priest puts the bowl of salt on the pentacle, and the tip of his athame in it, and says: '*Blessings be upon this Creature of Salt; let all malignity and hindrance be cast forth thencefrom, and let all good enter therein. Wherefore I bless thee and invoke thee, that thou mayest aid me, in the names of Cernunnos and Aradia.*'

He pours the salt into the High Priestess's bowl of water, and they replace both bowls on the altar. The High Priest leaves the Circle to join the coven in the North-East.

The High Priestess casts the Circle with the sword, proceeding deosil from North to North. As she passes the North-East, she raises the sword higher than the heads of the coven to leave a gateway. As she casts the Circle, she says:

'*I conjure thee, O Circle of Power, that thou beest a meeting-place of love and joy and truth; a shield against all wickedness and evil; a boundary between the world of men and the realms of the Mighty Ones; a rampart and protection that shall preserve and contain the power that we shall raise within thee. Wherefore I bless thee and consecrate thee, in the names of Cernunnos and Aradia.*'

She lays down the sword and admits the High Priest to the Circle with a kiss, spinning with him deosil. The High Priest admits a woman in the same way; the woman admits a man; and so on till all are inside. The High Priestess picks up the sword and closes the gateway with a deosil sweep of it.

The High Priestess names three witches. The first carries the bowl of water deosil round the Circle from North to North, sprinkling the perimeter. He then sprinkles each person in turn. If he is a man, he ends by sprinkling the High Priestess, who sprinkles him; if she is a woman, she ends by sprinkling the High Priest, who sprinkles her. The bowl is returned to the altar.

The second-named witch carries the smoking censer deosil round the Circle from North to North and replaces it on the altar. The third carries an altar candle round in the same way and replaces it.

All take their athames and face East, with the High Priestess in front. She draws the Invoking Pentagram of Earth (apex, bottom left, far right, far left, bottom right, and apex again) in the air before her, saying: '*Ye Lords of the Watchtowers of the East, ye Lords of Air; I do summon, stir and call you up, to witness our rites and to guard the Circle.'*

The rest of the coven copy her gestures with their athames.

The same to the South, saying: *'Ye Lords of the Watchtowers of the South, ye Lords of Fire; I do summon ...'* etc.

The same to the West, saying: *'Ye Lords of the Watchtowers of the West, ye Lords of Water; Lords of Death and of Initiation; I do summon ...'* etc.

The same to the North, saying: *'Ye Lords of the Watchtowers of the North, ye Lords of Earth; Boreas, thou guardian of the Northern portals; thou powerful God, thou gentle Goddess; I do summon ...'* etc.

All replace their athames on the altar, and the coven kneel in the South of the Circle facing North. The High Priestess stands with her back to the altar, with the wand in her right hand and scourge in her left, crossed over her breasts. The High Priest kneels before her and gives her the Fivefold Kiss, saying:

'Blessed be thy feet, that have brought thee in these ways' (kissing her right foot then her left).

'Blessed be thy knees, that shall kneel at the sacred altar' (kissing her right knee then her left).

'Blessed be thy womb, without which we would not be' (kissing her just above the pubic hair).

'Blessed be thy breasts, formed in beauty' (kissing her right breast then her left; she spreads her arms for this).

'Blessed be thy lips, that shall utter the sacred Names' (kissing her on the lips).

He then 'Draws Down the Moon' on her by kneeling again and touching her with his right forefinger on her right breast, left breast and womb; the same three points again; and finally the right breast. As he does so, he says:

'I invoke thee and call upon thee, Mighty Mother of us all, bringer of all fruitfulness; by seed and root, by stem and bud, by leaf and flower and fruit, by life and love do I invoke thee to descend upon the body of this thy servant and priestess.'

Still kneeling, he says:

'Hail, Aradia! From the Amalthean horn
Pour forth thy store of love; I lowly bend
Before thee, I adore thee to the end,
With loving sacrifice thy shrine adorn.
Thy foot is to my lip [kissing it], *my prayer upborns*
Upon the rising incense-smoke; then spend
Thine ancient love, O Mighty One, descend
To aid me, who without thee am forlorn.'

He stands up and takes a pace backwards. The High Priestess draws the Invoking Pentagram of Earth in front of him with the wand, saying:

> '*Of the Mother darksome and divine*
> *Mine the scourge, and mine the kiss;*
> *The five-point star of love and bliss —*
> *Here I charge you, with this sign.*'

The High Priest and High Priestess now both stand with their backs to the altar and deliver the Charge, as follows:

High Priest: '*Listen to the words of the Great Mother; she who of old was also called among men Artemis, Astarte, Athene, Dione, Melusine, Aphrodite, Cerridwen, Dana, Arianrhod, Isis, Brid, and by many other names.*'

High Priestess: '*Whenever ye have need of any thing, once in the month, and better it be when the Moon is full, then shall ye assemble in some secret place and adore the spirit of me, who am Queen of all witches. There shall ye assemble, ye who are fain to learn all sorcery, yet have not won its deepest secrets; to these will I teach things that are yet unknown. And ye shall be free from slavery; and as a sign that ye be really free, ye shall be naked in your rites; and ye shall dance, sing, feast, make music and love, all in my praise. For mine is the ecstasy of the spirit, and mine also is joy on earth; for my law is love unto all beings. Keep pure your highest ideal; strive ever towards it; let naught stop you or turn you aside. For mine is the secret door which opens upon the Land of Youth, and mine is the cup of the wine of life, and the Cauldron of Cerridwen, which is the Holy Grail of immortality. I am the gracious Goddess, who gives the gift of joy unto the heart of man. Upon Earth, I give the knowledge of the spirit eternal; and beyond death, I give peace, and freedom, and reunion with those who have gone before. Nor do I demand sacrifice; for behold, I am the Mother of all living, and my love is poured out upon the Earth.*'

High Priest: '*Hear ye the words of the Star Goddess; she in the dust of whose feet are the hosts of heaven, and whose body encircles the universe.*'

High Priestess: '*I who am the beauty of the green Earth, and the white Moon among the stars, and the mystery of the waters, and the desire of the heart of man, call unto thy soul. Arise, and come unto me. For I am the soul of Nature, who gives life to the universe. From me all things proceed, and unto me all things must return; and before my face, beloved of Gods and of men, let thine innermost divine self be enfolded in the rapture of the infinite. Let my worship be within the heart that rejoiceth; for behold, all acts of love and pleasure are my rituals. And therefore let there be beauty and strength, power and compassion, honour and humility, mirth and reverence within you. And thou who thinkest to seek for me, know thy seeking and yearning shall avail thee not, unless thou knowest the mystery; that if that which thou seekest thou findest not within thee, then thou shalt never find it without thee. For behold, I have been with thee from the beginning; and I am that which is attained at the end of desire.'*

All stand. The High Priest raises his arms wide and says:

'Bagahi laca bachahe
Lamac cahi achabahe
Karrelyos
Lamac lamec bachalyos
Cabahagi sabalyos
Baryolas
Lagozatha cabyolas
Samahac et famyolas
Harrahya!'

The High Priestess and coven repeat: *'Harrahya!'*

The High Priestess and High Priest face the altar with their arms raised in the Horned God salute (fists clenched, palms forward, first and little fingers pointing upwards). High Priest says:

'Great God Cernunnos, return to Earth again!
Come at my call and show thyself to men.
Shepherd of Goats, upon the wild hill's way,
Lead thy lost flock from darkness unto day.
Forgotten are the ways of sleep and night –
Men seek for them, whose eyes have lost the light.
Open the door, the door that hath no key,
The door of dreams, whereby men come to thee.
Shepherd of Goats, O answer unto me!'

The High Priestess and High Priest together say: *'Akhera goiti'*, lower their hands and say: *'Akhera beiti!'*

The High Priestess, High Priest and coven now form a ring facing inwards, men and woman alternately as far as possible, and link hands. They circle deosil chanting the Witches' Rune:

'Eko, Eko, Azarak,   )
Eko, Eko, Zomelak,   ) [repeated
Eko, Eko, Cernunnos,   ) three times]
Eko, Eko, Aradia!   )
Darksome night and shining Moon,
East, then South, then West, then North,
Hearken to the Witches' Rune –
Here we come to call thee forth!
Earth and water, air and fire,

Wand and pentacle and sword,
Work ye unto our desire,
Hearken ye unto our word!
Cords and censer, scourge and knife,
Powers of the witch's blade –
Waken all ye unto life,
Come ye as the charm is made!
Queen of heaven, Queen of hell,
Horned hunter of the night –
Lend your power unto the spell,
And work our will by magic rite!
In the earth and air and sea,
By the light of Moon or Sun,
As we do will, so mote it be.
Chant the spell and be it done!
Eko, Eko, Azarak,   )
Eko, Eko, Zomelak,   ) [repeated
Eko, Eko, Cernunnos,   ) till ready]
Eko, Eko, Aradia!   )

When the High Priestess decides it is time, she orders '*Down!*' and all
sit, still in a ring facing inwards.

Banishing the Circle

All take their athames and face East, with the High Priestess in front.
The High Priestess draws the Banishing Pentagram of Earth (bottom
left, apex, bottom right, far left, far right, bottom left again) in the air
before her, saying:
  '*Ye Lords of the Watchtowers of the East, ye Lords of Air; we do*
thank you for attending our rites; and ere ye depart to your pleasant
and lovely realms, we bid you hail and farewell ... Hail and farewell.'
  The coven copy her gestures and say the second '*Hail and farewell!*'
with her.
  The same to the South, saying: '*Ye Lords of the Watchtowers of the*
South, ye Lords of Fire; we do thank you ...' etc.
  The same to the West, saying: '*Ye Lords of the Watchtowers of the*
West, ye Lords of Water; ye Lords of Death and of initiation; we do
thank you ...' etc.
  The same to the North, saying: '*Ye Lords of the Watchtowers of the*
North, ye Lords of Earth; Boreas, thou guardian of the Northern
portals; thou powerful God, thou gentle Goddess; we do thank you ...'
etc.
  This completes the banishing of the Circle.

Bibliography

Andersen, Jorgen – *The Witch on the Wall* (George Allen & Unwin, London, 1977)

Apuleius, Lucius – *The Golden Ass* (Robert Graves translation, Penguin Books, Harmondsworth, Middlesex, 1950)

Ashe, Geoffrey – *The Virgin* (Routledge & Kegan Paul, London, 1976)

Beauvoir, Simone de – *The Second Sex* (*Le Deuxième Sexe*, 1949; English translation, Jonathan Cape, London, 1953; paperback Penguin Books, Harmondsworth, Middlesex, 1973)

Blavatsky, H.P. – *The Secret Doctrine*, Volumes I and II (Theosophical Publishing Co., London, 1947 reprint in one volume of 1888 original)

Bradford, Ernle – *Ulysses Found* (Hodder & Stoughton, London, 1963; paperback Sphere Books, London, 1967)

Branston, Brian – *The Lost Gods of England* (Thames & Hudson, London, 1957)

Budge, Sir E.A. Wallis – *The Book of the Dead* (2nd edition, Routledge & Kegan Paul, London, 1969). *Egyptian Magic* (Routledge & Kegan Paul, London, reprint 1972). *Egyptian Religion* (Routledge &

Kegan Paul, London, reprint 1972)

Burland, C.A. – *The Magical Arts: A Short History* (Arthur Baker, London, 1966)

Capra, Fritjof – *The Tao of Physics* (Wildwood House, 1976; paperback Fontana, London, 1976).

Carmichael, Alexander – *Carmina Gadelica, Hymns and Incantations, with Illustrated Notes of Words, Rites and Customs Dying and Obsolete* (Oliver & Boyd, Edinburgh; Volumes I and II, 1900; 2nd edition, Volumes I-VI, 1928 onwards). *The Sun Dances* (Floris Book, Edinburgh, 1977), a paperback selection from the English translations in *Carmina Gadelica*.

Chetwynd, Tom – *A Dictionary of Symbols* (Granada, St Albans, 1982)

Crowley, Aleister – *777 Revised* (Neptune Press, London, 1952)

Crowther, Patricia – *Lid Off the Cauldron* (Frederick Muller, London, 1981)

Deren, Maya – *Divine Horsemen* (Thames & Hudson, London, 1953; paperback under title *The Voodoo Gods*, Granada, St Albans, 1975)

Durdin-Robertson, Lawrence – *The Goddesses of Chaldaea, Syria and Egypt* (Cesara Publications, Enniscorthy, Co. Wexford, 1975). *The Goddesses of India, Tibet, China and Japan* (Cesara, 1976). *The Symbolism of Temple Architecture* (Cesara, 1978). *Juno Covella, Perpetual Calendar of the Fellowship of Isis* (Cesara, 1982). *God the Mother* (Cesara, 1982)

Farmer, David Hugh – *The Oxford Dictionary of Saints* (Clarendon Press, Oxford, 1978)

Farrar, Frank A – *Old Greek Nature Stories* (Harrap, London, 1910).

Farrar, Janet and Stewart – *Eight Sabbats for Witches* (Robert Hale, London, 1981). *The Witches' Way* (Hale, 1984). American editions of these two under titles *A Witches' Bible*, Volumes I and II (Magickal Childe, New York, 1984)

Farrar, Stewart – *What Witches Do* (originally published 1971; 2nd edition, Phoenix Publishing, Custer, Wa., 1983)

Fortune, Dion – *The Mystical Qabalah* (Ernest Benn, London, 1935). *The Sea Priestess* (Aquarian Press, London, 1957; paperback Wyndham Publications, London, 1976). *Moon Magic* (Aquarian Press, London, 1956; paperback Wyndham Publications, London, 1976). (Note: the paperbacks are slightly abridged.)

Frazer, Sir J.G. – *The Golden Bough* (Abridged Edition) (Macmillan, London, paperback 1974)

Ganz, Jeffrey (translator) – *The Mabinogion* (Penguin, London, 1976)

Garner, Alan – *The Owl Service* (Collins, London, 1967)

Gooch, Stan – *The Secret Life of Humans* (J.M. Dent, London, 1981)

Graves, Robert – *The White Goddess* (3rd edition, Faber & Faber,

London, 1952). *The Greek Myths*, Volumes I and II (Penguin, London, 1960 edition)

Gray, John – *Near Eastern Mythology* (Hamlyn, London, 1969)

Grigson, Geoffrey – *The Goddess of Love: the Birth, Triumph, Death and Rebirth of Aphrodite* (Constable, London, 1976; paperback Quartet Books, London, 1978)

Harding, M. Esther – *Woman's Mysteries* (Rider, London, 1971)

Harrison, Michael – *The Roots of Witchcraft* (Frederick Muller, London, 1973; paperback Tandem Publishing, London, 1975)

Hooke, S.M. – *Middle Eastern Mythology* (Penguin, London, 1963)

Irons, Veronica – *Egyptian Mythology* (Hamlyn, London, 1968)

Jacobi, Jolande – *The Psychology of C.G. Jung* (7th edition, Routledge & Kegan Paul, London, 1968)

Jansen, Sally E. – *A Guide to the Practical Use of Incense* (2nd edition, Triad Library & Publishing Co., St Ives, NSW, 1972)

Joyce, Donovan – *The Jesus Scroll* (Angus & Robertson, London, 1973; paperback Sphere Books, London, 1975)

Jung, Carl G. – *Synchronicity, an Acausal Connecting Principle* (translator R.F.C. Hull, Routledge & Kegan Paul, London, 1972)

Kinsella, Thomas (translator) – *The Táin* (Oxford University Press, London, 1970)

Larousse Encyclopaedia of Mythology (Hamlyn, London, 1959)

Leland, Charles G. – *Aradia: the Gospel of the Witches*, introduced by Stewart Farrar (C.W. Daniel, London, 1974)

Lethbridge, T.C. – *Witches: Investigating an Ancient Religion* (Routledge & Kegan Paul, London, 1962)

Lovelock, J.E. – *Gaia: a New Look at Life on Earth* (Oxford University Press, London, 1979, paperback 1982)

MacAlister, Stewart (editor and translator) – *Lebor Gabála Érenn, the Book of the Taking of Ireland*, Parts I-V (Irish Texts Society, Dublin, 1938-56). Commonly known as *The Book of Invasions*, this is a collection of medieval texts in which monks recorded very much older, originally oral, material.

MacCana, Proinsias – *Celtic Mythology* (Hamlyn, London, 1970)

MacNeill, Máire – *The Festival of Lughnasa* (Oxford University Press, London, 1962; paperback, two volumes, Comhairle Bheadolais Éireann, University College, Dublin, 1982)

MacQuitty, William – *Buddha* (Thomas Nelson, London, 1969).

Maple, Eric – *The Magic of Perfume* (Aquarian Press, Wellingborough, Northants, 1973)

Markale, Jean – *Women of the Celts* (Cremonesi, London, 1975)

Montet, Pierre – *Eternal Egypt*, trans. by Doreen Weightman (Weidenfeld & Nicolson, London, 1965)

Morganwg, Iolo (compiler) – *The Triads of Britain* (Wildwood House,

London, 1977)

Murray, Keith – *Ancient Rites and Ceremonies* (Tutor Press, Toronto, 1980)

Neumann, Erich – *The Great Mother* (2nd edition, Routledge & Kegan Paul, London, 1963)

Patai, Dr Raphael – *Man and Temple in Ancient Jewish Myth and Ritual* (Nelson, London, 1947). *The Hebrew Goddess* (Ktav Publishing House, New York, 1968).

Patrick, Richard – *All Colour Book of Greek Mythology* (Octopus Books, London, 1972). *All Colour Book of Egyptian Mythology* (Octopus Books, London, 1972)

Perowne, Stewart – *Roman Mythology* (Hamlyn, London, 1969)

Phillips, Guy Ragland – *Brigantia: a Mysteriography* (Routledge & Kegan Paul, London, 1976)

Phipps, W.E. – *Was Jesus Married* (Harper & Row, New York, 1970)

Pinsent, John – *Greek Mythology* (Hamlyn, London, 1969)

Poignant, Roslyn – *Myths and Legends of the South Seas* (Hamlyn, London, 1970)

Rawson, Philip – *Tantra: the Indian Cult of Ecstasy* (Thames & Hudson, London, 1973)

Reed, A.W. – *Aboriginal Myths: Tales of the Dreamtime* (Reed Books, French's Forest, NSW, 1978). *Aboriginal Legends: Animal Tales* (Reed Books, 1978)

Rees, Alwyn and Rees, Brinley – *Celtic Heritage* (Thames & Hudson, London, 1961)

Richmond, I.A. – *The Pelican History of England*, I: Roman Britain (Penguin, London, 1955)

Ross, Anne – *Pagan Celtic Britain* (Routledge & Kegan Paul, London 1967; paperback Sphere Books, London, 1974)

Schonfield, Hugo J. – *The Passover Plot* (Hutchinson, London, 1965; paperback Corgi, London, 1967)

St Clair, David – *Drum and Candle* (Macdonald, London, 1971)

Sety, Omm and Elzeini, Hanny – *Abydos: Holy City of Ancient Egypt* (LL Company, Los Angeles, 1981)

Shaprio, Max S. and Hendricks, Rhoda A. – *Mythologies of the World: A Concise Encyclopedia* (Doubleday, New York, 1979). UK edition under title *A Dictionary of Mythologies* (Paladin, London, 1981)

Shuttle, Penelope and Redgrove, Peter – *The Wise Wound: Menstruation and Everywoman* (Revised edition, Paladin, London, 1986)

Stone, Merlin – *The Paradise Papers* (Virago, London, hardback 1976; paperback 1977)

Sykes, Egerton – *Everyman's Dictionary of Non-Classical Mythology* (J.M. Dent, London, 1968)

Valiente, Doreen – *An ABC of Witchcraft Past and Present* (Robert Hale, London, 1973). *Natural Magic* (Hale, 1975). *Witchcraft for Tomorrow* (Hale, 1978)

Vinci, Leo – *Incense: its Ritual, Significance, Use and Preparation* (Aquarian Press, Wellingborough, Northants, 1980)

Warner, Marina – *Alone of All her Sex: the Myth and the Cult of the Virgin Mary* (Weidenfeld & Nicolson, London, 1976)

Wilhelm, Richard – *The I Ching or Book of Changes* (translator Cary F. Baynes, 3rd edition, Routledge & Kegan Paul, London, 1968)

Witt, R.E. – *Isis in the Graeco-Roman World* (Thames & Hudson, London, 1971)

Wood, David – *Genisis: the First Book of Revelations* (Baton Press, Tunbridge Wells, 1985)

Wood, Frederic H. – *This Egyptian Miracle* (John M. Watkins, London, 1955)

Index

To keep this Index within bounds, goddess names which appear only as alphabetical headings to entries in Part Three, Goddesses of the World, have not been included. So both lists should be consulted. Internal references in the Part III entries, however, have been included.